# Chekhov the Immigrant

Translating a Cultural Icon

# Chekhov the Immigrant

## Translating a Cultural Icon

EDITED BY

Michael C. Finke &
Julie de Sherbinin

Bloomington, Indiana, 2007

© 2007 by the authors. All rights reserved.

Cover illustration © 2007 by David Levine

Library of Congress Cataloging-in-Publication Data

Chekhov the immigrant : translating a cultural icon / Michael C. Finke and Julie de Sherbinin, eds.
   p. cm.
  Includes bibliographical references
  Summary: "Comprising the proceedings of a 2004 NEH-funded symposium marking the hundredth anniversary of Chekhov's death, Chekhov the Immigrant takes a multi-disciplinary approach to Chekhov's impact on American culture with: articles by literary scholars, contemporary authors of fiction and criticism, theater directors, and translators; transcripts of forums on translating Chekhov and Chekhov and medicine; and a DVD recording of a conversation about Chekhov with the eminent American physician and author Robert Coles."—Publisher's summary.
  ISBN 978-0-89357-345-4—ISBN 978-0-89357-340-9 (pbk.)
   1. Chekhov, Anton Pavlovich, 1860-1904--Criticism and interpretation--Congresses. 2. Chekhov, Anton Pavlovich, 1860-1904--Translations into English--History and criticism--Congresses. 3. Chekhov, Anton Pavlovich, 1860-1904--Appreciation--United States--Congresses. 4. Chekhov, Anton Pavlovich, 1860-1904--Knowledge--Medicine--Congresses. 5. Medicine in literature--Congresses. I. Finke, Michael C., [date] II. De Sherbinin, Julie W. III. Coles, Robert.

PG3458.Z9T373 2007
891.72'3--dc22

2006039684

Slavica Publishers
Indiana University
2611 E. 10th St.
Bloomington, IN 47408-2603
USA

[Tel.] 1-812-856-4186
[Toll-free] 1-877-SLAVICA
[Fax] 1-812-856-4187
[Email] slavica@indiana.edu
[www] http://www.slavica.com/

*To the memory of Marena Senderovich (1931–96)*
chekhoved, *teacher, friend*

# Contents

Acknowledgments ........................................................................................... v

From the Editors ............................................................................................ vi

Introduction ..................................................................................................... 1

Robert Louis Jackson
    On Chekhov's Art ................................................................................... 17

## Translating Chekhov's Prose

Forum on Translation

    Moderators Carol Apollonio Flath and Julie de Sherbinin;
    Translators: Peter Constantine, Richard Pevear, Larissa
    Volokhonsky ............................................................................................ 29

## Translating Chekhov's Drama

Laurence Senelick
    Seeing Chekhov Whole ......................................................................... 69

Michael Henry Heim
    Translating Chekhov's Plays: A Collaboration between
    Translator, Director, and Actors ......................................................... 83

Sharon Marie Carnicke
    Translating Chekhov's Plays without Russian, or,
    The Nasty Habit of Adaptation .......................................................... 89

## Chekhov and Anglo-American Letters

Julie de Sherbinin
    American Iconography of Chekhov ............................................................. 103

Katherine Tiernan O'Connor
    Writing in English with a Chekhov Muse ..................................................... 127

Andrew R. Durkin
    Hunters Off the Beaten Path: The Dismantling of
    Pastoral Myth in Chekhov and Crane .......................................................... 141

Anna Muza
    The Sound of Distant Thunder: Chekhov and Chekhovian
    Subtexts in Tom Stoppard's *Coast of Utopia* ............................................... 151

## Chekhov and American Writing

James McConkey
    My Chekhov ..................................................................................................... 165

Claire Messud
    Chekhov and Aspiring Writers ...................................................................... 169

Francine Prose
    Learning from Chekhov ................................................................................. 177

James Wood
    Chekhov's Simplicity ...................................................................................... 189

## Innovations in Chekhov Scholarship

Robert Louis Jackson
    Chekhov's "Rothschild's Fiddle": "By the Rivers
    of Babylon" in Eastern Orthodox Liturgy .................................................. 201

Svetlana Evdokimova
    Chekhov's Anti-Melodramatic Imagination: Inoculation
    against the Diseases of Contemporary Theater ......................................... 207

Cathy Popkin
    Doctor without Patients/Man without a Spleen:
    A Meditation on Chekhov's Practice ............................................................ 219

Spencer Golub

    Incapacity .................................................................................................. 239

## Performance Practice

Ellen Beckerman

    Finding the Boy Band in Chekhov's *The Seagull*:
    LightBox's *Gull* ........................................................................................ 253

Carol Rocamora

    Must There Be an Orchard in *The Cherry Orchard*?
    Understanding and Staging Chekhov ................................................... 259

## Seminar in the Medical Humanities

Robert Coles (Interviewed by Michael Finke)

    A Conversation with Dr. Robert Coles: Anton Chekhov and
    William Carlos Williams ......................................................................... 271

Michael C. Finke

    Heal Thyself, Hide Thyself:
    Why Did Chekhov Ignore His TB? ......................................................... 285

Conevery Bolton Valenčius

    Chekhov's *Sakhalin Island* as a Medical Geography ......................... 299

Richard Kahn, M.D.

    A Few Words on Chekhov and the Medical Humanities ..................... 315

Michael Finke and Richard Kahn, M.D., Moderators

    Seminar on Anton Chekhov and the Medical Humanities:
    A Discussion of Selected Chekhov Stories ............................................ 319

I. N. Altshuller *(trans. Eugene Alper)*

    About Chekhov *(excerpt)* ....................................................................... 337

Notes on Contributors ..................................................................................... 345

# Acknowledgments

A number of people have contributed to the appearance of this volume. We owe an enormous debt of gratitude to the National Endowment for the Humanities—especially to the readers and panelists who approved our proposal, and to Lydia Medici, who saw our *Chekhov the Immigrant* project through. Of the many involved in making possible the Chekhov Centenary Festival at Colby College in October 2004, we can here acknowledge only a few: Colby College President Bro Adams, Bets Brown, and Ed Yeterian, who as Dean of the Faculty provided a subvention for graphics in this volume. Nat Shed deserves special thanks for all he did to make the Festival run smoothly. Funding that we received for the Festival from the Maine Humanities Council also had its part in shaping this volume. George Fowler and Vicki Polansky of Slavica Publishers have been supportive collaborators from the start and deserve credit for the look of this book; needless to say, any imperfections remain our responsibility. Finally, we are very grateful to all of the participants who made the Chekhov Centenary Festival a success: those who presented their work in the symposium sponsored by the National Endowment for the Humanities and contributed pieces to the volume; our colleagues from the North American Chekhov Society who also gave papers at the Festival and responded to the NEH presenters; participants in the Medical Humanities Seminar from the Maine medical community; faculty and students and others with an interest in Chekhov who came to listen and respond. Some of their words are recorded here, at times, unfortunately, without attribution; others no doubt had their impact on the revised versions of the Symposium presentations printed here.

As American Chekhov scholars, we are most grateful to the many Russian *chekhovedy* who have shared generously with us over the years; we were saddened to learn of the death of Aleksandr P. Chudakov while this volume was in production.

## From the Editors

In order to produce a text easily negotiated by non-Russian speakers, we have rendered Russian names in commonly anglicized forms (Stanislavsky, Uncle Vanya, Sonya) and/or with a consistent, but anglicized transliteration system that reads easily and gives more pronunciation guidance than the Library of Congress method: soft signs are dropped, the /й/ sound is represented by "y," "-ий" endings are also spelled "y," and so on; here, for example, are the names of a few Chekhov characters: Anyuta, Ilovaiskaya, Obtemperansky, Yegor. Proper Library of Congress transliteration of names and titles will appear in footnote references that are cited from the original Russian.

Throughout the volume, references to Chekhov's fiction in Russian are cited from the most complete academic edition of his works, A. P. Chekhov, *Polnoe sobranie sochinenii i pisem v tridtsati tomakh* (Moscow: Nauka, 1974–83). That collection is divided into an eighteen-volume collection of Chekhov's writings (*Sochineniia*) and a twelve-volume collection of the letters (*Pis'ma*). Citations of Chekhov's writings will be followed by a parenthetical reference to *PssS*, which in turn will be followed by the volume and page number. For instance, a citation from the first page of "Lady with a Little Dog" will read "(*PssS* 10: 128)." By choice of the author, Chekhov's letters are cited either by the date of writing (according to the pre-Revolutionary calendar, unless otherwise noted), or by abbreviated reference to *PssP*, or both.

# Chekhov the Immigrant: Translating a Cultural Icon
## An Introduction

### Michael Finke, University of Illinois at Urbana-Champaign
### and Julie de Sherbinin, Colby College

No major Russian author has been more thoroughly assimilated by the American audience, none more eagerly naturalized, than the master of the short story, playwright, physician, and social activist Anton Chekhov (1860–1904). This interdisciplinary volume explores the cultural processes by which Chekhov becomes ours; or, at least, ours *too*. But let us not be misled by the first-person plural of that possessive pronoun: just as a Chekhov scholar (in Russian, a *chekhoved*) working in the Russian tradition might well object to how the author is viewed on our shores, the talented, cutting-edge representatives of several different disciplines who engage Chekhov in this volume each operate with their own particular images of the author. *Chekhov the Immigrant* talks about "translating" Chekhov—translation being its master trope—but it also stages that process, as Chekhov is variously rendered by contributors, each of whom makes the case for the aptness of his or her interpretation.

The volume issues from a symposium marking the one-hundredth anniversary of Chekhov's death, which was held at Colby College in Waterville, Maine, in October 2004. That meeting, sponsored by the National Endowment for the Humanities (NEH),[1] brought together literary scholars, historians, professional translators, theater critics and artists, authors of fiction and popular criticism, doctors and other health-care professionals—a wide range of thoughtful Chekhov-admirers. To convey something of the extraordinary polylogue that resulted, we offer here, in addition to articles based on the papers read by those participants, transcripts of discussion forums and digital video viewed during the symposium.

---

[1] The NEH symposium was part of a larger Chekhov Centenary Festival that also received support from: The Maine Humanities Council; The North American Chekhov Society; The Penobscot Bay Medical Center; The Kotlas Connection; REM-Waterville; and a number of Colby College offices and departments, including the Office of the Dean of Faculty and the Office of the President. The symposium was preceded by a one-day scholarly conference of the North American Chekhov Society; many of the participants in the NEH symposium also took part in that conference, and some refer to it in their papers here.

*Chekhov the Immigrant: Translating a Cultural Icon.* Michael C. Finke and Julie de Sherbinin, eds. Bloomington, IN: Slavica Publishers, 2007, 1–15.

The eagerness of many varied and distinguished figures to take part (as well as the enthusiasm of several who could not), and the NEH's decision to fund our proposal, validated our view of Chekhov's influence on this side of the world. Indeed, Chekhov has had a peculiarly strong hold on the American imagination ever since the early twentieth century, when the first English translations of his work crossed the Atlantic. Such major American writers as Tennessee Williams, William Carlos Williams, Eudora Welty, John Cheever, Raymond Carver, Joyce Carol Oates, and Walker Percy have acknowledged Chekhov's relevance to their work, and several generations of scholars and students have revered, analyzed, and imitated him. The 1990s and opening years of this new century have seen a proliferation of translations of Chekhov into English, and new biographies of Chekhov receive significant attention in the U.S. press.[2] Public intellectual figures such as Richard Gilman of Yale University and *The New Yorker*'s Janet Malcolm have made pilgrimages to Chekhov sites in Russia to better engage the author and then published books on him that received very wide regard.[3] As a playwright Chekhov figures second only to Shakespeare in frequency of performance on American stages.[4] Chekhov's drama has spawned scores of innovative theatrical spin-offs, such as the Wooster Group's *Brace Up!* (1989; based on *Three Sisters*), Ellen Beckerman's *Gull* (2000), Regina Taylor's *Drowning Crow* (2001), Alan Ladd's *Chekhov's Rifle* (2003), as well as a plethora of theater productions represented at the "Chekhov Now" drama festival in New York—which celebrated its fifth season in 2004.[5] Cinema has borrowed and reworked Chekhov in Louis Malle and Andre Gregory's stunning *Vanya on 42nd Street* (1994) and Richard

---

[2] Recent biographies include Donald Rayfield, *Anton Chekhov: A Life* (New York: Henry Holt, 1998); Philip Callow, *Chekhov: The Hidden Ground* (Chicago: Ivan R. Dee, 1998); and Rosamund Bartlett, *Chekhov: Scenes from a Life* (New York: Simon and Schuster, 2005). For some prominent review articles of these works see: Aileen Kelly, "Chekhov the Subversive," in *New York Review of Books* (November 6, 1997); Clare Cavanagh, "The Passion of Anton," featured on the cover of *New York Times Book Review* (March 15, 1998); Joseph Frank, "Why Sakhalin?" *London Review of Books* (February 17, 2005).

[3] Richard Gilman, *Chekhov's Plays: An Opening into Eternity* (New Haven, CT: Yale University Press, 1995); Janet Malcolm, "Travels with Chekhov," *The New Yorker* (February 21 and 28, 2000), 238–50, expanded into her *Reading Chekhov: A Critical Journey* (New York: Random House, 2001).

[4] Laurence Senelick, *The Chekhov Theatre: A Century of Plays in Performance* (Cambridge: Cambridge University Press, 1997), 1.

[5] The 2004 "Chekhov Now" Festival saw inventive stage versions of both drama and fiction, bearing such titles as "Firs' Dream," "3 Sisters Redux," "Uncle Victor," "Chekhov in Paris," "The Bet," and "A Teacup Full of Vodka." It included a Korean production of "Three Sisters" that was "interpreted through Grotowski Yoga and traditional Korean Mask Dance." See http://www.theatermania.com/content/show.cfm/show/107218 (accessed August 15, 2006).

La Gravanese's *Living Out Loud* (1998). And Chekhov has starred in the relatively new (and very American) field of medical humanities.[6]

If we in the West find Chekhov more like us than any of the nineteenth-century Russian greats, it is also the case that among us he has taken on shapes largely unknown to his native Russia, and when encountered, very often resisted.[7] This situation—perhaps best appreciated by academic Chekhov scholars in the United States, who have assimilated the major Russian scholarship—dramatizes the question of *why* we in North America understand Chekhov as we do; it raises fundamental questions, which the symposium aimed to address, regarding the processes of cultural exchange and naturalization across national borders. But genuine dialogue remains rare, too, between North American players in the various disciplines that claim Chekhov: specialists are often hindered from presenting their innovative visions of the inexhaustibly absorbable Chekhov to one another by their separate professional organizations, conferences and journals, as well as by their distinct idioms.

So it is that "Chekhov the Immigrant: Translating a Cultural Icon"—the symposium first, and now the volume—has staged multidisciplinary discussion of and critical reflection on Chekhov's impact on individual disciplines and disciplinary identities. The articles in this volume reflect on the various angles of vision that have produced the Chekhovs we now know, or think we know; they reveal how diverse American disciplinary methodologies move Chekhov in often varying, if not antithetical, directions. Their authors ask such questions as: What has it meant to import and make our own a cultural figure who, as an author, physician, self-made man, and philanthropist, serves Russians as the model of *intelligentnost'*? If for Russians Chekhov arguably defines what it is to be a humanist in the modern era, what have the man and his writings meant in the American cultural context of the last quarter century, and how and why has this varied across disciplinary boundaries? Ultimately such questions lead to more fundamental ones about the humanities. Taking seriously Chekhov's scientific education and practice as a physician, for example, involves exploring the humanities in contiguity and exchange with other fields of knowledge.

---

[6] Thus, a collection of Chekhov's stories has been published in the series "Literature and Medicine," oriented toward medical humanities curricula in medical schools; see *Chekhov's Doctors: A Collection of Chekhov's Medical Tales*, ed. Jack Coulehan, foreword by Robert Coles (Kent, OH: Kent State University Press, 2003).

[7] To the point, Michael Finke was told by a Muscovite painter: "Take on Tolstoy or Dostoevsky, but better leave Chekhov alone—he is the most Russian of Russian authors." See also the negative response to the innovative work of an "American Slavist" by the important Russian Chekhov scholar Vladimir Kataev, *If Only We Could Know! An Interpretation of Chekhov* (Chicago: Ivan R. Dee, 2002), 9.

If our experience at the NEH symposium is any guide, a wide variety of readers stand to benefit from such interchange. There scholars of Slavic literatures (like ourselves) very conversant with Chekhov's prose found—in American theater studies, for example, and in conversation with theater artists and also health-care professionals engaged with Chekhov—new perspectives and new possibilities for their own further research. Theater practitioners were well-served by exposure to discussions of the translator's art, since the scores of available translations represent Chekhov unevenly and those without access to the original lack important criteria for judging the quality of a translation. Translators who professed to avoiding scholarship on Chekhov were exposed to the latest theories of Chekhov's poetics, which could bear fruit in the future when they face the word choices that, ultimately, condition the English-language reader's access to the many layers of a Chekhov text. Our writers, most interestingly, spoke chiefly of teaching creative writing at the college level with the assistance of Chekhov; and what they had to say was quite illuminating to those teaching Chekhov under other rubrics. Finally, although there is a lengthy tradition of writing about Chekhov as a doctor (especially in Russia), in recent years the interdisciplinary of medical humanities has been producing sophisticated new theoretical approaches that are only beginning to find application to Chekhov. Literary scholars working the literature-and-medicine intersection in Chekhov clearly benefited from dialogue with clinicians and historians of medicine, and all were riveted by a video interview, produced specifically for the symposium and reproduced here, with a physician and author who, arguably, is one of the founders of the field of medical humanities, Dr. Robert Coles.

Over the past thirty years, there have been two scholarly gatherings devoted to Chekhov in the United States that might be called roughly analogous to ours; to our knowledge, however, there has never been a conference quite like the one whose record we offer in this volume. During the 1977–78 academic year at Cornell University a Chekhov Festival sponsored a series of lectures by leading Chekhov scholars and prominent American authors who happily acknowledged their debt to Chekhov. This symposium resulted in a volume of essays, *Chekhov and Our Age*, which was edited by James McConkey and included essays by Eudora Welty, John Cheever, Harold Brodkey, and Walker Percy.[8] The volume remains extremely valuable—as must any publication with original material on the craft and tradition of writing by such modern American masters—but the "age" has certainly changed over the past quarter century, and so too has the way in which Chekhov scholars frame their subject. The second major American conference devoted to Chekhov was the Third Symposium of the International Chekhov Society at Yale

---

[8] James McConkey, ed., *Chekhov and Our Age: Responses to Chekhov by American Writers and Scholars* (Ithaca, NY: Center for International Studies, Council of the Creative and Performing Arts, Cornell University, 1984).

University, in April of 1990, an academic meeting where specialists, some with a lifetime of engagement with Chekhov, addressed one another in a rather narrowly defined field. This conference too produced an enormously valuable collection of scholarly articles on Chekhov, edited by Robert Louis Jackson of Yale.[9]

Jackson, now *emeritus* and widely recognized as the dean of American Chekhov scholarship, participated in our NEH symposium, and his distillation of a lengthy career's study of Chekhov, "On Chekhov's Art," opens this volume. Here is a brief overview of what follows:

**Chekhov Translation**

Almost all American theater practitioners, audiences, writers, and readers encounter Chekhov only though the voice of a translator. It need hardly be said, then, that the element of interpretation inevitably involved in translation powerfully shapes the reception of this Russian writer in the English-speaking world. In recent years there has been a remarkable surge in American translations and adaptations of Chekhov. At the symposium, today's preeminent translators of Chekhov—indeed, of Russian literature generally speaking—discussed their craft.

For the better part of the twentieth century, translation of Chekhov into English was the unofficial domain of British translators. Most ubiquitous have been the translations by Constance Garnett, who published fourteen volumes of Chekhov's prose (approximately two hundred of an estimated five hundred stories), as well as Chekhov's major plays—all this between 1916 and 1924. Garnett's translations are still read widely today; perhaps because her work is out of copyright, major publishers continue to issue them in new collections selected and/or edited by American scholars and writers such as Ralph Matlaw (1979), Richard Ford (1998), Shelby Foote (1999), and Edmund Wilson (posthumous edition, 1999). Theorists of translation recognize that Garnett's Victorian inflections and free hand often seriously compromise the dense networks of meaning in Chekhov's work.[10] A British idiom continued to dominate the translation of Chekhov's prose from the 1960s through the 1980s. Ronald Hingley's Oxford University Press series and Ronald Wilks's renditions for Penguin both have many virtues; however, close allegiance to Chekhov's words is not always among them.

Recent American translators, by contrast, appear to take seriously the need to follow Chekhov's words carefully; this has been evident in translations of both the early tales (somewhat artificially defined as issuing from

---

[9] Robert Louis Jackson, ed., *Reading Chekhov's Texts* (Evanston, IL: Northwestern University Press, 1993).

[10] See Rachel May, *The Translator in the Text: On Reading Russian Literature in English* (Evanston, IL: Northwestern University Press, 1994), 35–36, 39–42, 100, 132.

1880–86) and the mature work.[11] In the forum on translation, translators Peter Constantine, Richard Pevear, and Larissa Volokhonsky discuss, among other topics: the questionable notion of an *American* English into which Chekhov's prose might be translated; inaccuracies and other flaws they have found in previous translations; how their methodologies avoid such infelicities; and the role of the market in their work. Scholars at the conference were eager to learn about the theoretical and pragmatic principles guiding these translators, but they were also not shy about challenging some of their word choices and laying out the interpretive possibilities that hinge on them.[12]

Even more may be riding on the translation of Chekhov's drama, given that the American public knows Chekhov primarily through his four major plays: *The Seagull, Uncle Vanya, Three Sisters,* and *The Cherry Orchard*. Oddly enough, however, it seems that theater personnel—not to mention their audiences—rarely consider the importance of translation in shaping the Chekhov that is delivered on stage. Our treatment of Chekhov's drama, by contrast, underscores the translation angle—"translation" in senses linguistic, theatrical, and cultural—in three pieces by major translators who are active in the theater and also distinguished scholars. Laurence Senelick (Tufts University), Michael Henry Heim (University of California at Los Angeles), and Sharon Carnicke (University of Southern California) offer fascinating pieces on their translation techniques and personal experiences in the world of the theater. Senelick, whose new translations of the complete body of Chekhov drama have come out since the symposium,[13] poses translation problems that illustrate the difficulties in conveying Chekhov's Russian in an English that is linguistically, tonally, and culturally accurate; his piece's title, "Seeing Chekhov Whole," emphasizes the imperative, in his view, of knowing intimately Chekhov's entire *ouevre* in order to understand, and accurately convey, words and phrases that appear repeatedly in his early and late plays, stories, and letters. Michael Henry Heim, who is perhaps best known among Chekhov devotees as the translator (in collaboration with Simon Karlinsky) of Chekhov's letters but has recently published translations of the major plays as

---

[11] With the exception of Paula Ross's poor translations for Prometheus Books: Anton Chekhov, *Stories of Women*, trans. Paula P. Ross (Amherst, NY: Prometheus Books, 1994), and *Stories of Men*, trans. Paula P. Ross (Amherst, NY: Prometheus Books, 1997).

[12] Roughly a year after the symposium an article about Pevear and Volokhonsky appeared in *The New Yorker*; for further discussion of their translations of Chekhov and other Russian classics, see David Remnick, "The Translation Wars," *The New Yorker*, November 7, 2005, 98–109.

[13] *Anton Chekhov's Selected Plays*, Norton Critical Edition, trans. and ed. Laurence Senelick (New York: W. W. Norton & Co., 2005); *The Complete Plays: Anton Chekhov*, trans. and ed. Laurence Senelick (New York: W. W. Norton & Co., 2005).

well,[14] shares observations from his collaborative work with directors and actors. And in "The Nasty Habit of Adapting Chekhov's Plays," Sharon Carnicke discusses the odd tradition in American Chekhov theater of staging Chekhov translations carried out by playwrights with no knowledge of Russian. Her contribution raises provocative questions about the ownership of text, arbitration of translation, and the effect of stardom on securing audiences and publishers for Chekhov's plays.

## Chekhov and Anglo-American Letters

This section offers pieces by four American Chekhov scholars and four American fiction writers and critics on Chekhov's relevance to American culture and literary practice. At the symposium the writers also took part in a discussion forum where they addressed one another and entertained questions from the audience; unfortunately, technical problems with the recording of that exchange prevent us from making a transcript available here.

Colleagues in Russia have begun the work of cataloguing allusions by anglophone writers to Chekhov, but there is as yet little by way of critical analysis.[15] In "American Iconography of Chekhov," conference co-organizer Julie de Sherbinin (Colby College) brings a critical eye to the numerous portraits, magazine sketches, and caricatures of Chekhov that have been painted and penned over the years by American illustrators in the print media; the canonized American iconography of Chekhov, she argues, is deeply at variance with the critically shrewd thinker Chekhov truly was, and most interestingly, very often diverges, too, from the particular view of Chekhov laid out in the pieces being illustrated. The contribution of Katherine Tiernan O'Connor (Boston University), "Writing in English with a Chekhov Muse," analyzes the literary tribute paid to Chekhov by an array of English, Irish, and American writers. Andrew Durkin (Indiana University) finds surprising correspondences between the near contemporaries Anton Chekhov and Stephen Crane in "Hunters Off the Beaten Track: The Dismantling of Pastoral Myth in Chekhov and Crane." He invokes yet another interdisciplinary field: the intersection between literature and environmental studies, an area of deep potential in regard to the ecologically minded Chekhov, but one that has largely

---

[14] *Anton Chekhov's Life and Thought: Selected Letters and Commentary*, trans. Michael Henry Heim and Simon Karlinsky, selection, commentary, and introduction Simon Karlinsky (Berkeley: University of California Press, 1975); Anton Chekhov, *The Essential Plays*, trans., introd., and notes by Michael Henry Heim (New York: Modern Library, 2003).

[15] See M. A. Shereshevskaia and M. G. Litavrina, "Chekhov v angliiskoi kritike i literaturovedenii"; I. M. Levidova, "Chekhov i sovremennye angliiskie novellisty (k probleme vliianiia)"; Patrick Miles, "Chekhov na angliiskoi stsene"; and I. M. Levidova, "Chekhov i literatura Irlandii," all in *Chekhov i mirovaia literatura*, ed. Z. S. Papernyi and E. A. Polotskaia (Moscow: Nauka, 1997), 369–540.

evaded research.[16] Last, Anna Muza elucidates the place of Chekhov among the rich nineteenth-century Russian cultural allusions in Tom Stoppard's trilogy, *The Coast of Utopia*.

One need not rely on Chekhov scholars, however, to find the figure of Chekhov in the fiction and essays of prominent North American authors. In his introduction to the volume that issued from the Chekhov Festival at Cornell University (1978–79), James McConkey wrote: "Touch a fiction writer or a poet, I have come to think, and you are likely to touch a Chekhovian."[17] Vladimir Nabokov produced his influential essay on Chekhov while teaching at Cornell. Chekhov (with Franz Kafka) is central to Philip Roth's *Professor of Desire*. Like Katherine Mansfield, who imagined herself to be "the English Tchekhoff," Raymond Carver identified closely with Chekhov's life—most famously in "The Errand," an imaginative recreation of Chekhov's death that, in retrospect, anticipated Carver's own. Joyce Carole Oates's "The Lady with the Pet Dog" is a deliberate analogue to Chekhov's story by that name. Contemporary American playwrights Wendy Wasserstein, David Mamet, Maria Irene Fornes, Michael Weller, Samm-Art Williams, John Guare, and Spalding Gray all participated in a project to write plays based on Chekhov's stories.[18] Joseph Brodsky published his poem "Homage to Chekhov" in *The New Yorker* (August 7, 1995).

Chekhov remains alive in American intellectual life today. Among notable recent publications by high profile figures—indications of Chekhov's salability, if not significant new contributions to the study of him—is the volume of Chekhov stories edited and introduced by the short-story writer and novelist Richard Ford and the 1999 volume of critical essays edited by Yale University's Harold Bloom.[19] We have already mentioned the prominent publications of Richard Gilman and Janet Malcolm; others who have published major articles on Chekhov in mainstream publications include symposium participant James Wood.[20] Short-story writers are dubbed

---

[16] But see Wallace Sherlock, "The Pastoral Theme in the Short Stories of A.P. Chekhov" (PhD diss., Cornell University, 1996); Stephen L. Baehr, "The Machine in Chekhov's Garden: Progress and Pastoral in *The Cherry Orchard*," *Slavic and East European Journal* 43: 1 (1999): 99–121; Jane Costlow, "Imaginations of Destruction: The 'Forest Question' in Nineteenth-Century Russian Culture," *The Russian Review* 62: 1 (2003): 91–118.

[17] James McConkey, introduction to *Chekhov and Our Age*, 2.

[18] See *Orchards* (New York: Broadway Play Publishing Inc., 1987).

[19] *The Essential Tales of Chekhov*, ed. and introd. Richard Ford, trans. Constance Garnett (Hopewell, NJ: Ecco Press, 1998); Harold Bloom, ed., *Modern Critical Views: Anton Chekhov* (Philadelphia: Chelsea House Publishers, 1999). The latter has been followed by other Chelsea House volumes on Chekhov prefaced by Bloom.

[20] Wood's major article, "What Chekhov Meant by Life," appears in his collection *The Broken Estate: Essays on Literature and Belief* (London: Jonathan Cape, 1999), 74–88.

"Chekhovian" when their work meets with critical approbation, and any number have been called the "American Chekhov," the "Canadian Chekhov," the "Indian Chekhov"—name your adjective of nationality. Chekhov continues to be read, studied, and emulated by students of writing in university courses on fiction-writing and M.F.A. programs. Assimilating Chekhov thus informs the practice of writing and criticism in contemporary American letters, and insofar as writers and critics conceive what they do in connection with a certain kind of attitude toward or relationship with this illustrious predecessor, Chekhov could be said to comprise an aspect of their very identity. This possibility is explored most profoundly in participant James McConkey's longstanding engagement with Chekhov.

Nevertheless, just as the American literary-cultural scene has undergone significant change in the past quarter century, the Chekhov who serves as a point of reference today is by no means the same Chekhov celebrated a quarter century ago. And while there has always been a disjuncture between the way writers and critics, on the one hand, and literary scholars, on the other, have read Chekhov's works and apprehended the author himself, this gap is itself worthy of critical reflection. Are fiction writers who feel attached to Chekhov aware of the scholarship plumbing ever more esoteric symbolic and psychobiographic dimensions to the oeuvre? Do scholars have a clue as to how influence really works with authors who actually create what they, the scholars, can only study and admire? As expected, the symposium dramatized the extent to which professional writers and popular critics turn to Chekhov with agendas different from those of Chekhov scholars in the academy; and yet the common area of what we all considered most important and interesting about Chekhov proved quite large. In his presentation the novelist and critic James Wood provided an overview of the role of free indirect discourse in Chekhov, which, were it not for its clarity and lack of jargon, would have done a Russian formalist or structuralist theoretician proud. Claire Messud and Francine Prose both treated the symposium audience with tales of using Chekhov in their university courses on creative writing; and in the version of her talk printed here, Messud has added a brief and very moving metaliterary reading of Chekhov's "Black Monk."[21]

**Innovations in the Scholarship on Chekhov's Prose and Drama**

Something of a revolution has taken place in Chekhov scholarship of the past two decades. New approaches to Chekhov's prose—largely pioneered by Slavists working in North America—have challenged the timeworn clichés of

---

[21] The symposium presentations of these authors were to have been recorded and transcribed for this volume, but technology failed us. As a result, some of the material published here varies significantly from what was heard at the symposium, and we have no record of the very lively exchange that took place among the participants and between them and their audience.

American, European, and Russian scholarship. Most significantly, Chekhov has been released from the straightjacket of mimetic understanding that long denied his prose the rich symbolic readings it deserves.[22] This is not to say that all American-based scholars are of one mind on Chekhov, however, and the contributions to this volume that touch on Chekhov's poetics further debate around fundamental questions regarding how Chekhov ought to be approached.

At the symposium we heard from the two American scholars who, in their own publications and through the graduate students they have trained and the dissertations they have directed, are most responsible for these new views of Chekhov. Savely Senderovich (Cornell University) laid out his controversial view of how we ought to understand apparently random, peculiar, and so-called "out-of-place" details of Chekhov's text—images, sounds, epithets, disconnected actions and utterances of characters, etc. Previous codifications of Chekhov's poetics had attributed a fundamentally mimetic function to such details: they cannot be understood as part of any textual pattern because their purpose is to convey the randomness of lived life. Senderovich instead has formulated a semiotic theory of poetic prose that privileges the seemingly incidental as key to a story's inner meaning. Only through attending to such details and the semantic networks they create, he argues, can the depths of a Chekhov text be plumbed.[23] Like Senderovich, Robert Louis Jackson has been offering finely nuanced symbolic readings of Chekhov's stories and plays for decades. These are readings that—while grounded in poetics—champion a deeply moral and humanistic view of Chekhov, and so diverge quite notably from the set of concerns characteristic of Senderovich's work. They also set Jackson's approach apart from those, particularly prominent in Russia in recent years, that view Chekhov as a writer for whom Russian Orthodox faith was central; for Jackson regards Chekhov's ethical orientation not as evidence of religious faith, but as a sensibility springing from the principles of Judeo-Christian morality. In addition to his "On Chekhov's Art," which leads off this volume, he offers an article illustrating his approach in the treatment of one Chekhov story, "Rothschild's Fiddle."

---

[22] The "mimetic" approach to Chekhov's poetics achieved its most sophisticated and influential articulation in the works of Aleksandr P. Chudakov, *Poetika Chekhova* (Moscow: Nauka, 1971; translated as *Chekhov's Poetics*, trans. Edwina Cruise and Donald Dragt [Ann Arbor, MI: Ardis, 1983]); and *Mir Chekhova: Vozniknovenie i utverzhdenie* (Moscow: Sovetskii pisatel', 1986).

[23] Unfortunately, we are unable to include Senderovich's paper in this volume. Key statements of his approach to Chekhov may be found in *Chekhov—s glazu na glaz: Istoriia odnoi oderzhimosti A. P. Chekhov. Opyt fenomenologii tvorchestva* (St. Petersburg: Dmitrii Bulanin, 1994), and "Poetics and Meaning in Chekhov's 'On the Road,'" in *Anton Chekhov Rediscovered: A Collection of New Studies with a Comprehensive Bibliography*, ed. S. Senderovich and M. Sendich (East Lansing, MI: Russian Language Journal, 1987), 135–66.

The next three articles stand well for the work of the succeeding generation of American Chekhov scholars. In "Chekhov's Anti-Melodramatic Imagination: Inoculation against the Diseases of the Contemporary Theater," Svetlana Evdokimova (Brown University) situates Chekhov against the cultural and social conventions of nineteenth-century Russian theater, explicating the "anti-theatrical" essence of his plays—in effect, his translation of drama into a new idiom. The next piece is by Cathy Popkin (Columbia University), who in recent years has published a series of studies on Chekhov's epistemologies as author and physician. In Chekhov's medical narratives, she shows, he often stages the epistemological insufficiencies of the medical gaze, and he dramatizes the complementary way of knowing that is represented by narrative art. In "Doctor without Patients/Man without a Spleen: Chekhov's Practice" she moves onto new ground, exploring the theme of professional and personal identity—fundamental in Chekhov's life and art—in an exquisite reading of one of Chekhov's last stories, "The Bishop," that relies on just the sort of symbolically weighted details Jackson and Senderovich have taught us to appreciate. And last, the contribution of Spencer Golub (Brown University) is a creative, *sui generis* treatment of the hypochondriac and obsessive-compulsive modes that he finds enacted in and by Chekhov's plays. His "Incapacity" is a piece that transgresses (if not obliterates) the boundary between literature and criticism in ways wonderfully consonant with the spirit of this volume and the NEH symposium from which it derives. In it he inhabits, as it were, the character of Epikhodov from Chekhov's *Cherry Orchard*, and compels us to think about the play and Chekhov's psychological poetics anew.

**Theater Practitioners on Chekhov**

The next segment comprises a "Forum on Performance Practice," in which theater practitioners share their experience-derived views on staging Chekhov. Ellen Beckerman, the young and extremely innovative artistic director of LightBox, staged *Gull*—LightBox's adaptation of Chekhov's *Seagull*—at Colby College during the NEH symposium. Her piece provides insight into the creative process behind that troupe's cooperative achievement. Beckerman's treatment of Chekhov is that of a sensitive reader and theater practitioner who does not have access to the original and claims total freedom to move Chekhov in ways that work for the current moment. At the symposium we heard from two other theater practitioners who, in contrast, strive to remain faithful to what they understand as the Chekhov theater tradition. Alexander Popov of the Moscow Art Theater spoke of bringing a still alive Stanislavsky method to budding American actors more than a century after that method's initiation.[24] In her contribution, Carol Rocamora (Tisch School of the Arts, New York University) told a similar story from the other side, as

---

[24] Unfortunately, we go to press without his contribution.

it were: she traveled to Moscow and consulted with Russian theater directors so as to immerse herself in the tradition of Chekhov's staging as a step toward her own staging of his plays.

## Chekhov and the Medical Humanities

The NEH symposium included a program in the medical humanities. While the literature on Chekhov invariably credits his identity and professional insights as a physician with a critical role in making him the writer he was, just why this was so has largely eluded us. In particular, we lack an understanding of the complexities of Chekhov's dual identity that might penetrate beyond truisms and include reflection on what Chekhov's mastery of literary art gave him as a physician. At the symposium we confronted these questions in a multidisciplinary arena that included health-care professionals, literary scholars with mastery of Chekhov's biography, and historians of medicine.

The conditions for fruitful dialogue would seem to have long been in place. A deep personal response to Chekhov as an author and colleague was already manifest among Russian physicians in Chekhov's lifetime. This was perhaps best demonstrated in 1902 at the Eighth Congress of the Pirogov Society—the Moscow-based association of Russian physicians—which celebrated Chekhov with what can only be called a secular version of an icon procession featuring his portrait, and at which the Moscow Art Theater performed *Uncle Vanya*, one central character of which is a physician.[25] Physician-colleagues were among the first memoirists of Chekhov, and they appeared eager to claim him as their own;[26] in both the former Soviet Union and in the West, monographs have been published by physicians for whom the study of literature—or in some cases, Chekhov himself—appears to be something of a second profession or hobby.[27] After a particularly difficult night of service as a third-year student at Columbia's College of Physicians and Surgeons in the 1950s, Dr. Robert Coles, from whom we will hear below,

---

[25] See N. I. Gitovich, *Letopis' zhizni i tvorchestva A. P. Chekhova* (Moscow: Khudozhestvennaia literatura, 1955), 692–93.

[26] See, for instance, the memoirs of G. I. Rossolimo, I. N. Al'tshuller, and V. V. Veresaev in *A. P. Chekhov v vospominaniiakh sovremennikov*, ed. N. I. Gitovich (Moscow: Khudozhestvennaia literatura, 1986).

[27] Some examples of works on Chekhov by physicians are: I. M. Geizer, *Chekhov i meditsina* (Moscow: Medgiz, 1954); E. B. Meve, *Meditsina v tvorchestve i zhizni A. P. Chekhova* (Kiev: Gos. meditsinskoe izd-vo USSR, 1961); B. M. Shubin, "Doktor A. P. Chekhov," in his *Dopolnenie k portretam* (Moscow: Znanie, 1998); M. B. Mirskii, *Doktor Chekhov* (Moscow: Nauka, 2003); William B. Ober, M.D., "Chekhov among the Doctors: The Doctor's Dilemma," in his *Boswell's Clap and Other Essays: Medical Analyses of Literary Men's Afflictions* (Carbondale, IL: S.I.U. Press, 1979); John Coope, *Doctor Chekhov: A Study in Literature and Medicine* (Chale, Isle of Wight: Cross Publishing, 1997); Elizabeth Loewald, *Sighting Anton Pavlovich* (Tenafly, NJ: Hermitage Publishers, 2004).

was given a volume of Chekhov stories by one of his teachers and told, "Chekhov should be every doctor's lifelong companion."[28]

Chekhov himself understood how reading stories might be a beneficial part of medical school education three-quarters of a century before such curricular innovations began to appear in the United States under the recently coined term "Narrative Medicine."[29] Thus, when it appeared that his book on Sakhalin might be accepted as a dissertation in medicine, making him eligible for a teaching position on the medical faculty of Moscow University, he told the neuropathologist Grigorii Rossolimo (who had been a medical school classmate), "If I were a teacher [at a medical school], I would try to draw my students as deeply as possible into the realm of the patient's subjective feelings, and I think that could really be of use to the students."[30] His proposal to de-objectify the patient in medical training was simultaneously a revelatory remark about narrative stylistics—perhaps the most interesting overt remark Chekhov ever made regarding the special value of *personal* narration as a feature of the poetics of fiction.

Meanwhile, among literary scholars today, there is great interest in participating in the relatively new academic field of medical humanities. In a gesture signifying consolidation of the field (and perhaps staking ownership to it), the Modern Language Association of America has recently published a volume meant to assist academics seeking to establish medical humanities curricula, *Teaching Literature and Medicine*.[31] Although humanities courses began appearing in medical school curricula in the 1960s in an attempt to "remedy an imbalance in medical education (and practice) in which too much emphasis was placed on the technological aspects of health care and too little on the human aspects of medicine and caregiving," the discipline of medical humanities as such—as a humanities discipline—is of more recent advent.[32] In part it has emerged from developments more or less internal to humanities: for example, an increased appreciation for the social and historical context of literary production (as in the New Historicism and Cultural Studies, and the tremendously influential work of the theorist and historian of medicine Michel Foucault) after a lengthy bias toward focus on the aesthetic object

---

[28] Robert Coles, "The Wry Dr. Chekhov," in his *Times of Surrender* (Iowa City: University of Iowa Press, 1988), 52.

[29] This formulation belongs to Dr. Rita Charon of Columbia University, who is also a Ph.D. in English.

[30] Reported by G. I. Rossolimo, "Vospominaniia o Chekhove," in *A. P. Chekhov v vospominaniiakh sovremennikov*, 436.

[31] *Teaching Literature and Medicine*, ed. Anne Hunsaker Hawkins and Marilyn Chandler McEntyre (New York: MLA, 2000).

[32] Anne Hunsaker Hawkins and Marilyn Chandler McEntyre, "Teaching Literature and Medicine: A Retrospective and a Rationale," introd. to *Teaching Literature and Medicine*, 4–5.

itself (the formalism of New Criticism, then Structuralism and Semiotics); and the imperative many humanists feel to find a practical justification for their work, as well as their canny grasp of an opportunity to associate themselves with medical schools, which are often centers of economic gravity and status in academic institutions.

Not surprisingly, however, there remain wide divergences between what literary scholars and historians see themselves as doing under the rubric of medical humanities and what such intellectual activity means to physicians who, like Chekhov, chase two hares at once, or to medical students subjected to coursework in the area. In spite of the lengthy tradition of doctors writing about Chekhov, there has been a veritable chasm between the approaches to Chekhov of literary scholars and those of physicians who have written about him. It is not a question of finding agreement; rather, of finding a common language in which to talk to one another, and genuinely hearing what the other says.

For physicians literature offers a comfortable venue for discussing moral and philosophical problems that are often better kept at arm's length during actual practice; they also often read works of fiction as monographs of psychopathology that are "better written than clinical case histories [and] often more complete" and comprise a kind of pseudo-enhancement of clinical experience.[33] And for practitioners in a field where personal selfhood can be overwhelmed by professional identity, there may be much potential gratification in reading stories about that self. Literary scholars, anthropologists and historians, on the contrary, speak in a jargon-filled language and refer to esoteric theories, remote from lived experience, in posing arguments that, if fully credited, might very well threaten to question, demystify, or perhaps even undo some of the epistemological foundations of medical discourse and, as a consequence, the very selves of its practitioners. Thus the editor of *Literature and Medicine* refused to publish a piece on one of Chekhov's medical stories by a symposium participant because, as she put it, she thought it might be offensive to the physicians among the journal's audience and editorial board.[34] Neither side is very open to the most radical insights of the other. Just as Chekhov did in his dual professional life, the medical humanities segment of the Chekhov conference will address that impasse.

The Medical Humanities part of the volume is divided into four sections.

The first provides a transcript of an hour-length interview—conducted specifically for the NEH symposium—with a stellar figure in the area of medicine and literature, Dr. Robert Coles of Harvard University. As a scholar of literature and professor of medicine, Dr. Coles was doing medical

---

[33] Andrew E. Slaby and Laurence R. Tancredi, "Literary Insights and Theories of Person," in *Medicine and Literature*, ed. Enid Rhodes Peschel (New York: Neale Watson Academic Publications, Inc., 1980), 113.

[34] Michael Finke, personal communication.

humanities long before the field existed in anyone else's imagination, and he more than any other individual must receive credit for its establishment as a discipline in the academy and an expected component of medical school training. As a prolific and creative author and social activist, Coles has been making the culture the rest of us only study. If Chekhov had been an American active in the last half of the twentieth century, he could not have been Chekhov, but he might well have been Robert Coles. At the NEH symposium a slightly edited version of this interview was screened for participants in a seminar on the medical humanities cosponsored by NEH, the Maine Humanities Council, and Penobscot Bay Medical Center. That video of the interview is included with this volume on a DVD.

There follow articles by one Chekhov scholar who has been working in the area of literature and medicine and one American historian of medicine. Conference co-organizer Michael Finke (University of Illinois at Urbana-Champaign) explores the complexities of Chekhov's multiple identities as author, physician, and patient in his speculative paper, "Heal Thyself, Hide Thyself: Why Did Dr. Chekhov Ignore His TB?" Historian Conevery Bolton Valenčius (Harvard University) situates Chekhov's longest and least understood book, *Sakhalin Island*, in the generic context of medical geography, thereby opening a frame of reference for that work to which literary scholars of Chekhov have hitherto been quite blind.

At the symposium, there was an open forum, in which many Maine health care professionals took part, for the discussion of several Chekhov stories; the stories—"Anyuta," "Ward 6," and "A Medical Case"—had been indicated in advance to registrants. The discussion was facilitated by one Chekhov scholar, Michael Finke, and one medical practitioner who has done work in medical humanities and been active in the Maine Humanities Council, Dr. Richard Kahn. A transcript of that discussion featuring the responses to Chekhov of doctors, nurses, counselors, and social workers, is offered here.

Last, through the good auspices of one of the symposium participants, the opportunity arose to include Eugene Alper's translation of the memoir of Chekhov by his Yalta physician, Dr. I. N. Altshuller, which to our knowledge has never before seen print in English. Altshuller cared for Chekhov in the last period of his life, when he was in sharply declining health. We have decided to include those parts of the memoir that touch on Chekhov's identity as physician and mortally ill patient.

# On Chekhov's Art

## Robert Louis Jackson, Yale University

Wisdom and platitude sometimes coincide. "Read slowly and deeply, looking forwards and backwards"—I once read in an old grammar. I have always read cautiously and, in learning Russian, developed a habit of examining words closely.

The study of Pushkin and Turgenev contributed especially to my reading of Chekhov's texts. Pushkin, like Chekhov, uses everyday speech in his prose and drama. The simple, colloquial dialogue in his plays, for example, in *The Stone Guest* (*Kamennyi gost'*), conveys complex and subtle thought.[1] E. A. Baratynsky, after reading in 1840 some of Pushkin's unpublished work and commenting on the "amazing beauty" of his verse, adds with surprise: "Can you imagine what marks all the last plays? Power and depth!"[2] How had Baratynsky, a poet and connoisseur of art, earlier missed the profundity of Pushkin's plays? (With the exception of *The Stone Guest*, Pushkin's dramas had been published.) Did the apparent simplicity of Pushkin's dialogue, of his language and style, veil the complexity of the work? Did Baratynsky not recognize, to borrow the words of Ralph Waldo Emerson in "Goethe; Or, The Writer" in *Representative Men*, "that the highest simplicity of structure is produced, not by few elements, but by the highest complexity"?

Some critics in the late nineteenth and early twentieth centuries viewed Turgenev as a great "stylist" of the Russian language and a faithful chronicler of social-cultural history in mid-century Russia, but considered his writing to be without much real depth. To some of these same critics Dostoevsky had a great deal to say, but said it badly. Yet Turgenev was a powerful thinker, as Dostoevsky was also a great stylist. What blocked the path of these critics to a deeper exploration of Turgenev's artistic thought? At the turn of the nineteenth century the Russian critic A. A. Andreevsky wrote of the "secret wealth of [Turgenev's] devilishly light and musical prose, one resembling the

---

[1] See my essay "Moral-Philosophical Subtext in *The Stone Guest*," in *Alexander Pushkin's Little Tragedies: The Poetics of Brevity*, ed. Svetlana Evdokimova (Madison: University of Wisconsin Press, 2003), 191–208.

[2] See Geir Kjetsaa's selection of Baratynsky's letters in his study, *Evgenii Baratynskii: Zhizn' i tvorchestvo* (Oslo-Bergen-Tromso: Universitetsforlaget, 1973), 623.

*Chekhov the Immigrant. Translating a Cultural Icon.* Michael C. Finke and Julie de Sherbinin, eds. Bloomington, IN: Slavica Publishers, 2007, 17–25.

verse of Pushkin whose profound inner content only a few people were able to disclose, and then at a very late date."[3]

Criticism, too, was slow in exploring the rich subtext of Chekhov's works and the means that he used to give expression to his artistic thought. Only in the past few decades has Chekhov scholarship begun to validate Sergey Bulgakov's prescient observation of one hundred years ago that after Tolstoy and Dostoevsky, writers who took as their chief theme "the basic questions of human life and spirit," Chekhov is "*the* writer of greatest philosophical significance."[4] Criticism acknowledged Chekhov's genius, but who would have placed Chekhov side by side with Tolstoy and Dostoevsky as a writer of the greatest *philosophical* significance?

Chekhov did not write any critical essays that called attention to his social or philosophical ideas or to his artistic method, nor was it his general practice to stage philosophical debates in his works, though there are some notable exceptions, such as *Ward No. 6*. Many of Chekhov's early critics, seeking in his stories the tendentious, the ideological, the judgmental, and finding none of these, charged him with "indifference." Some of these critics had an agenda. Others failed to grasp the nature of Chekhov's art. In this connection, Chekhov's paradoxical *poetics of seeing* is of especial interest. On the general theme of nature's impact on people, Chekhov wrote to Aleksei Suvorin, May 4, 1889:

> Nature is a very good tranquilizer. It reconciles, i.e., it makes a person indifferent [ravnodushnym]. And in this world one must be indifferent. Only indifferent people are capable of looking at things clearly, of being just [byt' spravedlivymi], and working. Of course, this applies only to intelligent and honorable people; as for egoists and empty people, you'll find plenty of indifference there. (Chekhov, *PssP* 3: 203).[5]

Indifference—we might substitute the words "detachment" or "equanimity"—enables a person to *see things clearly, truthfully, or justly,* and to *work* effectively. Chekhov's indifferent observer is a person of intelligence and ethical culture. One brings something to what one sees. What is striking here about Chekhov's approach to seeing or looking is the identification of *seeing with truth,* an ancient collaboration, to be sure, but one that goes to the heart of his poetics.

In Chekhov's conception of the artistic process, and of seeing in general, *point of view, how* one looks at reality, that is, one's vantage point of observa-

---

[3] See A. A. Andreevskii, "Turgenev: Ego individual'nost' i poeziia," *Literaturnye ocherki* (St. Petersburg, 1902); quoted in *Sobranie kriticheskikh materialov dlia izucheniia Turgeneva,* ed. V. Zelenskii (Moscow, 1910), 124.

[4] Sergei N. Bulgakov, *Chekhov kak myslitel'* (1904; repr., Kiev, 1910), 8.

[5] See Chekhov's letter of 8 May 1889 to his brother Alexander for a variant discussion on this theme of indifference (*PssP* 3: 210).

tion, telescopes with *point of view* as *outlook*. Here outlook on reality or the world is not a matter of answers, solutions, or judgments; rather it finds expression in and through depiction and narration ("question and intention" are immanent in the work of art), that is, through the artist's disposition of his materials, and through his imagery (the artist's specialty, according to Chekhov, is the creation of "images"; *PssP* 3: 45).

"I saw *everything*; hence the question now is not *what* I saw, but *how* I saw it" (Chekhov's italics), Chekhov wrote to Suvorin on the occasion of his departure from the island of Sakhalin, September 11, 1890 (*PssP* 4: 133). Chekhov's remark succinctly gives expression to his poetics of seeing and to his effort to impose on his writing—even a work as morally and socially volatile as that of his work in progress, *Island of Sakhalin. Notes of a Traveler* (1893)—a maximally artistic approach, that is, one of strict depiction and narration. Here in this remarkable multigeneric work, Chekhov's art of speaking in images combines in a unique way with rigorous scientific, scholarly, and journalistic objectivity—the kind that allows artistically-focused materials to speak for themselves.

Chekhov's poetics of seeing, of course, was not new in Russian literature. In a striking formulation, the young Leo Tolstoy insisted on the priority of artistic truth in literature. In contrast to Chekhov, however, he took as his point of departure an ethical-religious injunction: "The word of the Gospel, *'do not judge'*, is profoundly true in art: narrate, depict, but do not judge" (Evangel'skoe slovo: *ne sudi* gluboko verno v iskusstve: rasskazyvai, izobrazhai, no ne sudi), he wrote in his notebook April 10, 1857 (Tolstoy's italics).[6]

Tolstoy's dictum was not an idle one. It would later find dramatic expression in *Anna Karenina* and, in the first instance, in the novel's gospel-oriented epigraph: "Vengeance is Mine, I will Repay."[7] This injunction to the reader encoded Tolstoy's guiding poetic principle in his novel. At issue was not the *fact* of Anna's guilt, but *how* the author was going to present and relate that fact in a way that expressed his overarching point of view. The Russian critic N. N. Strakhov keenly discerned the "how" of the matter when he observed in a letter to Tolstoy of July 23, 1874: "You grasp everything from a very lofty point of view" (Vse vziato u Vas s ochen' vysokoi tochki zreniia). Strakhov again noted in a letter of January 1, 1875: "You do not idealize or

---

[6] See L. N. Tolstoi, *O literature: Stat'i. Pis'ma. dnevniki*, ed. F. A. Ivanova (Moscow: 1955), 41.

[7] See my discussion of this epigraph in my article, "On the Ambivalent Beginning of *Anna Karenina*," in *Semantic Analysis of Literary Texts: To Honour Jan van der Eng on the Occasion of his 65th Birthday*, ed. Eric de Haard et al. (Amsterdam: Elsevier, 1990), 345–52. For a discussion of Tolstoy's development of the tragic dimensions of Anna, see my essay "Chance and Design in *Anna Karenina*," in *The Disciplines of Criticism: Essays in Literary Theory, Interpretation, and History*, ed. Peter Demetz, Thomas Greene, and Lowry Nelson, Jr. (New Haven and London: Yale University Press, 1968), 315–29.

belittle [passion]. You are *the only just* person [Vy *edinyi spravedlivyi* chelovek], so that your Anna Karenina will arouse endless pity, but it will be clear to everyone that she is guilty" (Strakhov's italics).[8]

In his discussion of *Anna Karenina* in the July–August 1877 issue of *Diary of a Writer*, Dostoevsky recognized that Tolstoy's approach to Anna was not that of a prosecutor or judge, but of a *novelist* who viewed Anna's tragedy from a higher ethical-religious literary perspective. In Dostoevsky's analysis, Tolstoy presents Anna's drama in the great tradition of Greek and European tragedy. He perceives a conflation of Aristotelian and Christian concepts of tragedy in *Anna Karenina*.[9] The "human judge," he writes in illustration of Tolstoy's idea, should approach the drama of Anna with an awareness of a Law that is higher than human law and judgment. Referring to the "somber and terrible" denouement of Anna's drama, and focusing directly on the significance of the novel's epigraph, Dostoevsky wrote:

> The human judge himself ought to know that he is not the final judge; that he himself is a sinner; that the measure and scales in his hands will be an absurdity *if* he, holding measure and scales, does not himself submit to the law of the yet unsolved mystery and turn to the only solution—to Mercy and Love... In [Tolstoy's] picture [of Anna's moral and psychological fall] there is such a profound lesson for the human judge, for the one who holds the measure and the scales, that he will naturally exclaim in fear and perplexity, "No, Vengeance is not always mine, and it is not always for me to repay."[10]

What marks Tolstoy's depiction and narration of Anna's tragic fall is the organic unity of the esthetic and ethical: the *picture is the lesson*, and the *lesson is the picture*. The tragedy of Anna arouses feelings of fear and mercy, humility and love, and finally, "perplexity" (*nedoumenie*), that is, an awareness that the total truth of human conduct is inaccessible. Just this eminently *novelistic* picture-lesson (epitomized for Dostoevsky in the scene of reconciliation around the sick-bed of Anna) constitutes the highest moral-spiritual perspective in *Anna Karenina*.

---

[8] See L. N. Tolstoi—N. N. Strakhov, *Polnoe sobranie perepiski*, 2 vols., ed. A. A. Donskov et al. (Ottawa and Moscow: Slavic Research Group at the University of Ottawa and State L. N. Tolstoy Museum, 2003), 1: 171, 190. Strakhov emphasized in Tolstoy's approach to Anna's drama what Ralph Waldo Emerson in his essay on Goethe had posited as an artistic ideal: the attainment of "the just perspective, the seeing of the whole." Emerson, "Goethe; Or, The Writer," in *Representative Men* [1850], ed. Pamela Schirmeister (New York: Marsilio Publishers Corp., 1995), 193.

[9] For Dostoevsky's approach to this aspect of *Anna Karenina*, see F. M. Dostoevskii, *Polnoe sobranie sochinenii v tridtsati tomakh*, 30 vols. (Leningrad: Nauka, 1972–90), 25: 199–202.

[10] Ibid., 202.

Throughout his life Tolstoy strained against the limits of his poetic principle—depict, narrate, but do not judge. Chekhov, for his part, strictly holds to this principle. The ethical impulse is immanent in the way he sees and focuses reality. In this sense, one may say that Chekhov, like Tolstoy, *sees truthfully, justly*, and never in a spirit of moralistic triumphalism, never in judgment. Broad social or ideological "answers" or solutions are inimical to the spirit and practice of his art; this is true even as his work lifts the reader to the highest realms of moral, social, and philosophical awareness. In his important letter of October 27, 1888 to Suvorin, Chekhov warns his friend against confusing

> two concepts: the *solution of a problem* and the *correct posing of a question*. Only the second is obligatory for the artist. Not a single question is resolved in *Anna Karenina* or *[Eugene] Onegin*, but they completely satisfy one, for the very reason that all questions are correctly posed in them. The court is obligated correctly to pose questions, while it is up the jurors, each juror to his own taste, to decide them. (Chekhov's italics; Chekhov, *PssP* 3: 46)

In his remarkable correspondence, a monument to his life, thought, and epistolary art, Chekhov speaks his mind on a wide range of issues and questions concerning life, society, moral culture, history, literature, criticism, science, psychology, religion, philosophy, etc. We recognize the man and the artist. The full depth, breadth, and clarity of his insight and vision, however, are to be found in his belles-lettres and drama. Yet precisely in this imaginative realm the Chekhov we know from his correspondence is not immediately or directly apparent. The outwardly simple, tranquil, and everyday Chekhov text initially yields much less than the often garrulous and hyperactive texts of Tolstoy and Dostoevsky. Yet the apparent simplicity of Chekhov's text masks an art of astounding complexity and truth.

"Let everything on the stage be just as complex and at the same time just as simple as in life," Chekhov is reported to have said. "People dine, merely dine, but at that moment their happiness is being made or their life is being smashed."[11] Like Maeterlinck, Chekhov sought out the dramas of life not in melodramatic or super-dramatic actions, conflicts, or events, but in everyday life and actions.

In this connection, Chekhov's relation to Turgenev deserves mention. As we know, he often spoke critically and tartly of Turgenev, as writers often do of those who have strongly influenced them. Chekhov was particularly enamored of Turgenev in his apprentice years, though Tolstoy certainly displaced Turgenev as a literary mentor. Yet Chekhov surely found much in Turgenev's prose and drama that anticipated his own poetics. "Remember that however subtle and complex the inner structure of some tissues in the human body,

---

[11] "Vospominaniia D. Gorodetskogo," *Birzhevye vedomosti*, no. 364 (1904).

the skin, for example, nonetheless its appearance is comprehensible and homogeneous," Turgenev wrote to the young Konstantin N. Leontiev, October 3, 1860. "A poet must be a psychologist, but a secret one. He must know and feel the roots of phenomena, but represent only the phenomena themselves in their flowering and fading."[12] Further, in a letter to Countess I. E. Lambert, October 14, 1859, Turgenev advanced a way of looking at life that brings us to the threshold of Chekhov's tragi-comic drama:

> It recently occurred to me that in the fate of almost every person there's something tragic—only often this tragic element is concealed from the person by the banal surface of life. The one who remains on the surface (and there are many such people) often fails even to suspect that he is the hero of a tragedy. Some lady will complain of indigestion—and not even know that by these words she wants to say that her whole life has been shattered. Take here [on Turgenev's estate] for example: all about me are peaceful, quiet existences, but if you look closely you'll see something tragic in each of them—either something personal, or laid upon them by history, or by the evolution of the people.[13]

Chekhov took a close look at Russian life, at the banal surface of life, at life in all its everyday manifestations, forms, and detail; he went on to evolve an epic poetics of representation of reality, an art disclosing the organic relationship that exists between the seemingly unimportant detail or aspects of everyday surface reality and the essential drama of life underlying it.[14] In the cross-section of the moment, in life in all its fragmentary, fumbling, and chance-scarred manifestations, Chekhov sought out the longitudinal lines of truth—design and law: not what *had to be*, but what *has become*. Chekhov does not at all deny the presence and importance of accident or chance in life, in the exploration and development of situation and character in art, in the imaginative process. Chance is freedom. In the completed artistic drama of life, however, freedom is consummated: what was once accident now becomes design. There are no superfluous details. One may depict chance, accident, chaos in art, but *chaotic art* is a contradiction in terms.

---

[12] See Ivan Turgenev, *Polnoe sobranie sochinenii i pisem v dvadtsati vos'mi tomakh* [*Pss*, 28 vols.: sochineniia, 15 vols.; pis'ma, 13 vols.], *Pis'ma*, vol. 4 (Moscow-Leningrad: Izdatel'stvo Akademii nauk SSSR, 1960–68), 135. Turgenev's letter to Leontiev was first published in the journal *Russkaia mysl'*, no. 12 (1886): 83–85.

[13] Turgenev, *Pss, Pis'ma*, vol. 3, 354.

[14] For some earlier commentary on "detail" and "accident" in Chekhov's poetics along the line of my discussion, see M. P. Gromov, *Kniga o Chekhove* (Moscow, Sovremennik, 1989), 128–35. For other discussions on the "indissoluble connections between essence and details" in Chekhov's work, see Z. Papernyi, *Zapisnye knizhki Chekhova* (Moscow: Sovetskii pisatel', 1976), 91–125.

Less than two months before he died, Chekhov received from the literary critic and poet B. A. Sadovsky a poem, "The Leper" ("Prokazhennyi"), for evaluation. Chekhov found the content of the poem unconvincing. "For example," he wrote in a letter of reply, "your Leper says: 'I stand elegantly dressed / Not daring to look out the window.'" "It is unclear," Chekhov continues, "why does the leper have to dress in an elegant suit and why doesn't he dare look out the window? Overall, your hero's actions often lack logic, *whereas in art, as in life, there is nothing accidental*" (my italics—RLJ).[15]

Chekhov's remark echoes that of one of the characters in his story "On Official Business" ("Po delam sluzhby"), a person who has come to see life and people not as a mass of accidental disconnected detail and disjunctive lives but as a world imbued with a higher meaning. "Some kind of connection, invisible, but significant and necessary exists between both of [these people], between them and even Taunitz, and between everybody, everybody; in this life, even in the most desolate backwaters, nothing is accidental, everything is full of one general thought, everything has one soul, one goal, and to understand this it is not enough to think, not enough to reason, one must in addition, have the gift of insight into life, a gift, probably, that is not granted to everybody"(*PssS* 10: 99).

It was Chekhov who had that gift of insight, the gift of perceiving connections in the natural, social, and moral worlds, the gift of sensing the organic relation of the detail, the part, to the whole complex truth. In this respect Chekhov's work fulfilled Goethe's prescription for the highest form of cognition. "The highest thing would be to recognize that all fact is already theory." "Don't go looking for anything beyond phenomena, they themselves are the theory."[16] The process of *seeing* is itself an act of theorizing. As Goethe put it in the preface to his study of color: "Every act of looking leads to contemplation, every act of contemplation to reflection, every reflection to making connections, and thus we can say that every attentive glance we make in the world is already an act of theorizing."[17]

---

[15] "Voobshche v postupkakh Vashego geroia chasto otsutstvuet logika, togda kak v iskusstve, kak i v zhizni, nichego sluchainogo ne byvaet." A. P. Chekhov (*PssP* 12: 108).

[16] "Das Höchste wäre: zu begreifen, dass alles Faktische schon Theorie ist." See "Maximen und Reflexionen," in *Goethes Werke: Hamburger Ausgabe in 14 Bänden* (Hamburg: Christian Wegner Verlag, 1963), 12: 432 (no. 488). "Theory" here is not pure abstraction for Goethe. He goes on to say: "The blue of the sky reveals to us the basic law of chromaticism. Don't go looking for anything beyond phenomena: they themselves are the theory [Man suche nur nichts hinter den Phänomenen: sie selbst sind die Lehre]." "Die Lehre" in German can be used in the sense of "theory," "teaching," "science," "tenet," "precept," etc. The title of Goethe's study on color, *Zur Farbenlehre*, has been translated as *Theory of Color* or *Color Theory*.

[17] "Jedes Ansehen geht über in ein Betrachten, jedes Betrachten in ein Sinnen, jedes Sinnen in ein Verknüpfen, und so kann man sagen, dass wir schon bei jedem auf-

Chekhov is one of the greatest contemplators, connectors, theorizers in world literature.[18] Whether as writer of short stories and plays, as physician, journalist, cultural historian, or statistician (or all of these things, as in *The Island of Sakhalin*), Chekhov sifts through the multiple "incidents" and "accidents" of life and arrives at a sense of the whole, not as something amorphous and made up of isolated parts, but as something connected, unified in and through its parts and details. The sense that the reader or viewer carries away of Chekhov "hitting the mark," getting things "just right," of representing something in a way that "could not be expressed differently," is at root an intuitive recognition that where essences and final summations are concerned in art or life nothing is accidental, nothing arbitrary, nothing fortuitous, everything is felt to be "true." "What is the general?" Goethe asks. "The individual case. What is the specific? / A million 'cases.'"[19]

Chekhov's "thousand stories"—at least he once estimated that he had written that many—do not simply constitute a collection of isolated pieces;[20] they are a way of looking at the world, a way of knowing it, a way of representing the world of Russian life in its unity; in the broadest sense, his stories and plays are a way of affirming ethical, social, and spiritual "connections," what one character in "On Official Business" calls "one general thought." Chekhov, however, does not preach or characterize his thought. He embodies thought in images. Thus, the constant "walking" (*PssS* 10: 82, 98,

---

merksamen Blick in die Welt theoretisieren." See Goethe, "Vorwort," *Zur Farbenlehre* (ibid., 13: 316).

[18] Chekhov was not a "theorist" in any modern sense of the term, of course. He would doubtlessly have agreed with Goethe, however, that the "phenomena" themselves *are* the theory (see n. 16). He would certainly have shared Goethe's unease with theory-generated "abstraction." Goethe himself followed his comment on "theorizing" with this cautionary observation: "We should, however, undertake and do this theorizing consciously, self-aware, with freedom and, to use a daring word, with irony; such adroitness is necessary if the abstraction, which we view apprehensively, is to be harmless and the experimental results that we seek are to be live and useful" (Dieses aber mit Bewusstsein, mit Selbstkenntnis, mit Freiheit und, um uns eines gewagten Wortes zu bedienen, mit Ironie zu tun und vorzunehmen, eine solche Gewandtheit ist nötig, wenn die Abstraktion, vor der wir uns fürchten, unschädlich und das Erfahrungsresultat, das wir hoffen, recht lebendig und nützlich werden soll). Ibid.

[19] "Was ist das Allgemeine? / Der einzelne Fall. / Was ist das Besondere? / Millionen Fälle." Goethe, "Maximen und Reflexionen," 12: 432 (no. 489).

[20] "What seemed a 'fortuitous collection of facts,'" to many critics at the end of the nineteenth century, wrote Boris Eikhenbaum, "was in fact the realization of the basic principles of Chekhov's artistic work—the endeavor to embrace all of Russian life in its various manifestations." Eichenbaum, "Chekhov at Large," in *Chekhov: A Collection of Critical Essays*, ed. Robert Louis Jackson (Englewood Cliffs, NJ: Prentice Hall, 1967), 23. Eikhenbaum's original essay in Russian appeared in the Soviet journal *Zvezda* in 1944.

99) of the simple unidealized figure of Loshadin in "On Official Business"—this lowly delivery man and messenger is forever on the move, going about, "walking from person to person" (khodit ot cheloveka k cheloveku), "and he will forever and continuously be walking and walking" (navsegda i budet vse khodit' i khodit'), fulfilling some errand or service—establishes a pattern of crisscrossing connections that are social and ethical in content. This constant walking provides the clue to the "general thought." In the language of the Old and New Testaments, Loshadin is *walking in the ways of the Lord*. "This is the way, walk you in it" (Isaiah 30:21). Or, as Loshadin, in completely unbiblical language, puts it when asked if his work was not at times fearful: "It's fearful, sir, but really that's our work—service, there's no walking away from it" (Strashno, barin, da ved' nashe delo takoe—sluzhba, nikuda ot nei ne uidesh', *PssS* 10: 90). "Sluzhba"—*service*, in the deepest sense, Loshadin's sense, is not just "administrative service," but service of one's fellow human beings—that is the "official business" of every individual.

There is a magic simplicity to Chekhov's word and style. In a first reading of Chekhov one seems to glide across his text. Yet when we follow the first reading with a new one, and then with another and another, the depth and density of Chekhov's imaginative world and the complexity of his language and thought become evident; what seemed a smooth surface no longer seems quite so smooth, and Chekhov's artistic word and world no longer appears quite so plain or direct.

Yet all the same Chekhov's text continues to exercise its magic power—that magic that induced Vladimir Mayakovsky to say of Chekhov's work: "[His] language is as precise as 'Hello!' as simple as 'Give me a glass of tea.'"[21] What Mayakovsky did not add was what Chekhov had to say about such simple actions as dining or drinking tea: at such moments "people's happiness is being made or their life is being smashed."

Mayakovsky follows up his comment on Chekhov's language by suggesting that the compact form in which Chekhov conveys the idea of a story is "the urgent cry of the future— 'Economy!'"[22] If there is an urgent cry of the future, however, it is not just for economy in writing. As Chekhov once put it, "I know how to write briefly about big things."

---

[21] Vladimir Maiakovskii, "Dva Chekhova," in *Polnoe sobranie sochinenii* (Moscow: Khudozhestvennaia literatura, 1955), 1: 301.

[22] Ibid.

# Translating Chekhov's Prose

# Forum on Translation

Moderators: Professor Carol Apollonio Flath, Duke University
and Professor Julie de Sherbinin, Colby College

Participants: Peter Constantine, New York, Richard Pevear,
Paris, and Larissa Volokhonsky, Paris

JULIE DE SHERBININ

It is my pleasure to introduce an event that many of us have been particularly anticipating: a discussion of the translation of Chekhov into English—and, specifically, into American English—by three preeminent translators: Peter Constantine, Richard Pevear, and Larissa Volokhonsky. And we have Carol Flath of Duke University to provide some framework for the forum. She has written on the theory of translation and has the practical experience of having translated, and interpreted, from both Russian and Japanese.

Peter Constantine first came to my attention in 1996, when his translations of Chekhov's early stories were published in *Harper's* magazine. He did something extraordinarily enterprising, which was to realize that some of the early Chekhov had never been translated into English; he found these stories, translated them, and assembled them into what eventually became a very elegant volume, *The Undiscovered Chekhov*.

Richard Pevear and Larissa Volokhonsky, who work in Paris, are broadly acknowledged as today's premier translators of Russian literature into English. This morning the question arose as to whether one can do valid literary analysis based on a translation. In my opinion, the Chekhov translations of Pevear and Volokhonsky invite real analysis, for they are precise in a way that translators have rarely been before. Many translators have been lyrical or smooth or good at colloquial phrasing; but not necessarily precise. With Chekhov, above all, you need that precision.

With no more ado, then, I'll turn the floor over to Carol.

CAROL APOLLONIO FLATH

The question of translation is of course at the heart of Chekhov's legacy in the American tradition, but it's also at the heart of all communication. I'm delighted to take part in this symposium with these outstanding translators of Russian literature, and particularly Chekhov, into English. I've been asked to give a little bit of background on Chekhov translation, and after

*Chekhov the Immigrant: Translating a Cultural Icon.* Michael C. Finke and Julie de Sherbinin, eds. Bloomington, IN: Slavica Publishers, 2007, 29–66.

that we'll launch into what I'm sure is going to be a wonderful discussion about the specifics of translation. Although Julie mentioned "theory of translation" when introducing me, in today's discussion we're going to be more interested in praxis. We have a wonderful opportunity to learn what and how Chekhov translators DO, and how they FEEL about it. To that end, our translators have brought some particularly interesting or problematic passages from Chekhov and are prepared to explain why they rendered them as they did.

Before turning to our translators, however, let's briefly review the history of Chekhov in English. This discussion will doubtless continue tomorrow during what promises to be a very stimulating panel on drama, but today we will focus on prose works.

In 1900 Chekhov wrote a short letter to one of his first translators, the young and energetic Olga Vasilyeva, to whom he was sending a copy of "The Lady with the Dog." His first order of business was to thank Olga for a rug that she had picked up for him in, of all places, Algiers. The second order of business in Chekhov's letter was to respond to her question as to what English journal would be the best outlet for her translation of his "Little Trilogy" (the cycle of stories "Man in a Shell" ["Chelovek v futliare"], "Gooseberries" ["Kryzhovnik"], and "About Love" ["O liubvi"]). Chekhov responds: "Alas, I absolutely do not know how to respond to your question. I don't read English, I do not see English journals, and I don't know them. And it seems to me that I have so little to offer the English public that it makes absolutely no difference to me whether I am published in an English journal or not" (*PssP* 9: 97). Can we take Chekhov at his word? How would he have reacted a century later to the enormous and ever-increasing body of his work in English, produced by a throng of translators who, like Chekhov's own characters, manifest the full range of human virtues and failings?

By the way, in spite of Chekhov's apparent lack of enthusiasm, Olga Vasilyeva did translate Chekhov into English, and she sent him copies of her translations. But where are they today? Does anyone here know?

I think it may be possible—as much as this sort of thing is possible, and from the distance of this centennial of Chekhov's death—to divide the history of his translations into three fifty-year chunks, the third one of course beginning today. Let us give the due honor that is so rarely granted to translators and call these periods: the Garnett era, the Hingley era, and the current era, which might well be named the Pevear-and-Volokhonsky era. The first era begins with the translation Isabel Hapgood published as "Philosophy 'at Home'"—undoubtedly a rendering of Chekhov's 1887 story "At Home" ("Doma")—which appeared in the October 1891 issue of the New

York publication *Short Stories, a Magazine of Fact and Fancy*.[1] There followed a spate of anonymous translations, many of which are lost to us at this point, but including what was probably the first translation published in England, an anonymous and enigmatically titled diptych, "The Biter Bit" and "Sorrow" ("Gore"), published in *The Temple Bar: A Magazine for Town and Country Readers* (May 1897). C. E. Long's version of *The Black Monk and other Stories* (1903) is acknowledged as the first signed translation published in England.

These and other individual works sink into the shadow of Constance Garnett's monumental achievement: the thirteen volumes of Chekhov's stories that she produced between 1916 and 1922. Garnett dominates this first period, both in England and in the United States. Thanks to their high quality and the convenience of copyright expiration, her translations remain in print and continue to multiply to this day. Critics point out a certain Victorian reticence and, speaking pejoratively, decorum in her style,[2] but she outclasses her contemporaries on many levels, including those of fidelity, grace, and—speaking approvingly now—consistency. She is the patron saint of translation of Russian literature into English. I want to read to you a description of her working by D. H. Lawrence. "Sitting out in the garden, turning out reams of her marvelous translations from the Russian, she would finish a page and throw it off on a pile on the floor without looking up and start a new page. The pile would be this high—really, almost up to her knees. And all magical."[3] One of my questions to the translators will be: How do you work? Does your working style resemble what D. H. Lawrence recalls of Mrs. Garnett? I might add that in the summer of 1904, which is a period that is of course on our minds today, Constance Garnett was actually in Russia. She was making her second and final trip to Russia; so that, figuratively and literally, she was actually taking Chekhov's place—he was in Badenweiler at the time.

The first fifty years is brought to a close by three milestones: the end of World War II; the death of Constance Garnett in 1946; and, conveniently,

---

[1] Avrahm Yarmolinsky, foreword to Anna Heifetz, *Chekhov in English: A List of Works By and About Him*, ed. Avrahm Yarmolinsky (New York: The New York Public Library), 1949, 4.

[2] See Rachel May, *The Translator in the Text: On Reading Russian Literature in English* (Evanston IL: Northwestern University Press, 1994), 38–42. May perceptively analyzes Garnett's translation of deictic features of Chekhov's work, in which the narrator's voice is shown to take over territory that in the original belongs to other narrative levels. The result is a bias in translation toward omniscience.

[3] Richard Garnett, *Constance Garnett: A Heroic Life* (London: Sinclair-Stevenson, 1991), 133.

the publication of the New York Public Library's bibliography of Chekhov in English in 1949 (it covers the period through July 1, 1948).[4]

During the second half of the twentieth century a number of excellent translators—many of them educated in post-war language schools—turned their attention to Chekhov. Chekhov aficionados are familiar with the names of David Magarshack, Jessie Coulson, Harvey Pitcher, and Ann Dunnigan, as well as those of their collaborators. The "giant" in this set is of course Ronald Hingley, whose nine-volume Oxford Chekhov (1966–79) stands as the centerpiece of the post-Garnett half-century, in spite of all the other excellent translations that came out in that period.[5] Like Garnett, Hingley offers his own distinctive style—like Garnett's, very British—which is firmly anchored in a mastery of the original Russian. His work is, however, in Schleiermacher's terms, a reader-oriented translation.[6]

The third era of Chekhov translation into English begins, in my scheme, in the late 1990s—the centennial of Chekhov's own maturation as a storywriter and playwright. If you look in *Books in Print*, as I did last week, you'll find 97 prose works and 110 works of drama in print. I might add that it's a sort of sad parlor game to go into *Books in Print* and click on the individual listings of these works;[7] it's sad because the translator continues to be anonymous, even today. The full description includes, among other things: ISBN number, binding format, several classification categories, a detailed list of contents, a Library of Congress number, the wholesalers through which the book can be obtained, the price (of course), the book's physical dimensions in inches; but, in the majority of these listings, the translator's name is not to be found.

Today all of the early short stories, from 1880–85, have been translated. A number of them exist already in the 1987 Raduga collection, translated by Ivy Litvinov and Alex Miller.[8] Any story not translated anywhere else can

---

[4] Heifetz, *Chekhov in English*.

[5] Anton Chekhov, *The Oxford Chekhov*, 9 vols., trans. and ed. Ronald Hingley (London: Oxford University Press, 1965–75).

[6] "Either the translator leaves the writer alone as much as possible and moves the reader toward the writer, or he leaves the reader alone as much as possible and moves the writer toward the reader." Friedrich Schleiermacher, "On the Different Methods of Translating," trans. Waltraud Bartscht, in *Theories of Translation: An Anthology of Essays from Dryden to Derrida*, ed. Rainer Schulte and John Biguenet (Chicago: University of Chicago Press, 1992), 42.

[7] "Author: Chekhov," http://www.booksinprint.com.

[8] Anton Chekhov, *Collected Works in 5 Volumes*, vol. 1, *Stories 1880–85*, trans. Alex Miller and Ivy Litvinov (Moscow: Raduga, 1987).

be found in Peter Sekirin's *The Complete Early Chekhov*.[9] These two works are more valuable as initial reference sources than as armchair reading.

Now that everything has been translated, the real question—as Michael Heim has pointed out[10]—is that of re-translation. What is it that new translators are adding to this tradition? It is an achievement just to have been the first to do it; but I think all of us know, having read first-time translations, that they don't necessarily have to be excellent to be useful. Peter Constantine's 1998 versions of several early stories give the early Chekhov a much-needed boost—the biggest it has gotten since Harvey Pitcher's superb collections, which also continue to be reissued (one of them as recently as this summer).[11] Penguin, Oxford, and other publishers continue to release Chekhov in new editions and reprints. Garnett's translations continue to abide. There are numerous centenary year publications, including one curious phenomenon: the nicely produced, though hastily translated books in Hesperus Press's slim, colorful, and endearingly titled "100 Pages" series, which includes Chekhov's "Story of a Nobody" ("Rasskaz neizvestnogo cheloveka," translated by Ronald Wilks, 2004).

You will notice that many of these translators hail from the other side of the Atlantic. How might we focus our attention on the American Chekhov that has been advertised as our topic? Let me say a few words about the Pevear/Volokhonsky team's really remarkable achievement: they've gained the success of name-recognition, which few translators do. Their translations are becoming definitive editions, certainly in American classrooms, for many of the Russian writers. This will certainly be the case for those who are reading Dostoevsky, for example, because of the literalism of their approach. And of course it is their translation of Tolstoy's *Anna Karenina* that Oprah Winfrey chose to promote—and I think that we're all grateful to you and to Oprah for directing everybody's attention to the inimitable *Anna*. We're very grateful to you for turning your attention to Chekhov, and we're looking forward to more. And we also have to thank Peter for bringing the early Chekhov to the popular reader, as well as to the readers in this room, in a volume that has recently come out in paperback.[12]

I'd like to begin the discussion with a quotation from D. S. Mirsky, to whom those of us who studied Russian literature in college were certainly exposed. Mirsky writes:

---

[9] Anton Chekhov, *Complete Short Stories of Anton Chekhov, 1880–85*, 4 vols., trans. Peter Sekirin (Toronto: Megapolis Publishing Company, 2001).

[10] See his piece in this volume.

[11] Anton Chekhov, *Chekhov: The Comic Stories*, trans. Harvey Pitcher (London: André Deutsch, 2004).

[12] Anton Chekhov, *The Undiscovered Chekhov: Forty-Three New Stories*, trans. Peter Constantine (New York: Seven Stories Press, 2000; rept.1998).

> Chekhov's English admirers think that everything is perfect in Chekhov. To find spots in him will seem blasphemy. Still [there is] a complete lack of individuality in his characters and in their way of speaking [that…] is especially noticeable when he makes his characters speak at length on abstract subjects. […] Another serious shortcoming is Chekhov's Russian. It is colorless and lacks individuality. He had no feeling for words. No Russian writer of anything like his significance used a language so devoid of all raciness and nerve. This makes Chekhov […] so easy to translate. Of all Russian writers, he has the least to fear from the treachery of translators.[13]

I'd like to hear our translators' reaction to Mirsky's words.

RICHARD PEVEAR

Well, you sent us this by e-mail, and I sat and scratched my head and tried to think: What works is Mirsky thinking of that could be described in this way? And I couldn't come up with any, not even in passages where you get long ideological conversations—and there aren't very many of them. I think Mirsky's completely wrong, and I don't know what he had in mind when he said that. Nabokov does agree with Mirsky in a sense. He says that Chekhov is the most colorless of great Russian writers. Nabokov was a great friend of Mirsky's, a prince among princes. But I don't find this a very accurate description of Chekhov's writing. In fact, the more we have worked on him, the less I would agree.

CAROL APOLLONIO FLATH

Mirsky is still everywhere though.

RICHARD PEVEAR

He was a wonderful man. I love his book. He was simply wrong in this case.

PETER CONSTANTINE

I feel that even in the earliest works, when Chekhov was just out of his teens, as it were, there is a sharpness and a pacing, and complete control. There is that well-known incident recalled by Korolenko where he said, more or less, "Show me an ashtray, and I can write a story about an ashtray." He seems to have had this gift of getting it right. If you look at his manuscripts as well, there are very few changes, so I feel that he's very much in control. And reading the later stories, where he's a very different kind of writer from the early Chekhov—his is a beautiful, powerful Russian, you really feel that every word is just *there*. So I'm an admirer of Chekhov, and I'm too stunned by Mirsky's words to respond.

---

[13] D. S. Mirsky, *A History of Russian Literature* (New York: Viking, 1958), 383.

LARISSA VOLOKHONSKY

It's never bland or monotonous. If you take, for instance, the rather lengthy monologues of von Koren and Laevsky in "The Duel," their language is completely different. Even in my wildest imagination I couldn't say that his characters lack individuality...

RICHARD PEVEAR

You should remember, by the way, regarding the value of such judgments, that Tolstoy, after reading *The Brothers Karamazov*, said, "They all sound the same..."

CAROL APOLLONIO FLATH

All those Russians... I have a quote that Peter might find interesting. Chekhov wrote to Suvorin (19 January 1895), "Little stories, because they are little, are translated, and forgotten, and then again translated, which is why I'm translated in France more than Tolstoy." What is your reaction to this comment by Chekhov? Also, do you feel a certain kind of "fingerprint" whenever you're working with Chekhov? I think that authors have a certain fingerprint or stylistic constant that remains palpable throughout their work. You mentioned this difference between the early and late Chekhov; but do you feel a real qualitative difference between the early and late Chekhov?

PETER CONSTANTINE

Well, I wonder about that letter, whether he's not being playful and stylish, as a letter writer, or if he really means that. In France the very early translations were done in a great mass by Denis Roche, Chekhov's first translator, who did volume after volume: the French Garnett. Roche was eight years younger than Chekhov. I've even heard that Constance Garnett might have used his work as a crib, or done her translations from his French translations. I don't want to dethrone her.

LARISSA VOLOKHONSKY

Garnett does sometimes feel as if she was using the French version.

RICHARD PEVEAR

She uses French spellings of names.

CAROL APOLLONIO FLATH

You know, another fascinating little fact about Constance Garnett and the way she worked is that she was tutored in Russian by exile terrorists. For instance, she worked with the quite extraordinary Kravchinsky-Stepniak — and also with Felix Volkhovsky. These were terrorists: Kravchinsky-Stepniak had stabbed the police chief of St. Petersburg to death in 1878. So there was little Constance Garnett, with her bad eyesight, pursuing her garden activities in such company...

RICHARD PEVEAR

She was also somewhat sympathetic toward them.

CAROL APOLLONIO FLATH

Yes, the Garnetts ran in a liberal circle. But these garden-mates were most definitely murderers as well. And she was kind of domesticating them, as translators do.

RICHARD PEVEAR

I don't want to denigrate Garnett, because I think her work is extraordinary, but she didn't work alone, and she never acknowledged any help. I know of at least one woman, Natalie Duddington, who was a ghost for her. If you've ever done any translating of these books from Russian, and then you contemplate the quantity of work that she did, it's not only staggering but simply impossible.

CAROL APOLLONIO FLATH

She did two novels a year, basically.

RICHARD PEVEAR

Yes; she had help.

CAROL APOLLONIO FLATH

I think we all have help, don't we? Is it really an activity that one can do all by oneself?

RICHARD PEVEAR

No, but this picture of her heaping up piles of paper ... is pure Lawrence!

CAROL APOLLONIO FLATH

So, he made it up?!!

PETER CONSTANTINE

Speaking of the early stories: The very early ones, I sometimes think, are quite different from what you get in the mature Chekhov. To quote... Oh, I can't find it in the book right now, but it goes like this: "I was chased by 30 dogs, 7 of which were white, 8 gray, and the rest black...." Do you know that one? Something as wild as that. There's absolutely no connection between that and the later Chekhov, no traceable "fingerprint." And these early pieces were later looked down upon, particularly by scholars like Ronald Hingley, who discouraged us from reading them: In his biography of Chekhov he calls them twaddle and balderdash. They were deprecated all around—in Germany, in France—that is, until recently. And now they're finally appearing. I think it's vital to have a full picture of what Chekhov was doing.

CAROL APOLLONIO FLATH

That full picture does exist now, meaning that all of his prose works, as far as I know, are translated into English. This raises the question: Which stories do you think need to be translated again? How did you choose the stories you translated? Was it because they had been poorly translated before? Was it because you loved them and wanted to put your own voice to them? For example, how did you—Richard and Larissa—choose the stories for your first collection?

RICHARD PEVEAR

We wanted to make a representative collection, and we also wanted to have our favorite stories in it. We chose the stories we thought were Chekhov's best, but also some that showed something special or unique. I personally dislike "The Black Monk," but it's an interesting story, an interesting aberration of Chekhov's.

CAROL APOLLONIO FLATH

So it's in there?

RICHARD PEVEAR

Yes, it's there. So it wasn't only a question of what we admired the most, but also what best represented Chekhov. But anyone who dares to say such a thing—to make a selection from the work of a man who wrote as many stories as he did—must recognize that there have to be arbitrary choices.

CAROL APOLLONIO FLATH

You know, at a panel yesterday there was a conversation about the meaningless words Chekhov uses sometimes—for the most part, as onomatopoeia: those kinds of clanging sounds and so on.

RICHARD PEVEAR

Oh yes; there's a lot of noise in Chekhov, banging, birds...

LARISSA VOLOKHONSKY

"Tara-ra boom-biya!"[14] [laughter]

CAROL APOLLONIO FLATH

This aspect of Chekhov makes me think of a very interesting translation theorist, Douglas Robinson, who has written a book called *The Translator's Turn*. He suggests a very different way of viewing translation—a whole series of tropes for translation, which he calls the "tropics of translations."[15]

---

[14] From *Three Sisters*.

[15] Douglas Robinson, *The Translator's Turn* (Baltimore: Johns Hopkins University Press, 1991).

According to him, one can do a translation without taking into account the lexical meaning of the words. That leads to something like a phonetic translation, where the sounds are reproduced with completely new meaning in the second language. The classic example here is Zukofsky's translation of Catullus[16] — some of you may know it — where he just takes the words...

RICHARD PEVEAR

He *almost* just takes the words.

CAROL APOLLONIO FLATH

Yes. In the resulting translation the sounds are the same as the original; there's an occasional smattering of the original lexical meaning, but the result, a "sound" translation, is entirely new. Robinson calls this sort of translation "metonymic." And all this leads to a question in Chekhov's regard. So much of his meaning is in the rhythm. I know, Richard, that in your forward to the stories you and Larissa translated, you comment on the importance of rhythm in Chekhov. That's not anything that has to do with lexical meaning.

RICHARD PEVEAR

No, you're right, it's not. But it's something that a translator should pay attention to. One of the bad habits of translators from Russian into English is to rearrange the rhythm of a sentence. There's a wonderful line in "The Lady with the Little Dog," where Gurov is eating the melon...

LARISSA VOLOKHONSKY

Yes, yes. «На столе лежал арбуз. Гуров отрезал себе ломоть и стал есть не спеша. Прошло, по крайней мере, полчаса в молчании.» It's three short sentences with very specific rhythm. It's very important to make them three, and also to convey this unhurriedness: He began to eat unhurriedly.

RICHARD PEVEAR

It's also the distinctness of these three acts: "There's a melon on the table. He cut a slice. And began to eat." And I saw a translation that said, "Gurov cut a slice from the melon that was on the table." It's the same meaning, but it's wrong. And what's wrong is the rhythm, because the rhythm expresses Gurov's attempt at total detachment. She's weeping her head off and he's eating melon for half an hour. But the rhythm of the sentence shows that. Now, it's wrong to think that a writer says, "I'm going to make the rhythm of the sentence show this...." No writer writes that way. But Chekhov felt it that way. That's how he saw it, and how it sounded to him. And he wanted that effect, it simply came to him in that rhythm. It's very easy to change it — to say, "Well I could do that a little better" — without paying attention to

---

[16] *Catullus*, trans. Louis Zukofsky and Celia Zukofsky (London: Cape Goliard, 1969).

*why* he did it. But I think that's a mistake. A translator must often do consciously what the author did unconsciously—because it "went right," as Robert Frost said. That's one difference between an author and a translator.

CAROL APOLLONIO FLATH

So the translator approaches the text from the cerebral side of things, like a critic? From the science side, as opposed to that of feeling?

RICHARD PEVEAR

Not quite. Because you have to sense that, and then feel it within you. Since we're talking about rhythm, perhaps we can look at a passage from Chekhov I've prepared for this forum: the opening of "Gooseberries." We have the original and our translation, and also a couple of other renderings.

PETER CONSTANTINE

Yes, I also want to look at the opening of "Gooseberries."

CAROL APOLLONIO FLATH

Yes, let's turn to "Gooseberries." Let's compare a couple of translations and hear about your particular approaches to this passage.

LARISSA VOLOKHONSKY

I'll read a sentence, toward the middle of the paragraph, from the Russian original: "Далеко впереди еле были видны ветряные мельницы села Мироносицкого, справа тянулся и потом исчезал далеко за селом ряд холмов, и оба они знали, что это берег реки, там луга, зеленые ивы, усадьбы, и если стать на один из холмов, то оттуда видно такое же громадное поле, телеграф и поезд, который издали похож на ползущую гусеницу, а в ясную погоду оттуда бывает виден даже город" (*PssS* 10: 55).

RICHARD PEVEAR

Here is the translation of Avrahm Yarmolinsky: "Far ahead were the scarcely visible windmills of the village of Mironositzkoe; to the right lay a range of hills that disappeared in the distance beyond the village, and both of them knew that over there were the river, and fields, green willows, homesteads, and if you stood one of the hills, you could see from there another vast plain, telegraph poles and a train that from afar looked like a caterpillar crawling, and in clear weather you could even see the town."[17] That's pretty good.

This is a new one, by Rosamund Bartlett: "A long way ahead you could just about see the windmills of the village of Mironositskoe. To the right there was a series of hills, which stretched away and then disappeared far

---

[17] Anton Chekhov, *The Portable Chekhov*, trans. and ed. Avrahm Yarmolinsky (New York: The Viking Press, 1968), 371.

beyond the village. And they both knew that this was the riverbank where there were meadows, green willows and estates. If you stood on the top of one of the hills you could see another equally enormous stretch of open countryside, as well as telegraph poles, and a train creeping along in the distance like a caterpillar, while on clear days you could even see the town."[18]

And then our translation: "Far ahead the windmills of the village of Mironositskoe were barely visible, to the right a line of hills stretched away and then disappeared far beyond the village, and they both knew that this was the bank of the river, with meadows, green willows, country houses, and if you stood on one of the hills, from there you could see equally vast fields, telegraph poles, and the train, which in the distance looked like a crawling caterpillar, and in clear weather you could even see the town."[19]

What I noticed in working on that passage is this linking simply by the word "and." Everything is put together only by the word "and," and the syntax doesn't establish any relation between the parts. I had noticed this already in a number of Chekhov's later stories, a tendency to put things in sequences with the word "and," without any subordination. Things are happening at the same time, but they're not inwardly connected…

LARISSA VOLOKHONSKY

Everything is on the same level. It creates a certain tone, this level tone—it sounds bland.

RICHARD PEVEAR

Somehow, it also describes this vastness of the Russian countryside, this "and, and, and" stretching out. Armand Robin described Charles Péguy's verse as being like the furrows in the fields of the Beauce, where he was born. There's a rhythm that represents the landscape, and that also represents the relation of events within the story, which as you all know, is a story about nothing going together. It's all put together in the same room, but there's no inner connection. So it's important for a translator to notice that and not to change it, especially the long phrasing of the whole passage. It's a simple enough thing; what is strange is that translators sometimes don't do it, indeed, very often don't.

CAROL APOLLONIO FLATH

And Peter also has a passage for us to discuss.

---

[18] Anton Chekhov, *About Love and Other Stories*, trans. Rosamund Bartlett (Oxford: Oxford University Press, 2004), 147.

[19] Anton Chekhov, *Stories*, trans. Richard Pevear and Larissa Volokhonsky (New York: Bantam Books, 2000), 311.

PETER CONSTANTINE

> Well, last week I translated "Za iablochki" ("Because of Little Apples") for Cathy Popkin's forthcoming Norton Critical Edition of Chekhov. My first reaction was actually to feel that Chekhov was a joy to translate; I really couldn't think of any problems. But then while working on the story I saw how it could really trip one up in some significant ways. So I want to read to you the opening lines, to demonstrate some of the problems a translator has to deal with. The story begins, "Между Понтом Эвксинским и Соловками, под соответственным градусом долготы и широты, на своем черноземе с давних пор обитает помещик Трифон Семенович." So even this beginning brings the translator up short. I was wondering what to do with "*Pont Evksinskii*" and "*Solovki.*" What would you do with something like that? I decided just to call them "Black Sea" and "White Sea." Let me read you my version, and let's see if you agree, because it's a work in progress.

LARISSA VOLOKHONSKY

> I'll tell you what I think about this: If you don't do it as you said—"Black Sea" and "White Sea"—you have to have two footnotes.

PETER CONSTANTINE

> Yes, which is a problem, I think. I prefer not to use footnotes, especially for the first sentence of a story. So my beginning goes: "Between the Black Sea and the White Sea, at a certain longitude and latitude, the landowner Trifon Semenovich has resided since time out of mind." Another translator of this story, Peter Sekirin, whose *Complete Early Short Stories of Anton Chekhov*, we mentioned earlier, decided to translate the opening this way: "Between Pont Evskinsky to the south and the Solovetsky Monastery to the north, on the corresponding longitude and latitude, lives Trifon Semyonovich the landowner."[20] That, in a sense, loses the point, from my perspective. No American reader would understand the reference.

LARISSA VOLOKHONSKY

> What did you do with "*na svoem chernozeme*"?

PETER CONSTANTINE

> I rendered it as "black earth," which I think works—you can keep that in English, right? People will understand.

---

[20] *The Complete Early Short Stories of Anton Chekhov: "He and She" and Other Stories*, vol. 1, *(1880–82)*, trans. Peter Sekirin (Toronto: Megapolis Publishing Co., 2001), 21.

LARISSA VOLOKHONSKY

Also, I would try—I don't know if others would agree—to say "nice little landowner." Because the Russian diminutive, "*pomeshchichek*" immediately introduces the attitude of the narrator.

PETER CONSTANTINE

Now you can see that there are things you have to deal with straight off.

RICHARD PEVEAR

I like the one here that says "between the Pontus Euxinus…"

PETER CONSTANTINE

"Pontus Euxinus" is in fact Ancient Greek: *Pontos Euxeinos*. That was the joke behind it—which perhaps the readers of the time might have been able to tap into, calling the Black Sea by its lofty Ancient Greek name. But for current readers of Russian literature in English, you really need to find some way to render it that will keep some of the joke, perhaps, though in a different way. It's a wonderful problem.

CAROL APOLLONIO FLATH

You've come up with a very interesting solution. It reflects the original, but it also reminds the reader to consider these potential symbolic meanings. There's been a lot of discussion around this issue over the past two days. Is it possible in translation to keep all—or if not all, an equivalent wealth, let us say—of the nuance? To retain symbolic meaning, or the meaning that comes through rhythm and sound? I think that may even be the biggest question facing translators of Chekhov. Do you agree?

RICHARD PEVEAR

Facing translators of anything! It's the great loss that every translator knows and is faced with most immediately: the loss of the sound of the original. You don't have it in your translation and never can.

CAROL APOLLONIO FLATH

But can you compensate in some way?

RICHARD PEVEAR

I think you can, but too strenuous an effort to compensate is also bad. You have to do what's natural in English. This dialogue between English and Russian is a very subtle thing. You've twice used the word "literalism." I wrote it down, because I don't conceive of what we do as at all a literal translation. Professor Saul Morson, who isn't here, once wrote a very negative review accusing us of merely translating literally.

CAROL APOLLONIO FLATH

Do you have an "-ism" to describe what you do?

RICHARD PEVEAR

No! [*much laughter*] But I can assure you that a literal translation would read very differently from what we've published. There is a leaning toward the original language as far as possible without becoming strained, and that's a very subtle question.

JULIE DE SHERBININ

Might I suggest opening things up here to comments and questions from the audience? I see opportunities for further discussion that might pass us by if others aren't invited to jump in.

PROF. VLADIMIR GOLSTEIN, BROWN UNIVERSITY

I have a question about your translation of "Because of Little Apples." In the previous session, on Chekhov's poetics, a tremendous amount of attention was paid to religious symbolism—to all the symbolism in Chekhov's texts. I think your proposed translation goes in the wrong direction. What we're talking about there is Solovki Monastery, a very important concept for Russians—the monastery—and for the story, which deals with a kind of punishment and a kind of justice, and portrays a non-religious character who wants to act rather like God. If you throw away the Greek imagery and the Russian Orthodox dimension and leave just White Sea and the Black Sea, you flatten Chekhov's complexity and what the story's all about.

PETER CONSTANTINE

Your point suggests another way of doing it. Nabokov did say, to come back to that, that he wants footnotes skyscraper high. That would be one way of achieving a reading that is going to be close, which will bring out the many, many subtexts. I recall talking with Julie de Sherbinin five or six years ago about the pity of what one has to lose in order to make a story work in English. As regards this translation, which is to be included in a Norton Critical Edition, I can discuss it with my editor, who's sitting over there [*Peter Constantine points to Cathy Popkin*], and decide what should be kept in—perhaps with footnotes—and what not. For me, what's important in this story is the fun, the lightness, the things that would speak to an American audience. You'll notice that Yarmolinsky's translation didn't catch the monastery on the islands in the White Sea. Nor did Sekirin, who also drops whole sentences from paragraphs; indeed, anything that seems to be difficult just disappears in his translations, which is one way of doing it so that you keep it "for the people," as it were, maximally accessible. But I would also like to stay as close to the text as possible, and some critics have said that I stay too close to the text. Others might say that I'm too creative, but one does try to do as much as one can.

ROBERT L. JACKSON, YALE UNIVERSITY

On the footnote matter: A splendid translation of Chekhov might have many, many footnotes, but I think the point is that people have to be afforded the opportunity, in a certain sense, to seek further. And I wanted to say that one of the great virtues of Richard and Larissa's translations is that they have—apart from a sensitivity to the issues that they were just talking about, rhythms and so on—they have a sensitivity to the meaning of a particular word and its role in the text. As I was saying at lunch, when in Dostoevsky somebody says *"chert,"* he means the devil, and he knows that *"chert"*... When someone says *"chert voz'mi"* (the devil take it), you don't translate that as, "Oh, the hell with it." You have to strive to get that devil in. So there is a point, I think, to what Volodya Golstein was saying. One doesn't want to be clumsy—one doesn't want to be literal to the extent of clumsiness, but to get in that idea of the Solovetsky Monastery is an interesting one.

PETER CONSTANTINE

Do you think that that was important to the story?

ROBERT L. JACKSON

Yes. I think it's interesting...

PETER CONSTANTINE

Because I wonder why the orchard would be between the Ancient Greek *Pontos Euxeinos* and the Solovetsky Islands. I mean, if there is a way of capturing all the ambiguities here I'd love to find the key to that. But if you have *Pontos Euxeinos* and the Solovetsky islands meaning different things to different readers even at the time—then what is Chekhov actually doing? I thought he was being witty. I smiled when I read it, so I wanted the English reader to smile as well.

VLADIMIR GOLSTEIN

If you think about the story, though, it's precisely that this guy, this "little landowner," takes it upon himself to punish. It's a play on the theme, more or less, of original sin. They steal something, and he tells them to start punishing each other, and after they beat the hell out of each other they begin to hate each other so much that they run away from each other. I'm actually using Robert Jackson's idea, that the landowner acts like God, and the characters become like Adam and Eve and run away, without any desire...

PETER CONSTANTINE

And you think the monastery's name...?

VLADIMIR GOLSTEIN

It's about sin, punishment, justice. The monastery's name connects with Orthodox Christian notions about it, and the ancient Greek, perhaps, with the Greek idea of justice...

MICHAEL FINKE, UNIVERSITY OF ILLINOIS AT URBANA-CHAMPAIGN

Remember, too, this story, like the myth of the fall, is about exile. And the Solovetsky Monastery and the Black Sea coast are two famous sites of exile, in the latter case of Ovid.

LARISSA VOLOKHONSKY

I think that in this particular case science is intruding on art. I agree with what you said about our translation, but I think that in Peter's case, in the case of this story, it's not so important. Translation in many ways is almost a "weighing," "*garmoniia*." Valery Larbaud said that a translator must have a very sensitive balance in his head. Often you have to weigh what is more important. And I think in this particular case, it's more important to be amusing and light.

ROBERT JACKSON

What is important, also, is to convey what Chekhov is trying to convey. In other words, I don't think you can file this story under the category of "amusing and light." The story has a satirical quality. There's even a ponderous quality to the text and to the prose, and it's very heavy in its satire. I think that if Chekhov had wanted to say, "the White Sea and the Black Sea," he could have managed to say it. He evidently used other words that almost mythologize the story, and myth is one of the very central elements in the story, "Because of Little Apples": it has Christian myth, Dulcinea, *bogatyrs*, and so on. Words come up that stretch the imagination, and I think that if Chekhov used those words, he meant to. Now, if the reader has to ask, "What does this mean?"—well, then, that's what it takes to understand him. Why does Chekhov use a piece of Latin? Why does he use it in his text? In his plays? They're in the plays, and we could put it all in English, but the use of Latin is very important in a variety of ways. We're getting a bit of Kulygin [from *Three Sisters*] here...

PETER CONSTANTINE

If I understand Larissa's point, I think one deals with these complexities on a case-by-case basis. I don't believe in ironing out. I *would* like to keep everything that's possible, but the way I read it, the question is what was important to Chekhov here, as a twenty-year-old writer at the time (this was 1880), who was very witty and sharp and just getting started. I read the story as very light, witty, maybe in a Trollopean way, maybe in a Wodehousean way. I don't see it being as deep and complex as Chekhov's later stories. The earlier stories are masterpieces, but I don't think you should read them through the darker prism of the late stories.

ROBERT JACKSON

At twenty Chekhov was forty or fifty. [*much laughter*]

CATHY POPKIN, COLUMBIA UNIVERSITY

I think it's not just a question of translation. If I'm not mistaken the *Polnoe sobranie* (Complete Works) has notes to those two items in the Russian. It's not just people reading it in translation who have difficulty.

PETER CONSTANTINE

Actually what I do with the next line might be even more shocking; it goes: "Фамилия Трифона Семёновича длинна, как слово *естествоиспытатель*, и происходит от очень звучного латинского слова, обозначающего единую из многочисленнейших человеческих добродетелей." And this is what I did with it: "His family name is as long as the word overnumerousness and derives from a songless Latin word referring to one of the countless human virtues." By way of comparison, here is what Sekirin does: "His family name is so long it is difficult to pronounce. It's based on the Latin word meaning 'talent.'"

LARISSA VOLOKHONSKY

Not much talent there…

PETER CONSTANTINE

Yarmolinsky, on the other hand, who is usually a stickler about these things, has dropped Chekhov's sentence completely, possibly because it's problematic for the translator, and you wonder, "What do you do?" Do you translate *estestvoispytatel'* directly as "naturalist," which in English isn't a long and tongue-twisting word, or do you choose another word that has eighteen or nineteen letters in it and keep the joke somehow? Even though it's a different kind of joke—an equivalent one, perhaps?

CAROL APOLLONIO FLATH

Here's one more. This one is from Robert Payne's collection: "His surname was as long as a barge pole, and derived from a very resounding Latin word designating one of the innumerable human virtues."[21]

PETER CONSTANTINE

Another little problem in this story is the tongue twister that Trifon Semenovich has come up with in order to show his stance towards humanity. It goes, "Мужики, простачки, чудачки, дурачки проигрались в дурачки"

---

[21] Anton Chekhov, *The Image of Chekhov: Forty Stories by Anton Chekhov in the Order in Which They Were Written*, trans. Robert Payne (New York: Alfred A. Knopf, 1967), 3.

(*Soch.* 1: 40). Well, let's look at how the other translators have handled this. In his translation, Sekirin just dropped it. He didn't deal with it at all. As for Payne's translation… Do we have that? [*finds paper and reads*] "All fools, clodhoppers, simpletons / Ruin themselves by playing at dunce." And then there's a footnote: "An untranslatable pun. *Durachki* (dunces) is also the name of a card game." So what I did with that was: "Foolish fools fooled foolishly by foolish fools."

RICHARD PEVEAR

How does this sound: "Country bumpkins dump rumps on stumps and trump trumps." [*everyone laughs*]

JULIE DE SHERBININ

May I interject a question here? Peter, you just said you turned for inspiration to others, and I know you meant that in quotation marks. But I'd like to ask you all: to what extent are you aware of the translation history of a text you translate, and to what extent does such knowledge either liberate you or bind you?

LARISSA VOLOKHONSKY

When I do my first version—which I call a "literal version," though I don't think it's literal at all, since there's already some linguistic work done before I produce it—I don't look at any other translations, because the moment I look at them, I think they are better than mine. So I produce a "literal version" that is as close to the text as I can make it, trying to follow the syntax of the Russian sentences as much as possible. Then I give it to Richard, and I think he looks at other translations.

RICHARD PEVEAR

I do—when I can find them, when I have them… Especially when we started, I would have all of them—except for *Crime and Punishment*, which is a difficult case because there are so many of them; so I would eliminate a certain number. I generally work and then look at the other translations. I do a version, then I look at others, and sometimes say, "My God, I've completely misunderstood that," or, "They're right," or, "That was better." And I'll even steal! I think it was Theodore Roethke who once said, "Bad poets borrow; good poets steal." So I sometimes "lift" something, but usually I'm checking other translations just for confirmation. In any case, I am certainly aware of the translations that have been done. By the way, we haven't looked at the work of one good translator of Chekhov, Ann Dunnigan, an American. I think she's the best that I've seen.

MAN FROM AUDIENCE

Could you tell us some more about how the two of you work together? The actual sit-down, next-to-one-another, work?[22]

RICHARD PEVEAR

Yes. We actually work on two sides of the same wall. Larissa over here, and I'm over there, and she does a completely literal translation.

LARISSA VOLOKHONSKY

Though never in the garden. [*everyone laughs*]

RICHARD PEVEAR

We haven't got a garden.

ROBERT L. JACKSON

You don't throw the paper on the floor?

RICHARD PEVEAR

No. And it never piles up that high. [*gesturing, he indicates a height*]

LARISSA VOLOKHONSKY

Sometimes it's pretty high!

RICHARD PEVEAR

It's getting higher... Larissa does a completely literal version, with all kinds of commentaries: "This is strange. This is odd. This is Old Church Slavonic. This is a slip of the tongue. He meant to say this, but he said that." And I work with that.

LARISSA VOLOKHONSKY

I look for hidden biblical quotations, for instance. Chekhov is full of liturgical quotes—or not quotes, but hidden allusions to liturgical texts, to biblical texts, and I look for that.

CAROL APOLLONIO FLATH

What version of the Bible do you use? Do you then take it literally out of a certain version of the Bible?

LARISSA VOLOKHONSKY

That depends. When Chekhov has something in Slavonic, I usually go to the King James Bible to find it, but if it's something that is quoted by memory and therefore formulated in or closer to modern Russian, then I use the Revised Standard Version.

---

[22] A year after the NEH Chekhov Symposium, David Remnick published "The Translation Wars" in the *New Yorker* (November 27, 2005; 98–109). There Pevear and Volokhonsky further discuss the process of working together on translations.

RICHARD PEVEAR

Sometimes it's misquoted.

MAN FROM AUDIENCE

When you do find a misquotation from Shakespeare or the Bible, or something in English, do you correct it, do you footnote it, or do you print it the way the author translated it?

RICHARD PEVEAR

I give the misquotation a footnote. Anyway, after Larissa has done her version, I make one of my own. So there's a complete version—and by the way, written in pencil—that Larissa gives me, and I work from that and make another complete version, with all my questions on it: "Can this be right? He couldn't have said that." You know, we were once criticized by another eminent Slavist (who's not here, luckily), who said, "Their translation is very good, but occasionally they lapse into banality." And then he quoted from *Crime and Punishment*, a wonderful sentence: "It was a very simple matter, and there was nothing complicated about it."

LARISSA VOLOKHONSKY

And incidentally, there is almost exactly the same sentence in Chekhov somewhere.

RICHARD PEVEAR

When I took Larissa's literal version, I looked and said, "That can't be. It's stupid to say that—"It was a very simple matter, and there was nothing complicated about it." We went to the original and checked— that's exactly what Dostoevsky wrote.

LARISSA VOLOKHONSKY

"Это было очень простое дело, в нём не было ничего сложного."

RICHARD PEVEAR

What could I do? I translated it, and Professor Fanger said, "Aha! The occasional banality." That's one of the risks translators run... In any case, we work in that way. We go over the new version and all my questions. Then we produce another version, which we read through together, comparing it with the original, and making final corrections. Then we turn it over to the editors, who have their own ideas... which must be resisted.

ROBERT L. JACKSON

Yes, what do they do with it? They probably try to wrench things around a bit?

RICHARD PEVEAR

That depends on the editor. In the beginning we got "wrenched around," but now they hardly edit us at all—which is sometimes a mistake! There are things that could have been caught.

LARISSA VOLOKHONSKY

*Anna Karenina* was heavily edited. I mean, they tried to…

RICHARD PEVEAR

They failed.

LARISSA VOLOKHONSKY

They tried to rewrite it.

RICHARD PEVEAR

We were given an excellent piece of advice by Olga Carlisle—Olga Andreeva Carlisle. We asked her about this, and she said, "Always listen to the editor. Smile and say you will do everything, and then do as little as possible."

PROF. ANDREW DURKIN, INDIANA UNIVERSITY

You said that one of you does the "first version," and then there are questions and so forth. Particularly in regard to longer works—maybe not for Chekhov's stories, but for the novels, like "The Duel"—does each of you do the entire text through, or do you proceed chapter by chapter?

RICHARD PEVEAR

No, we each do the whole text.

ANDREW DURKIN

So, each step you do the whole text. Then back to the next project?

RICHARD PEVEAR

Yes.

MAN FROM AUDIENCE

My question is, how do you prepare to do the translations? Do you spend some preparatory time looking at biography? Do you read any of the criticism or scholarship that is out there? You've noted that you often look at previous translations, and no one person sees everything, so do you familiarize yourself with the secondary literature on these writers?

LARISSA VOLOKHONSKY

No. You know, it's our work, in a sense—I'll have to speak about ourselves—and what we bring to it is the result of the entire human experience.

RICHARD PEVEAR

Well, not all human experience—ours. [*laughter*]

LARISSA VOLOKHONSKY

Yes, we bring our personal experience, as readers, and Richard's experience as a writer in his own right. So we don't feel that any specific preparation is necessary. Whatever additional information we need, we try to get it as we proceed, as we encounter problems.

PROF. RALPH LINDHEIM, UNIV. OF TORONTO

Which aspects of Chekhov do you find easiest to translate? Which features are most difficult?

LARISSA VOLOKHONSKY

Here is one problem: Chekhov changes the aspect and tense of verbs.

RICHARD PEVEAR

It's verbal aspect—the imperfective and perfective, which doesn't exist in English.

LARISSA VOLOKHONSKY

This is very often spoken about among scholars. When he has a narrative that implies repeated or habitual action, "She used to get up in the morning and have coffee"—it implies that this has been going on for several days or months or years. And then all of a sudden there intrudes a specific situation, and the tense changes, either into present or into past. He does it very imperceptibly. All of a sudden a habitual behavior becomes a specific behavior, like in this story that I've prepared to discuss today…

PETER CONSTANTINE

"Ward Six?"

LARISSA VOLOKHONSKY

There are some instances in "Ward Six," but I have an example from "The Story of an Unknown Man," when Zinaida Fyodorovna comes to the narrator every morning, and they have conversations, and she says, "Yes, there were big doings at Poltava, my sir, there were indeed." And then all of a sudden… [*to Richard*] yes, you read it, from chapter 17. You can skip to "It even happened…"

RICHARD PEVEAR

"It even happened that I wouldn't meet her for whole days. I'd knock timidly and guiltily at her door—no answer; I'd knock again—silence… I'd stand at the door and listen; but then a maid goes by and announces, coldly: '*Madame est partie.*'" Suddenly it shifts from: "I would do this." "I kept doing this" to "The maid goes by," and back to: "Then I'd pace the hotel corridor, pace, pace... Englishmen of some sort, full-breasted ladies, garçons in tailcoats... And when I've looked for a long time at the long striped carpet that stretches all down the corridor, it occurs to me that I'm playing a strange, probably false role in this woman's life, and that I'm no longer able to change this role; I run to my room, fall on my bed, think and think, and can't think anything up, and it's only clear to me that I want to live, and that the more unattractive, dry, and tough her face becomes, the closer she is to me, and the more strongly and painfully I feel our affinity."[23]

LARISSA VOLOKHONSKY

And then there is this specific thing. [*she points to the passage*]

RICHARD PEVEAR

"Then I go out to the corridor again, listen with anxiety... I don't have dinner, don't notice how evening comes. Finally, past ten o'clock, I hear familiar footsteps, and Zinaida Fyodorovna appears at the turning by the stairs.

'Taking a stroll?' she asks, passing by. 'You'd do better to go out... Good night!'"

This shift of verbal aspect is a tricky thing that can sometimes work in English, but sometimes has to be given up, because it becomes too strange."

PROF. CONEVERY VALENČIUS, HARVARD UNIVERSITY

I'd be really interested to hear how all three of you each approach slang. Especially because there are a lot of places in stories where he is trying to indicate that someone is being evasive in their breeziness. I'm thinking about this, because I'm a historian of the nineteenth century, and I read stuff like Jane Austen, where, when someone picks up a teacup, that's telling me something really important—which I don't usually get—about where that person is socially. It might indicate that someone is more uncouth than they should be, but I don't get it, because it's coming out of a social world that has an elaborate set of rules that I don't fathom. I was thinking about this when I was reading a lot of the short stories that you translated. And slang is so easily dated. How do you pick what kind of "slanginess" to use?

RICHARD PEVEAR

It's a great problem, because, as you said, slang gets dated. Sidney Monas, whom I love, did a translation of *Crime and Punishment*, and he uses—as did William Arrowsmith, in his translation of Aristophanes—American G.I. slang. So Razumikhin becomes Raskolnikov's "pal." It simply grates on my ear—I can't listen to it. It's too specific. Or there's David Magarshack: he

---

[23] Anton Chekhov, *The Complete Short Novels*, trans. Richard Pevear and Larissa Volokhonsky (New York: Alfred A. Knopf, 2004), 315.

translated the whole of Smerdiakov into Cockney English. What on earth brought Smerdiakov to Cockney English?

ROBERT L. JACKSON

Nabokov does that too—he uses "pals" in his Lermontov translation.

RICHARD PEVEAR

He had a bad ear for English slang. It's very tricky. I tend to try to tone it down, because any marked slang is going to die. It is simply the wrong linguistic realm. For instance, it introduces a Cockney mentality where there wasn't any.

MAN FROM AUDIENCE

Bernard Gilbert Guerney also did that to a great extent.

RICHARD PEVEAR

Yes, in his much-praised translation of Gogol's *Dead Souls*...

PETER CONSTANTINE

In British translations we often find *muzhik*s [peasants] out in the steppes of Russia speaking a Somerset dialect, or with a regional or Scottish accent, which actually in Scotland has created much ill will—Scots, I mean the Germanic language considered a close cousin of English, has recently been recognized by the European Union as an official minority language. The Scots are not pleased to have British translators using their language to render ungrammatical peasant speech. So in Britain it is now also a question of political correctness. In the Russian, when a character says things that are very, very strange to a Russian ear, strange and colorful things that are not standard Russian, then perhaps they can be translated into something equally strange and outlandish in English. I think that's part of what we're talking about.

LARISSA VOLOKHONSKY

Yes, to come up with something natural...

PETER CONSTANTINE

Because the characters do sometimes say some really outlandish things that are funny. The comedy of many of the earlier stories lies in the speech of the characters. The stories from the 1880s are very different in this from the stories of the 1890s.

PROF. MARTIN BIDNEY, SUNY BINGHAMTON

I've done a little bit of translating, and I've noticed that it's very tiny little decisions, thousands of them, going on all day. When you just read that last paragraph, I thought, "Let's see, 'I am no longer able to change this role,'" and I thought, "If I had done it—I like to economize—I would have said, 'I can no longer change this role.'" But there could be problem there, because you have a "k" and there are no other "k" sounds: "I am no longer able to change this role" has a tremendous flow to it, nothing so hard as a "k," and "able" and "change" create a type of assonance. Did you want that, or did you just not think of "can"? It's economy versus a certain kind of rhythm…

RICHARD PEVEAR

Yes, it's an interesting question. I think that in working on a translation—and this is inevitably a subjective thing, for a person writing in English, for me—the character acquires a voice. He has a way of phrasing things. Once you hear his voice, he begins to speak through you. This is how this rather—I don't know what to call him—"unknown man" speaks. He has a way of excusing himself that's rather formal and slightly false: "I am no longer able to change this role…" He's gotten this woman into a completely horrible situation; he takes no responsibility, and keeps a slight moral distance, and so the way I rendered it sounds more formal, more distant: "I am no longer able…" This reminds me of a passage in *Crime and Punishment*. Raskolnikov looks in the mirror or a window before he goes to kill the old pawnbroker, just before he knocks on her door, and says, "Am I not pale, too pale?"

LARISSA VOLOKHONSKY

"Не бледен ли я, не слишком бледен?"

RICHARD PEVEAR

And again a "helpful" critic said, "You should make that much more spoken: 'Maybe I'm too pale.'" But I just didn't hear it that way. I didn't hear Raskolnikov saying that. Why I decided that, I don't know, but ultimately a translation of mine, if it has any coherence or authenticity as an original text, will have *my* voice in it. There's no way I can get out of that. Otherwise it won't have any voice at all. Amy Mandelker said of our translation of *Anna Karenina* that we "put it into a crisp modern English." I never thought of putting anything into crisp modern English. I translated the novel from Russian into English. Whatever qualities the translation has come partly from Tolstoy, partly from my language. It had nothing to do with trying to find some crisp, new, fresh, or American way. I don't think there is such a thing as an American translation. At least I'd never set about making one. It would be like Cocknifying Smerdiakov.

MAN FROM AUDIENCE

Getting back to the question of humor: There are some instances in your originals, of course, which are impossible to translate—puns and plays on words and so forth—and you just have to give up. However, later on, when you come across something that you could turn into humor, which might not have been in the original, do you feel that if it's in the vein that Chekhov is trying to explore, that it's alright for you to add humor that's not there in the original, perhaps in order to compensate for what you've not been able to translate?

PETER CONSTANTINE

I would say that this might be a good idea. In other words, if in one part of the paragraph there is a joke, and you can perhaps do it one or two sentences later, that might be permissible in certain cases. It means that you would save the fun. I think I'm a little conservative when it comes to translation, though: I like to stay as close as I can. Maybe you disagree with that. The idea is to try and recreate in English what is in the Russian, to bring it into English with the same kind of wit, if it's there, or dullness, if it's there. We're not really supposed to be creating beyond what Chekhov is creating.

SAME MAN FROM AUDIENCE

I'm thinking specifically of the Scott Moncrieff translation of Proust, where he does that. He will put in humor that is not there, because he can't translate some of the humor that is there. And I notice that in some of the new translations that have been done recently, they've taken all that out and tried to get back to a more literal translation, but I think a lot is lost.

PETER CONSTANTINE

Well, I can see that to do that as a policy can be dangerous—to tamper—but there must be certain cases where it can be done. Let's say that Trifon Semenovich, the landowner, has a certain way of speaking: snide, witty (or he thinks so); he talks down. You can sustain that, and perhaps play a little bit with the wit. If you can't do it in one place, you can do it a sentence or two later.

RICHARD PEVEAR

Here's the alternative case. What do you do with humor that occurs only in English? We were translating the interrogation of Mitya Karamazov. They ask him: "What happened to that little bag around your neck?" He said, "I dropped it right there."

LARISSA VOLOKHONSKY

He "lost it."

RICHARD PEVEAR

"Where, exactly?" "In the square, in the square somewhere. Devil knows where in the square!" [*everyone laughs*] That rhyming isn't there in the Russian, but it works well in English, it's the correct translation, and it suits the spirit of Mitya's responses to his interrogators. And so we kept it.

PROF. CYNTHIA MARSH, UNIVERSITY OF NOTTINGHAM

I think you've made a lot of good points about intonation and rhythm. But you've said that there's no such thing as an American translation. I think that I've been in the States for thirty-six hours, and I've been sitting here absolutely compensating for the different intonations and rhythms that I'm hearing. And I'm sure that you have to compensate for what I'm saying, because of my particular intonations and rhythms. And I'm wondering if a reader doesn't come to a translation as a collaborator, as I'm sitting here compensating. A reader actually brings to a translation a whole set of compensations. How much do you take that into account in the act of translating? How much does it allow you to think, "Perhaps we can get away with this," as it were—either not moving too far from the text or staying close to the text. Tomorrow in the panel on drama the question of rhythms and intonations of spoken language will surely come up, and I have a whole other set of arguments for that. But the point here is that while you have been reading out extracts from translations, I've actually been having difficulty understanding them, asking myself, "What did they say?" So I think there are all sorts of issues here—theoretical issues that perhaps we can't explore right now—but I wonder how much reader expectation and reader compensation figure into what you're doing.

RICHARD PEVEAR

I think it depends on the reader, because the reader first has to trust the text, and then give herself or himself to it. If the translator can't achieve that trust, then he's failed—there's nothing to talk about. But how British readers learn to read my translations is beyond me. I can't control that. I can't manipulate it. There's no way I can be aware of it. If what I'm reading to you sounds American, apart from my accent—if it sounds rhythmically American—then it is. It's like what Borges said about being Argentine: it's either a fate or an accident. Whatever I write, I write in the only way I can. But I do want, on the other hand, to make readers think that it's a bit Russian and not so much me. I'd like to manipulate them a little towards a strangeness, because it is a translation, and the fun of translating is that you're between languages. English can draw something from Russian, draw some enrichment. English narrative prose in America, I think, is at this point a rather threadbare thing. Almost all in the first person: "I got up. I brushed my teeth. I went out. Agnes came in. She said 'kiss me.' I kissed her." There's no style. If you can draw some kind of richness from another language, that is the best thing a translation can do. I would hope our work might influence American writers, among others.

WOMAN FROM AUDIENCE

I just have a follow-up question. You, Richard, are also a creative writer, working in English?

RICHARD PEVEAR

I used to be.

SAME WOMAN FROM AUDIENCE

And I don't know whether others of you at the table are as well. Have you written your own works since you've been working as a translator? I'm just wondering how living within that voice—or in that place where the Russian and the English come together—how that affects you when you're writing your own creative work in English. If that's something that any of you do…

RICHARD PEVEAR

I haven't written… All my creativity goes into translation.

LARISSA VOLOKHONSKY

You write prefaces. And footnotes.

RICHARD PEVEAR

Yes, the footnote is one of my favorite forms. It's very difficult. It's a poetic form. [*laughter*]

JULIE DE SHERBININ

Could you tell us about the market aspects of publishing? When did you start to publish? And Peter, what is your particular story? How did you convince a publisher to publish another—indeed, yet *another*—translation of a classic Russian author?

RICHARD PEVEAR

We had a great deal of difficulty. We were rejected by all the major publishers, who said just that: "Who needs another translation? Garnett lives forever!" There was a lucky chance. I had been writing—publishing poetry, publishing essays—and I had made acquaintances, mainly through the mail. You remember—we all used to write letters… Then we finally sent our samples with some supporting letters—one of them from Professor Jackson—to North Point Press, which was an excellent small press. They sent the translation samples out for review to two people. One of them was Clarence Brown, and the other was Guy Davenport—two writers who wrote for them, and who happened to be literary acquaintances of mine. The press didn't know that. Nor did I know until some time later that they had been asked to read our samples. Anyhow, they both recommended publishing the translation. So it happened by that strange coincidence—though it's not entirely coincidence, because if I hadn't published anything, North Point wouldn't have happened upon that "community of peers." That was lucky, and they did a wonderful job of publishing the book. They went out of business as a result. [*laughter*] Not really as a result, but they did put all of their last money into it. They made a press kit. We got reviewed all over the country because of it. There was a wonderful review in

Wichita, Kansas, in the Wichita *Eagle*, with a big photograph on one side and a full-page review on the other. The title was "Dostoevsky Still the Best," and the picture was of—Tolstoy! A full-page photograph of Tolstoy with a big scowl. We got all kinds of reviews, because the press kit practically wrote the reviews itself, so all they had to do was fill in their copy.

CAROL APOLLONIO FLATH

But now you can choose what you do.

RICHARD PEVEAR

We always did!

CAROL APOLLONIO FLATH

Good point.

PETER CONSTANTINE

My editors keep asking, "Oh, can you translate this work for us?" Things have definitely changed.

JULIE DE SHERBININ

So how did you get into it?

PETER CONSTANTINE

I had initially translated some stories by Thomas Mann that were not known in English. And that book created quite a fanfare when it came out. I had spoken to Cathy Popkin, and asked her about all the Chekhov stories that had never been translated before. I asked her if this was true, and if they were worth translating. She was extremely encouraging. So I translated a couple of stories and started sending them around, and they were turned down everywhere, the idea being that these stories were too playful: they were not serious Chekhov, *good* Chekhov. Some editors even suggested, "Would you consider doing later stories, not these?" And then Seven Stories Press accepted the project and decided to publish it under the title *The Undiscovered Chekhov: Thirty-Eight New Stories*, and before it was published *Harper's* Magazine came out with nine of the stories, the "lost" Chekhov stories—there was an enormous fanfare. There were parties, there were television interviews, in Russia, here, everywhere. It got out of control. What happened then is that all the publishers came running and wanted to do the book. The interest that *Harper's* had stirred up on the literary scene made the publishers reevaluate the stories. All this happened very, very quickly, because of *Harper's*. It really was an incredible thing. And then Seven Stories Press published an expanded edition, and an even more expanded edition came out in Britain. I thought that these stories would not be well received in England. I was really worried about Britain, because there is a tendency there for the press not to like American translations. Even though I'm originally English I've lived here for twenty-one years, and I do write, I think, like an American, with American rhythms. But the British press was kind. One critic did call my translation "scintillating American"—it was George Steiner, actually. [*laughter*] So that's how that started.

MICHAEL FINKE

I'm curious… Could you give us an idea of how Chekhov is selling? What kind of print runs do these books have?

RICHARD PEVEAR

I don't know about the *Short Novels*, which just came out.

LARISSA VOLOKHONSKY

Two thousand copies a year.

MAN FROM AUDIENCE

Unless it makes Oprah's list.

CYNTHIA MARSH

Is that worldwide? In all the English-speaking markets in the world?

RICHARD PEVEAR

This is a Bantam book. It's an American edition, and probably they're not pushing it. There are a lot of competing Chekhov translations out there.

PETER CONSTANTINE

I'm told that my Chekhov translation has been selling quite well. I know that one statement has thirty thousand copies, which is why I was so pleased at the excitement the book has generated.

CAROL APOLLONIO FLATH

So what are your next projects, all of you? What about you Peter, are you going to be taking up Chekhov again?

PETER CONSTANTINE

Seven Stories has asked me to do a collection of Chekhov stories, the ones that Richard and Larissa didn't choose.

CAROL APOLLONIO FLATH

There's a lot of those.

ROBERT L. JACKSON

We have to contend with the fact that around 1900, when Chekhov was asked, "How many stories did you write," he answered, "*Tysiacha*," one thousand!

PETER CONSTANTINE

It's well over six hundred... well up there. So that's one thing that I've thought of doing. I'm also doing a volume of Machiavelli's works for Modern Library. I have translated Tolstoy's *Cossacks* and Gogol's *Taras Bulba* for them, and they are about to bring out my new translation of Voltaire's *Candide*.

CAROL APOLLONIO FLATH

What about you, Larissa and Richard? More Chekhov?

LARISSA VOLOKHONSKY

I've started *War and Peace*.

PETER CONSTANTINE

You're going to be very busy.

LARISSA VOLOKHONSKY

I'm on page 276. There are 1600 in my edition.

WOMAN FROM AUDIENCE

And what do you do, Richard, while you're waiting for the rest of it?

RICHARD PEVEAR

Actually, I'm translating *The Three Musketeers*. That's not a joke. With French I can work on my own, which gives Larissa time to produce her first version.

CAROL APOLLONIO FLATH

Well that does bring up another question. Is there a special feel to Russian, since all of you translate from other languages too?

PETER CONSTANTINE

A special feel?

CAROL APOLLONIO FLATH

A special feel to it...

RICHARD PEVEAR

Of course there is. But it's very hard to define.

PROF. GEORGE PAHOMOV, BRYN MAWR

Just a practical question: There are names of artifacts, in Chekhov and other Russian writers, which are historically bound—the tools have disappeared, horse culture has disappeared: types of harness, where you harness this horse, where you harness that horse. Where to you go to find out what those things are in English, because they're not in dictionaries—not even hundred-year-old dictionaries. What do you do? And horses are so central to lots of stories.

RICHARD PEVEAR

Yes, especially with Tolstoy. Sometimes you can find the right words, if you know something about harnesses and horses. There are special dictionaries. I don't have any, but they do exist. Otherwise, as Father Alexander Schmemann, whom Professor Jackson mentioned this morning, used to say, "If you can't find something to say, say something religious." I say something that sounds "horsey."

LARISSA VOLOKHONSKY

Most of the terms in Russian I find in Dal''s dictionary.[24] Dal' is very good. I go to Dal', and then I try to explain to Richard what it is that I found in Dal'.

RICHARD PEVEAR

Sometimes by putting it on... [*all laugh*] We also use the *Oxford English Dictionary*. I recommend that. Because I will never use a word that Tolstoy or Chekhov couldn't have written, a word, for instance that only entered English in 1920. It offends me to do that. I love the historical definitions. Like Emile Littré's French dictionary. Half of French literature is quoted in it.

MAN FROM AUDIENCE

I have a shelf full of pre- and immediately post-revolutionary English-Russian and Russian-English dictionaries, which will give you the word, but the word is often obsolete, and if you put it in your translation the reader will not know what that word means, and you will have to footnote again. I think a wonderful case of this is Nabokov's insisting that the title of Gogol's story "Shinel'" ("The Overcoat") should be translated "The Carrick," because that is in fact the tailor's term in the Regency for a caped overcoat, but *shinel'* is a perfectly normal Russian word and *carrick* is a perfectly grotesque English word, and you can't do that.

RICHARD PEVEAR

No, that's right.

LARISSA VOLOKHONSKY

We call it "Overcoat."

ANDREW DURKIN

Actually, my question is going to be along the same lines. To go back to your comment about the art form of the footnote: I was thinking of "Dama s

---

[24] Vladimir Dal', *Tolkovyi slovar' zhivogo velikorusskogo iazyka*, 4 vols., first published 1863–66.

sobachkoi" (The Lady with the Little Dog), where they have dinner at the *kurort* (spa) and they meet at the Slavyansky Bazaar Hotel when she comes to Moscow. How much cultural information that is obsolete for both cultures, or that may still be meaningful to a Russian reader but is just out of the cultural orbit for an English speaker, do you explain for them? How often do you just put problematic material out there, implicitly suggesting that they can find out about it elsewhere? And how much do you maybe gloss over?

RICHARD PEVEAR

I would prefer to footnote everything culturally important, everything that the ordinary English reader wouldn't know—if it plays a role in the story. It's important to know why a person says this, and as we've been saying all day, it's always important. So I would tend to use footnotes like that. But the real problem now is: Where do you stop? Can you refer to the Prodigal Son without giving a footnote? I was teaching the story of Pushkin, "The Stationmaster." You'll recall the cheap prints of the Prodigal Son on the wall. Pushkin mentions it twice. If Pushkin says something twice it must be important. I started asking my students—because the story is a reversal of the Prodigal Son, and it's very funny—I kept saying, "Why are these prints on the wall?" Finally one of them said, "Who is the Prodigal Son?" And I said, "How many people here do not know?" And they all put their hands up. The point is, when do you stop footnoting? You can't give them the entire Western Civilization in footnotes.

CAROL APOLLONIO FLATH

Nabokov tried to do that.

RICHARD PEVEAR

Nabokov is a great artist of the footnote. I love his *Eugene Onegin*. It's unreadable; and he said that when he revised it, he made it worse. [*laughter*]

PETER CONSTANTINE

Larissa and I were discussing earlier when Mitya in "Za iablochki" (For Little Apples), as a prank, puts tar on the gate, which is an indication that the woman who lives there is a fallen woman or immoral. It probably needs a footnote, or maybe qualities, such as "the cross of shame" or "immorality." So that would perhaps be two ways of doing it: either sending the reader down to look at a footnote, or adding something that will incorporate the missing information.

LARISSA VOLOKHONSKY

I think it should be "tar," because tar is important.

PETER CONSTANTINE

No, "tar" is what Chekhov says, but one might add "a cross of..." in order to introduce the moral component...

RICHARD PEVEAR

That's the kind of thing where readers might understand what it means on their own, if they just pay attention.

PROF. KATHERINE O'CONNOR, BOSTON UNIVERSITY

I'm just curious: When one works for a long time with a particular author, as you have just been working with Chekhov and Tolstoy, do you—quietly, among yourselves—ever talk about what you honestly admit are irritations with that author's style, his use of rhetoric, tone, quirks?

RICHARD PEVEAR

Yes. Especially with Tolstoy. Tolstoy is an extremely annoying writer. He's very crude, very heavy-handed. He's repetitious. He makes mistakes. He makes simple grammatical mistakes.

LARISSA VOLOKHONSKY

He omits subjects or objects.

RICHARD PEVEAR

Especially in *War and Peace*. So I keep hearing from the other side of the wall: "Oh Lev Nikolaevich! How could you write that? And what do we do with it?"

LARISSA VOLOKHONSKY

And with Chekhov, I became very, very sad, when we were translating him. I asked, "Why am I so sad?"

RICHARD PEVEAR

I'm so depressed; why am I so depressed?

LARISSA VOLOKHONSKY

And then you leave off translating Chekhov.

RICHARD PEVEAR

If you want to feel good, translate Bulgakov.

PETER CONSTANTINE

Although I must say, the early witty stories were lots of fun, so I have no complaint at all. Especially doing these translations after Thomas Mann, whose stories were convoluted and problematic.

JULIE DE SHERBININ

And Babel?

PETER CONSTANTINE

Babel was a very difficult writer. We were talking with Larissa about this. He does word-gymnastics, which I had to try to figure out how to render. Babel in that sense was far, far more challenging than Chekhov, because he tricks you often—maybe going a little bit too far sometimes. [*to Larissa*] What do you think as a Russian reader of Babel—of the images and the ideas?

LARISSA VOLOKHONSKY

He's very difficult to translate, but that doesn't mean he goes too far.

PETER CONSTANTINE

Grammatically sometimes... grammatical errors, well not errors, perhaps, but...

LARISSA VOLOKHONSKY

It's all deliberate, and it's worked out. And when you as a translator read an author, as Richard said, you have to trust him. Babel is our great writer. We can trust him, so it's not perceived as...

PETER CONSTANTINE

Translating Babel, you have to try to create a new language almost...

LARISSA VOLOKHONSKY

Then what do you do with Platonov?

PETER CONSTANTINE

I think those times—1917, 1918—were very exciting in Russia.

LARISSA VOLOKHONSKY

It creates a whole new perception of the world, this kind of language; but you can't say he goes too far.

PETER CONSTANTINE

Oh, I didn't mean it as a criticism.

LARISSA VOLOKHONSKY

I understand.

PETER CONSTANTINE

I'm a fanatic Babelist... But he was harder than...

RICHARD PEVEAR

"Babelist!" What an unfortunate name! [*laughter*]

JULIE DE SHERBININ

I have a frivolous question. What was the Oprah matter all about?

RICHARD PEVEAR

Ask her. [*points to Larissa Volokhonsky*]

JULIE DE SHERBININ

Were you on the Oprah show?

RICHARD PEVEAR

No, no! I didn't know who she was. Our editor called, laughing her head off, and said, "I love telling you guys this, because you don't know what I'm talking about." And I said, "Well, tell me!" She said, "Do you know who Oprah Winfrey is?" And I said, "No." I said, "I think she's a Country-Western singer." Grand Ole Oprah… That was as close as I came.

CAROL APOLLONIO FLATH

Did you watch the show?

RICHARD PEVEAR

No. I didn't even get the website. Our editor did it for us.

CONEVERY VALENČIUS

A historian's question: I'm really surprised, Peter, to I hear you talking about translating stuff not only from this wealth of languages, but also from a variety of different historical eras. So many of our questions have been directed at how you translate, not only from a whole different language and culture, but from another time, dealing with what is now archaic technology, for instance—the whole horse-culture problem. What are your approaches to picking an era or avoiding it? You're jumping around in time, translating from people who are writing in a lot of very different time periods as well as…

PETER CONSTANTINE

As far as Russian is concerned, I feel happiest dealing with the 1880s to the early 1900s. That language is a language in itself. Babel was a whole new language, a new Soviet language. In high school in the 1970s—I went to an international high school in Greece, where half my classes were in Russian, the idea being to impart a Russian education to the Polish, Bulgarian, and Rumanian diplomats' kids. However, our teachers were White Russian, so we did Nabokov, we did Babel. When I went to Leningrad afterwards with the idea of studying literature, I was very surprised at the curriculum—I knew that there wasn't going to be any Nabokov in the U.S.S.R. then—but it was *very* different. In high school we did have to deal with socialist realism and its language to some extent, but the teachers themselves were not all that comfortable with it—they were émigrés, so it wasn't really their thing. I wonder whether that conditioned my preferences. Also, I haven't lived in a Russian situation for twenty years. And it's been a long time since I've spoken the language, though reading and speaking are very different things. In Russian, I would say that I like the period from Chekhov to Babel, and I've never translated beyond that, though I did one Pelevin story and one Shalamov story. But they were quite difficult to do. I've recently translated two new novels by Brina Svit from Slovene, and I am working right now on a novel for Knopf by a very, very young German author, Benjamin Lebert, he's twenty-two. I like translating modern literature—the newest things—but not in Russian.

RICHARD PEVEAR

Actually Russian literature has a rather compact time period—it began in the nineteenth century. But the further you go into the past, the more adaptation is justified, because the original culture is so different, so distant—as Homeric culture is different from American culture. I don't know if any of you have read Christopher Logue's translations—sort of translations—of Homer. They're very exciting and very interesting, but of course dreadful as translations. I mean, they're not translations, but I think that's more justifiable. I feel rather close to the culture of the nineteenth century, except for these lost implements and things like that, which can mostly be found.

LARISSA VOLOKHONSKY

I don't feel any separation from that time. Because I grew up reading all these books many times. They are my past, somehow. And I don't see it as distant history—it's my personal history.

RICHARD PEVEAR

Larissa said to me the other day that she realized that all of her family in Russia learned to speak from reading Tolstoy. They talk to each other like Tolstoy characters, not like Dostoevsky characters.

LARISSA VOLOKHONSKY

Not in his language exactly, but with his way of thinking, and in his somewhat platitudinous form, uttering these truths about life: Life is this way, life is that way…

CAROL APOLLONIO FLATH

I think we've probably run out of time. There will undoubtedly be many more questions, and I think they can perhaps come and ask you them after the session. It's just been a delightful conversation. I really appreciate it, and thank you again to the organizers for putting it all together.

# Translating Chekhov's Drama

# Seeing Chekhov Whole

## Laurence Senelick, Tufts University

When I was a graduate student in Comparative Literature at Harvard in the palmy days of Harry Levin and Renato Poggioli, a riddle circulated through the department. Who is the greatest Russian writer of the nineteenth century, it asked. Answer: Constance Garnett. Certainly, for Anglophone readers in the first half of the twentieth century, and for some time afterwards, it was her genteel English voice that emanated from the pages of the Russian classics. "Seventeen volumes of Turgenev, thirteen volumes of Chekhov's *Tales* and two volumes of his *Plays*, thirteen volumes of Dostoyevsky, six volumes of Gogol, four volumes of Tolstoy, and six volumes of Herzen,"[1] not to mention occasional renderings of Goncharov, Gorky, Ostrovsky, and a collection of folk songs, issued from her hand. These heroic labors were carried on between 1893 and 1922 by a Cambridge-educated wife and mother in poor health, who did her own gardening, cooking, and entertaining and who visited Russia only twice, briefly.

Such familiarity with the Russian greats would suggest that Constance Garnett was a shrewd evaluator of their qualities. Who knows? She never wrote about them. It was her husband Edward who penned the introductions to the Turgenev and Gorky volumes and who published a book about Tolstoy. Yet Constance Garnett had the inestimable advantage of knowing firsthand the texts of these masters. Close acquaintance should have enabled her to make critical pronouncements of considerable acumen. Instead, she left evaluations to literati such as Arnold Bennett, E. M. Forster, and Katherine Mansfield, who, of course, based their judgments on her translations and those of others. And, because of her haste and her less than indigenous knowledge of Russian, Garnett tended to make all her authors sound like one another, neutralizing their individual qualities.

In this respect, Garnett is hardly an isolated case. Since the current practice in the theater is for playwrights and directors to undertake so-called "translations" of languages they don't know, few questions are asked about the specificity of a text. Yet even someone with a solid knowledge of the Russian language should be aware that in the translation of Chekhov what is be-

---

[1] Carolyn G. Heilbrun, *The Garnett Family* (New York: Macmillan, 1961), 183.

*Chekhov the Immigrant: Translating a Cultural Icon.* Michael C. Finke and Julie de Sherbinin, eds. Bloomington, IN: Slavica Publishers, 2007, 69–82.

ing translated is not Russian *per se*—it is Chekhov's wielding of Russian.[2] One is dealing not only with a language which is not one's own, but with the artistically wrought language of a creative artist. Working on a translation, it is essential for one to inquire into the precise connotation of a word or a phrase at the turn of the nineteenth century *as it is used by Chekhov*.

For instance, in *Uncle Vanya*, when Voinitsky complains that Elena's faithfulness to her husband is *fal'shivyi*, to translate this by the English "false" is to select what used to be called a *"faux ami,"* a seemingly exact but actually imprecise counterpart. The word appears in Chekhov's writing only in such phrases as *fal'shivaia moneta, fal'shivye bilety*—counterfeit money—and therefore what is meant here is something like "phoney," "fake." Or note, in the first version of *Ivanov*, how Count Shabelsky cannot address Anna without a Yiddish exclamation or an anti-Semitic joke. So, in Act I of the last version of *Ivanov*, the one that is always translated, when we hear the Count's voice from inside the house, railing at Anna's piano technique, "You've got no more ear for music than a *farshirovannaia ryba*," the reference is not taxidermic, but culinary. All previous translators have rendered this as "stuffed fish" or "stuffed trout," but the *zhidovka* (Jewess) is being rebuked for having no more ear than a *gefilte fish*.[3]

In the process of translating, I try to be alert to such hidden jokes. Whenever I attend a Chekhov performance in Russia, I pay close attention to when the audience laughs, and try to prompt a similar response in English. One has to be careful in this respect, however. Some older Russians have a hard time keeping a straight face at Sonya's famous image at the end of *Uncle Vanya*— "Мы увидим все небо в алмазах" (We shall see all heaven in diamonds)— because in Iosif Kheifets's popular 1958 movie, *Dorogoi moi chelovek* (My Dear Man) an abusive father keeps threatening his family that he will make them see all heaven in diamonds.

Admittedly, one can go overboard in searching for idiosyncrasy. A French translator of Pirandello, Jean-Loup Rivière, thought he detected an asthmatic impulse in Pirandello's structure of linked short sequences which suddenly explode into a long one. He was disappointed to learn that the Italian dramatist did not suffer from asthma, but he did discover that Pirandello smoked a hundred cigarettes a day.[4] Did shortness of breath affect his dramatic construction? Can one perceive a tubercular cause for Chekhov's prose style or his preference for short forms?

Taken as a whole, Chekhov's dramatic output continually reflects back on itself. A remarkably ecological writer, Chekhov recycled not only ideas but

---

[2] Jean-Michel Déprats, in Jean-Michel Déprats, Éloi Recoing, Jean-Loup Rivière, and Cathérine Treilhou-Balaude, "'C'est le poète qui commande': Table ronde," *Registres de l'Institut d'études théâtrales, Sorbonne nouvelle* 3 (September 1998): 111–12.

[3] There is no common Russian term for a stuffed fish in the taxidermic sense.

[4] Jean-Loup Rivière, in Jean-Michel Déprats et al., "'C'est le poète qui commande,'" 10.

expressions. The same phrases crop up in his letters and his stories as in his plays, which abets the notion that Chekhov's is a closed world. One of his favorite juvenile quotations, the phrase "obscured by the veils of ignorance," has never been tracked down to a particular source, but turns up on Lopakhin's lips the year of Chekhov's death. *Play without a Title* (*P'esa bez nazvaniia*; usually called *Platonov*) and *Along the Highway* (*Na bol'shoi doroge*) are stockpiles of Chekhovian themes and phrases. Glagolev Jr. with his thirty-five telegrams from Paris is a forerunner of Ranevskaya's lover as well as Yasha in *The Cherry Orchard*. Voinitsev has been offered a job but it is speculated that he won't take it, because he is too lazy, as Lopakhin will later say of Gaev. Merik in *Along the Highway* describes someone as like a "retarded kid with a new toy"; Lebedev uses the term to describe Shabelsky in *Ivanov*.

George Steiner used to claim that, interviewing candidates for Oxford, he was favorably impressed when a prospective student admitted to having read the complete works of a given author. Seeing Chekhov whole, examining how he used the language throughout his writing, can only aid a translator in making choices. Even if Constance Garnett failed to distinguish the individual traits of authors or to capitalize on her familiarity with the writers she put into English, much may be said for translating the whole body of a writer's work. After Garnett, the next aspirant to her laurels has been David Magarshack, whose output, largely disseminated by Penguin Books in the 1950s and '60s, temporarily supplanted hers. In the matter of Chekhov, he was outdone, however, by Ronald Hingley, who produced the *Oxford Chekhov* between 1964 and 1983. It was not a truly complete edition, since Hingley omitted most of the early humorous fiction, the journalism, the letters, and the first version of *Ivanov*; but it did provide notes, variants, and commentary on publication history, all of which was lacking in Garnett's volumes.

The chief problem with Hingley's translations—and this holds true for those of Magarshack as well—is that they sought to assimilate Chekhov to a supposititious English common reader. They attempted to de-Russify the text. Hingley, in particular, seems to have made the perverse decision whenever possible not to follow Chekhov's sentence structures or word order, and to rely on English clichés and catchphrases when confronted with particularly flavorsome Russian idioms. He made no effort to preserve the careful repetition of words, let alone the rhythms, in Chekhov's later writing. Hingley went so far as to translate "peasants" as "the locals," and to change Russian names to English ones—Pavel and all its diminutives, Pasha, Pava, Pavochka, etc., to Paul, for instance. He was not consistent in this, however, which makes the practice all the more awkward. Although Hingley was more aware than his predecessors (and many of his successors) that Chekhov writes in a very colloquial language, his renderings sound nowadays, especially to an American ear, like a disoriented P. G. Wodehouse.

Pointing out the flaws in other people's translations is a pleasant enough indoor sport, but there is something more cogent to be discovered than incompetence or wrongheadedness. If one were to examine all the renderings of Chekhov's plays into English from Max Mandel and George Calderon to the present, one could trace in them the history of translation and of the Anglophone world's relationship to Chekhov and the evolution of modernist ideas of theater. Translation contains in itself the conditions of its emergence. It puts a text into a state of crisis that is stimulating and provocative. Every attempt at translation is relative, bound to circumstances; the translator must stop at a given moment even though he would like to rework his text endlessly. A translation always needs to be redone.

Two years ago, I was approached by W. W. Norton to revise their Critical Edition of Chekhov's plays, edited and translated by the late Eugene Bristow. Having thirty-five years' experience of translating and re-translating the major plays for various productions, I persuaded them to start from scratch, with an edition that would include more plays and fresh renderings based on the thirty-volume Chekhov issued by the U.S.S.R. Academy of Sciences in the 1980s, along with a different selection of critical essays.[5] The customary practice among publishers is to combine Chekhov's Big Four in one volume, occasionally including the final version of *Ivanov*. The one-act plays are usually lumped together in a separate volume. This may make marketing sense, since the average reader may not be looking for more than a nodding acquaintance with the plays. For the serious student who does not have access to Russian, it creates a false impression. The close interaction between the one-acts and the full-length plays, their variations on themes, become clearer when they are offered in chronological order.

The need to present Chekhov's plays as a totality led me a step beyond. I am presently putting the finishing touches on a *Complete Plays* of Chekhov to be published in one volume by W. W. Norton. "Complete" is, of course, a weasel word, but this edition intends to be fuller than any previously in print. I have included those early comic pieces which are laid out like plays, as well as the first version of *Ivanov* and *The Power of Hypnotism*, a vaudeville Chekhov sketched out with his friend Ivan Leontev-Shcheglov and which has not been published in any language since 1911. A copious number of variants are also included, along with thorough annotation.

This is not to say that Chekhov is like Ibsen in regarding his dramatic output as chapters of a single book. Ibsen, during his tenure as dramaturg in Bergen, had learned how to turn out a five-act play annually, and, later in his career, every two years. In his realistic phase, the plays constitute a debate with one another. *An Enemy of the People* argues against lying to the public; the next play, *The Wild Duck*, argues for the necessity of illusion. Chekhov, however, saw himself primarily as a writer of short fiction, with drama as a side-

---

[5] The resulting volume, *Anton Chekhov's Selected Plays*, trans. and ed. Laurence Senelick (New York: W. W. Norton & Co., 2005), includes translations of *The Bear, Ivanov, The Wedding, The Celebration, The Seagull, Uncle Vanya, Three Sisters,* and *The Cherry Orchard*.

line. His early plays are occasional, prompted by requests to provide material for actors or a theater, and only later inspired by his own creative urgency. Everyone knows that he once said that medicine was his legitimate wife, literature his mistress. In that case, playwriting was a series of one-night stands.

Plays in pre-Revolutionary Russia had to undergo two censorships, one for publication and one for performance. What is striking about the language of *Platonov* and *Along the Highway*, two plays never performed in Chekhov's lifetime, is the freedom of the dialogue. Words and phrases, not to mention situations, which would never pass the stage censorship, are used in abundance, giving the dialogue a vivacity that does not correspond to the standard notion of what is Chekhovian. (The plebeian idiom of *Along the Highway* may come more from literary sources than from things heard, though; there is something artificial about its folksy vernacular.) In both cases, the language is more forceful, more slangy, more audacious than anything one would expect from a beginner. I would suggest that, as Chekhov became more familiar with the conventions of the professional stage, he exercised a kind of self-censorship. His sops to Cerberus can be seen in his replacement of certain lines in *The Seagull* concerning Arkadina's affair with Trigorin and in *The Cherry Orchard* concerning Trofimov's past and his views of serfdom. As he famously wrote to Olga Knipper, "The things that worried me most were the second act's lack of action and a certain sketchy quality in Trofimov, the student. After all, time and again Trofimov is being sent into exile, time and again he is being expelled from the university, but how can you express stuff like that?" (19 October 1903). Nevertheless, *these* revisions concern content, not form.

Even as early as *Platonov*, Chekhov realized the dramatic power of a verbal leitmotiv. Retired Colonel Ivan Ivanovich Triletsky enters in Act I, blithely saying, "God is patient and hasn't punished me." He vanishes from sight until the end of the play, when he has the last line, "God has lost patience and is punishing me." For the most part, however, Chekhov's attention to language in his playwriting came late. Several of the early vaudevilles were dashed off in a couple of hours or days, as Chekhov himself boasted in his letters. The same holds true for the first version of *Ivanov*, which was composed in a week and a half, almost on a bet. In that notorious case, Chekhov spent the rest of his life revising and touching up his burst of creativity; but his revisions had more to do with clarification of character and motive than with the niceties of dialogue. Even his radical alteration of the last act and the protagonist's suicide were made with an eye to the actors' capabilities and the audiences' responses, not to Chekhov's artistic imperatives.

In *Ivanov*, as later, Chekhov's tendency is to excise the over-explicit and the redundant, to prune away excesses. In the first version, many of the lines end in exclamation marks, but in the rewriting for the Alexandra Theatre in St Petersburg, these are replaced by ellipses. Chekhov's next major play, *The Wood Goblin*, is remarkable for a thoroughgoing revision of the third-act peripeteia and a consequent new fourth act, which transforms it from a society melodrama to a comedy. Its next avatar, *Uncle Vanya*, shows a new attention to detail, concision, and, particularly, a linguistic organizing principle.

Two parenthetic statements here: I choose to translate Dr. Khrushchev's nickname "Leshii" as "Wood Goblin" because "Wood Demon" makes too diabolic an impression. The mischievous sprite whom the ancient Slavs and their posterity believed inhabited the forests is closer to Puck or Robin Goodfellow in his fondness for leading travelers astray and imitating the sounds of various animals. In Chekhov's day, Russians said *"leshii voz'mi"* as a mild expletive, the way an Englishman might say "Deuce take it."

Also, in turning *Wood Goblin* into *Uncle Vanya*, Chekhov committed an oversight. You may recall Astrov's mentioning his *fel'dsher* or medical attendant, who never says *"idet,"* but always says *"idët"* (*PssS* 13: 82). Then Astrov remarks, "Мошенник страстный" (An awful crook). How can a hospital orderly be an awful crook? In *Wood Goblin*, the mispronunciation is attributed to a bookkeeper, someone more likely to misappropriate money.

*Uncle Vanya* is knit together by words formed on *dukh* and *dykh* (spirit and breath), to provide a sense of oppression. In the very first lines of dialogue, Astrov declares, "It's stifling" (*dushno*), and variations on that sentiment are struck with regularity. Vanya repeats it and speaks of Yelena's attempt to muffle her youth; the Professor begins Act II by announcing that he cannot breathe, and Vanya speaks of being choked by the idea that his life is wasted. Astrov admits he would be suffocated if he had to live in the house for a month. The two young women fling open windows to be able to breath freely. During the first two acts, a storm is brewing and then rages; and Vanya spends the last act moaning *"tiazhelo mne,"* literally "It is heavy on me," "I feel weighed down." At the very end, Sonya's "We shall rest" (My otdokhnem) is etymologically related to *dushno* and connotes "breathing freely." The standard English translation, "We shall rest," unfortunately ends with a decisive dental sound, and not a long-drawn-out and softer vocable. I tried to ameliorate it in the Norton Critical Chekhov as "We shall be at rest," but for the Complete Chekhov I have translated it as "We'll be at peace," the same number of syllables, ending in a sound that can be protracted, and spelling out what is implied in Sonya's aria.

Another important verbal motif in *Vanya* is folkloric: with a nod to the earlier *leshii*, the dialogue refers to the *domovoi* (house goblin), the *vodianoi* (water goblin), and the *rusalka* (water sprite). As in *Seagull*, the *rusalka* is mentioned in connection with an *omut*. Treplev refers to Pushkin's unfinished verse play *Rusalka* in regard to Nina, and later Nina says that both he and she have fallen into the *omut*. In this context, *omut* might be translated as "whirlpool" or "maelstrom," but its use in *Vanya*, the suggestion that Elena dive plop! into an *omut*, reveals that its alternative meaning is intended: a "millrace," precisely the body of water into which Pushkin's heroine threw herself to become a *rusalka*. Similarly, when Astrov remarks of Elena, "Она прекрасна, спора нет" (She's beautiful, no question), he is quoting Pushkin's version of *Snow White*, the "Tale of the Tsar's Dead Daughter and the Seven Warriors"; the evil Tsarina turns to her mirror with the question whether she is really the fairest in the land and the mirror replies: "Ты прекрасна, спора нет..." ("Fair art thou, no contest there..."). These are what I call embedded quotations, less obvious than the explicit citations from Lermontov and Nekrasov; but a translator must be alert to them in order to preserve the thematic flavor of the original.

The tighter construction of language in the later plays comes from the fact that Chekhov, now reasonably comfortable financially, no longer regarded the stage merely as a financial milch-cow to provide royalties while he concentrated on his fiction. Writing from his newly-purchased farmstead in Melikhovo to Suvorin, who had founded a theater in St. Petersburg, Chekhov announced, "I too shall write a play especially designed for your circle [...] I will write something strange. For the State and for money I have no desire to write. For the time being I am comfortable, and can afford to write a play for which I shall get nothing; if circumstances alter, then, of course, it'll be a different tune" (5 May 1895). This is believed to be the first mention of what would turn out to be *The Seagull*. By not writing for the Imperial theaters or for the box-office, Chekhov was able to suit himself and to devote more time to crafting his language.

In this new attention to detail, a commonplace uttered in the first act may return to resonate with fresh significance. Astrov complains that when people can't understand him, they call him "strange" or "peculiar" (*strannyi*); later, Yelena uses that very word to describe him, thereby revealing that she doesn't understand him. The same holds true for *chudak* (crackpot) and its derivatives.

As in *Uncle Vanya*, the incohesive elements of *The Seagull* are held together by language. Whatever their naturalistic psychologies and social positions, the characters are largely composed of linguistic tics and obsessions—Sorin's "*v kontse kontsov*" (when all's said and done), and Masha's "*pustiaki*" (nonsense, trivia). These artificial formulas, the sense that each character is programmed to keep saying the same thing over and over again, contributes to the illusion of reality. The recurrence of the same idea or an identical phrase is not simply the sign of the protagonists' boredom or the mark of a morbid "compulsion for repetition": it structures the text by reducing it to a finite series of themes, constantly resumed or varied. Certain words, iterated six or seven times, characterize an individual; others crystallize an obsession or a general neurosis, such as the words *talent* (*talant*), *know* (*znat'*) and its derivatives (such as *uznat'*, *to find out*). The repetition of these words bespeaks a general desire to be recognized by others as a loving person and, for Treplev, Arkadina, Trigorin, and Nina, as an artist. (Incidentally, Chekhov rarely uses the word "art," but prefers talent as his signifier for genius and ability).

The characters communicate or fail to communicate through recollection, quotation (not just literary but of one another), inarticulate sounds such as Dorn's humming and Sorin's whistling. As in Chekhov's vaudevilles, the characters talk past one another, without any genuine attempt to persuade anyone else. Rather than expressing a given character, language escapes them to be relayed and transmitted by the character along a subtextual underground railway. Often, the verbal dialogue breaks off at the very moment when the characters are just about to make a statement. As Patrice Pavis puts it, the peculiar power of Chekhov's text originates in a sort of teasing, never explaining, never providing the key to the quotations or to the characters.[6]

Echo is one of Chekhov's favorite effects. It suggests to the spectator, placed in the position of omniscient auditor, that an action, a situation, an expression has already been put in evidence and the repetition makes some sense. Echo is also a more or less masked citation of one's own or someone else's remark. "It gets you going in circles!" declares Medvedenko to Masha about his paltry salary at the start of the play, and Dorn picks up the phrase, when the schoolmaster starts complaining about the price of flour in the next act: "It gets you going in circles!" When Nina Zarechnaya characterizes Konstantin's play as a *"chitka,"* a mere "read-through," we realize that she must have picked up this bit of backstage slang from listening closely to Arkadina. In Act I, Konstantin offers to stand outside Nina's house and stare at her window; in Act IV, he speaks of standing for hours outside her hotel, while Nina herself haunts the grounds of the estate and fails to come in.

The translator must be alert to the echoic effect between different characters who were not on stage at the same time but who come to the same conclusions. In the first act, Konstantin describes Trigorin's writing as "Charming, talented ... but ... compared to Tolstoy or Zola, a little Trigorin goes a long way." In Act II, Trigorin describes his own writing as: "Charming, but a far cry from Tolstoy."

The same principles of linguistic construction apply to Chekhov's last two plays. In *Three Sisters*, the prevalent state of mind is regularly expressed by *"nadoelo"*—"I'm sick and tired," "fed up." In his brief interlude alone with Masha in Act II, Vershinin blames the average local *intelligent* for being "sick and tired of his wife, sick and tired of his estate, sick and tired of his horses"; but he is clearly characterizing himself, for he soon draws a picture of his own wretched marriage. Masha, whom Vershinin would exempt as an exceptional person, is "sick and tired of winter," and when her husband proclaims his love with "I'm so happy," she bitterly spits back, "I'm sick and tired, sick and tired, sick and tired," thus aligning herself with the fellow-townsmen she detests. Even the genteel Olga pronounces herself "sick and tired" of the fire. The unanimous response to this spiritual malaise is a commonplace fatalism.

---

[6] Patrice Pavis, "Commentaires et notes" to Antoine Tchékhov, *La Mouette*, trans. Antoine Vitez (Paris: Actes Sud, 1985), 99–103.

Chebutykin's dismissive *"Vse ravno"*—"It doesn't matter"—reverberates through the other characters as well. Vershinin uses it to deny differences between the military and civilians; Tuzenbakh describes his resignation from the army in those words; Solyony denigrates his love for Irina with the phrase. According to Irina, Andrei's debts "don't matter" to Natasha. This deliberate insouciance is the counterbalance to the equally deliberate velleities about the future. Chekhov's intention to employ this leitmotiv is evident from the fact that, in his final revision of the play, he inserted *"vse ravno"* into Chebutykin's dialogue six separate times.

In *The Cherry Orchard*, every character speaks in a particular cadence. Compare Pishchik's short asthmatic phrases with the run-on grandiloquence of Trofimov or with Anya's iambic meters. Changes are rung on *neschast'e* (unhappiness, misfortune), from Epikhodov's nickname "Twenty-two Misfortunes," to Ranevskaya's narrative of her unhappy past, to Firs' characterization of the emancipation of the serfs. Of course, an umbrella misfortune overhangs the whole play, the sale of the estate. After much searching, I decided to replicate this recurrence with "troubles": Epikhodov becomes "Tons of Trouble," Ranevskaya speaks of her troubles, and Firs refers to the freeing of the serfs as the "Troubles."

Another important repetition is the earthy term *nedotepa*, uttered regularly by Firs and which is the last line in the play. Translators grow gray over the word: earlier English versions have "good-for-nothing," "rogue," "duffer," "job-lot," "lummox," "silly young cuckoo", "silly old nothing," "nincompoop", "muddler," "silly galoot," "numbskull," "young flibbertigibbet." In fact, *nedotepa* was not a Russian word when Chekhov used it; it was Ukrainian for an incompetent or a mental defective. Chekhov may have remembered hearing it in his childhood; it does not appear in Russian dictionaries until 1938, and then Chekhov is cited as the source.[7] The first English translator of the play George Calderon seems to have confused it with the obscure Russian word *nedotiapa*, from *ne-* (not), and *dotopiat'* (to finish chopping), which makes great sense in the context of the play.[8] The critic Batyushkov considered the whole play to be a variation on the theme of "nedotepery," each of the characters representing a different aspect of life unfulfilled.

Herein lies the paradox. Seeing Chekhov whole enables one to see the details close up. Scrutinizing the details one begins to see the whole pattern. This may be why critics have so often had recourse to painting for an analogy. Chekhov's first English translator George Calderon likened his style to that of the Acmeists. The poet Randall Jarrell compared Chekhov's technique in

---

[7] E. A. Polotskaia, *"Nedotepa i vrazdrob'* (o trudnostiakh perevoda p'esy)," *Russkii iazyk* 4 (364) (23–31 January 2003): 7–15.

[8] George Calderon, "Introduction to Tchekhoff," in *Two Plays of Tchekof* (London: Mitchell Kennerley, 1912).

*Three Sisters* to that of Edouard Vuillard: "[T]he foundation areas on the canvas are made less emphatic by the swarms of particles that mottle the walls with rose-printed paper, the rugs from swirls, the lawns with pools of sun and shade. From such variation and variegation comes his cohesion."[9] My own preferred comparison is with the pointillists, each point of color distinct in itself yet contributing to a greater whole, once one steps away.

The translator's duty to preserve these individual speckles of the verbal motifs is not exclusive to Chekhov. It was insisted upon by George Bernard Shaw, who wrote to Siegfried Trebitsch, the German translator of his plays:

> The way in which you translate every word just as it comes and then forget it and translate it some other way when it begins (or should begin) to make the audience laugh, is enough to whiten the hair on an author's head. Have you ever read Shakespeare's *Much Ado About Nothing*? In it a man calls a constable an ass, and throughout the rest of the play the constable can think of nothing but this insult and keeps on saying, "But forget not, masters, that I am an ass." Now if you translated *Much Ado*, you would make the man call the constable a Schaffkopf. On the next page he would be a Narr, then a Maul, then a Thier, and perhaps the very last time an Esel.[10]

This was such a salient principle for Shaw that he hammered at it the following month: "I tell you again and again most earnestly and seriously, that unless you repeat the words that I have repeated, you will throw away all the best stage effects and make the play unpopular with the actors... Half the art of dialogue consists in the echoing of words—the tossing back & forwards of phrases from one to another like a cricket ball..."[11] What is true for Shaw is true for Chekhov.

Nearly forty years later, the American critic Stark Young, when he set out to translate *The Seagull* for the Lunts, was surprised to find that the "tone, which in a dramatic work is a diffused and intangible but final quality that reveals its general characteristic" had been falsified in earlier English translations of Chekhov. He too singled out "those balances, repetitions for stage effect, repetitions for stage economy, theatrical combinations and devices, time-patterns, and so on, that are the fruits of much intention and technical

---

[9] Randall Jarrell, "About *The Three Sisters*. Notes," in *The Three Sisters* (London: Macmillan, 1969), 105–06. There had been an impressionist show in Moscow in 1896, and Tolstoy had characterized Chekhov's technique as a story writer as impressionism. Édouard Vuillard (1868–1940), a Parisian painter, enjoyed a long and successful career; his domestic interiors use the linear techniques and vibrant colors of Japanese prints.

[10] *Bernard Shaw's Letters to Siegfried Trebitsch*, ed. Samuel A. Weiss (Stanford, CA: Stanford University Press, 1986), 30 (26 December 1902). The words translate as "sheep's head," "fool," "muzzle," "beast," "ass."

[11] Ibid., 36 (15 January 1903).

craft, and that are almost totally absent from the translation."[12] Of Constance Garnett, he observed that "She has a way of missing the point just enough to spoil the more immediate economy, as it were, of a theatrical moment." Greater attention needed to be paid to Chekhov's style.

Everyone knows Mies van der Rohe's aphorism "God is in the details." Less familiar may be Vladimir Nabokov's "There is no delight without the detail." But most apposite to Chekhov is a notation which Stendhal made in his journal: "Everyone acknowledges that whoever tells a story must appear to be speaking the truth, but to do this one must have the courage to go into the slightest details. This, I think, is the only means of overcoming the reader's distrust." Chekhov, especially in the latter part of his literary career, was a very careful writer and a very economical one; wherever one sinks the probe into his writing, it hits something solid. The best way to understand Chekhov is not to proceed from general assumptions about intention or meaning, but to inquire closely into the choice of words, the structure of sentences, the rhythms of the prose. This may sound like a retreat to formalism or structuralism, a New Critical or purely aesthetic co-optation of an author whom many would prefer to enroll under the banner of progress and humane activism (ecology and conservation, to name one of the latest movements). Yet it is, I believe, the appropriate method for dealing with an author so evasive and self-effacing.

"The shock of the new" in Chekhov's handling of familiar topics contributed mightily to his reputation in his lifetime. Chekhov's newness tends to be lost or overlooked, and may be recovered by sharper attention to the novelty of his dialogue. As my mentor Nils Åke Nilsson pointed out, Chekhov is an unacknowledged precursor of the Futurists and their launching of a *zaumnyi* or "transrational" language. He cites as examples the phrase *"Ty i tak nagavrililsiu"* (You've Gavril-ed it up enough) in *Ivanov*, the "tram-tram-tram" exchange in *Three Sisters*, and Gaev's billiard jargon, calling this a "new dramatic syntax."[13]

Even Stark Young, eager to be faithful to Chekhov, trembled before this novelty. He had to admit that "Chekhov's dialogue is perhaps a trifle more colloquial than mine. Certainly it is more colloquial than I should ever dare to be; for in a translation any very marked colloquialism is always apt to hurt the economy of effect by raising questions as to what the original could have been to come out so patly as that."[14]

---

[12] Stark Young, "Translating *The Sea Gull*," in *"The Sea Gull," A Drama in Four Acts*, trans. Stark Young (New York: Samuel French, 1950), xii–xv.

[13] Nils Åke Nilsson, "Two Chekhovs: Mayakovsky on Chekhov's 'Futurism,'" in *Chekhov's Great Plays: A Critical Anthology*, ed. Jean-Pierre Barricelli (New York: New York University Press, 1981), 251–61.

[14] Young, "Translating *The Seagull*," xix.

Young took as an example Trigorin's remark that, when he gets a whiff of heliotrope, *"skoree motaiu na us"*—"quickly I wrap it around my moustache." Any good Russian-English dictionary will tell you that this is a figure of speech meaning "I make a mental note of something." Perhaps, as Stark Young feared, it is as wrong to translate it literally as it might be to translate "he got my goat" literally into Russian. Nevertheless, to translate it as Young does, "Quickly I make note of it," is to substitute the bland for the colorful. My own solution, bearing in mind, first, Chekhov's fascination with facial hair (every one of his major plays contains remarks about whiskers), and next, that Trigorin is an avid fisherman, is: "I instantly reel it in on my moustache." His following phrase, *"Lovliu v sebia i vas na kazhdoi fraze,"* Young renders awkwardly as "Every sentence, every word I say and you say, I lie in wait for it." However it ought to continue the piscatorial imagery, since Chekhov may have had in the mind the biblical idiom, "to fish in troubled waters," in Russian *"lovit' rybu v mutnoi vode."* It is well known that from his long boyhood experience as a chorister under his father's tutelage, Chekhov's mind was well-stocked with scriptural commonplaces. My solution goes "I'm angling in myself and you for every phrase."

I find it striking that these stylistic and linguistic aspects of Chekhov's work are the most neglected by critics, as well as translators. There is a clear preference for the biographical, the thematic, and the compare-and-contrast approaches. In the English-speaking world, this inattention to Chekhov's language, whether prose or dialogue, is due, in part, to the fact that a great deal of the commentary is written by those who cannot read him in the original. Such otherwise sophisticated commentators as V. S. Pritchett, Richard Gilman, and J. L. Styan have had no qualms about dilating on Chekhov, secure in the belief that translation will give them all they need. It would be unheard-of to write an intensive study of Proust without knowing French or of Goethe without knowing German, but somehow Chekhov's appeal is so great that enthusiasts choose to ignore the linguistic aspect in the belief that Chekhov's qualities lie in essential, "universal" issues. Styan's book, *Chekhov in Performance*, is sedulous in comparing different translations of given lines in order to arrive at some notion of the original;[15] but this method is hardly likely to produce precise results. It may be compared to playing the piano with gloves on.

In the theater, this has led to the absurd practice of having someone competent in the language of origin (though not necessarily well versed in the playwright) translate "word for word" and someone competent in the language of reception then produce an acting version. This practice is of long standing, with Alexander Koiransky working for Guthrie McClintic in the 1940s, Leonid Kipnis for Tyrone Guthrie and Ariadne Nicolaeff for John

---

[15] J. L. Styan, *Chekhov in Performance: A Commentary on the Major Plays* (Cambridge: Cambridge University Press, 1971).

Gielgud in the 1960s, Marina Lavrova for Jean-Claude Carrière in the 1980s. The result is always two loosely related translations: the first, from the language of origin, into flat, deliberately "un-speakable" English, and the latter a transcription of it into good, presumably "stageworthy" English. The process takes one farther and farther from the original. To exacerbate this, the director often means to function as the author or *auteur*, which voids the implicit contract with the spectator. After all, if the publicity reads that the play is by Chekhov, the public has a right to see that play and not a fantasia concocted by an adaptor or director.

At present, there is a fashion for "rough" translation, which chops long speeches into telegraphic phrases, simplifying the language and making it easier for the actors. Using this method and a trot provided by a so-called Russian specialist, dramatists remote from Chekhov's sensibility, language and concerns, such as Pam Gems, Edward Bond, David Mamet, Trevor Griffiths, Peter Barnes, Lanford Wilson, David Hare, Brian Friel, and Richard Nelson, warp him into new shapes that express their own preoccupations. This need of English-speaking playwrights to wrestle Chekhov to the mat has become a compulsively Oedipal rite of passage.

Ultimately, individual choices may be less important than general principles. In conclusion, let me offer a few maxims for anyone planning to translate Chekhov's (or, for that matter, anyone's) plays.

> It is not the translator's job to correct or improve the author.
> Where the characters are incoherent, don't try to make them make sense.
> Where they are slangy, ungrammatical, or substandard, don't try to regularize them.
> Where Chekhov is effusive, don't try to restrain him. When a character speaks in rambling sentences, full of parentheses, as Ivanov, Trigorin, and Lopakhin are prone to do, don't break them up into smaller units. Trust the author's punctuation.
> Where Chekhov places an operative word at the beginning or end of a sentence, don't lose it in the middle of the sentence.
> Where a series of words have the same length and endings, e.g., *-no* in Russian adverbs, try to replicate that effect.
> Where a phrase seems unusual or grotesque, try to ascertain if it is a quotation or a cultural reference.

A translator should bear in mind that his task is to be less a creator than an interpreter, an interpreter keenly conscious of the intrinsic frailty of this singular mode of interpretation. This is why established dramatists are dangerous when they undertake translation, for they are unwilling to subordinate their own instincts. The essence of a dramatic text lies in its language. Each language creates a particular affective relationship with what the sounds evoke. The hope that this peculiar encounter of sound and sense can be reincarnated in another language is always utopian. On the level of sounds, the experiment of translation is an experiment in uprooting, of problematic transubstantiation, the essential energy of translation consisting in detaching the sense from the letter.

Every act of communication is itself a translation. You are translating my words as you read them into something meaningful to you. (And if students are anything to go by, you are misreading and misinterpreting in the process.) Time, distance, variation in viewpoint and reference only increase the difficulty of transmission. In translating from another language and another time, one feels always in transition, off balance. There is, however, a recompense. Rather than seeing a translation as a deficit in the original language, we can take it as a gain in our own language. By submitting the text to so close an inspection and so careful a transplantation, we are enriching our culture. We are bringing the text closer to ourselves.

# Translating Chekhov's Plays: A Collaboration between Translator, Director, and Actors

## Michael Henry Heim, University of California at Los Angeles

I wasn't going to talk about the "t" word—yes, I mean "theory"—but it has come up a few times today, so I've changed my mind. I'm not a theorist by nature and won't go on about it, but I'd like to set forth a few ideas I've developed through the practice of translation to show you why I feel a little theory will not be amiss.

I'm old-fashioned in the sense that I still believe that the central issue a translator must face is to decide how literal or free the translation of each word or phrase or sentence is going to be. The theoretical contribution I'd like to make—and I don't believe I've read or heard anything along these lines before—is that we can look for the solution in the source text; that is, I would suggest that the source text provides hints for how literal or free the translation should be.

Let's start at the macro level and talk about genre. Drama, a genre that by definition is meant to be spoken, cries out for as free a translation as possible. True, there can be mitigating circumstances. One of the plays I've translated, a play by Milan Kundera called *Jacques and His Master* (*Jacques et son maître*), comes with an introduction by the author that contains a rather transparent indication of how he wants the play to be translated. The entire introduction is a caveat against rewriting, and of course the translator is the arch rewriter. Kundera says: "I wish to cry out with Jacques's master: 'Death to all who dare rewrite what has been written!... Castrate them and cut off their ears!'"[1] A clarion call, one no translator will want to ignore.

At the micro level the source text can provide all sorts of hints about how literal or free a translation is wanted. Let me move to another genre to illustrate what I mean. When translating Vassily Aksyonov's *Island of Crimea* (*Ostrov Krym*),[2] I felt that the freewheeling ebullience of the diction, which was meant to show up the wooden quality of Sovietspeak, was as important as the novel's unorthodox, fantastical content. While we have all read many examples of wooden English, it is less prevalent than wooden Russian during

---

[1] Milan Kundera, *Jacques and His Master: An Homage to Diderot in Three Acts*, trans. Michael Henry Heim (New York: Harper and Row, 1985), 9.

[2] Vassily Aksyonov, *The Island of Crimea*, trans. Michael Henry Heim (New York: Random House, 1983).

*Chekhov the Immigrant: Translating a Cultural Icon.* Michael C. Finke and Julie de Sherbinin, eds. Bloomington, IN: Slavica Publishers, 2007, 83–88.

the Soviet period. To give the English-language reader the same feeling of freedom that the Russian-language reader got from the novel, I felt the English diction had to be over the top in terms of, well... *ebullience*. And that meant handling the original with a great deal of freedom.

Another important theoretical issue is function, the function the translation is meant to serve. As obvious as this may seem, I don't think I've ever heard anybody come out and say it. And I believe it's one of the reasons that we have so many translators of Chekhov in this room, and why we *need* so many translators of Chekhov. A translation conceived for one function will differ from a translation conceived for another. That's why it makes perfect sense that Laurence Senelick plans to redo the translations he did for the Norton Critical Edition when he publishes them as translations for the stage. I hope you will pardon the overstatement, but when you're doing a translation for the Norton Critical Edition you have to keep in mind that, in a sense, the text exists for the sake of the notes, the prime audience being college students reading in an academic context. They are not only reading; they are learning. You might even say that the background (the notes) becomes foregrounded, and the text of the plays must be translated in such a way as to "illustrate" the notes.

The function of the Chekhov translations that I've done was clear to me from the start because they originated in requests from directors for a stageworthy text. In 1975, when the Mark Taper Forum in Los Angeles commissioned the first of them, *Three Sisters*, there was a vague awareness in this country that Chekhov the dramatist had not been well served by his translators. Theaters were using two approaches to remedy the situation. The first was for directors and/or dramaturges to place as many translations as they could muster side by side and say, "I'm going to take this line from this one, that line from that one, and another line from the third or fourth"; or, "I don't like any of the possibilities, so I'm going to do what I sense is right"—all this without recourse to the original. The second was for theaters to commission a trot, a pony, a crib—call it what you will—as a basis for "what-I-sense-is-right" emendations.

The Mark Taper commissioned just such a "literal" (that was the jargon word for the trots at the time) from me. But I said to myself, "Ha! They may want a literal, but I'm going to give them a text they can put on the stage as is." It turned out they did just that: they didn't change a word. I got my wish. Don't always get your wishes, though...

When the theater invited me to the dress rehearsal, I was appalled. And I realized that to a large extent I was to blame. The reason was this: I had a mission (which, as we all know, is a dangerous thing). My mission was to create an American version of Chekhov.

At the time the only American translator of Chekhov I knew of was Stark Young. While preparing this talk, I happened to mention him to a colleague at UCLA who turned out to be related to him and told me a few things about him. Young learned Russian for one reason: to translate Chekhov. He had a lot going for him: he was a poet in his own right and a short-story and essay writer. (By the way, he was also a southerner, and southerners have been particularly attracted to Chekhov. You may have heard of *The Wisteria Trees*, written by Joshua Logan in about 1950 as a southerner's post-bellum take on *The Cherry Orchard*. Young had an analogous "twilight Russia" view of Chekhov.) But if you study Russian for one purpose and one purpose only, you're not quite yet at home with the language and mistakes creep in. Then, too, you are likely to lack the cultural context that comes with reading Russian literature from cover to cover, a luxury that only we "professionals" can afford.

Unfortunately, Los Angeles was not the ideal place for my militantly American Chekhov. We have a stable of highly trained actors waiting for the next movie or television role, and they're perfectly willing to do "legitimate theater" while they wait. Still, their training does not necessarily prepare them for the classical stage, and the diction I fed them gave them leave to "American it up," to slouch, if you will; and slouch they did. In other words, the decorum needed for Chekhov went *by* the boards instead of *onto* the boards. Now I was working against the kind of decorum I had seen in previous American Chekhov productions, which was the faux-Shavian decorum foisted on American actors by the language they received from Constance Garnett or other British translators. All the American Chekhov I had seen was very definitely British-accented. But Chekhov's *dvorianstvo* isn't the aristocracy, it's the gentry, a different caste altogether. When I read Chekhov's plays in Russian, I had the feeling the characters weren't speaking a language that had dated much, and when I asked Russians whether they felt the same they would invariably answer, "Yes, yes. There are very few words and constructions Chekhov's characters use that we can't use now"—"we" being intelligent, well-educated people in everyday conversation. That's what I was trying to bring across. But I had gone too far—with disastrous results.

Luckily, I was vouchsafed another chance. A director who had seen the script but not the performance recognized its possibilities, and I wound up doing the other three major plays for his theater. Let me go into the translation methodology we worked out together. It was based on the methodology Simon Karlinsky and I came up with when we collaborated on a translation of Chekhov's letters. It was on the basis of that translation, published as *Anton Chekhov's Life and Thought* (and still in print after thirty years),[3] that the Mark Taper Forum turned to me for the *Three Sisters* crib. The way Simon and

---

[3] *Letters of Anton Chekhov,* trans. Michael Henry Heim in collaboration with Simon Karlinsky, ed. Simon Karlinsky (New York: Harper and Row, 1973); republished under the title *Anton Chekhov's Life and Thought: Selected Letters and Commentary* (Berkeley: University of California Press, 1975; repr., Evanston, IL: Northwestern University Press, 1997).

I worked was as follows. In the morning I would go to the library and translate as much as I could; in the afternoon I would go to his office and read my English out loud while he, a native speaker of Russian, followed the Russian text. The moment he felt the match less than perfect, he would challenge me: "Why this? Why not that?" I had to defend myself. After which he defended himself. We had some knock-down-drag-out arguments, let me tell you, but in the end we would come to an agreement. And at the very end we agreed that I had learned a lot about Russian, he a lot about English. I hope Chekhov profited as well.

I proposed a similar process to the director. Like most Americans he knew no foreign language well enough to work professionally with it, so we had to alter the process somewhat. I read the English text aloud to him, and he was the native speaker of—well, I suppose you could call it "the stage." It was important for me to read the text aloud because I immediately heard things I was amazed I had written. He would stop me if he had any questions about the language, at which point I would become the "Karlinsky" and refer to the Russian text, but he would also stop me if he had any question about the culture, any question about the context, any question about the characters, and so on. It took about three days of intense and intensive work, twelve-to-fifteen hour days. But this time *I* learned something about English, because he would say: "No actor can make that work!"; and I would realize he was right. I also learned what the American audience (or any non-Russian audience) would have trouble conceptualizing—elements of Russian life that I took for granted (because I'd studied the culture for so long), but that would trip up both the actors and the audience.

The second stage of what I have called our methodology was to take the script to the actors. I wanted very much to be present, but after the first time we decided that I should hold off until the rehearsal had been underway for a day or two, because as the author's surrogate I might take over, and no director would be happy about that. What I did basically was to spend two or three days listening to the actors read and answering their questions. And they had many questions: I had the original with me, after all; I had the Bible. Often the questions went beyond linguistic niceties. I remember an actress once asking me what she—that is, her character—read before she went to sleep. But as much as they learned from me, I learned from them. I kept an ear out for their misreadings, not only so I could correct them, but also so I could correct the translation: they often unwittingly put things in their own way—which was *the* way, and I amended my text accordingly.

Sometimes the gift I received from the actors was a *mot juste*, which involved substituting one lexical item for another, but more often than not it had to do with something less concrete, something all but ineffable: rhythm. From hearing lines recited over and over I learned that a phrase of fifteen syllables can move faster than a phrase of ten if it happens to be the natural way of saying what needs to be said. Numbers don't always count. And rhythm is paramount. Flaubert once said that the rhythm of a sentence often came to him before the words (and consequently before meaning itself). When I first read that, I thought Flaubert was proselytizing art for art's sake or merely exaggerating. But the more I translate, the more I see how right he was: I often find myself fitting words to a pre-existing prosodic pattern. One of the most enlightening sessions I've ever had with actors came, oddly enough, with amateur actors. It happened many years ago, at Dartmouth. All of a sudden I heard the text read in a way I only then realized I had missed, and it had everything to do with the rhythm. The kids were supremely conscious of how the words sounded; they were all but parsing them. When I expressed my gratitude to the director, she said, "Oh, yes, we have a man come once a week from New York to teach elocution." Elocution! Now there's a concept that's virtually disappeared, but it made an enormous difference to the actors and helped me no end.

You now have an idea, I hope, of why I find working with actors so productive. I might add that it is important for me to hear the translation early in the rehearsal process, because I want to catch what they say *before* they memorize their parts. As they internalize lines, even lines that are less than speakable, they are obliged to make them work. In my experience even faulty diction can work on the stage provided the actors are talented enough: talented actors can somehow bring it to life. But not all actors are talented enough, and the ones who are may have to spend all their creative energy on getting around awkward lines instead of on acting. The translator needs to provide actors with a text that is as speakable as possible so they can concentrate on the matter at hand—the play as a whole. I'm reminded of what Sharon Carnicke said today about the transgressive text: if you start with a text that's transgressive and don't recognize it as such, you're starting on very much the wrong foot. Working with the actors for a day or two helps me to start them on the right foot. By the time I hand them back to the director, I want the text to be as "transgression-free" as I can make it.

The process works so well that I write it into the contracts I make with theaters: three days preparatory work with the director, three days work with the actors. If you're tempted to follow suit, you should be aware that it can backfire—monetarily at least. I once did a contemporary Czech play for a theater that shall remain nameless, and I flew twice to *gorod N* (the city of N, "a certain city," as Russian nineteenth-century novelists were wont to say), first to work with the director, then to work with the actors. Everything was fine, everything was dandy, until the theater suddenly went under. The play must go on, and go on it did, but not only did I fail to receive the translation fee, I had to pay the airfare and hotels out of pocket.

Let me conclude on a more optimistic note by citing two concrete examples of how collaborating with directors and actors has influenced my work. The first is quite specific. It has to do with the play within the play in *The Seagull*. In the first act Kostya is flying high: he believes his play will catapult him to fame; Nina is in the doldrums: she longs to go on the stage, but is unsure of herself. By the last act it's clear that Kostya hasn't gone anywhere, literally or figuratively; it's not clear that Nina is going to be a great actress—not by any means—but she has at least broken away from her parents. He is on the way down, she on the way up. But let's go back to the first act. The only way we're going to care about them, get involved with them, is if the play within the play has a spark to it: Kostya must show promise as a playwright; Nina must show promise as an actress. Listening to the actress recite my first version of the text, I realized it sounded too much like gibberish, too clumsy. So I went back to the Russian and what did I find but a certain rhythm to the prose. For example, "i éta bédnaia luná naprásno zazhigáet svoi fonár'" is a perfectly regular iambic line. I therefore transferred the meter to the English: "And this poor moon has lit its lamp in vain. No more do cranes wake calling in the meadow." Now Kostya demonstrates he has an ear, and Nina has something to work with.

The second example is more general and goes back to the mistake I made when trying to wave the flag. After the Mark Taper debacle, I decided that that rather than go to the other extreme—I still felt the Shavian tone to be wrong-headed—I would aim for a mid-Atlantic variety of English, an English neither markedly British nor markedly American. I did so not so much because I wanted the translations to be acceptable on both sides of the Atlantic (though they have in fact been performed both here and there), as because I wanted to create the illusion that the audience was listening to Chekhov in Russian. Much as we suspend disbelief when we read a novel or watch a play (we know the action is artificial, yet we accept certain literary conventions and therefore accept the action as "real"), we suspend disbelief when we read or—especially—*hear* a translation. If the diction is obviously American or obviously British to us, we are jerked out of our "disbelief": we think, consciously or unconsciously, "They're American, not Russian," or "They're British, not Russian." If it's as neutral as possible, our disbelief is more likely to remain intact.

Just as in my capacity as teacher I've had the luxury of reading through the Russian canon many times over, so in my capacity as translator I've had the luxury of working with many directors and hearing many sets of actors read through my renderings of the Chekhov plays. In the acknowledgments I published in The Modern Library edition of the translations, which came out nearly thirty years after my first attempt at *Three Sisters*,[4] I could not mention them all by name, but they were all instrumental in shaping the outcome and I am grateful to them all.

---

[4] Anton Chekhov, *Chekhov: The Essential Plays*, trans. Michael Henry Heim (New York: Modern Library, 2003).

# Translating Chekhov's Plays Without Russian, or The Nasty Habit of Adaptation

## Sharon Marie Carnicke, University of Southern California

Rather than shed new light on Chekhov's plays *per se*, this essay shares some observations concerning the currently widespread theatrical practice that encourages well-known English-language playwrights with little or no knowledge of Russian and Russian culture to translate and adapt Chekhov's plays. My topic unfolds like a two-act play. The first act concentrates on the playwrights, whose versions are often hailed publicly as revelations about Chekhov but which, on closer inspection, like Rorschach tests reveal more about the playwrights than their model. The second act takes place at the professional theaters, where directors tend to prefer playwrights' versions to more traditional translations.

A short prologue concerning the history of Chekhov's reception in the United States sets the scene for these two dramatic acts. During 1923 and 1924 the Moscow Art Theatre toured the United States with productions of *Ivanov*, *Uncle Vanya*, *Three Sisters*, and *The Cherry Orchard*, significantly increasing Americans' exposure to Chekhov.[1] Prior to the Russian company's tour, audiences in the United States had seen only three professional productions of Chekhov's plays in English.[2] While U.S. critics applauded the Russian-speaking actors, they were far less enthusiastic about Chekhov, whose artistic and cultural sensibilities seemed more exotic than the sound of his native language. While on the one hand the foreign language was only one of the

---

[1] Over the course of 52 weeks during 1923 and 1924, the Moscow Art Theatre gave 380 performances in the United States, half of which were Chekhov's plays. N. V. Mints, "O vliianii khudozhestvennogo teatra na mirovoe teatral'noe iskusstvo," *Ezhegodnik Moskovskogo Khudozhestvennogo Teatra: 1943* (Moscow: Muzei MKhAT, 1945), 602.

[2] In 1908, Vera Kommissarzhevskaya toured in a Russian-language *Uncle Vanya*. In 1915 and 1916 the Washington Square Players in New York City produced *The Bear* and *The Seagull*. Victor Emeljanow, ed. *Chekhov: The Critical Heritage* (Boston: Routledge & Kegan Paul, 1981), 4–5, 8–10; see also Laurence Senelick, "Russian Drama and Performance in the U.S. Prior to the MAT Tour of 1923," in *Wandering Stars: Russian Émigré Theatre, 1905–1940*, ed. Laurence Senelick (Iowa City: University of Iowa Press), 203–18; and Sharon Marie Carnicke, "Stanislavsky's Production of *The Cherry Orchard* in the US," *Chekhov Then and Now*, ed. J. Douglas Clayton (New York: Peter Lang, 1997), 19–30.

*Chekhov the Immigrant: Translating a Cultural Icon.* Michael C. Finke and Julie de Sherbinin, eds. Bloomington, IN: Slavica Publishers, 2007, 89–100.

many "details of behaviour" that comprised the acting, and hence "an inability to understand it is no particular bar to comprehension," on the other hand "the plays of Chekhov, the very cornerstone upon which this admirable, this exemplary Moscow Art Theatre was built [sic], leave English-speaking peoples cold, and perhaps inclined to resentment."[3] While the actors bridged the cultural gap, the Russian playwright seemed to widen it through his display of "the Slavic temperament [which] feeds upon self-deprecation, upon pessimism."[4] Chekhov struck American critics as "a bastard product of Byronic (or Puskinian) Romantic pessimism, Mallarmé and French Symbolism, and Zolaesque naturalism."[5]

Today, one hundred years after Chekhov's death, it is hard to imagine an English-language theatrical tradition without him. His plays often inspire the same passionate enthusiasm, the same claims of universality, that surround those of Shakespeare. And yet, despite the enthusiasm, an aftertaste of the 1920s opinion of Chekhov as strange, pessimistic, even boring lingers into the present. The late Paul Schmidt complained of a persistent sense of "exoticism" in Chekhov among theater professionals who stage him. Actors and directors, Schmidt noticed, are "willing to dismiss strangeness and incomprehensibility as 'Russian.'" For example, during Broadway rehearsals of Michael Frayn's version of *Platonov* (entitled *Wild Honey*), Schmidt noticed that American actors would react to unfamiliar British terms in Frayn's translation as if they were part of Chekhov's unfamiliar culture. When Schmidt explained to one that "goods train" in Britain is a "freight train" in the U.S., the actor responded with, "Oh, I thought it was just some strange Russian expression." Schmidt comments that "With almost any other playwright, I'm sure the actors would have asked, what does this mean?" Moreover, Schmidt observes, "Too many productions emphasize this strangeness, the remove from our own experience."[6]

While drafting this essay, I visited the drama section of a large bookstore in Los Angeles. As I browsed, I overheard two young people exclaiming happily whenever they found a play that might provide them good material for their acting class. "Here's Chekhov," said one. "Oh no," said the other, "I hate Chekhov!" While putting the book back on the shelf, the first student added,

---

[3] Russell McLauchlan, "*The Cherry Orchard* with Two Bright Stars," no paper, no date. (Clippings, New York: The Performing Arts Research Collections, New York Public Library).

[4] John Corbin, review of *Three Sisters*, *New York Times*, 31 January 1923, quoted in Emeljanow, *The Critical Heritage*, 241.

[5] Burton Roscoe, "Controversy Stirred by *The Cherry Orchard*," no paper, no date. (Clippings, New York: The Performing Arts Research Collections, New York Public Library).

[6] Paul Schmidt, "Translating Chekhov All Over Again," *Dramatists Guild Quarterly* (Winter 1997): 19–20.

"My friend took a class and they spent the whole term just on Chekhov." "What a nightmare!" the other responded. "I would have dropped that class immediately." These two students, I fear, are not unique. Many potential spectators would nod their heads in agreement.

The two acts that comprise my topic mirror the ambivalent context of praise and aversion that greets Chekhov in English-language theaters today. Even as playwrights honor Chekhov, indeed flatter him through imitation, directors and producers anticipate the aversion and guard against empty houses by linking his name to those of hot, new playwrights.

## Act I: The Playwrights

Nowhere does the high opinion of Anton Pavlovich's worth as a dramatic writer register as loudly as it does among English-language playwrights who take him on. A list of those who have "translated" and adapted Chekhov reads like a who's-who of modern and contemporary drama. A few among the American playwrights are Clifford Odetts, who prepared a 1939 version of *The Three Sisters* for the Group Theatre; Tennessee Williams, with his adaptation of *The Seagull* (entitled *The Notebook of Trigorin*); Jean Claude Van Itallie, who has given us versions of all the major plays; Lanford Wilson, whose *Three Sisters* was commissioned in 1984 by director Mark Lamos for the Circle Repertory Company; and David Mamet, who fashioned his version of *The Cherry Orchard* in 1985 for the New Theatre at Chicago's Goodman Theatre. Among those from Great Britain are David Hare, Edward Bond, Pam Gems, and Tom Stoppard, who baldly admits, "I've always felt very envious of Chekhov."[7]

Even playwrights who do not work on Chekhov's texts openly acknowledge their debt. Writers as various as Irwin Shaw, William Inge, Paddy Chayefsky, Lillian Helman, and Arthur Miller cite Chekhov as one of their models. The influence is so extensive that playwright Robert Anderson observed, "American playwrights have gone around, trying to be the American Chekhov."[8]

Do those who translate and adapt Chekhov express their anxiety of influence by becoming his English-language ghost writers? Reviewer Ryan McKittrick suggests as much when he sees them as "channeling Chekhov."[9] Or perhaps playwrights can break free of his influence only by confronting him. Senelick writes that an entire "generation" was "haunted by Chekhov's

---

[7] "Stagewrite Productions Archive," *National Theatre Education*, http://www.nt-online.org (accessed August 2002).

[8] Laurence Senelick, *The Chekhov Theatre: A Century of Plays in Performance* (Cambridge: Cambridge University Press, 1997), 284.

[9] Ryan McKittrick, "Channeling Chekhov," *The American Repertory Theatre Homepage*, http://www.amrep.org (accessed August 2002).

spectre, and needed to exorcise his influence."[10] Three case studies suggest how literally we may take these two eerie metaphors.

When Van Itallie first took the Chekhov challenge in 1972 with *The Seagull*, he worked from a myriad of published English and French translations.[11] As he describes his creative process, he does indeed sound as if he were "channeling" Chekhov.

> [I] read to myself a single phrase in both English and French, let its meaning "flow through" me [...]. Then, as the character I would perform aloud a version of the phrase to my assistant (almost always an actor), who would write it down and then read it back. Listening to the rhythm of the spoken phrase, I would refine it and speak it back again. We repeated the process for each speech, scene, and act. My goal was to deliver Chekhov as fresh and alive as possible, without my own idiomatic imposition. I wanted Chekhov in English to flow from the actors' mouths like clear water.[12]

Despite his lack of Russian and his use of others' work, Van Itallie presents his version as faithful translation, assuring his readers that, "Vitaly Vouluff, the renowned Russian Chekhov scholar and translator of Tennessee Williams into Russian, has kindly scoured each line of these versions for accuracy to the original."[13] Despite Vouluff's warranty, Van Itallie has drifted quite far from the Chekhov I know in Russian. Senelick finds that in *The Seagull* "difficult phrases, obscurities or literary allusions were cut, until the play lost its bearings in the world of art, and every character began to sound like every other."[14]

David Mamet, to his credit, openly calls his Chekhovian versions adaptations and acknowledges their translators by name in his publications.[15] Yet, as he works, he too "channels" Chekhov by projecting himself imaginatively

---

[10] Senelick, *The Chekhov Theatre*, 302.

[11] Van Itallie was asked to translate *The Seagull* by Princeton's McCarter Theatre; his translation was later staged by Joseph Chaikin of The Open Theatre in 1975. Van Itallie also provided the translation for Andrei Serban's much touted production of *The Cherry Orchard* at the Vivian Beaumont Theatre at Lincoln Center (produced by The New York Shakespeare Festival) in 1977. Meryl Streep first came to critical attention in this production as Dunyasha. As reported by Laurence Senelick in "Chekhov's Plays in English," *North American Chekhov Society Newsletter* (Spring 2000), 13, Ann Dunnigan accused Van Itallie of plagiarism from her translation of *The Cherry Orchard* in 1978.

[12] Jean Claude Van Itallie, *The Major Plays* (New York: Applause Books, 1995), ix.

[13] Ibid., xii.

[14] Senelick, *The Chekhov Theatre*, 294. Vouluff must have had a better grasp of English when he translated Williams than when he vetted Van Itallie's Chekhov.

[15] In David Mamet and Anton Chekhov, *The Cherry Orchard* (New York: Grove Press, 1987) the literal translator is given as Peter Nelles.

into the Russian's mind. Mamet assumes that, as fellow playwrights, he and Chekhov share a kindred thought process. Of *The Cherry Orchard*, Mamet writes:

> Chekhov has thirteen people stuck in a summer house. He has a lot of brilliant scenes. [He needs ...] a pretext which keeps them in the same place and "talking" to each other for a while. [... He thinks]: "Gosh, this material is fantastic. What can I do to just keep the people in the house?" [...]
>
> One can have a piece of jewelry stolen, one can have a murder committed, one can have a snowstorm, one can have the car break down, one can have The Olde Estate due to be sold for debts in three weeks unless someone comes up with a good solution.
>
> I picture Chekhov coming up with this pretext and saying, "Naaa, they'll never go for it." I picture him watching rehearsals and "wincing" every time Lopakhin says (as he says frequently), "Just remember, you have only three (two, one) weeks until the cherry orchard is to be sold." [...]
>
> "Oh no," [Anton] must have thought, "I'll never get away with it." But he did, and left us a play we cherish.[16]

It is as if Mamet wants to play the role of Chekhov, "channeling" him much as an actor conjures a character by stepping into the other's shoes.

Lanford Wilson took on *Three Sisters* at the behest of a director who saw Chekhov in Wilson. Like a true exorcism, the process of confronting Chekhov proved painful. "The only thing I knew about the Russian language," Wilson admits, "was that it used a different alphabet." With the help of Berlitz, he continues, "It took me about a year to get through the play. It took Chekhov three months to write *Three Sisters*. He had the benefit of knowing the language."[17] To Wilson's credit he strove for fidelity. "Within that damning limitation," he resolved, "I tried to translate this play as accurately as I could."[18] But is it any wonder that the finished product lacks the depth of nuance that Chekhov's Russian displays? "Imagine," Senelick exclaims, "a Muscovite taking a score of English lessons to turn Tennessee Williams into playable Russian."[19]

Whether "channeling" or "exorcising" Chekhov, whether translating or adapting him, playwrights put their own stamps upon his plays. While one

---

[16] Ibid., xiv–xv.

[17] Anton Chekhov, *Three Sisters*, trans. Lanford Wilson (Lyme, NH: Smith and Kraus, 1984), x.

[18] Ibid., xi.

[19] Senelick, *The Chekhov Theatre*, 302. Senelick's comment strikes me as particularly apt given the choice of Williams's translator (cited above) to vet Van Itallie's translations of Chekhov.

could argue that all translators reflect themselves through the inevitable linguistic and cultural compromises that the very act of translating entails, I would argue that playwrights do so in spades. Unlike professional translators who expect to become the invisible medium of an author, playwrights struggle over the course of their careers to develop recognizable voices of their own. Their reputations depend upon it. Playwrights can ill afford to lose themselves in Chekhov.

In 1997, Paul Schmidt, himself a playwright, meditated on the pitfalls of translation and complained, "I've spend much of the last three years translating Chekhov's plays ... which means I haven't done much work on plays of my own."[20] When Schmidt published his Chekhov translations that year, he displayed through them his mission to banish the distanced exoticism which so irked him. The versions he thus produced, with their easy rhythms and their familiar jargon, made Chekhov seem a contemporary American author. Of Schmidt's translations Senelick writes, "They have been much admired and much produced; personally (and I speak as an old friend) I find them too willing to mow down Chekhov's carefully-planted repetitions and to insert new stage directions and emphatic punctuations which impose interpretations on actors."[21] In such impositions Schmidt reveals the playwright in himself.

Those who openly admit that their work on Chekhov is adaptation (as does Mamet), or imply that it is (as does Stoppard when he calls his *Seagull* a "version"), defend themselves against the scholars among us who seek fidelity to the Russian, even as they deftly secure for themselves creative latitude. Thus, their work best exemplifies the dramatic strategies through which playwrights can retain their own voices as they "channel" or "exorcise" their mentor.

Mamet's idiosyncratic reading of *The Cherry Orchard* as an early prototype of "revue-plays" like Schnitzler's *La Ronde* reflects Mamet's own thematic interests. When he sees in *The Cherry Orchard* a "series of scenes about sexuality, and particularly frustrated sexuality,"[22] I am reminded of *Sexual Perversity in Chicago* (1974), *Speed the Plow* (1988), about the Hollywood casting couch, and *Oleana* (1992), about sexual harassment. To help us see sexuality in *The Cherry Orchard* Mamet uses linguistic innuendo. Varya's lack of appeal as a virginal "convent girl" (Mamet 9) suggests why Lopakhin can not propose, and Charlotta's allure as she offers to turn "tricks" (Mamet 24, 58–59) suggests an explanation of her mysterious and clouded past that might surprise Chekhov.

---

[20] Schmidt, "Translating Chekhov All Over Again," 18. Schmidt's translations were first published in *The Plays of Anton Chekhov* (New York: Harper Collins, 1997).

[21] Senelick, "Chekhov's Plays in Translation," 13.

[22] David Mamet, in Mamet and Chekhov, xiv, x. Page numbers to Mamet's version of *The Cherry Orchard* are noted parenthetically as "Mamet" and page number in the text.

Mamet's adaptation also reveals his dramaturgical interest in controlling his actors through rhythms and graphics. In his own plays phrasings, repetitions, broken sentences, capital letters, italics, and punctuation are meant to insure specific line readings and intonations. He famously asks his actors to trust his texts. He transfers this technique to Chekhov as well, in effect directing the plays that he adapts. For example, using clearly Mametian rhythms and emphasis, Gaev says in Act I, "Because my *sister* married a commoner and then proceeded to *comport* herself—we can't say very virtuously, can we? No. But who is withal ... but whom I love. My glorious sister. Of whom we must say, with all the mercy in the world ... comports herself—*wantonly, viciously* ... in whose every act we must say, we find depravement and..." (Mamet 30). Compare Gaev's speech in any Russian edition of the play and you will find a man who speaks more fluidly, more grammatically, without italics, pausing only once as Anya enters behind him. In short, Mamet's adaptation, as Senelick rightly says, is "thoughtful," and "ingenious," but ultimately "reductive" and "downright inaccurate" because it is after all "personal."[23]

Unlike Mamet, Tom Stoppard has adapted a full volume's worth of plays from various languages that he does not know.[24] Like Mamet, he approaches Chekhov without a Slavic language and with an interpretive sensibility. On the first count, although Stoppard was born in Czechoslovakia, he became a refugee at the age of two and freely admits, "I spoke only toddler's Czech."[25] On the second count, as his recent biographer observes, Stoppard "exhibits the chameleon skill of an adaptor, rather than the slavish role of translator."[26] Stoppard states that for Chekhov he did not seek "a translation as scrupulous as a ledger—that is, where everything on the Russian side of the line is accounted for on the English side."[27] Moreover, Stoppard revises Chekhov in ways that continually recall his own talents and reputation.

Stoppard crafted *The Seagull* for a London production in 1997 directed by Sir Peter Hall and starring Felicity Kendal, at that time Stoppard's wife. He used translations by Joanna Wright and four others, including that of Pam Gems who had herself worked from yet another translation. In it, Stoppard invokes his own reputation as an erudite, witty, and language-loving playwright. Taking his cue from Chekhov's quotation of *Hamlet* in Act I of *The Seagull*, when Treplev and his mother spar using Shakespeare's lines, Stoppard shows his easy familiarity with the bard by adding more references to

---

[23] Senelick, *The Chekhov Theatre*, 303.

[24] Among these is the often produced *On the Razzle*, based on a German play by Johann Nestroy. Stoppard's translations/adaptations including *The Seagull* are published as Tom Stoppard, *Plays*, vol. 4 (London: Faber and Faber, 1999).

[25] Ira Nadel, *Tom Stoppard: A Life* (New York: Palgrave, 2002), 37.

[26] Ibid., 309.

[27] Ibid., 485

the mix. For example, Treplev begins by remembering Hamlet's fear of suicide and thus foreshadowing his own: "Harken, ye ancient and hallowed shades [...] send us a sleep, perchance to dream of what will be in two hundred thousand years from now!"[28] Arkadina exposes her knowledge of *King Lear* and *Macbeth*, when she calls Sorin you "foolish, fond old man" (Stoppard 4: 418) and asks Dorn to "Read on, Macduff" (Stoppard 4: 423). When, disgusted with reading Maupassant, she borrows from yet another of Hamlet's soliloquies: "There is something in my soul o're which my melancholy, etcetera" (Stoppard 4: 424). Since Chekhov and Shakespeare are so often compared and since Stoppard's first major success as a playwright in 1966 was *Rosencrantz and Guildenstern* (in effect a back story from *Hamlet*), Stoppard's inclusion of more Shakespearean lines registers as ironic self-reference.

Stoppard also delights in further expanding Chekhov's frame of reference. Consider Treplev's description of his stage in Act I: "Now there's a theatre for you. Curtain—wings—then nothing but empty space" (Stoppard 4: 403). This apparently inadvertent reminder of the title of a book, *The Empty Space* by the Russian-born British director Peter Brook,[29] places Treplev squarely into the history of successful theatrical reform. Stoppard also exercises his own famous wit when Dorn speaks of his "pick-and-choose sort of life" (Stoppard 4: 420) and Treplev describes Trigorin as "having no backbone, he was able to bend both ways" (Stoppard 4: 458). Critics frequently cited these specific phrases as recognizable signs of Stoppard's personal writing style.

German translator Reinhard Kaiser sees all translation as analogous to theatrical production, with each translation representing a new "staging" of the text. "Even if it were possible," he muses, "we wouldn't be very happy to go to a theater and see there nothing but historical, original, contemporary productions. As interesting as they might be, they certainly would not satisfy us completely."[30] Non-Russian speaking playwrights who "stage" Chekhov by re-translating him produce distinctly Brechtian "performances." They do not lose themselves in the role of Chekhov, but rather stand beside him as fellow playwrights and personally comment on his spirit by embodying his texts.

## Act II: The Theaters

The theatrical milieu provides the motive behind the creation of such Brechtian "performances." Most playwrights who take on Chekhov without Russian

---

[28] Stoppard, *Plays*, 4: 411. Citations to Stoppard's adaptations of Chekhov are noted parenthetically as "Stoppard," followed by volume and page number.

[29] Peter Brook, *The Empty Space* (New York, Avon Books, 1968).

[30] Reinhard Kaiser, "The Dynamics of Re-Translation," *Translation Review* 63 (June 2002): 84–85.

do so at the behest of directors, producers, or high profile actors. Note the argument that occurred between director Mike Nichols and actor Meryl Streep in advance of their much anticipated August 2001 *Seagull* in New York's Central Park. Nichols had commissioned a version from American playwright Richard Nelson, who had proved his mettle with a translation of *The Three Sisters* for the Guthrie Theatre and a dramatization of James Joyce's *The Dead* on Broadway. Streep insisted on Stoppard's version and won the argument. Significantly, neither Nichols nor Streep sought a direct translation by someone who knew Russian.[31]

True, an aesthetic desire often prompts a theater to commission a new translation. For example, Mark Lamos had hoped to emulate the process of active collaboration that can occur during rehearsals for a new play when he asked Lanford Wilson to translate. "I wanted [...] to have a living playwright's involvement," Lamos said, and expected Wilson "to 'find' his translation within the process of production."[32] More often, however, a less idealistic motive is at work. As translator John E. Woods points out, retranslation becomes desirable whenever "there's a buck to be made."[33] On the commercial level, versions of Chekhov by famous names are simply more marketable than those by unknowns.

Moreover, their market value derives, in large part, from their perceived ability to combat the sense that Chekhov on his own spells boredom. Critical reviews, often quoted on the back covers of paperback editions,[34] best reveal this barely hidden assumption. In *The Seagull* Van Itallie produces a "sublimely understood Chekhov, absolutely true to the original" (from the *New York Post*); his *Three Sisters* "captures Chekhov's exuberance, music, and complexity" (from *The Village Voice*); and his *Cherry Orchard* is "a classic restored to the hands, mind and blood of the creator" (from the *New York Times*). "Wilson's translation [of *Three Sisters*] is a revelation. It sings in an actor's mouth. Fluent, funny, sexy, supremely actable [...] a perfect translation—that is, not a translation at all, but seemingly the original" (from playwright Emily Mann). Mamet "will help to undermine our silly critical notions of 'definitive Chekhov'" (*The Three Sisters*, back cover) and "allow us to see [him...] in totally new and surprising ways" (*The Cherry Orchard*, back cover) through "contemporary, highly accessible" language (*The Three Sisters*, back cover). Stoppard's *Seagull* is "brilliant, dazzlingly as clever as you'd like,

---

[31] At the time of the production's premiere, nearly all reviewers related the story of this controversy. See Nadel, *Tom Stoppard*, 485, 530.

[32] Wilson, *Three Sisters*, vii.

[33] John E. Woods, "A Matter of Voice," *Translation Review* 63 (June 2002), 86.

[34] The following quotations are cited from the back covers of the following editions: Van Itallie, *The Major Plays*; Mamet's version of *The Cherry Orchard*; David Mamet and Anton Chekhov, *The Three Sisters* (New York: Grove Press, 1990). In parentheses following each quotation is the source as given on the back covers.

as colloquial as Chekhov's realism demands."[35] Despite Stoppard's lack of Russian, he "remains utterly faithful to the original while giving it the lightest dusting."[36] In short, hot, contemporary playwrights can make Chekhov interesting even for those who, like the two reluctant students mentioned above, hold a 1920s opinion of him.

## By Way of Conclusion

In 2002 *Theatre Journal* graphically, if inadvertently, depicted the heated debate inspired by my topic when the editors placed two performance reviews side by side. The first damned a production of Ibsen's *Hedda Gabbler* for its use of an "unacceptable script," created from a "literal" translation used as "a crib to arrive at a playable acting text." The reviewer notes that the producers were following a theatrical practice that had become common for Chekhov's plays. The second review praised playwright Thomas Kilroy's version of *The Seagull* set in Ireland. When Masha answers the famous first question in the play ("Why do you always wear black?") with "It's because I'm so sad. Black is for sadness," the reviewer observes that Kilroy "signals transgressively right at the outset that authoritative authorship is up for grabs." While the first reviewer mourns the loss of a familiar author's voice, the second enjoys transgression as an effective means to "almost reveal the [Chekhov] play for the first time."[37]

Like *Theatre Journal*, I too can intellectually embrace both opinions. On the one hand, as a Russian scholar who has tried to echo Chekhov's voice through my own translations, I want to criticize theaters for their hubris in commissioning non-Russian speakers. Since all translators, however faithful to the original, must necessarily make linguistic and cultural compromises as they work, playwrights who revise someone else's translation produce texts that seem to me a kind of theatrical hearsay. As words are passed from Chekhov to a first so-called "literal" translator, and then to a playwright, the content, tone, and rhythms of the original are inevitably transformed. Schmidt spoke my mind when he wrote, "I love Chekhov, I always have [...] and I want to make sure he's treated right."[38] I applaud when British playwright and translator Michael Frayn, who learned Russian during his stint in the British National Service, says, "Translating's hard enough if you can

---

[35] Steve Capra, review of *The Seagull*, directed by Peter Hall, August 1997, http//www.xlnt-arts.com (accessed August 2002).

[36] Bill Hagerty, review of *The Seagull*, directed by Peter Hall, *News of the World*, 18 May 1997, http//www.aol.com/actorssite2 (accessed August 2002).

[37] Jon Robin Baitz, review of *Hedda Gabler*, Ambassador Theatre, New York City, October 2001; and Steven Dedalus Burch, review of *The Seagull*, Pittsburgh Irish and Classical Theatre, Pittsburgh, 25 August 2001, *Theatre Journal*, 54: 3 (2002): 486–87 and 487–89 respectively.

[38] Schmidt, "Translating Chekhov All Over Again," 18.

understand the original. Trying to do it from someone else's literal translation would be like performing brain surgery wearing thick gloves."[39]

On the other hand, as a theater practitioner I also champion productions that make Chekhov live anew, that shake up tired interpretations, that startle contemporary audiences with fresh perspectives on the sometimes all too familiar dramas. Since the beginning of the century when directors such as Meyerhold challenged the opinion that a director must serve the play as written, productions that build interpretive concepts from existing texts have become the creative motor in Western theaters. Recent productions of Chekhov in his native land seek transgression as readily as those in the West.[40] Moreover, whether a production is transgressive or not, it succeeds only when it speaks to living spectators. As David Cole eloquently observed nearly thirty years ago, theater "provides an opportunity for experiencing imaginative truth as present truth."[41]

Hanging in the balance between the scholarly and theatrical points of view, however, I ask a slightly different question. Does the desire for transgressive production necessarily entail transgressive translation? While theater revels in the interpretive work that directors and actors do when they stage a familiar play, what does it mean when a company builds its interpretation from a script that is itself a playwright's interpretation of the play? Conceptual productions of Chekhov in Russian, like productions of Shakespeare in English, can create delicious tension between staged interpretations and the audience's *a priori* knowledge of the original texts. As Schmidt explains, if Shakespeare is subject to a directorial concept that "treats him wrong" on stage, "he always bounces back [...] because we can read English, [and] we know what he was up to."[42] I would add, so it is with Chekhov in Russia today; he "bounces back." But on English-speaking stages, Schmidt reminds us, "Most theatre people can't read Russian, so when they're dealing with Chekhov they have to rely on what someone else tells them."[43] Is it any wonder that Chekhov in English may not "bounce back" as readily as he does in Russian? Because translations and adaptations vary so much in their accuracy and stylistic approaches to the original texts, Chekhov can get lost in the interaction between a director's vision and a playwright's remaking of him.

In the final analysis, my divided loyalties lead me to hope that professional theaters will reconsider the current practice of commissioning play-

---

[39] Michael Frayn, interview with *The London Times*, 10 Oct. 2001.

[40] John Freedman, theater reviewer for *The Moscow Times*, regularly examines new productions of Chekhov in Russia. They are too numerous to cite here and so frequent that in his column on 16 July 2004, Freedman called Chekhov "the come-back kid."

[41] David Cole, *The Theatrical Event: A Mythos, A Vocabulary, A Perspective* (Middletown, CT: Wesleyan University Press: 1975), 5.

[42] Schmidt, "Translating Chekhov All Over Again," 18.

[43] Ibid., 18.

wrights without Russian to translate Chekhov and begin to build their productions on more direct reflections of his plays.[44] Perhaps my hope springs from the fact that, emotionally speaking, I always want my Chekhov as direct as I can get him.

---

[44] Perhaps it goes without saying that I prefer my own translations of Chekhov plays, all of which were created for specific productions and polished in rehearsal. (Producers contact me directly for permission to stage them.) Of the many published versions I have used for classes over the years, I find Ann Dunnigan's American and Michael Frayn's British translations to be helpful. I have not yet had the opportunity to review the recently published translations of my colleagues Michael Heim and Laurence Senelick, whose talks on translation appear in this volume and whom I highly respect.

# Chekhov and Anglo-American Letters

# American Iconography of Chekhov*

## Julie de Sherbinin, Colby College

> "Braz continues to paint me. [...] The head is almost done; they say that there's a good resemblance, but the portrait doesn't interest me. There's something in it that's not me, and something of me is lacking [chto-to est' v nem ne moe i net chego-to moego]."
>
> —Letter to M. P. Chekhov, 28 March 1898
> (*PssP* 7: 193)

The well-known 1985 *New Yorker* cartoon titled "Influences" at once satirizes and celebrates the notion of Chekhov's supreme authority as a short-story writer in the world of American letters (Figure 1 on the following page). The cartoon implies, of course, that the epithet "Chekhovian" has become so diffuse in American culture that it signals *worth* independent of any actual relationship to Chekhov—such that a baseball player or garage mechanic becomes consequential by association with the writer. The broad and amorphous net cast by Chekhov's name accounts, too, for the inordinate frequency with which writers are deemed Chekhovian: Eudora Welty is "the Chekhov of the south"[1] and John Cheever is "the Chekhov of the suburbs," while Andre Dubus, Alice Munro, Peter Taylor and scores (perhaps hundreds) more have also been compared to Chekhov. This trend looms so large that a satirist in *The Utne Reader* includes Chekhov in a "ten most overrated" list: "It's time to put him away for a while so American short stories can recover from their Chekhov-induced addiction to little epiphanies of wistful middle-class pain."[2] In a recent iteration David Sedaris earns the Chekhovian acco-

---

* My thanks to the artists whose work is presented here, and to Nikolai Likhodedov and Dalia Bseiso for technical assistance. Permission for reproduction of the graphics has been obtained whenever possible.

[1] The South has boasted, as well, of the "Chekhov of Alabama" (Mary Ward Brown) and the "Chekhov of East Texas" (Horton Foote). See www.wual.ua.edu/phplalbound/ reviews/mary_ward_brown.html; www.bostonphoenix.com/archive/theater/99106/10/The_Death_of _Papa.html (both accessed August 10, 2004).

[2] Jon Spayde, "Don't Bother," *The Utne Reader*, May–June 1998, 55. America has also managed to reduce Chekhov to a paint-by-number writer: "Learn how to paint com-

*Chekhov the Immigrant: Translating a Cultural Icon.* Michael C. Finke and Julie de Sherbinin, eds. Bloomington, IN: Slavica Publishers, 2007, 103–26.

Figure 1. Sidney Harris, artist, *The New Yorker*, April 8, 1985. © *The New Yorker* Collection from cartoonbank.com. All Rights Reserved.

lade in an advertisement for his book, *Dress Your Family in Corduroy and Denim* (Figure 2 opposite). The *New York Times* critic Michiko Kakutani actually wrote in her review of the book that materials in this volume "yield a more Chekhovian brand of comedy"[3] — yet the publisher's astute marketing team grasped the power of the name alone to attract sales. The graphic on Sedaris's book cover unwittingly suggests the dangers of mindless borrowing: it can strip a writer down to nothing.

Chekhov, whose mind was so finely tuned to both the humor and dangers of the hackneyed image and timeworn phrase, himself readily became the victim of cliché. This paper is an attempt to sort through the various paradigms constructed around Chekhov that have defined public American understandings of the writer over the last century. And because it is in my interest — as one familiar with the remarkable discoveries in Chekhov scholar-

---

plex characters through dialogue from the short story master and dramatist Anton Chekhov. Read the passage, follow the prompts, and build a dramatic scene of your own." *Literary Cavalcade*, February 2004, 30.

[3] Michiko Kakutani, review of *Dress Your Family in Corduroy and Denim* by David Sedaris, *New York Times*, June 11, 2004.

**Figure 2.** Advertisement for David Sedaris' book *Dress Your Family in Corduroy and Denim*, Little, Brown and Company, 2004

ship over the last twenty-five years —to promote a vital and multi-layered Chekhov, I will highlight some bright points where public critics have reached toward the underlying layers of thought that are the real stuff of his work. I've chosen to undertake this brief survey with reference to the intersection between printed criticism and graphic representations of the author—or American iconography—both because it offers a circumscribed field of investigation, and because this intersection reveals the core components of popular understandings of Chekhov in American (intellectual) culture. Graphic artists are apt to reveal a fairly unmediated account of how a writer is perceived by a culture; and Chekhov gave us a high standard for assessing the semiotic complexity of the visual image, a standard we can bring to bear on representations of the author himself.

Reference to portraiture appears ubiquitously in Chekhov's prose—in the form of paintings, icons, *lubok* prints, photographs, lockets, magazine clippings, and so forth. Savely Senderovich first uncovered the dense semantic weight of the visual image in Chekhov, acquired through its association with religious iconography (icons, incidentally, served as the major narrative texts for a largely illiterate peasantry in Russia). Senderovich has analyzed the pervasive duality associated with pictorial images in Chekhov—the icon always appears in an environment of contrast between the sacred and the profane, either as "part of a series of images that contain internal contradictions" or affiliated with "a double with an opposite and profane meaning."[4] My work

---

[4] Savely Senderovich, "Chudo Georgiia o zmie: Istoriia oderzhimosti Chekhova odnim obrazom," *Russian Language Journal* 39 (1985): 196–97. Senderovich—a participant in

on inversions and displacements of the Marian image (i.e., the virgin and the harlot) in Chekhov's prose suggests that Chekhov insistently psychologizes the act of viewing: impulses toward veneration go awry time and again as the interpretive equipment of the observer constructs any given visual text according to his or her own experience and needs.[5] A fixed master image, with its claims to an authoritative representation of the subject, fragments into the many personalized private narratives that viewers imagine, narratives deeply shaped, of course, by cultural habit. This question of viewing gets even more interesting if we consider Michael Finke's recent psychobiography of Chekhov as physician and artist, in which he argues that "seeing and being seen, showing and hiding, prove absolutely central to Chekhov's life and works."[6]

The essence of cultural translation, similar to the characters' acts of viewing icons and pictures in Chekhov's prose, involves importing an image and seeing it in terms of one's own orientations, in relationship to what is culturally familiar. Laurence Senelick has given us a brilliant account of how Chekhov's drama was imported into America's theaters, in ways that ranged from naive imitation of Moscow Arts Theatre norms to Chekhov's reflection in various post-war theatrical trends and in the mirrors of the styles of various American directors.[7] My far less comprehensive account of American "iconography" tracks a not dissimilar evolution from broadly accepted national clichés to interpretive slants borne of individual artists and reviewers whose opinions in one way or another engage the reigning paradigm(s). It is no surprise that an American upbringing leaves its stamp on the pictorial images and criticism that purveys Chekhov to the public; in his native land, too, the popularly lauded Chekhov is clearly a product of a specific, culturally relevant set of predispositions, critical prejudices, and publishing conventions. And the immigrant, after all, assimilates.

Portraits and photographs of Chekhov from Russia were not only the first depictions of the author to appear in the American press in the early twen-

---

the 2004 Chekhov Symposium whose presentation, "Two Opposing Approaches to the Problem of Incidental Detail in Chekhov's Poetics," unfortunately could not appear in this volume—is a foremost innovator concerning Chekhov's poetics. For some of his work in English, see "A Fragment of Semiotic Theory of Poetic Prose (The Chekhovian Type)," *Essays in Poetics* 14: 2 (1989): 43–64, and two essays—"Poetics and Meaning in Chekhov's 'On the Road'" and "Anton Chekhov and St. George the Dragon Slayer"— in *Anton Chekhov Rediscovered*, ed. Senderovich and Munir Sendich (East Lansing, MI: Russian Language Journal, 1987), 135–87.

[5] Julie W. de Sherbinin, *Chekhov and Russian Religious Culture: The Poetics of the Marian Paradigm* (Evanston, IL: Northwestern University Press, 1997).

[6] Michael C. Finke, *Seeing Chekhov: Life and Art* (Ithaca, NY: Cornell University Press, 2005), 15. (See Finke essay in this volume.)

[7] Laurence Senelick, *The Chekhov Theatre: A Century of the Plays in Performance* (Cambridge: Cambridge University Press, 1997).

tieth century, but—naturally enough—have served as the foundation for the work of illustrators to this day. The most famous painting of Chekhov is that by Repin's student I. E. Braz that was commissioned by Pavel Tretyakov and has been displayed in the Tretyakov Gallery in Moscow since it was painted in 1898 (Figure 3). I'll come back to this portrait in more detail later. For now, suffice it to register Chekhov's joke about Braz's effort: "If I've become a pessimist and write dark stories, then it's because of my portrait."[8]

**Figure 3.** I. E. Braz, portrait of A.P. Chekhov, 1898

---

[8] Letter to M. A. Chlenov, 13 February 1902 (*PssP* 10: 195).

It is, perhaps, axiomatic that Russian literature was regarded as one big dark and brooding treatise on the unpleasant notion of suffering by American readers during roughly the first half of the twentieth century. Early reception of Chekhov in America corresponds fully, then, to the author's joke about the Braz painting.[9] With surprising consistency the presiding view from his death to mid-twentieth-century had Chekhov pegged as a "recorder of lost illusions" (1912), a "master of the gray short story" (1921), and "a pessimist, a profound pessimist" (1923).[10] A number of early-century American reviews are accompanied by murky gray or black and white head-shots of the author, a reflection of the state of technology, to be sure, but depictions that also seem to confirm these glum evaluations.

This (mis)understanding of Chekhov was in good measure an import from Russia via Prince Mirsky (who called Chekhov's prose "poison"), Princess Vera Toumanova's biography, *Anton Chekhov: The Voice of Twilight Russia* (1937), and even Lev Shestov's tag, "the poet of hopelessness."[11] The familiar epithet that attached itself to Chekhov was "gray." This color association was absolutely persistent. In a 1904 obituary Christian Brinton proclaims: "If his palette was grey, if the monotony of the steppe, the disillusion and disenchantment of the Russian soul colored his canvas, it is because they were factors in contemporary life."[12] Fifty years later, *Time* magazine reports in an anonymous notice entitled "Power of Negative Thinking" that Chekhov "wears his rue with a difference: it's not black, only charcoal grey."[13] This adjective is profoundly ironic given that Chekhov not only explodes the paradigm of black-and-white thinking in many stories;[14] he also locates ultimate value in the color gray. Recall that Anna Sergeevna's eyes and her favorite dress in "Lady with the Little Dog" are gray; it becomes apparent that the color gray denotes a point of perceptive synthesis for Gurov, the collapsing of his dichotomous understandings of a world based on the exalted and the

---

[9] The Braz portrait may well have been known to America; it appears early on in a British journal that circulated in the United States. See *The Outlook* 87 (26 October 1907): 421.

[10] Unsigned, "Chekhov, Recorder of Lost Illusions," *Lippincott's Monthly Magazine*, September 1912, 363–70; N. B. Fagin, "Master of the Gray Short-Story," *Poet Lore* 32 (September 1921): 416–24; Alexander Kaun, "Chekhov's Smile," *Bookman* 57 (March 1923): 95.

[11] See "Is the Art of Chekhov a Distilled Poison?" *Current Opinion* 71: 4 (October 1921): 505; and John Cournos, "Golden Age and Twilight," *The Virginia Quarterly Review* 13: 3 (1937): 440–43.

[12] Christian Brinton, "Anton Chekhov," *The Critic* 45: 4 (October 1904): 319.

[13] "Power of Negative Thinking," *Time*, May 9, 1955, 114.

[14] See, for instance, Marena Senderovich, "The Symbolic Structure of Chekhov's Story 'An Attack of Nerves,'" in *Chekhov's Art of Writing*, ed. Paul Debreczeny (Columbus, OH: Slavica Publishers, 1977), 11–26; and de Sherbinin, "The Nature of Illusion in 'The Teacher of Literature'" in *Chekhov and Russian Religious Culture*, 107–24.

defiled.[15] Gray, for Chekhov, becomes a valuable middle ground between extremes—extremes preached vocally by Russian writers that he eschewed in favor of ambiguities and thoughtfully discovered meanings.

Shades of gray define one of the earliest (if not the earliest) graphic representations of Chekhov in an American publication. The sketch by T. Egri appeared in *Theatre Arts Monthly* under the title, "New York's favorite dramatist of the 1929 season" (Figure 4).

**Figure 4.** T. Egri, artist, *Theatre Arts Monthly*, August 1930

---

[15] Julie de Sherbinin, "The Poetics of Middle Ground: Revisiting Chekhov's 'Lady with a Little Dog,'" in *Anton Chekhov: Poetics, Hermeneutics, Thematics*, ed. J. Douglas Clayton (Ottawa: The Slavic Research Group at the University of Ottawa, 2006), 179–91.

The modernist/constructivist bent of Soviet poster art stamps Egri's version of an 1890 photograph of the thirty-year-old Chekhov. It appears adjacent to a notice announcing "the first Soviet Union Olympiad of the Theatre," suggesting that the left-leaning inclinations of the Western artistic world would willingly import Chekhov with the unnuanced *bogatyr*-like status of the Soviet superhero.[16] (Incidentally, a host of Soviet-era portraits and sculptures of Chekhov create of him a proto-megawriter, erasing any traces of his individuality.[17]) Thus, the first half of the century was characterized either by truisms about Chekhov that represented an amalgam of Russian (and British) predispositions—and an American antipathy for that which was not upbeat—or by a Soviet hero-making impulse. Few readers found their way past this wall.

One who did was Robert Littell who, in *The New Republic* in 1927, bemoans his countrymen's preference for the "red-blooded-national-weekly point of view," calls Chekhov "profoundly un-depressing, un-sordid, un-dreary," and suggests that a fine literary craftsman might take a handful of Chekhov stories, "change the names, Americanize the dialogue (which is strongly English in Mrs. Garnett's translation), lay the scene in Oshkosh, Springfield, Fairview, or Maplehurst, and, leaving all the delicate marrow intact, sail into fame on the pure, if narrow waters of the 'quality' magazines."[18] How interesting that a perceptive critic understood the problem of reception as one of both linguistic *and* cultural translation. Littell predicted that Chekhov would eventually "come into his own" in America; and so he does in the post-war period, but the question remains as to whose "own" he comes into.

It would be a mistake to make too much of periodization; at the same time, American post-war publications do something new with Chekhov. By mid-century photographs had come to dominate U.S. magazines. The author of *Celebrity Caricature in America* writes, "Designers, who had once adapted modern art for covers, features, and advertising, turned increasingly to photography for its innovative look or its perceived sense of realism."[19] Generally speaking, from the 1950s through the 1970s, Chekhov catapults from the category of pessimist to the category of realist (i.e., a "reflector of life as it is lived")—a critical prejudice cemented in by A. P. Chudakov's *Chekhov's Poet-*

---

[16] T. Egri illustration, "Anton Tchekov," *Theatre Arts Monthly* 14: 8 (August 1930): 641, 643.

[17] See *A. P. Chekhov v portretakh, illiustratsiiakh, dokumentakh*, ed. V. A. Maniulov (Leningrad: Gos. uchebno-pedagogicheskoe izd. ministerstva prosveshcheniia RSFSR, 1957).

[18] Robert Littell, "A Chekhov Miscellany," *The New Republic*, June 22, 1927, 124–25.

[19] Wendy Wick Reaves, *Celebrity Caricature in America* (Washington, DC: National Portrait Gallery, Smithsonian Institution; and New Haven: Yale University Press, 1998), 275–76.

*ics* (1971; published in English in 1983). The realist critical orientation of this period is conveyed by photographs used to accompany reviews and commentaries in *Life*, *Newsweek*, *The New York Times Magazine*, *The Saturday Review*, and other magazines. At this point in time, a variety of photographs of Chekhov had become available through the auspices of *Sovfoto*, photos that by now are highly familiar to us through repeated reproduction in books.

Perhaps not surprisingly, in 1952 the more rarified atmosphere of the trade journal *Theatre Arts* produces a fortunate pairing of an essay and graphic both more nuanced than the norm, suggesting that the artist Gardner Leaven coordinated his illustration with the author's ideas (Figure 5). Henry Popkin (then an English professor at Brandeis) writes, "This idea that Chekhov's plays consist mainly of unrelieved gloom is as mistaken as it is widespread," and ascribes to Chekhov the role of "the ironic spectator."[20] Leaven's painting, accordingly, depicts a slightly mischievous Chekhov with

**Figure 5.** G. Leaven, artist, *Theatre Arts*, March 1952

---

[20] Henry Popkin, "The Ironic Spectator," *Theatre Arts* 36 (March 1952): 17.

layered shading—a realistic image with a derivative Norman Rockwell bent, but one with nuance and opinion. While in time Chekhov-as-ironist was to become yet another cliché, in the context of mid-century criticism the joint Popkin-Leaven effort looks to have been refreshing.

For about three decades—through the era of the photograph—we find little by way of sketch or caricature. Artists' renditions of Chekhov reemerge roughly in the last decade of the twentieth century, in accordance with a surge of publications demanding reviews. It is worth noting that Chekhov— who as a young writer collaborated with illustrators and caricaturists to create some very funny vignettes that appeared in the lowbrow press—loved a good parody. In today's busy America, there is little time for collaboration: the exigencies of non-staff writers and graphic artists, deadlines, electronic submissions, etc. do not foster cooperative efforts. As a result, mismatches prevail between illustrators' depictions and the substance of the reviews they illustrate. While these odd pairings themselves have something of Chekhovian humor—and Chekhovian internal contradictions—to recommend them, more to the point here are the ways that they demonstrate, or challenge, various *a priori* constructs of Chekhov known to America.

David Levine, by far the best known of the illustrators who have applied their hand to Chekhov, penned his caricature in 1986 to accompany John Bayley's review of Henri Troyat's Chekhov biography (translated by Michael Henry Heim) for the *New York Review of Books* (this graphic is reproduced on the cover of this book—alternatively as the frontispiece of the hardcover edition). Bayley and Levine seem to be at odds from the outset. The former dubs Chekhov the male equivalent of one of Barbara Pym's "excellent women" (a "subdued heroic figure whose life is usually ignored by and depended on by everybody") and reports, via Troyat, that Chekhov was "possibly sterile through the effects of tuberculosis."[21] This laudable-and-benevolent-self-sacrificing-man version of Chekhov has an enduring appeal to America. Levine, however, enlarging on the Chekhov depicted in one of the 1901 photos with Tolstoy at Gaspra (Figure 7 opposite), dresses Chekhov in garb that distinctly evokes the American icon of virile masculinity, a sheriff or cowboy (the broad-brimmed hat, pointy-toed boots, and the elongated string on the pince-nez that calls to mind a lasso)—America's "excellent man," perhaps? Levine seems to be contesting the review and holding out for a more vigorous Chekhov. Possibly, too, he contests cultural space: the British (Bayley) and French (Troyat) may not see through to the sturdy Chekhov who an American reviewer, some years earlier, had compared to Davy Crockett.[22]

---

[21] John Bayley, "An Excellent Man," review of *Chekhov* by Henri Troyat, trans. Michael Henry Heim, *New York Review of Books* 33: 19 (December 4, 1986): 21.

[22] "Spread before us in these letters is the irreproachable life of Anton Chekhov, whose success story is a model and might even be set to music, to the tune of 'Davy Crockett.'" Henry Popkin, "Self-Portrait," *Commonweal* 62 (June 24, 1955): 310.

**Figure 6.** See the illustration reproduced on the front cover of this book (alternatively, as the frontispiece in the hardcover edition). David Levine, artist, *New York Review of Books*, December 4, 1986. Compare with Figure 7 at the left.

**Figure 7.** Photograph of Chekhov with Tolstoy at Gaspra, 1901

If this is an example of Chekhov being constructed literally in the likeness and image of America, then it is a witty one.

The reverse situation pertains to the Chekhov that graces the cover of the March 15, 1998, *New York Times Book Review* (Figure 8 on the following page), and reappears in a slightly different pose later in the issue (Figure 9 on p. 115). It was created by D. B. Johnson to accompany the Slavist Clare Cavanagh's review of Donald Rayfield's biography. The sketch could draw from at least three different sources: the 1902 head shot of Chekhov photographed in Yalta; a two-thirds body-shot of Chekhov sitting in a claw-armed chair; and the Braz portrait, which decorates the cover of Rayfield's biography, *Anton Chekhov: A Life* (1997).[23] It is worth returning to the Braz painting (Figure 3 on p. 107) for a moment, since it points to issues potentially relevant to an interpretation of these later graphics.

Although Chekhov's ultimate dislike of the Braz is legendary, he seems to have been flattered by the original commission: in spite of Braz's failed first portrait attempted at Melikhovo, the author agreed to sit for a second portrait

---

[23] Donald Rayfield, *Anton Chekhov: A Life* (New York: HarperCollins, 1997).

**Figure 8.** D. B. Johnson, artist, *The New York Times Book Review*. Cover Illustration, March 15, 1998

in Nice (a time-consuming enterprise) and he wrote to friends with a certain tone of pride about the commission and the Tretyakov Gallery.[24] This duality fits well with Michael Finke's analysis of Chekhov's ambivalence about seeing and being seen, for Chekhov's initial impulse toward self-importance gives way to a vehement hatred of the portrait that could well have to do with the painting's exposure of his ailing body.

During the sittings for the portrait, Chekhov wrote to A. A. Khotiaintseva: "Braz is painting me. His studio. I sit in an armchair with a green velvet

---

[24] Letter to A. S. Suvorin, 27 January 1898 (*PssP* 7: 160); letter to V. M. Sobolevsky, 21 October 1898 (*PssP* 7: 304); letter to Liza Mizinova, 24 October 1898 (*PssP* 7: 308); letter to V. F. Komissarzhevskaya, 2 November 1898 (*PssP* 7: 318).

Figure 9. D. B. Johnson, artist, *The New York Times Book Review*, March 15, 1998

back. *En face*. A white tie. They say that the tie and I look much alike, but my expression—just like last time—makes it look as if I've sniffed some horseradish."[25] Unlike the vast majority of photographs, the portrait portrays Chekhov's *body*. His joke about his own resemblance to a white tie suggests possible anxiety about facial pallor exposing his illness; the crack about horseradish draws attention to the inordinately red nose, one that involuntarily evokes the alcoholic red nose on Mussorgsky in Repin's 1881 portrait,

---

[25] Letter to A. A. Khotiaintseva, 23 March 1898 (*PssP* 7: 190–91).

Figure 10. I. E. Repin, portrait of the composer M. P. Mussorgsky, 1881

where the composer is depicted ill and disheveled in the hospital, on the brink of death (Figure 10).

This link would be no more than speculation but for a watercolor by Khotiaintseva herself that depicts Chekhov at the Tretyakov in line to view the Braz portrait of himself—and in the background the only other recognizable portrait seems almost certainly to be that of Mussorgsky (Figure 11 opposite).[26] A veil of illness becomes associated with the Braz portrait, which was painted in Nice, where Chekhov wintered in 1898 because of his fragile health.

The major "incident" in 1902 concerning the portrait is related, if indirectly, to Chekhov's illness. When a congress of doctors presented a large

---

[26] Michael Finke generously shared this painting with me, and made the Mussorgsky identification, prior to the publication of *Seeing Chekhov*—it appears on the cover of his book. See Finke's discussion of the Braz and Khotiaintseva paintings, 198–200.

**Figure 11.** A.A. Khotyaintseva, painting of Chekhov viewing the
I.E. Braz painting at the Tretyakov Gallery, 1898

photographic reproduction of the Braz to the Moscow Art Theatre in thanks for a special performance, Chekhov wrote to the theater instructing them to replace the portrait with a photograph taken at Opitets on Petrovka in Moscow. This was either a head-shot, which did not expose his body, or, more likely, the portrait in the claw-armed chair in which Chekhov's shoulders look broad and solid as they rise above the back of the chair (Figure 12 on the following page). Incidentally, in 1923 Stark Young wrote of "the first picture of himself that he had given Madame Tchehov [Olga Knipper]—a three-quarters likeness" with "an impish consciousness of self, or better perhaps a kind of loose alertness."[27] This would confirm the idea that Chekhov was concerned with conveying images of his most favorable, potent self. In Braz, Chekhov's shoulders appear thin and are dwarfed by the armchair. A congress of doctors may have been particularly unwelcome viewers, for, as Michael Finke suggests, "the self Chekhov aspired to be—in particular his professional identity as a physician—very much hinged on his being the one who sees, rather than the patient of the medical gaze."[28]

---

[27] Stark Young, "Tea with Madame Tchehov," *The New Republic*, May 23, 1923, 343.

[28] Finke, *Seeing Chekhov*, 6.

Figure 12. Photograph of A.P. Chekhov, 1902

If Chekhov's hostility toward the Braz portrait did, indeed, have to do with what it exposed, then the publisher's choice to place the portrait on the cover of Rayfield's biography is doubly ironic: it reveals ill health in a biography touting sexual vitality; and it suggests that Rayfield duplicates Braz's act of exposure by advertising private matters to the inquisitive eye of the public. Here we return to the *New York Times* book review with the nearly sensationalist cover lead-in, "Gentle Chekhov, Meek and Mild. But hot blood runs in his veins"; and the review title, "The Passion of Anton: Believe it or not, Chekhov had a sex life." The cover portrait by D. B. Johnson seems to play on this headline by depicting a "mild" version of the writer, deep in thoughts that do not appear to have to do with women. But given this news, it is discordant that the interior black and white sketch, also by D. B. Johnson, shows Chekhov in what looks like pajamas (a version of his pin-striped suit) and a wheelchair (rounded arms and lines that intimate spokes—from the Opitets claw-armed chair?). Hardly a Don Juan, this wary-faced Chekhov looks as if he is a patient in a convalescent home wheeled out for his daily airing. The church cupolas in the background, shorthand signifier of Russia, speak of a conservative moral grounding rather than the sexual freedom flaunted by the biography and review. D. B. Johnson captures one Chekhov of tradition, an image of the writer as a frail individual armed only with a potent pen. On the other hand, Rayfield's Chekhov is obsessively fixated on sexuality in a highly reductive manner.[29] While his corrective to the legend of Chekhov's celibacy is welcome, Rayfield's book in effect attempts to create a new icon—a hot-blooded, passionate Chekhov—with a lack of the kind of nuance with which Chekhov must necessarily be treated.

Little known to America is Antosha Chekhonté, the pseudonym under which Chekhov penned hundreds of slapstick anecdotes and hilarious stories in his twenties as a means to support himself and his family. Donald Fanger's review of Peter Constantine's *The Undiscovered Chekhov* (1998) celebrates Chekhov's early humorous bits and pieces. Incongruently, then, Thomas Libeti's sketch of Chekhov (Figure 13 on the following page) accompanying the review—which in another context would have done good justice to Chekhov's layeredness (note the repeated but varied cheek and jowl lines)—portrays a haggard face. Fanger actually comments on Constantine's book cover itself (Figure 14 on p. 121):

> All [these stories] were dashed off by the man whose photograph appears on the dust jacket of this collection—clean shaven, young, fleshy, thick-haired, thoughtful-eyed, a far cry from the familiar photos of a decade later, which show the bearded, rather prim-looking (is it the pince-nez?) and masklike face of the writer who for too long was stereotypically hailed as the melancholy bard of autumnal, futile, unmoving Russia.[30]

---

[29] It should be noted that Rayfield's biography (with the help of A. P. Kuzicheva's rich archival findings) does deliver new and more complicated information about the author's life; he simply drives the idea about Chekhov as a Don Juan far too hard. Robert Brustein critiques Rayfield's biography for "expos[ing] the huge chasm that lies between diligent scholarship and imaginative criticism." "The Sex Life of Anton Chekhov," review of *Anton Chekhov: A Life* by Donald Rayfield, *The New Republic*, March 2, 1998, 27.

[30] Donald Fanger, "Back by Popular Demand," review of *The Undiscovered Chekhov* by Anton Chekhov, trans. Peter Constantine, *The New York Times Book Review*, March 14, 1999, 12.

Figure 13. Thomas Libeti, artist, *The New York Times Book Review*, March 14, 1999

Indeed, recent scholarship has increasingly engaged the work of the young Chekhov. Yet the received image, which the illustrator passes on, is a somber likeness at utter odds with the spirit of the translation and review, encouraging the transient reader to latch onto the recognizable rather than to embrace a less familiar sense of the author.

We encounter another conundrum in Elizabeth Hardwick's review in *The New Republic* of Pevear and Volokhonsky's first volume of Chekhov translations.[31] The review offers fairly quotidian coverage of Chekhov—mostly paraphrase of his stories, the cliché of Chekhov's "evanescence," and a clear preference for the familiar and yet imprecise translations of Constance Garnett—

---

[31] Elizabeth Harwick, "The Disabused," review of *Stories* by Anton Chekhov, trans. Richard Pevear and Larissa Volokhonsky, *The New Republic*, November 27, 2000, 24–27.

**Figure 14.** Cover of Peter Constantine's translations,
*The Undiscovered Chekhov*, Seven Stories Press, 1998

yet Vint Lawrence's graphic depicts Chekhov as a sort of proto- intellectual intellectual in a pose of concentrated and profound thinking (Figure 15 on the following page). The illustration has far more evocative potential than does the review, but the pairing deflates it. Moreover, the essay itself raises a question that may contribute to the divide between public criticism and scholarly norms: What are the limitations of reviewers assessing a translation when they have no access to the language of the author?

An interestingly apt match appears in Henrik Drescher's illustration to A. O. Scott's review of Janet Malcolm's *Reading Chekhov* (2001) (Figure 16 on p. 123). Drescher depicts a quasi-Freud look-alike (penning Chekhov's name

**Figure 15.** J. Vinton Lawrence, artist, *The New Republic*, November 27, 2000

next to the illustration lest there be any mistake?), as if the fame Malcolm gained for writing on psychoanalysis had a primary bearing on her understanding of Chekhov. The title of Scott's review—"The Good Doctor Decoded"—repeats the illustrator's gesture, as seemingly does, too, his analysis of Malcolm's book: "The hidden meaning of his stories is that he is hidden so well within them as to escape detection altogether, which is how you know he's there"; "Though she is suspicious of the pushiness of biographers, she does discreetly pry into the writer's own character, which begins to seem in its combination of forthrightness and reticence, like an uncanny mirror of her own."[32] Chekhov is constructed to resemble the reputation of the book's

---

[32] A. O. Scott, "The Good Doctor Decoded," review of *Reading Chekhov: A Critical Journey* by Janet Malcolm, *The New York Times Book Review*, December 9, 2001, 12.

**Figure 16.** Henrik Drescher, artist, *The New York Times Book Review*, December 9, 2001

author! Malcolm herself, one of the few public critics to write on Chekhov after extensive reading of scholarship, actually abstains from psychoanalysis in her wide-ranging engagement with Chekhov.[33]

---

[33] In an apt reflection of the current scholarly trends, Malcolm ends her book with the observation: "We do not ask such questions of the other realists, but Chekhov's strange, coded works almost force us to sound them for hidden meanings [...] We don't want to get too fancy. But we don't want to miss the clues that Chekhov has scattered about his garden and covered with last year's leaves. These leaves are fixtures of Chekhov's world (I have encountered them in the gardens of no other writer), and exemplify Chekhov's way of endowing some small quiet natural phenomenon with metaphorical meaning." Janet Malcolm, *Reading Chekhov: A Critical Journey* (New York: Random House, 2001), 205.

Philip Hensher, in *The Atlantic Monthly* (January 2002), disputes the worth of Malcolm's book. Oddly enough, Hensher's review ("Incomparable Naturalism") is illustrated with Mark Summers's view of Chekhov, a figure stylized in ornate baroque purple curly-cues, most studiedly fashioned and not at all naturalistic (Figure 17). Summers' illustration captures Chekhov's mythological dapperness; and, while he gratuitously elongates his subject's face into a contemporary version of the strikingly handsome middle-aged male, his representation of Chekhov's glasses—one seeing eye, one blotted out lens—points to the author's complex vision and reflects a critical discussion about Chekhov's literal and figurative eyesight.[34] Hensher, on the other hand, holds on to the Chekhov of A. P. Chudakov in *Chekhov's Poetics* when he writes that Chekhov's lavish details are "simply lists of objects": "Each object appears unnecessary and even surprising in so frugal a writer; cumulatively, though, they create not just a world of unprecedented solidity but the sensation of human lives lived in that world."[35] Scholarship that engages the "deeper reaches" of Chekhov finds that there is no place for the notion that words in Chekhov could be "simply lists of objects";

**Figure 17.** Mark Summers, artist, *The Atlantic Monthly*, January 2002

---

[34] Savelii Senderovich, *Chekhov—s glazu na glaz: Istoriia odnoi oderzhimosti A. P. Chekhov. Opyt fenomenologii tvorchestva* (St. Petersburg: Dmitrii Bulanin, 1994); Michael Finke, *Seeing Chekhov*, esp. 4, 178, 202.

[35] Philip Hensher, "Incomparable Naturalism," review of *Translations of Anton Chekhov* by Ronald Hingley, and *Reading Chekhov* by Janet Malcolm, *The Atlantic Monthly*, January 2002, 128.

the realization that there is no such thing as incidental detail in his texts informs much of the best recent criticism.[36]

Just as in Chekhov there is nothing random about detail, nothing random about supposed "mismatches," so here, too, a cultural context is at work that has constructed Chekhov in specific ways and operates off of those constructs. America has stocked its larder with a few set images of Chekhov. With few exceptions, artists and reviewers each take what they have—a set of received preconceptions that see Chekhov variously as pessimistic and gray, or an ironic wit, or the ideal of a compassionate human being, a sickly and sober individual of genius—and expand the myth of the writer's somber-faced identity on that foundation. Many of these assessments, all penned by an extraordinary array of talented artists,none the less exhibit an element of built-in conservatism: the Chekhov (or whoever) of our university training is usually the author who stays with us for the long haul. All of these images feed into the naturalistic fallacy that has haunted Chekhov—by which I mean the tendency to read him as a realist who feeds us back "life as it is," and a dour life at that, in his prose.

The "delicate marrow" of Chekhov's stories, on the other hand, is what attracts the Chekhov epicure, be s/he translator, writer, or scholar. Marrow is a life-giving substance and it is hard to get at. Chekhov commentary over the last few decades—written by participants in this Symposium and others, and available in English—has opened up terrain inhabited by an unexpected and utterly vital Chekhov, a Chekhov who plumbs the depth of human phenomena, whose writing is saturated with highly charged (yet utterly iconoclastic) symbolic images and, just as importantly, a Chekhov who engages in a sustained meditation on the psychology behind the ways that human beings read received symbols and construct meaning for themselves. This scholarship has little impact on public perceptions for one obvious reason: scholarly work can look turgid, inaccessible, and downright uninteresting from the outside, and it takes time to master. But in its best iteration, new thinking crosses frontiers and moves into new realms. What might a public criticism informed by the cutting-edge ideas of the scholarly world look like?

A higher degree of integration would require that more Slavists find ways to bring their wares to the marketplace. In so doing, scholars would need to learn a more inclusive idiom: the trade-off for decreased detail of analysis would be wider exposure for their ideas. And who better to write reviews of translations than those who know both languages? Meanwhile, public critics might pay heed at least to the trends in scholarship. And a tip-off to illustrators concerning the ideas put forth in reviews of new work could

---

[36] The term "deeper reaches" references the first volume of scholarship that generated much new thinking on Chekhov. See Savely Senderovich, "Toward Chekhov's Deeper Reaches," in *Anton Chekhov Rediscovered*, 1–8. Senderovich is the foremost pioneer of the symbolic function of so-called "incidental detail" in Chekhov. See n. 4.

clue them into the changing faces of the author. Finally, scholars, most of us teachers, might bring the perceptions of public critics into our classrooms and thinking in order to excite students about the relevance of Chekhov outside a narrowly academic realm. It captures their interest to know that Cornel West has a Chekhov obsession ("If I have to choose between Chekhov and most hip-hop, I'll go with Chekhov"[37]).

Ultimately, we need to recognize that in most depictions of the immigrant Chekhov—through the exigencies of many forms of translation—there's something that's not Chekhov, and something of Chekhov that is lacking. As he himself astutely knew, on so many levels we fill in ourselves—our preoccupations, prejudices, perceptions, and language—to frame that which is not us. To the extent that critics of any ilk succumb to clichés and replicate American iconographic ideas about Chekhov, it is because they are part of our cultural penchants and ways. But, when we're lucky, something that *is* Chekhov is also there. Seeing beyond—to the phenomenological view of the world that Chekhov proffers—is a matter of effort and awareness.

---

[37] Quote from Cornel West under "Chekhov's Legacy," *Nebraska Center for Writers*, http://mockingbird.creighton.edu/NCW/chekleg.htm; hear West's radio commentary, "Chekhov's Legacy," from *The Tavis Smiley Show*, August 11, 2004, at the National Public Radio website, www.npr.org.

# Writing in English with a Chekhov Muse

## Katherine Tiernan O'Connor, Boston University

Around the time when I first became attentive to how frequently and consistently Chekhov's name showed up in the *New York Times Book Review* and the *New Yorker*, I read the following reference to him in a review (by Will Blythe) of Tom Perrotta's novel *Little Children*:

> Sometimes it seems a little antiquated to praise an author for sympathizing with his characters, for treating them in their difficulties with a tenderness that few gods have shown their humans. The author as executioner feels more realistic, more modern. And it is standard to compare to Chekhov writers who do show such kindness. And yet with *Little Children*, what is Tom Perrotta but an American Chekhov whose characters even at their most ridiculous seem blessed and ennobled by a luminous human aura? They're all chumps, it is true. But we wish them well.[1]

This description makes Chekhov seem, at least to me, too familiar and friendly: that is, avuncular and toothless, and thus his alleged "distinguishing characteristic," namely, *kindness,* starts sounding like a virtue one wants to disavow. Moreover, how does one defend Chekhov against such a charge? By insisting that he is not nice to his characters and does not lend them "a luminous human aura"? What is disquieting about such comments is that they make Chekhov seem too accessible, too open to false identification, too ready an analogue.[2] It is ironic that a Russian author who was so reticent about disclosing information about himself and whose work was often criticized by his Russian readers for not having a clear point of view is perceived as being so familiar and *kindly* a presence by his English-speaking readers. However, given that reticence or elusiveness in anyone can also be read as an invitation to privileged access, this may not be so ironic after all. Although the type of *kindness* ascribed to Chekhov in the above-cited review may make one

---

[1] Will Blythe, "All the Children Are Above Average," *The New York Times Book Review* (5 September 2004), 6.

[2] One is reminded of the *New Yorker* cartoon that shows stars from various professions naming those who have had the greatest influence on them, and every one of them, even a baseball player, includes Chekhov in his list! (See de Sherbinin essay and figure 1).

*Chekhov the Immigrant: Translating a Cultural Icon.* Michael C. Finke and Julie de Sherbinin, eds. Bloomington, IN: Slavica Publishers, 2007, 127–39.

cringe, one could argue that a number of English-speaking authors who have written works inscribed with a Chekhov watermark are, in fact, expressing their gratitude to Chekhov for the *kindness* he has shown them simply by being who they perceive him to be.[3] How it is that such texts reflect their obvious indebtedness to Chekhov is what I should now like to examine. The texts I have chosen bear no surface resemblance to each other, but they all, each in their own way, celebrate the affinities their authors have felt with their respective muses, each of whom goes by the name of Chekhov.

Our discussion of the relationship between some English-speaking authors and Chekhov begins with a revisiting of the interesting and some would say infamous example of Katherine Mansfield and her story "The-Child-Who-Was-Tired." Although it is true that there has been much debate over the years about the nature of her indebtedness to Chekhov, even to the point of accusations of plagiarism on her part (particularly in regard to the above-mentioned story), I am ultimately most interested in her own self-perceived sense of connectedness to Chekhov and what that reveals about her and about the Chekhov seen through her eyes.[4] To restate the obvious: the question of literary influence—however one defines what constitutes influence—is a vexed one indeed. However, it may also on occasion engender as much if not more anxiety in the critics who debate it than in the authors said to reflect it. That seems to me to be the case with Katherine Mansfield and her life-long reading of and frequently acknowledged love of Chekhov, as a human being and as a writer.[5] In short, Chekhov's works (his letters and his stories) seem to have been part of her reading life throughout her writing life.

"The Child-Who-Was-Tired" was the first story that Mansfield published in England (in 1910). Although Chekhov would soon come into vogue in England, starting with the production of his plays, Mansfield was clearly exposed to him and to "Tired" (my translation of "Spat' khochetsia"),[6] in particular, before his stories began to be translated regularly into English. That her first exposure to Chekhov seems to have come from a German translation that she read while in Germany is echoed in the fact that her variation on the

---

[3] In other words, the kind of literary influence I'm referring to here is markedly different, I would contend, from the "anxiety-producing" kind celebrated by Harold Bloom in *The Anxiety of Influence* (New York: Oxford University Press, 1973).

[4] Katherine Mansfield's connection to Chekhov, along with the various opinions regarding it held by different scholars and critics, has been explored in detail in an unpublished dissertation by Charanne Carroll Kurylo, "Chekhov and Katherine Mansfield: A Study in Literary Influence" (University of North Carolina, 1973). As my notes will show, my discussion of Mansfield and Chekhov is indebted to the information and commentary found in that study.

[5] For her proprietary response to Chekhov and her sense that she is the English Chekhov, see Kurylo, "Chekhov and Katherine Mansfield," 150.

[6] "Spat' khochetsia" has also been translated as "Sleepy" and "Let Me Sleep."

story is given an imprecise but definitely German setting.⁷ (In Chekhov's story, the 13-year-old servant girl Varka, deprived of sleep by the constant demands of her masters, ends by strangling the crying baby in order to get some sleep; in Mansfield's variation, the nameless Child tends the household of Frau and the Man day and night, until she, too, takes the life of their baby boy in order to rest.) Thus, although there can be no question that Mansfield's story is a variation in her own idiom on the Chekhov original or, rather, on a German translation of the Chekhov original, it is, I think, pointlessly labeled a plagiarism since it marks the beginning of a literary intimacy that is soon openly and proudly acknowledged. Moreover, given the fact that the phrase "the child who was tired" is not embedded in the text of Mansfield's story, I would argue that her hyphenated rendering of this phrase in her title constitutes an implied acknowledgement of the story's prior existence in someone else's text. Furthermore, Katherine Mansfield, who was from New Zealand, chose to launch her own professional writing career in England with a story that speaks to the very issue of "foreign origins." One wonders, of course, what it was about this particular Chekhov text that inspired Mansfield to want to write it in her own idiom without any trace of parody.⁸ There are many passages in her letters in which she elaborates on why she finds Chekhov so appealing, and many of them could be said to be exemplified by his "Tired." The problem—if it is a problem—is that these passages were written *after* the publication of "The Child-Who-Was-Tired," and after she had immersed herself more thoroughly in Chekhov's stories and knew more about his life and about the affinities she perceived them as sharing by virtue of his having had, as did she, tuberculosis:

> I really have suffered such AGONIES from loneliness and illness combined that I'll never be quite whole again. I don't think I'll ever believe they won't recur—that some grinning Fate won't suggest that I go away by myself to get well of something!! Of course externally and during the day one smiles and chats & says one has had a pretty rotten time, perhaps but God! God! Tchekhov would understand: Dostoevsky wouldn't. Because he's never been in the same situation. He's been poor and ill & worried but enfin—the wife *has* been there to sell her petticoat—or there has been a neighbor. He wouldn't be alone. But Tchekhov has known just EXACTLY this that I know. I discover it in his work—often.⁹

---

⁷ Kurylo, "Chekhov and Katherine Mansfield," 71–73.

⁸ The theme of human isolation combined with that of a suffering and exploited child would certainly appear to account for Mansfield's attraction to the Chekhov text. Moreover, the changes and additions that she made to the story make it appear more obviously socially conscious than the Russian original. See ibid., 76–78.

⁹ Quoted in ibid., 164.

And later to her friend Samuel Solomonovich Koteliansky, who had further acquainted her with Chekhov: "I shall try and get well here. If I do die perhaps there will be a small private heaven for consumptives only. In that case I shall see Tchekhov."[10] Mansfield's initial attraction to "Tired" foreshadows what will be her life-long sense of shared affinities with Chekhov. It is, after all, a story about being alone and being "tired unto death," and about striking out against that which is perceived to be responsible for one's suffering. Moreover, Mansfield's letters, especially those written "in exile" while she was trying to find a cure, often convey the kind of desperation and aloneness that she might have initially attributed to the young heroine of "Tired."[11] Chekhov, on the other hand, as both the author of the story and as a letter-writer, especially in his letters "in exile" when he too was seeking a cure, seems, at least on the surface, more detached from his suffering than either Mansfield or the young girl in the story.[12] It is also true, however, that Chekhov seems to have provided Mansfield with the kind of relief and comfort that both his young heroine and hers had been denied: "Oh, darling Tchekhov! I was in misery to-night—ill, unhappy, despondent, and you made me laugh... and forget, my precious friend!"[13]

That Katherine Mansfield felt drawn to Chekhov both as an artist and as a human being with whom she felt she could identify on many levels is beyond question. Moreover, it seems pointless in this case to try and draw too sharp a distinction between the artistic and the personal, even though it is clear that in her opinions about other writers she did indeed often draw such a distinction. Consider, for example, this comment on Turgenev: "I simply cannot believe that there was a time when I cared about Turgenev. Such a poseur! Such a hypocrite! It's true he was wonderfully talented, but I keep thinking what a good cinema play *On the Eve* would make."[14] The syntactic logic of her *but* is not immediately apparent unless what she means is that *On the Eve*

---

[10] Quoted in ibid., 168.

[11] Many of Mansfield's letters are poignant in this regard. For specific examples, see letters written to J. M. Murry (30 and 31 January 1918, and 3 and 4 February 1918) and to Ottoline Morrell (24 May 1918) in *Katherine Mansfield: Selected Letters*, ed. Vincent O'Sullivan (New York: Oxford University Press, 1989), 67–68; 71; 93–94.

[12] I explore the persona that Chekhov conveyed in the letters he wrote in the months and days preceding his death in "Chekhov's Death: His Textual Past Recaptured," *Studies in Poetics*, ed. Elena Semeka-Pankratov (Columbus, OH: Slavica Publishers, 1995), 39–50. Mansfield herself argued that "if one reads 'intuitively'[Chekhov's] last letters they are terrible." Quoted in Kurylo, "Chekhov and Katherine Mansfield," 176. For the entire text of this letter see *Katherine Mansfield: Selected Letters*, 270–72. Mansfield, in other words, chose to read Chekhov's last letters in a spirit that conformed to her own more openly expressed horror at the thought of approaching death.

[13] Quoted in Kurylo, "Chekhov and Katherine Mansfield," 170.

[14] Quoted in ibid., 105.

would be better as a "cinema play" than as a novel. The mystery of syntax aside, however, it is clear that Mansfield's antipathy to Turgenev's persona as she discerned it coexisted with and was distinct from her recognition of his talent. In the case of Chekhov, however, that distinction never had to be made.

If "The Child-Who-Was-Tired" marks the beginning of Mansfield's lifelong engagement with Chekhov and his work, then "The Garden-Party," one of her late and great stories (1922), might be said to reflect that engagement in its culminating stage.[15] Not surprisingly, the connections between this text and its Chekhov antecedent "The Name-Day Party" ("Imeniny") are much less apparent. In fact, Mansfield's story is dramatically unlike Chekhov's in virtually all respects. It describes, as does Chekhov's story, a party given on a summer day by an upper-class family, but on the surface that's about the extent of the connection between the two stories. The reverse is obviously the case with "The Child-Who-Was-Tired" and "Tired." One would, in fact, have to be alerted to a Mansfield-Chekhov connection and to be on the lookout for traces of it in order to recognize the fascinating—precisely because it is so subtle and inverted—connection between Mansfield's "Garden-Party" and Chekhov's "The Name-Day Party." Moreover, the death that occurs in each story only further serves to dramatize how different they are. In "The Name-Day Party" Olga, the hostess, goes into premature labor after the tension and stress brought on by the party, and she and her husband Pyotr lose their baby. The story ends with them both overcome by the depression and guilt that ensues. In "The Garden-Party," on the other hand, the accidental death that occurs—that of a young laborer who has no personal connection to the Sheridan family hosting the party but who lives with his family in a cluster of "mean, little cottages" at the bottom of the hill—only serves to highlight the vast chasm that separates the world of the Sheridans from that of the cottage-dwellers.[16] Laura, the artistic daughter of the family, is touched by the news of the death and feels guilty (unlike the rest of her family) about proceeding with such a happy and festive event under the circumstances. However, the party does take place as planned and is a great success. Furthermore, when Laura is later called upon to deliver leftover goodies from the party to the bereaved family and sees the body of the deceased laid out on a bed, she is both moved and exhilarated by how peaceful, remote, and beautiful he looks. His death, in other words, and the deliverance from earthly realities (his poverty

---

[15] Mansfield died a year later in 1923. The fact that "this last period [of Mansfield's life] was also the period of her heaviest borrowing from Chekhov is difficult to understand or to justify," says Kurylo (ibid., 176). I would argue, however, that no justification is needed, given that this is also the period in which Mansfield wrote some of her greatest stories—"The Garden-Party" among them.

[16] Katherine Mansfield, "The Garden-Party," *Stories*, intro. Jeffrey Meyers (New York: Vintage Books, 1991), 294.

and her privilege and guilt) which it seems to signify frees Laura to exult in the joy of life: "'Isn't life,' she stammered, 'isn't life—' But what life was she couldn't explain. No matter. He [her brother Laurie] quite understood. *'Isn't it, darling?'* said Laurie."[17] Thus, in Mansfield's story the death of a stranger brings on a feeling of release from guilt and exhilaration with life, whereas in Chekhov's story the death of the baby brings on both guilt and depression. However, both the hyphenated "Child-Who-Was-Tired" and the hyphenated "Garden-Party" reflect that they are borrowed Chekhov titles. True, "garden-party" is not an exact translation of "imeniny" ("name-day party" would be a more literal translation), and "garden-party" as a noun conjures up an English rather than a Russian (or a foreign) occasion. That is as it should be, however, given that Mansfield's story is very much an English story. Furthermore, from a certain point of view "garden-party" is a fitting translation of the Chekhov title given that Chekhov's "name-day party" is an all-day affair that takes place on a country estate. To my knowledge, "garden party" is not customarily a hyphenated noun in English, but it is made so in Mansfield's title because, I suggest, she is again highlighting her gratitude to Chekhov even when, or perhaps *because* the story she has now written is so completely her own.

Joyce Carol Oates's story "The Lady with the Pet Dog," included in a collection entitled *Marriages and Infidelities* (1973), which won the National Book Award, is an obvious reworking of the famous Chekhov story of the same name ("Dama s sobachkoi").[18] Moreover, since Chekhov is now a writer long familiar to educated English-speaking readers, and since this particular story is one of his most famous, we presume that a number of Oates's readers are aware that this story shares a title with a prior Chekhov text. Furthermore, when we read Oates's story alongside Chekhov's, we see how obviously intentional and elaborate her refashioning of the Chekhov text is. One could argue, in fact, that her story is more interesting as creative revisionist criticism of a particular Chekhov text than as self-standing fiction.

To begin with, she Americanizes Chekhov's locales (turning Yalta into Nantucket) and adopts the viewpoint of the woman rather than the man. Rather than being the pale figure of Chekhov's story who is seen only through Gurov's eyes (or gaze), Anna is now at the center of the story, and it is through her gaze that we see her lover, who is never even named. However, by reversing the story's perspective and making Anna its dominant presence, it is clear that Oates is not making any kind of feminist statement— on the contrary. What her story does demonstrate, however, is how totally unlike Chekhov she is as a writer. She writes with a kind of breathless, melodramatic, often sexually charged intensity that could hardly be described as

---

[17] Ibid., 297.

[18] Joyce Carol Oates, "The Lady with the Pet Dog," *Marriages and Infidelities* (Greenwich, CT: Vanguard Press, 1972), 327–44.

Chekhovian. That may be the point, however, for it is obvious that Oates is an astute reader of Chekhov who is attuned to what it is about Chekhov that makes him Chekhov, and, complementarily, what it is about him that makes her want to want to flaunt her difference. For example, Anna's boredom with her husband and her desire to live life in a different way translates in Oates into a woman who is what we might call clinically depressed and who is even tempted on one occasion to "[draw] a razor blade lightly across the inside of her arm, to see what would happen."[19] I stress, however, that there is nothing parodic about Oates's ratcheting up of the emotional intensity level of the Chekhov story, for her transformed characterizations sound like vintage Oates and yet also seem to harmonize in general terms with Chekhov's characterizations. For example, it is not hard to imagine that Chekhov's Anna might be more depressed than he chooses to spell out in the story, even though it is indeed impossible to imagine his Anna doing practice runs with a razor blade.

Oates's manipulation of narrative time in her story is much more elaborate than Chekhov's is in his. Chekhov employs a linear chronology and events occur in his narrative in the same order in which they occur in his characters' (Gurov's in particular) lives. The conscious degree to which Oates manipulates time in her narrative becomes more obvious, in fact, when one compares her text to Chekhov's. The romantic and emotional highpoints of Chekhov's story occur after a long lead-in, and they stand out by virtue of the fact that they seem to come as a surprise to the characters themselves. Oates's story, on the other hand, begins with one of these romantic highpoints, namely, the moment when Gurov goes to the provincial town where Anna lives and surprises her in the theater. Moreover, since Oates's narrative is circular and has multiple frames, this is only the first of many dramatic and intense moments in a story which runs along at fever pitch, at least when compared with Chekhov's. What is also striking, however, despite the glaring contrasts between the two texts, is how obviously and cleverly Oates makes her text conform to Chekhov's. In both her story and Chekhov's, two married people meet, start an affair that does not end when they expect it to, resume the affair in a more serious way in a different locale (where Anna lives), and face an uncertain future despite the strength of their love and their mutual awareness of how much they mean to each other. Oates's Anna has gone to her family's beach house in Nantucket to escape temporarily from her husband and her marriage. She, like Chekhov's Anna, is childless, and she meets her Gurov on the beach. He too is vacationing without his spouse, but he is accompanied by one of his children, a blind son, and a "small yipping dog, a

---

[19] Ibid., 331.

golden dog."[20] A perfect inversion of Chekhov it appears: it is the man who is seen through the woman's gaze and it is he who has the pet dog. Oates's alterations of the Chekhov text are, moreover, sometimes highly entertaining and one imagines that she must have enjoyed doing with Chekhov what she did. For example, when the "small yipping golden dog" is later identified as a golden retriever, one laughs and applauds. Golden retrievers grow up to be bigger dogs than Chekhov's "little dog" ("sobachka"), but by having first introduced the dog to us as a "small yipping dog," Oates teases us into thinking that her dog is a duplicate of its Chekhov model when in fact it is not. Another clever feature of her story is how she makes Chekhov's title apply to her story even though she is telling it from Anna's point of view, and the pet dog belongs to the man and not to Anna. Again, Oates manages both to invert the Chekhov text and at the same time to salute it by going to ingenious extremes to adhere to it. For example, one day on the beach before the affair commences, Anna's about-to-be-lover takes up a pad and begins to make a series of sketches of her holding and playing with his dog. After telling her to "take the one she likes best," he then entitles his drawing "lady with pet dog."[21] Thus, the initial discordance which seems to exist between Oates's variation on the story and the Chekhov title is resolved in a way that suggests that the joke is once again on us (or at least on those of us familiar with the Chekhov model). It's as if Oates were saying, "I bet you wondered how I was going to pull that off. Well, see!" Moreover, the artistic inclinations of Anna's about-to-be lover mirror Gurov's original (and subsequently abandoned) intention of becoming an opera singer. Throughout her story, therefore, Oates demonstrates her critical appreciation of and fondness for a Chekhov text that has provided her with the perfect opportunity to replay it in a very different idiom.

In contrast to Katherine Mansfield, whose connection with Chekhov seems more complex and personal and also more constant a feature of her reading and writing life, Joyce Carol Oates's engagement with Chekhov appears more detached and literary, less compounded by a sense of shared emotional and experiential affinities—rather the reverse, in fact. One senses that it is the attraction and challenge of a particular Chekhov text rather than the seduction of the Chekhov persona and biography that has inspired Oates.

Raymond Carver's famous story "Errand," which appeared before his death (in 1988), reflects an engagement with Chekhov that is both complex and highly personal.[22] A kind of hybrid creation, both fictional and non-

---

[20] Ibid., 334. The fact that Oates' "Gurov" has a blind son who is with him during his stay on Nantucket is also a clever twist on the Chekhov story since it is Anna's husband's unspecified eye trouble that prevents him from joining her in Yalta.

[21] Ibid., 337.

[22] William L. Stull's very useful biographical essay on Raymond Carver, which initially appeared in *The Dictionary of Literary Biography* and was accessed on the fol-

fictional, the story begins with the one-word sentence *Chekhov*, almost as if Carver is summoning him to attendance. What then follows is a condensed and affecting summary of the final years of Chekhov's life, starting with 1897, when he began hemorrhaging from his mouth while dining with his friend Suvorin in Moscow, and ending with his death scene in the German spa Badenweiler. Henri Troyat's biography of Chekhov appears to be Carver's source.[23] However, when Carver turns to Chekhov's actual death scene, he introduces certain details that suggest that he was an actual presence in the hotel room where the death occurred.[24] The version of "Errand" that originally appeared in the *New Yorker* (1 June 1987) ends with Olga's description of being alone in the hotel room with Chekhov's body when dawn breaks: "There were no human voices, no everyday sounds, there was only beauty, peace, and the grandeur of death."[25] Thus concludes Carver's only slightly fictionalized version of a biographical account of Chekhov's death. It is, therefore, as if the very retelling of the story of Chekhov's death itself constitutes a form of tribute to him. Moreover, the fact that Carver himself, who knew that he was very ill, died on 2 August 1988, a year after the story had appeared in the *New Yorker* and only two months after it appeared in *Where I'm Calling From*, his last book of stories, suggests that a more complex kind of biographical and creative interpenetration is being enacted here. Even more interesting, the version of "Errand" in *Where I'm Calling From* is not the same version that appeared earlier in the *New Yorker*. Rather than end with Carver's retelling of the biographical story of Chekhov's death, it ends with a fictional epilogue to Chekhov's death. It is only then that the significance of Carver's title becomes evident. His epilogue begins with the reappearance of the young blond waiter, a character of Carver's creation, whom we earlier saw bringing the champagne that Doctor Schwöhrer (Carver's spelling) had so famously called for when he saw how dire Chekhov's condition was. Since Troyat's biography is mute about who actually brought the champagne, one could argue that Chekhov's death scene (as Carver perceived it through

---

lowing website, discusses Carver's admiration of Chekhov and his sense of their shared affinities, both artistic and personal. See http://www.whitman.edu/english/carver/biography1.html.

[23] In the discussion following my presentation of the paper on which this article is based (NEH symposium at Colby College, 8 October 2004), my colleagues alerted me to the fact that it was Troyat in particular who appeared to be Carver's biographical source. The specific details given and the sequence in which they appear replicate Troyat's account. See Henri Troyat, *Chekhov*, trans. Michael Henry Heim (New York: Dutton, 1986).

[24] Raymond Carver, "Errand," *Where I'm Calling From* (New York: Atlantic Monthly Press, 1989), 512–26. See, in particular, his description of the careful and studied way in which the doctor checked Chekhov's pulse after his breathing had stopped (520).

[25] Ibid., 521.

Troyat) invited the insertion of just such a character.[26] The illusion continues, therefore, that Carver himself was present at Chekhov's death and is thus able to comment on details and events "missed" by Chekhov's biographers. Although Carver did not actually place this young waiter at Chekhov's death scene (he exits from the room after delivering the champagne; thus he is absent when Chekhov dies), he now has him reappear in the morning when Olga is alone in the hotel room with Chekhov's corpse. Looking considerably more well-groomed than he had hours earlier, the waiter comes ostensibly to collect the glasses, ice bucket, and tray and also to present Olga with three long-stemmed yellow roses. He is apparently not aware that Chekhov has died and is, therefore, perplexed to find that Chekhov's wife is so distracted and unmindful of what he is telling her. Before Olga catches on to the waiter's cluelessness, and before she informs him of what has happened, the waiter himself becomes distracted by the champagne cork lying on the floor near his shoe—the champagne cork that had so famously popped out of the bottle when Olga was first alone with her husband's body. Olga finally pulls herself together, informs the waiter that Chekhov is dead, and tells him about the *errand* she wants him to perform, namely, to go and find "the most respected mortician in the city ... a mortician, in short, worthy of a great artist."[27] After listening to Olga's instructions, the waiter then imagines every possible detail of his going on such an errand without ever actually doing it. The errand is, in fact, anticipated in such painstaking detail that it is hard not to forget that everything being described is merely the waiter's imagined scenario of what he thinks will happen if he does perform the errand. Finally, the champagne cork on the floor catches the waiter's attention once again and interrupts his thoughts. He muses further on future probable actions: "To retrieve [the cork] he would have to bend over, still gripping the vase [with the three yellow roses]."[28] This time, however, the waiter actually does what he imagines he will have to do, and the next and final sentence of the story is, "Without looking down, he reached out and closed it in his hand."

The fact that the waiter Carver conjures up manages to secure a memento or talisman from Chekhov's death scene before allegedly going off to fetch an appropriate mortician suggests that Carver is staging a kind of metaphorical reenactment of his own complex engagement with Chekhov and is perhaps appropriating Chekhov's death in order to face his own more easily. The story could certainly be said to be Chekhovian in that it invests prosaic details with a sense of both random casualness and purposeful placement.[29] The

---

[26] See Troyat, *Chekhov*, 332.

[27] Carver, "Errand," 524.

[28] Ibid., 526.

[29] Stull describes the fictional story that Carver appends to the biographical part of "Errand" as a "Chekhovian fiction." He also notes that the retrieval of the fallen cork is a "gesture [that] brings the story to a faultless Chekhovian close." See Stull, 2 (essay

champagne cork certainly invites comment. Since Olga is alone in the room with Chekhov's corpse when the champagne cork is said to have popped out of the bottle, she is obviously the sole source for this part of the biographical account. Moreover, given that Chekhov had a fondness for suggestive sound effects in his plays, and given that Olga had acted in them, one can't help wondering if the popped cork isn't her own creative contribution to the story of Chekhov's death. However, even if it is, one would have to concede that it is a brilliant insertion worthy of Chekhov himself. Carver's own manipulations of the errant cork invite additional speculations. Since Carver was a recovering alcoholic who had stopped drinking during the last decade of his life, it is interesting that it is the cork from a half-full bottle of champagne that his waiter cups in his hand at the end of "The Errand." Conventional wine-cork mementoes are usually associated with wine drunk, but this is hardly a conventional memento. Moreover, the story ends with this gesture of retrieval. Carver's young waiter never does have to go out and find a proper mortician because a "mortician worthy of a great artist" has already been found, and he hardly aspires to prepare Chekhov for burial. On the contrary, Carver has made Chekhov a character in a story which does not end with his death. Furthermore, Carver appears so identified with Chekhov in the story that it also appears to hold promise of Carver's own future appearance in a story (or stories) not yet written.

However different they are as writers, Carver shares with Mansfield what I would describe as a deep engagement with both Chekhov's art and his persona. Their engagement with Chekhov also reflects a kind of gratitude for the *comfort* which they seem to have derived from the example of his life, particularly when facing deteriorating health and imminent death. "The Lady with a Pet Dog," on the other hand, reflects Oates's critical astuteness about how Chekhov's story works and about what constitutes its finest moments while at the same time demonstrating how unlike Chekhov she is. Thus, she *knows* the Chekhov text but appears less engaged with the author himself.

The final text to be considered here, John Ford Noonan's two-act, two-character play *Talking Things Over With Chekhov*, is a comic reenactment of the kind of intertextual and interauthorial engagement (even intimacy) that we have, in part, been discussing.[30] Its humor is derived from its self-conscious and bemused appreciation of just how ubiquitous and "influential" a presence Chekhov has been in the work and in the hearts and minds of so many authors. The play's two characters, Jeremy, a playwright, and his ex-wife

---

accessed on website provided in n. 22). I, however, am not so much interested in the alleged Chekhovian qualities of the Carver story as I am in the implications associated with his having created the kind of hybrid text that he did—part Chekhov life (and death), part Carver fiction.

[30] John Ford Noonan, *Talking Things Over with Chekhov* (New York: Samuel French, 1991).

Marlene, meet by accident in Riverside Park and reconnect briefly if acerbically to rehash their failed relationship and to read the script of a play which Jeremy has just written about the break-up of their relationship. Marlene, an actress whose career has been on hold after having once been "the best Masha [the critics] ever saw in *Three Sisters*," has a selfish interest in Jeremy's new script, and Jeremy nurses a hope that it will write Marlene back into his life.[31] Although Jeremy and Marlene are hardly Anton and Olga, one can't help thinking of the two couples in relation to each other and that adds to the humor of the play. Jeremy is, moreover, obsessed with Chekhov, invoking him constantly and seemingly regarding him as a kind of "secret friend" whom he talks things over with and who gives him writing tips. (Similar sentiments were, I might add, also expressed by Katherine Mansfield, but obviously not in a comic vein: "Ach, Tchekov! Why are you dead? Why can't I talk to you in a big darkish room at late evening—where the light is green from the waving trees outside? I'd like to write a series of Heavens: that would be one."[32]) Noonan's familiarization of Chekhov is funny, however, not because he is parodying Chekhov but because he is parodying the familiarization of Chekhov that has taken place. Remarkably, however, Chekhov emerges as both appealing and amusing, and hence Jeremy's attachment to him seems fully justified. Consider the following excerpt from the play:

> *Jeremy.* [...] I know if he were still alive, he and I would've been close friends.
> *Marlene.* Great artists never have close friends.
> *Jeremy.* I would've been his first!
> *Marlene.* First what?
> *Jeremy.* Chekhov's first close friend. A great artist needs one. I see us out in Yalta. He coughs. Makes a joke about the weather. I get up. Get him his tea. I come back. His blanket has slipped off. I put it back on. He says, "Thank you" in English. We talk about Tolstoy. I explain how much I love *Anna Karenina*. Chekhov laughs. I ask him why. He only smiles. I smile back... He asks about America. I tell him about Brooklyn. He asks why I came all the way to Yalta. "Someone has to take care of you!" I say. "My wife would," says Chekhov, "but she's in Moscow rehearsing my new play." He bows his head. I ask what's wrong. He says, "As the end approaches, I cry at the silliest things." I take his hand. He whispers, "Thanks, close friend."[33]

Needless to say, if one knows about Chekhov's life in Yalta and about his relationship with his wife, Noonan's dialogue becomes even more amusing. Given that the biographical literature sometimes comes down rather hard on

---

[31] Ibid., 13.
[32] Quoted in Kurylo, "Chekhov and Katherine Mansfield," 165.
[33] Noonan, *Talking Things Over with Chekhov*, 14–15.

Olga for being an absentee wife in Moscow when her husband was ailing in Yalta, Jeremy's desire to travel to Yalta to "take care of" Chekhov becomes an implied criticism of Olga while at the same time being expressive of Jeremy's obvious devotion to Chekhov. Moreover, Jeremy's wife, Marlene, hardly comes across as a nurturing wife, so one senses that Jeremy is also projecting his own sense of abandonment by her onto his portrayal of Chekhov in Yalta. The dialogue also highlights Chekhov's famed elusiveness and reserve and the challenge that that posed for anyone wanting to get close to him. Furthermore, the allusion to Chekhov's laugh (when Jeremy refers to his love of *Anna Karenina*), followed by his smiling refusal to explain why he has laughed, evokes all the complexities of Chekhov's relationship with and changing attitude toward Tolstoy. It is thus entertainingly suggestive if one is aware of both the biographical literature and of the obvious connection between Chekhov's "Lady with a Pet Dog" and Tolstoy's *Anna Karenina*. One could imagine that Chekhov's cryptic laugh and smile is also meant to reflect his sense of Jeremy's naiveté and possible ignorance regarding his (Chekhov's) own textual "response" to *Anna Karenina*. The concluding lines of the dialogue are funny in yet a different way. The image of a weepy and highly sentimental Chekhov who is reduced to tears by virtually anything is amusing because it is so at odds with the conventional view of the Chekhov persona. What's also appealing about these lines, however, is that we can imagine that Chekhov might have felt weepy (secretly, as it were) even if he didn't act weepy.[34] Moreover, by putting these preposterously unChekhovian words into Chekhov's mouth, Jeremy seems to be projecting once again and implying that in such a situation (with the end approaching), he would be in tears all the time.

As already noted, it is not Chekhov who is parodied in Noonan's play but rather the *familiarization* of Chekhov that has taken place. The play also conveys a genuine fondness and admiration for Chekhov the artist and for the Chekhov persona. Thus, Noonan implies that the familiarization of Chekhov is understandable. It is also hardly in danger of making Chekhov seem any less elusive or infinitely interpretable. And so, Noonan's play highlights the absurdity of thinking that one can domesticate Chekhov while at the same time conceding that there's a powerful temptation to try.

To conclude, it is both understandable and curious, both ironic and not, that Chekhov, the writer whose work has sometimes been said to highlight man's *inability* to communicate with man, has been perceived to be communicating so directly and so personally to so many of our English-language authors. Or, as Noonan's Jeremy would say, "he's speaking Russian but somehow I hear it in English."[35]

---

[34] See n. 12.

[35] Noonan, *Talking Things Over with Chekhov*, 26.

# Hunters Off the Beaten Track: The Dismantling of Pastoral Myth in Chekhov and Crane

## Andrew R. Durkin, Indiana University

Anton Pavlovich Chekhov (1860–1904) and Stephen Crane (1871–1900), despite the manifest differences in their origins, languages, and cultures, exhibit certain oddly intriguing affinities in their lives and works, a sort of mirroring that suggests certain parallels in Russian and American literature and culture in a period of modernization and urbanization. Both began their literary careers at twenty and as relative outsiders, writing on the literary margins, the medical student Chekhov as a contributor to the Russian satirical journals, the young Crane, who had studied at Syracuse University, as the author of short sketches for the *New York Tribune*. Both maintained ties to the world of journalism throughout their careers, Chekhov rising through the various strata of the Russian journalistic world of his day to the literary elite, Crane working, or trying to work, as an active reporter, as well as a poet and an author of fiction, throughout his brief and turbulent career, and ending in England on close terms with the likes of Henry James and Joseph Conrad. Both married rather unconventionally, Chekhov to an actress, Crane, ever more extreme, to a woman with what might have been charitably termed a somewhat shady past. In an odd final and fatal coincidence, both died of tuberculosis (complicated by malaria in the case of Crane) in the German sanatorium town of Badenweiler, Crane in June of 1900, Chekhov in July of 1904.

Apart from these biographical near-parallels, Chekhov and Crane can be placed among the first truly modern writers in their respective cultures. In this paper I would like to focus on what might be taken as a primary indication in the early career of each writer of a movement away from the literary and cultural system of the past, namely their respective rejection of the pastoral tradition that played such a large part in the literature and culture of the nineteenth century in both Russia and America. In Russia, the works of writers such as Turgenev, Aksakov, and Tolstoy privileged interaction with nature, particularly in the form of the hunt. In America, as we know from such landmark studies as Leo Marx's *The Machine in the Garden*, pastoral was more variable, but if anything even more pervasive. It is perhaps difficult to find a work of the early and mid-nineteenth century in which the American wilderness, often so ominous in the colonial period, or some displacement of that wilderness, does not take on overtones of a pastoral Peaceable Kingdom. From the frontier idyll of Cooper's Leatherstocking novels and Melville's

*Chekhov the Immigrant: Translating a Cultural Icon.* Michael C. Finke and Julie de Sherbinin, eds. Bloomington, IN: Slavica Publishers, 2007, 141–50.

South Pacific paradise in *Omoo* and *Typee,* to the perspectival pastoral in Thoreau that finds restorative nature everywhere, and to Sarah Orne Jewett's Maine stories (inspired in part by Turgenev's *Sportsman's Sketches*), the pastoral orientation reappears like a hardy perennial. (And in visual arts we might also mention the Hudson River School and Frederick Church.) Even Mark Twain, who viewed Cooper's mythologizing of the frontier and its settlers as a pernicious chivalrous fraud, himself feels the powerful tug of pastoral in such works as *Tom Sawyer* and *Huckleberry Finn.* However, writers of a younger generation in both countries seem to resist the attraction of pastoral in favor of an outlook that rejects the privileging of nature and the partitioning of space into distinct realms with divergent values, Chekhov in several early comic pieces, Crane in a series of sketches set in the Sullivan County area of New York State that were among his first published works.

With Chekhov, this assertion of the non-differentiation of space occurs most overtly and most pointedly in two early stories, from 1881 and 1882, each written to mark the date on which the hunting season opened in Russia, June 29, the feast of Saints Peter and Paul, and referred to as St. Peter's Day. The titles of the stories, "St. Peter's Day" ("Petrov den'," 1881) and "June 29th" ("Dvadtsat' deviatoe iunia," 1882), as well as their date of publication (June 29 in both cases), reflect the calendrical ordering of topics that underlay the constantly varying yet never changing carnivalistic world of the Russian satirical journals. Unlike more typical calendrical stories in these journals, which were related to events and activities in which the readers of the journals themselves participated, or perhaps aspired to participate (for instance the opening of the theater session or the move to a dacha for the summer), these stories assume complete ineptitude in matters of the hunt and/or lack of interest on the part of the implied reader. The original mock dedication of "St. Peter's Day" makes this explicit: "Dedicated with pleasure to those hunters who shoot badly or who do not know how to shoot" (*PssS* 1: 567). As we know from the attention devoted to hunting or fishing equipment, to weather conditions and other environmental factors, and to the accumulated individual and collective experience of hunters in such works as those by Aksakov, Turgenev, and Tolstoy, one of the hallmarks of Russian pastoral, for which hunting was the paradigmatic interaction with nature, is precisely the acquisition of experience and skill (*opyt* and *opytnost'* in Aksakov's treatment).[1] The notion of hunters lacking mastery of their sport verges on a contradiction in terms. Yet this is precisely what Chekhov's first story depicts, a gaggle of inept landowners and their hangers-on whose clumsy attempts to engage in the sport of their forebears degenerate quite literally into a farce, with most of them drunk. The leader of the whole expedition, the overbearing landowner

---

[1] See Andrew R. Durkin, *Sergei Aksakov and Russian Pastoral* (New Brunswick, NJ: Rutgers University Press, 1983).

Yegor Yegorovich Obtemperansky,[2] races home to find the local psalm reader under his wife's bed (he had expected to find the doctor, a member of the hunting party who disappears from the group). Among the other *dramatis personae* of this little comedy, perhaps three should be mentioned as most indicative of the re-valuation of pastoral inscribed in the story. The oldest member of the hunting party, born at the end of the eighteenth century and a man of the people (*meshchanin*), is the only participant who actually possesses any hunting skill—the others respect his ability to hit a twenty-kopeck coin tossed in the air. Tellingly, this relic of the pastoral hunting tradition is summarily forgotten when the party suddenly decides to move to a different location. The youngest member, a *gymnasium* student, instead of being initiated into the solemnities of the hunt, is plied with beer and vodka and winds up drunk and sick. The one character who freely concedes that he does not know how to hunt, and indeed admits to having no interest in hunting, is the fore-mentioned doctor (perhaps significantly, given that Chekhov was a medical student at the time and may have viewed the members of his future profession as figures of urban modernity). Significantly, the issue is again one of ability: "I don't know how to shoot, I don't even know how to hold a shotgun... I can't stand firing" (*PssS* 1: 69). Indeed, the doctor withdraws from the general comedy, goes to sleep under a tree, and later walks home alone, vowing never again to give in to social pressure to go on a hunt. This refusal on the doctor's part to participate in the sham of interaction with nature clearly functions as an inscribed norm of appropriate modern behavior as the other characters idiotically attempt to enact conventions and rituals they no longer understand or esteem. The "characters" at the other end of the natural-social spectrum, the hunting dogs, also vote with their feet, bolting for the security and comfort of home at their earliest opportunity.

"St. Peter's Day" displays the farcical desacralization of what had been, in the hunting pastoral of earlier Russian literature, the central ritual binding man and nature, as well as of the literary mode that celebrated that bond. As such, it provides a model or template for much of Chekhov's anti-pastoral, as well as that of early Crane. One further feature of the story seems to be a recurrent element in both authors' stories. "St. Peter's Day" (as well as "June 29th") recapitulates its own stylistic history and inscribes its ideological structure. In its opening paragraphs, the text echoes and appropriates the quasi-poetic style of earlier pastoral prose only to collapse this into the farce of the main part of the story: "The stars faded and grew hazy... Somewhere voices could be heard... From village chimneys poured blue-grey, acrid smoke"

---

[2] As has been suggested by Savelii Senderovich, the name George, of which Yegor (*Egor'*) is a variant, held particular significance for Chekhov. In the present case, the significance is clearly inverted. This George is no dragon-slaying saint; he only wings a quail. *Chekhov—s glazu na glaz: Istoriia odnoi oderzhimosti A. P. Chekhov. Opyt fenomenologii tvorchestva* (St. Petersburg: Dmitrii Bulanin, 1994).

(*PssS* 1: 67). With their interpunction, inversion, and poetic vocabulary of visual perception ("faded," "grew hazy," "blue-grey"), these phrases recapitulate the nature prose of Turgenev in particular, but the expectations they encourage are quickly inverted and dispelled. The opening paragraph of "June 29th" is even more clearly in the pastoral stylistic key, ending with an implied congruence between the natural and human realms: "Above the grass and above our heads, with even strokes of their wings, soared kites, red-footed falcons, and short-eared owls. They were hunting...." (*PssS* 1: 224). The final word "hunting" (*okhotilis'*—from *okhitit'sia*, the same word that is used for hunting by humans and in the derivative form *okhotnik*—hunter—appears in the titles of works by both Aksakov and Turgenev) suggests a congruence and continuum with the world of human hunters, to whom the focus immediately shifts. Nothing however could be further from the truth. The human hunters in this story are even more removed from the world of the true hunt than those of "St. Peter's Day," if not by utter lack of skill, then by their disposition. Oblivious to the fraternal camaraderie of true hunters (the temporary effacing of class boundaries among hunters focused on a common quarry is an important component of earlier Russian hunting pastoral), the hunters in this story engage in endless bickering; the doctor (in "St. Peter's Day" the one character who does not participate in the farce of hunting) is here a glutton who in no way differs from his companions. Hunting, rather than a quasi-ritual, degenerates into a pretext, equivalent to card-playing or other activities, for sociopathological conflict.

If these early hunting stories depict the degeneration of the pastoral sensibility (and imply the inappropriateness of pastoral prose in a modern context), two others reverse the spatial trajectory of pastoral, namely the movement, motivated by the hunt in many cases in Russia, into the world of nature. In both "At the Wolf-Baiting" ("Na vol'chei sadke," 1882) and "In Moscow on Trubnaia Square" ("V Moskve na Trubnoi ploshchadi," 1883), nature is brought into modern urban space, indeed into Moscow itself, with perhaps predictably disastrous results. In "At the Wolf-Baiting," which describes an actual public wolf-baiting held in Moscow in January of 1882, participation in the archetypal Russian hunt (cf. the famous wolf hunt in Tolstoy's *War and Peace*), with implications of both union with and mastery over nature, has been replaced by spectacle, in which a series of rather battered captive wolves are released only to be quickly run to ground and dispatched for the entertainment of an urban audience that is only superficially removed from the blood-thirsty audience in the Roman Coliseum. The hunt, that most direct activity, is transformed into spectacle—*zrelishche* (*PssS* 1: 117)—in violation of the intensely participatory quality of the hunt as presented in the hunting pastoral tradition. This pseudo-hunt or "quasi-hunt" (*quasi-okhota*) (*PssS* 1: 119)[3] is matched by the pseudo-urbanity of the Moscow audience, which, in its ignorance of the hunt, sees it as something equivalent to a bullfight or cockfight. The only figures not swept up in the voyeuristic frenzy of the crowd is the narrator, the representative of true modernity, who describes himself as a total non-hunter, unfamiliar with any but toy guns, and who views the whole event as atavistic; and a *gymnasium* student, whose non-comprehension of what is taking place and disturbed reaction to what he sees provide a defamiliarizing moral perspective.

The other story presents a somewhat more complex interplay between the pastoral world and urban existence. In its description of the animal market that was held on Trubnaia Square (Chekhov's first apartment in Moscow was adjacent to the square), the commodification of various wild creatures, including songbirds, pigeons, hares, rabbits, hedgehogs, guinea pigs, weasels, fish packed into in barrels and buckets that are "an utter hell" (*PssS* 2:245); and even frogs, snails, and beetles. The horror of this reduction of the things of nature to the things of commerce is summed up in an initial emblematic question from a buyer: "How much for a skylark? (*A pochem zhavoronok?*)" (*PssS* 2: 247). This (in Russian) two-element formulation, with the realm of money and commerce in the predicate (placed first) and the world of nature (as well as perhaps poetry) in the subject, yet with the two bound in a single statement, encapsulates the awful reality of the market. The oxymoronic or paradoxical nature of the question pervades the entire text. In the eyes of true amateurs, the songbirds that are the quietest in the company of other birds at the market are the most likely to sing once they are alone, and if a pigeon fancier is spotted, the hawkers of pigeons tout one bird as "An eagle, not a pigeon!" (*PssS* 2: 246). Despite the frantic trading taking place at the market, few, if any, sellers or buyers know the correct price of the living goods, guessing at what the market will bear. This in part arises from the incommensurable quality of creatures of nature versus articles of trade, the uncertainty over prices reflecting the slippage between the two categories. Only a few specialists and skilled amateurs can assess true value, but these values are not primarily monetary. The two "amateurs" who are described are themselves living oxymorons, the first a tattered elderly man, significantly without a kopeck—that is outside the economy of this market—but who nevertheless inspects the wild birds and fish passionately; referred to as "a character" (*tip*), he is in fact the hunter of the literary tradition, trapped in an alien urban reality, as well as in an alien genre, the urban sketch or feuilleton. He visits Trubnaia Square only in the colder months; in the summer he reverts to the zone of nature (and the past) outside Moscow, where he "hunts quail by

---

[3] For a brief description of the technical aspects and requisite skill involved in the traditional wolf hunt, see S. T. Aksakov, "Gon'ba lis i volkov," in *Sobranie sochinenii v 4-kh tomakh* (Moscow: Khudozhestvennaia literatura, 1956; henceforth, *SS*), 4: 556–60.

piping for them and angles for fish" (*PssS* 2: 247–48).⁴ This remnant of the true hunting tradition is matched by another "amateur," but one from the other end of the spectrum, a *gymnasium* teacher known to the market in mockery of bureaucratic titles as "Your Pronounness." If the old hunter is a hunter without a hunt, a living relic forced to seek out the market for its metonymic traces of the world to which he belonged but with which he loses touch (at least in the winter), "His Pronounness" seems to be a different sort of oxymoron, the essence of modern bureaucratic abstraction and modernization who nevertheless comes to life only in the contemplation of fancy pigeons. His passion is not for a trace of an earlier mode of existence, but an alternate world to that of titles and uniforms. Although the exact value of the pigeons to him is not made explicit, they would seem to be some sort of inverted metaphor, something as *unlike* the abstracted, de-essentialized modern world that he and other living pronouns (the part of speech with no intrinsic referent or meaning, but always relational and situational) inhabit. Trubnaia Square is thus a tiny "slice of Moscow, where people love animals so tenderly and where they torture them so" (*PssS* 2: 248); but also a place where, paradoxically, the participants in the market become like the objects of their trading; reduced to the Gogolian metonymy of their clothes and headgear (sheepskin coats, topcoats, fur caps, top hats: largely animal products), they "teem, like crayfish in a colander" in their own "utter hell" (*PssS* 2: 245). The animal market, like the racetrack that is the scene of wolf-baiting, is a place where the disjunction between nature and modern urban life is exposed, but the market suggests that for all the distortions of the market place, there is still an irreducible link between the two realms.

Turning at last to Stephen Crane and the set of pieces that are collectively known as his Sullivan County stories or sketches, certain congruencies with the concerns and devices of Chekhov's hunting stories can be noted, as well as some clear differences. The eighteen pieces were apparently written as a continuing series of linked sketches, with the same general setting, in a number of cases the same characters, and the same general thematics. Like Chekhov's early pseudonymous stories, the sketches appeared, for the most part anonymously, in the *New York Tribune* from February to July 1892, although a few first appeared in other publications in 1892 or posthumously.⁵

---

⁴ For some details on the traditional hunting of quail by this method, see S. T. Aksakov, *Zapiski ruzheinogo okhotnika Orenburgskoi gubernii* (*SS* 4: 370) and the English translation, *Notes of a Provincial Wildfowler*, trans. Kevin Windle (Evanston, IL: Northwestern University Press, 1998), 204. For angling, see S. T. Aksakov, *Zapiski ob uzhen'e ryby* (*SS* 4: 9–146) and the English translation, *Notes on Fishing*, trans. Thomas P. Hodge (Evanston, IL: Northwestern University Press, 1997).

⁵ Attribution of most of the sketches to Crane was made only in the 1960s; for specifics on publication, see the commentary to the individual sketches in Stephen Crane, "Sullivan County Sketches," in *Tales, Sketches, and Reports: The University of Virginia*

The Sullivan County stories thus represent the twenty-one-year-old Crane's first attempt at a more or less sustained project of pieces on a single theme, a form to which he returns on several occasions (as in his Whilomville stories) and perhaps reflects the close links between his writing and the endlessly renewed present tense of the newspaper. Although Chekhov's hunting pieces are related to the calendrical concerns of the satirical journal, Crane's sketches are much more insistently a series of successive variations on a limited number of themes, forming a sort of supertext in which a single organizing principle is more easily traced.

In general, two main phases in the development of Crane's sketches are apparent. The first seven sketches are in large part non-narrative, alternately focusing either on the past of Sullivan County (and the mythologizing of that past) or on the game that can, or formerly could, be found in the area, as the titles make clear: "The Last of the Mohicans"; "Hunting Wild Hogs"; "The Last Panther"; "Not Much of a Hero"; "Sullivan County Bears"; "The Way in Sullivan County"; and "Reminiscence of Indian War." The primary "program" of these stories is the ironic reversal or rejection of the myths of the American past, historical, literary, and what we might term natural or pastoral. The first story evokes James Fenimore Cooper's construction (or canonization) of the native American as the noblest of Noble Savages only to deconstruct that figure. Instead of Cooper's hero, Uncas, that bronze god in a North American wilderness, the last Mohican known to Sullivan County was a nameless, homeless beggar whose only ambition was "to beg, borrow, or steal a drink" from the whites who had supplanted him and his people (Crane 8: 200). The dominant role of irony in this first sketch (as well as in various ways throughout the series) is explicit. Cooper's work "is of course a visionary tale and the historical value of the plot is not a question of importance," but the "pathos lies in the contrast between the noble savage of fiction and the sworn-to claimant [to the title of Last Mohican] of Sullivan County" (Crane 8: 200).

From the outset Crane creates a new fictional world in which the illusions of the past, including the literary-mythic past, dissolve in the light of the reality of direct experience and perception. Like Chekhov in his hunting works, Crane, writing for and publishing in the medium of direct observation, the modern newspaper, opts for the truth of mundane reality, or at least for the less obviously inflated myth, for the Sullivan County version of the Last Mohican is itself the product of the mythologizing work of oral tradition. In a sort of reverse equal opportunity, the most celebrated eliminator of the supposed threat of the Native American is shown to have been (as the title of the story devoted to him announces) "Not Much of a Hero." Instead of "the Indian Slayer, the Avenger of the Delaware" of local legend and epitaph, the

---

*Edition of the Works of Stephen Crane* (Charlottesville, VA: The University of Virginia Press, 1973), 8: 847–61.

hero of dime novels inspiring adolescents to go west to eliminate yet more Indians, Tom Quick is exposed as the killer of "only" fifteen Indians (as opposed to the hundred of legend), who shot his victims in the back, or while they were peacefully fishing, hunting, or sleeping, and who even killed women and children. The sketch ends by suggesting three possibilities: Tom Quick the Indian Slayer is a complete mythologization of an otherwise blameless early settler; he was a pathologically vengeful killer (supposedly his parents were killed by Indians); or he was "purely and simply a murderer" (Crane 8: 215).

Finally, in "A Reminiscence of Indian War," a Revolutionary War massacre of American forces by Tories and Indians is made possible by the courage instilled in the American forces by the false rhetoric ("Let the brave men follow me. The cowards may stay behind"; Crane 8: 223) of a man who takes no part in the crucial battle. As with the culture-shaping myths concerning the personages and events of the past, so too with the myths of the hunt. In the Sullivan County of today, the fiercest animal is not some indigenous beast but the imported European wild boar, of which a few have escaped and have all probably been shot ("Hunting Wild Hogs"). The most dangerous animal present in the past, the cougar (mountain lion or "panther") has been eliminated ("The Last Panther"). Despite tales of the animal's ferocity and cunning, the "last of the panthers ... in this part of the country was killed in 1829 by a negro who ... received from the hands of the admiring authorities ... the munificent reward of $15" (Crane 8: 207). Even allowing for inflation, this bounty would seem a somewhat paltry sum for the elimination of so formidable a beast. In the hunt that is described in the conclusion of the story, a panther cornered in a cave is axed and knifed by a "small lad" able to crawl into the space, and the animal's carcass is carried home by the "army" (that had pursued it) who "thereupon cheered and went home and told about the killing of the panther" (Crane 8: 211), thus beginning the process of legend-building once again. That this supposed deadliest of creatures is dispatched by socially marginal figures (a black, a child) suggests that the panther's reputation may be more the product of mythologization than of reality. Bears, in fact now more numerous than in the days of early settlement and clearing ("Sullivan County Bears"), are revealed as "the shyest of all the animals which naturally live in these woods" (8: 216) and must be chased and cornered before they will turn on a hunter so that "it is difficult to reconcile the bear of fiction with the bear of reality" (Crane 8: 219). Finally, in "The Way in Sullivan County," the full mechanism of the formation of hunting legend (a.k.a. lies) is revealed: six different men claim to have shot three bears at one time in the same way, and a bear and panther are goaded by shots into attacking each other, only to have the survivor (the panther) shot by the onlooking hunter. Crane thus deflates the literary and historical myths of the erstwhile frontier, suggesting that they are more the product of mindless repetition than of valid experience, and turns the ferocious beasts of legend, if not back into the reclining creatures of a Peaceable Kingdom, at least into denizens of the forest that are basically harmless if left to their own devices.

After clearing the space of the accumulation of myths concerning the realm of nature, in the remaining Sullivan County stories Crane populates this newly liberated space with a new cast of characters in a new literary mode. In place of the pseudopastoral and pseudoheroes of the tradition, Sullivan County now becomes the stage on which four characters, from the city and neophytes in the world of nature, enact a recurrent comic plot, though one with inverse thematic relations to the discarded narratives of the past. In each story, the four encounter some new aspect of Sullivan County, imagine it full of dire and unknown dangers (largely drawn from literary and legendary stereotypes), and end up by having their illusions dispelled by a prosaic reality. Rather than rehearsing each story, I will point only to the first story, "Four Men in a Cave," which provides the paradigm and the fullest expression of the model. After entering an unknown cave, the four, trembling with fear, encounter a shaggy human denizen of the cave whom they variously imagine to be some sort of "vampire," "ghoul," "Druid before a sacrifice," or "shade of an Aztec witch doctor" (Crane 8: 228). Instead, this supposedly dreadful figure of the supernatural or atavistic turns out to be a half-demented local who, having become a compulsive gambler, engages one of the quartet in a game of poker (and in fact cleans out his chosen victim). This descent into a Plato-like cave of ignorance and illusion, the projection of fear upon the murky unknown, and the comic reversal and recognition form the basic pattern for most of the stories. This pattern parallels the *kazalos'/okazalos'* structure that has been identified by Vladimir Kataev as characteristic of Chekhov's early "epistemological" stories,[6] but in Crane what is gained is not so much a specific truth (adults lie; gentlemen friends may be cruel and indifferent) as the realization that truth itself is provisional. The characters are variously beset by a drunken fishing guide ("The Octopush"); by another haggard local eager to find someone who can calculate what he should charge for his potato crop ("A Ghoul's Accountant"); by a seemingly supernatural black dog that howls not because of a death (though one dramatically occurs in the story) but because it is hungry ("The Black Dog"); by a bear that becomes entangled in a tent and sends it crashing down the mountainside ("Tent in Agony"); and by a farm woman whose brood of brats have been made sick by eating flypaper and who tries to exact physical vengeance on one of the hapless quartet rather than on the peddler who is in fact responsible ("An Explosion of Seven Babies"). In the *reductio ad absurdum* of the pattern, a huckleberry pudding made with tainted ingredients sends one of the four into howls of stomach pain, which his companions, in the dark in more ways than one, ascribe to a raging wild animal and fear that the man

---

[6] V. B. Kataev, *Proza Chekhova: Problemy interpretatsii* (Moscow: Izd. Moskovskogo universiteta, 1979).

who is in fact the source of the noise has been the deadly creature's victim ("The Cry of a Huckleberry Pudding: A Dim Study of Camping Experiences"). This last story suggests stories of Chekhov in which an overdose of experience results in physical illness, such as "Grisha"; the man who gets ill is the only one to eat the pudding, and in fact prepared it. Two of these intrepid adventurers gradually emerge from the quartet, a little man (Billie) and a pudgy man, who become the Laurel and Hardy (or Estragon and Vladimir) of this endlessly deceptive landscape, in which each new adventure ends in painful and/or humiliating contact with and recognition of the decidedly prosaic world of Sullivan County. Thus the narrative Sullivan County sketches differ somewhat from Chekhov's hunting stories; in Chekhov a residual sense of the existence of a realm, if not of a traditional sublime pastoral, at least of nature as a zone of value still obtains. The problem for Chekhov is that for the most part we are too trivial in mentality or at least too assimilated to the world of modernity to respond to it appropriately. For Crane, perhaps an even more thorough-going modernist and ironist, once our notion of the natural world is stripped of the inherently false myths in which we have enveloped it, once the light dawns both literally and figuratively, that world is nothing more than the same sort of comic, prosaic, and absurd world as the rest of reality.

Chekhov and Crane thus both use narratives of the hunt and more broadly of nature to dismantle the assumptions of the very narratives that they appropriate, rejecting some of the most powerful myths in their respective cultures concerning both the nature of nature and the nature of our relationship to it. Although perhaps slight in themselves, these early works by both authors not only suggest the orientation of each author's larger project, but also mark a crucial stage in the emergence of a fully modern sensibility in their respective cultures.

# The Sound of Distant Thunder: Chekhov and Chekhovian Subtexts in Tom Stoppard's *The Coast of Utopia*

### Anna Muza, University of California at Berkeley

According to Tom Stoppard, *The Coast of Utopia*, a vast dramatic cycle chronicling the lives of radical Russian intellectuals of the mid-nineteenth century, grew out of a "very abstract desire to write a play in the manner of Chekhov."[1] Talking to the Russian journal *Knizhnoe obozrenie*, Stoppard expressed particular admiration for Chekhov's ability to write "about real people and not about language or anything like that."[2] References to Chekhov's theater form a rich and heterogeneous subtext in Stoppard's trilogy, ranging from direct quotations to suggestive allusions, from the hopeful cry "To Moscow!" to gardens, fishing rods, and foreign governesses to the recurrent "sound of distant thunder," echoing, perhaps, the sound of a broken string. But if the traces of Chekhov's immigration onto the Coast of Utopia are unmistakable, his being there appears to be superfluous to the design and meaning of the dramatic whole. The "real people" who came to inhabit *The Coast of Utopia*, Alexander Herzen, Mikhail Bakunin, Vissarion Belinsky, and others with their militant philosophies and intense and scandalous lives do not invite a Chekhovian treatment; in its epic expanse, historical focus, and direct political engagement Stoppard's work suggests a theatrical lineage going back to Brecht, G. B. Shaw, and even Shakespeare, rather than to the "manner of Chekhov." Moments such as the one when the young Bakunin explains to his father that he has resigned from military service "on grounds of ill health, Papa. I'm sick of the Army" (*Voyage*, 14)[3] also suggest that "language" and Oscar Wilde may have prevailed over "real people" in Stoppard's theater of history.

---

[1] Dominic Cavendish, "The Long Voyage of Sir Tom," *Telegraph*, 29 June 2002, http://www.telegraph.co.uk/ (accessed December 2004). *The Coast of Utopia*, comprised of *Voyage*, *Shipwreck*, and *Salvage*, was originally staged by the National Theatre in London in 2002 in its nine-hour-long entirety.

[2] "Ia ne mechtal sest' v tiur'mu za svoi p'esy," interview conducted by Petr Favorov, *Knizhnoe obozrenie*, http://www.book-review.ru/news/news293.html (accessed December 2004).

[3] All references in the text, given in parentheses, are to *Voyage*, *Shipwreck*, or *Salvage* and page number from Tom Stoppard, *The Coast of Utopia*, 3 vols. (London: Faber and Faber, 2002).

*Chekhov the Immigrant: Translating a Cultural Icon.* Michael C. Finke and Julie de Sherbinin, eds. Bloomington, IN: Slavica Publishers, 2007, 151–62.

wever, Stoppard's use of Chekhov in *The Coast of Utopia* is neither ˛ental nor superfluous but conceptual and consistent. Stoppard en- ˛es, I believe, a paradox implicit in Chekhov's modern condition. Over the ˛urse of a century, Chekhov's characters, images, and situations have ˛ecome a mainstream, proverbial presence in the English-speaking world: Laurence Senelick has compared "the acceptance of Chekhov as a readily recognizable cultural totem" to the "domestication" of Picasso in the overall flattening of the original modernist experiment.[4] At the same time, Chekhov's art has been expanded from the confines of the brooding Russian soul to what Martin Esslin has called an "infinitely ambiguous image of the human condition."[5] Thus, in the twentieth century Chekhov has both lost and gained in depth. I wish to show that Stoppard involves both the "flat" and the "deep" Chekhov in shaping several key themes of *The Coast of Utopia*, and that if the former serves his treatment of art and language, historical authenticity and artistic illusion, the latter informs Stoppard's own ambiguous image of the human condition.

The Chekhovian clue to the opening play of the trilogy, *Voyage*, is so obvious that one British reviewer has renamed it *The Four Sisters*.[6] Here, as elsewhere, Stoppard's pedantic factual accuracy does not prevent him from suffusing his writing with literary reminiscences, and as a result, events of a Russian family chronicle merge into a Chekhovian fantasy. Set for the most part on the Bakunin country estate, *Voyage* has all the trappings of a dear and familiar play from the Chekhov canon, with four sisters and a brother, a Russified German Baron, a garden and a lake, endless philosophizing, and an occasional mention of Pushkin. The Chekhovian potential of the setting and cast of characters is enabled through the patterns of speech and behavior, and Chekhov's characteristic "mood" is emulated by means of sunsets, awkward pauses, and "doleful piano music" (*Voyage*, 28). The family atmosphere is akin to that of *The Three Sisters*, with the conspicuous figure of the Bakunins' father filling in the gap left by the late General Prozorov; but in its tragicomic kaleidoscope of unhappy and misplaced romantic attachments *Voyage* has a deeper affinity with *The Seagull* and its frustrated and mismatched lovers.

Despite the stylistic gap that separates the exclamation "To Moscow!" on Mikhail Bakunin's lips from the more subdued Chekhovian moments in *Voyage*, the play's overall effect depends on the commonplaces of the Chekhov convention. In an early sketch Chekhov drew a parodistic inventory

---

[4] Laurence Senelick, "Chekhov and the Bubble Reputation," in *Chekhov Then and Now. The Reception of Chekhov in World Culture*, ed. J. Douglas Clayton (New York: Peter Lang, 1997), 13.

[5] Martin Esslin, *The Theatre of the Absurd*, 3rd ed. (Harrisburg, VA: Penguin/Pelican Books, 1983), 417.

[6] Jonathan Coall, "Revolutionary Talk," http://www.nationaltheatre.org.uk/?lid=2477 (accessed December 2004).

of "Elements Most Often Found in Novels, Short Stories, Etc.," such as impoverished noblemen, governesses, doctors, butlers in service for generations, impounded estates, heavenly summits, and so on, many of which he subsequently came to use and which have become emblematic of his own writing.[7] Stoppard's use of the elements most often found in Chekhov is both reassuring and disconcerting. On the one hand, the Chekhovian pastiche smoothes the audience's transition to an alien and remote world, and if Stoppard mocks his public's anticipation that a play from Russian life will look and sound like Chekhov, he nevertheless grants his viewers the particular, nostalgic, as well as culturally flattering, pleasure of recognizing the familiar in the unknown. (It is perhaps not unrelated to the effect of that pleasure that several critics have found *Voyage* to be the best play of the trilogy.) On the other hand, however, seeing the "real people" of the 1830s through Chekhov's pince-nez is pointedly anachronistic. Mikhail Bakunin's "To Moscow!" and his sisters' embrace predate *The Three Sisters* by a much more considerable stretch of time than the fourteen years by which the mise-en-scène of *Déjeuner sur l'herbe*, formed by the members of the Herzen household in 1849, anticipates the painting by Manet in *Shipwreck*. The insertion of popular images into the frame of "historical reality" suggests, among other things, a post-modernist "flattening" of history itself, history reduced to recycled, trivial postcards. The entanglement of reality, historical memory, and art has been a central, defining theme of Stoppard's work,[8] and although his project asserts rather than denies the accessibility of history, it also recognizes the blinding force of the familiar and ready-made. Stoppard does not push his irony to the extremes of Woody Allen, who had cheerleaders dance on the battlefield of Borodino in his *Love and Death*, but Chekhov-before-Chekhov does point to the flaws and failures of our vision. Stepping into the prepared, processed words and images, Stoppard's characters expose not their own, but *our* inauthenticity. Thus, somewhat paradoxically, Stoppard uses "Chekhov" both as a familiarizing and estranging device, and undermines the very familiarity of the Chekhov idiom on which he relies.

It is no less paradoxical that while the misplaced "Chekhov" underscores the modernity of *The Coast of Utopia*, Chekhov's theatrical language is also used by Stoppard to impart a timeless and utopian quality to some of his characters and conflicts. Ever since Meyerhold discerned "puppet buffoon-

---

[7] *PssS* 1: 17–18. For the English translation, see *The Undiscovered Chekhov: Thirty-Eight New Stories*, trans. Peter Constantine (New York: Seven Stories Press, 1998), 175–77.

[8] Following the quasi-historical circus of *Travesties* (1974), Stoppard's major plays of the 1990s, *Arcadia* (1993), *Indian Ink* (1994), and *The Invention of Love* (1998), have been devoted to historical figures and circumstances, always presented in a double frame exposing the mechanisms of historical memory and representation.

..der the surface of *The Cherry Orchard*,⁹ Chekhov's continuous reenact-
and critical scrutiny have brought to light the presence of venerable
conventions beneath the "organic flow of life" in his drama, and
realed the features of stock theater types behind his "real people."¹⁰ Stop-
ard endows some of his historical characters with physical properties and
mannerisms that refer them to their Chekhovian prototypes and, ultimately,
theatrical masks. Vissarion Belinsky and the "young philosopher" Nicholas
Stankevich—in their lack of social grace, their clumsiness, and in the disparity
between their lofty visions and human myopia—strongly resemble two characters from *The Cherry Orchard*: the eternal student Petya Trofimov and
Petya's grotesque counterpart, the learned clerk Yepikhodov with his two-
and-twenty misfortunes; they all ultimately merge with the *emploi* of the sad
clown, the suffering yet funny Pierrot. Belinsky enters the stage in *Voyage*
only to immediately fall over his valise and thus introduce himself as a "fool"
(*Voyage*, 29); in similar fashion, Yepikhodov appears on stage with a bouquet
of flowers that he instantly drops. The "flamboyant bathrobe," ill fitting
Belinsky's image, which Stoppard's character suddenly craves in the Parisian
"swamp of bourgeois greed and vulgarity, " becomes an emblematic costume,
a metaphor of the clown's garb (*Shipwreck*, 28). Like nearly all material details
in *The Coast of Utopia*, however minor, the bathrobe has not been invented by
Stoppard but picked out from the historical closet and turned into a larger-
than-life stage prop.¹¹ In its stage function, Belinsky's bathrobe is identical to
Petya's old galoshes, the exaggerated footwear of a clown, which he cannot
find and then pointedly puts on amidst the commotion of general departure
in Act IV. Unlike Petya, however, Belinsky never gets to wear his property
onstage: it is Ivan Turgenev who tries on the bathrobe and thus strips his
ascetic friend's "false" identity through a purely theatrical symbolic exchange
of costume. Turgenev's own clownish trait, shooting at imaginary hunting
targets, replicates Gaev's imaginary game of billiards. Stoppard also associates Turgenev with the characters and motifs of *The Seagull*, the play about art
and artists in which Turgenev himself is a motif.¹² Turgenev's shooting tic lets

---

⁹ Vsevolod Meyerhold, "The Naturalistic Theater and the Theater of Mood," in *Meyerhold on Theater*, trans. and ed. Edward Braun (New York: Hill and Wang, 1969), 28.

¹⁰ "Theatricalization" of Chekhov is amply evidenced and discussed in Laurence Senelick's history of Chekhov performance, *The Chekhov Theatre: A Century of the Plays in Performance* (Cambridge: Cambridge University Press, 1997).

¹¹ The bathrobe is described in some detail by Pavel Annenkov in his *Literaturnye vospominaniia* (Moscow: Sovetskii pisatel', 1989), 349. English translation: *The Extraordinary Decade: Literary Memoirs*, ed. Arthur P. Mendel, trans. Irwin R. Titunik (Ann Arbor, MI: University of Michigan Press, 1968), 232–33.

¹² Explicit references to Turgenev in the play include Trigorin's remarks in Act II about Turgenev as a model imposed on him by the critics, and Nina's recital of a

out his passion for hunting which, though appropriate for the author of *A Sportsman's Sketches*, also corresponds to Trigorin's passion for fishing. In *Salvage*, Turgenev's walking on stage with a gun and firing at birds mirrors Treplev's appearance with a gun and a slain seagull in Act II. In accordance with Chekhov's dictum, the gun fires, and the fact that Turgenev's shooting offstage is mistaken by Natalie Ogaryov for her husband's suicide provides yet another reference to the Treplev theme. Herzen's concluding remark, "It's some kind of dream" (*Salvage*, 70), is identical to Nina's words closing Act II, "It's a dream!"—a happy phrase that follows her long talk with Trigorin in the presence of the dead bird. A host of Chekhovian clues deprives Turgenev of some measure of historical and human reality, and places him among the types of Chekhov's human comedy, a Russian commedia dell'arte. The Chekhovian genealogy of Stoppard's characters compromises their historical origins: "Chekhov" becomes a means of converting history into a performance of history.

Thus Stoppard returns the cosmopolitan and universal Chekhov to his Russian origins only to expose the theatrical artifice of his native and "natural" tongue and to turn the historical setting into a theatrical playground. Situated between Russia and Europe, organic life and artistic form, face and mask, Chekhov functions as a mediator, a translator that allows Stoppard to speak Russian and English at the same time. Translation or conversion is a prominent, symbolic activity on the coast of utopia, where everyone is a link in the Great Chain of Translation, beginning with Herzen's deaf-mute son Kolya, who has to be taught to interpret human speech. Revolutionaries struggle to convert ideas and philosophies into life, lovers live out works of literature, and artists translate life into language and image. In that regard, Chekhov's counterpart or substitute in *The Coast of Utopia* is Turgenev—a real writer and a metaliterary, metaphoric figure that negotiates all kinds of transitions from nature to artifice. One of the very few names in the trilogy familiar to the Western public, Turgenev is duly featured as the author of his best-known works: *A Sportsman's Sketches*, *A Month in the Country* (referred to as a play that "takes place over a month in a house in the country" [*Shipwreck*, 78]), and, of course, *Fathers and Sons*, which he comes to compose after a chance encounter with a young "nihilistic" doctor, the transparent prototype of Bazarov. Stoppard develops Turgenev's mention of the "figure of a young provincial doctor that had struck [him]"[13] into a full episode in order to

---

passage from *Rudin* in her last speech in Act IV. Turgenev's presence in *The Seagull* and in Chekhov's writing and literary consciousness in general was "deconstructed" by Peter M. Bitsilli, *Chekhov's Art: A Stylistic Analysis*, trans. Toby W. Clyman and Edwina. J. Cruise (Ann Arbor, MI: Ardis, 1983), esp. 22–28.

[13] In a piece titled "Apropos of *Fathers and Sons*" ("Po povodu 'Otsov i detei,'" 1869) Turgenev mentions the "remarkable young man" in defending his novel's truthfulness

present Turgenev as an incisive artist observing and capturing life. Turgenev's main quality as a writer in *The Coast of Utopia* is his detached objectivity which confounds his contemporaries: to the question "who wins" in the romantic rivalry in *A Month in the Country*, the author replies, "No one, of course" (*Shipwreck*, 78); and to a revolutionary inquiring, "So you don't take sides between the fathers and the children?" he responds, "On the contrary, I take every possible side" (*Salvage*, 96). Turgenev's "clear, finely discriminating, slightly ironical vision" was championed by Isaiah Berlin in his *Russian Thinkers*, a major source for, and influence on, Stoppard's work;[14] but in turning his Turgenev into an "observer without illusion" Stoppard has emphasized and enlarged a feature most immediately and commonly associated, in Russian letters, with Chekhov. Turgenev's literary self-appraisal, "People complain about me having no attitude in my stories. They're puzzled. Do I approve or disapprove? Do I want the reader to agree with this man or that man?" (*Shipwreck*, 24) "anticipates" Chekhov, as does his play about "a month in the country."[15] In an essay titled "The Influence of Dostoevsky and Chekhov on Turgenev's *Fathers and Sons*," Donald Fanger has argued that Turgenev's "gift of a dispassionate and penetrating observer" is "one that we perceive, inevitably, through the prism of Chekhov," and that Berlin's reading of Turgenev's "truthful genius" had been equally shaped by Chekhov.[16] As an impartial Chekhovian artist Turgenev greatly appeals to Stoppard, who nevertheless also places him in grotesque situations that ridicule and undermine the very idea of art's truthfulness to life. In the complicated mise-en-scène based on *Déjeuner sur l'herbe*, Turgenev appears as the painter: he "is at first glance sketching Natalie but in fact sketching Emma" (*Shipwreck*, 74). A painting-within-a-painting-within-a-play, Turgenev's sketch reflects the illusory nature of all experience. The artist's ambition as an interpreter of life is emptied of all meaning in Turgenev's effort at providing Karl Marx with the best translation, into English, of his "ghost of Communism." In addition to various political connotations of the disembodied sig-

---

to Russian reality. Quoted from Ivan Turgenev, *Fathers and Sons*, trans. Michael R. Katz (New York: W. W. Norton and Company, 1996), 161.

[14] Isaiah Berlin, "Fathers and Children," in his *Russian Thinkers* (New York: The Viking Press, 1978), 293. In his acknowledgements, Stoppard calls Berlin "one of the two authors without whom [he] could not have written these plays" (the other one being E. H. Carr).

[15] The view of *A Month in the Country* as a major predecessor of Chekhov's drama has by now become standard, but it is curious to note that in 1926, having seen its first English staging (by Tyrone Guthrie), Constance Garnett's son David wrote to his mother: "It is as good as Tchehov and it is extraordinarily like Tchehov in its dramatic method." Quoted in: Richard Garnett, *Constance Garnett. A Heroic Life* (London: Sinclair-Stevenson, 1991), 337.

[16] Donald Fanger, "The Influence of Dostoevsky and Chekhov on Turgenev's *Fathers and Sons*," in Turgenev, *Fathers and Sons*, 328.

nified, the Russian writer's struggle with English "spirits" and "spooks" mirrors Stoppard's own chase after the phantoms of Russian history (*Shipwreck*, 40–44). In *Salvage* Turgenev the hunter is impatient to test his new shotgun and, for the lack of "any birds of prey in Fulham," he shoots at a boy's kite (*Salvage*, 70). The substitution of a bird by a kite, of the "real thing" by an artificial likeness is emblematic of the artist's trade. Turgenev cannot find a bird and misses the kite, as he misses the right word in his translation of the "ghost of Communism," finally settling on "hobgoblin." Comprising historical, literary, and symbolic identities, Turgenev's protean character changes with the shifts in the viewer's perspective: it seems that Stoppard is sketching Turgenev but he is in fact sketching Chekhov or Trigorin or his own self-portrait. In *The Coast of Utopia* "Turgenev" is a topos of Chekhov's and Stoppard's convergence.

Referring to Chekhov and his characters, Stoppard's Turgenev also refers to himself as a motif in Chekhov's drama. This tour-de-force application of Borges's idea about the writer as a creator of his precursors has a larger relevance to Stoppard's own literary strategies.[17] Unlike Shakespeare and other authors often evoked in Chekhov's drama, Turgenev still remains a "real" figure from a recent past: Professor Serebryakov in *Uncle Vanya* can recall Turgenev's gout, and Trigorin in *The Seagull* cites the unflattering comparison, "A good writer, but Turgenev was better,"[18] all of this enhancing the "reality" of the fictional characters. At the same time, "Turgenev" has already become a figure of speech, a "readily recognizable cultural totem." Trigorin's self-epitaph bears traces of Chekhov's own frustration with the critical commonplace, and Astrov in *Uncle Vanya* uses a Turgenev cliché trying to persuade Yelena to give herself to him "here, in the lap of nature": "Here there is the plantation, the dilapidated country houses in the style of Turgenev...."[19] Astrov's use of "Turgenev" as a panderer is extremely cheap (*poshlyi*), but in a larger context the reference acknowledges the style of Turgenev in Chekhov's own play about a month in the country. Turgenev's dual status in Chekhov's world is similar to Chekhov's role in Stoppard's. As a ready-made sign, Chekhov is available to all, and in reproducing the utmost cliché of the Chekhov vocabulary the anarchist Mikhail Bakunin exposes himself as a conformist. Stoppard relies on Chekhov as a dramatic idiom, a well-defined discourse that can be used to reveal rather than conceal the mechanisms of art and representation.

Yet the Chekhovian signs and symbols on the map of *The Coast of Utopia* also point to a different kind of Chekhov presence in Stoppard's concept—not

---

[17] Jorge Luis Borges, "Kafka and his Precursors," in *Labyrinths: Selected Stories and Other Writings*, ed. Donald A. Yates and James E. Irby (New York: New Direction Publishing, 1964), 199.

[18] *Chekhov: The Major Plays*, trans. Ann Dunnigan (New York: Signet, 1964), 135.

[19] Ibid., 225.

as a strategy but as an inherent influence. The debate that lies at the core of the trilogy concerns historical teleology, progress, and the meaning of collective and personal happiness; Alexander Herzen, Stoppard's ironic "modern" hero, comes to renounce any purposefulness in the march of nature and history: "There is no libretto! History knocks at a thousand gates at every moment, and the gatekeeper is chance" (*Salvage*, 118). However, life as it unfolds on the coast of utopia over the span of thirty-five years suggests a more ambivalent and unsettling view of it than does any theoretical scheme, including Herzen's. Enacting the failure of human intellect against the oddity of life Stoppard creates a variation on a quintessential Chekhovian theme, and appeals to Chekhov as a playwright who has found a dramatic form for the elusive and strange in human experience.

Writing at a time when Chekhov was being created as a forerunner of the Absurdists, Charles B. Timmer has distinguished Chekhov's unique blend of hope and despair, and associated his belief that life is neither intelligible nor absurd with the technique of the "bizarre": "a statement, or a situation, which has no logical place in the context or in the sequence of events," a "playful, whimsical strangeness."[20] Timmer's apt term may be applied to coincidences, repetitions, and various peculiar events in Chekhov's drama that present a challenge to rationalization of experience. Situated on the borderline between necessity and chance, bizarre correspondences tease human beings with an insight into the hidden order of things, which, however, can never be identified with certainty. Preoccupied with the future, Chekhov's characters perpetually reenact the past, and live out the eternal return in all of its literal and metaphoric modes, from homecoming to nostalgia and reminiscence. This "retrogressive" quality has mostly been seen as a token of a particular weakness of the Chekhovian people unable to confront the unknown. In his seminal essay on *The Seagull*, Robert Louis Jackson has written about the failure on the part of Treplev and other Chekhov characters to relinquish their "golden childhood and the dream of innocence before the bitter necessity of knowing reality."[21] However, the Return may equally suggest a pattern of fate in which the future becomes but a mirror-image of the past: thus, even Treplev's suicide closing *The Seagull* is only a repetition of an earlier event. But when the events appear fateful and predetermined, a bizarre incident thwarts the march of destiny: in what is an exact reversal of the tragic action in *The Cherry Orchard*, Simeonov-Pishchik is rescued from financial ruin by deus-ex-machina Englishmen. Chekhov's characters are sensitive to what they see as messages of fate, to omens, games of chance, and uncanny sounds,

---

[20] Charles B. Timmer, "The Bizarre Element in Chekhov's Art," in *Anton Čechov*, ed. T. Eekman (Leiden: E. J. Brill, 1960), 278.

[21] Robert Louis Jackson, "The Empty Well, the Dry Lake, and the Cold Cave," in *Chekhov: A Collection of Critical Essays*, ed. Robert Louis Jackson (Englewood Cliffs, NJ: Prentice Hall, 1967), 111.

but they often fail to notice, or are denied access to, the actual events and connections that shape their lives. Contrary to a major convention of the Western theater, Chekhov's drama does not rely on the discovery of a hidden secret: if there is a secret in Chekhov, its bizarre effect is that it rests undiscovered. In *Uncle Vanya*, Sonya, relying on Yelena's advice and help in her love for Astrov, remains ignorant of the mutual attraction between her stepmother and Astrov, and of the idealized Astrov's active interest in another man's wife. Yelena's husband also remains blissfully unaware of the double courtship that threatens his marriage. The Professor's concluding remark, "After all that's happened, I've lived through so much and turned over so many things in my mind these last few hours, I believe that I could write an entire treatise on how people ought to live for the edification of prosperity,"[22] is particularly ironic in this context, as his conceited readiness to explain away life rests on a limited access to "all that's happened." In *The Seagull*, it is the play's central image that escapes the understanding of its characters. Scholars have commented on the inherent ambiguity of the seagull's progress from an "ethereal creature" to a "stuffed bird,"[23] yet it has hardly been noticed that the three co-authors of the image—Treplev, Trigorin, and Nina—have an incomplete knowledge of their respective contributions. Trigorin does not know that Treplev has killed the gull as a portent of his suicide ("Soon, in the same way, I shall kill myself"[24]); Treplev never learns of Trigorin's sketch of a short story and never understands Nina's subsequent identification with the seagull; Nina does not know of the stuffed bird or of the (famous) lapse of Trigorin's memory. No one will learn of Nina's visit to Treplev, preceding and partly prompting his suicide, nor that the suicide turns the stuffed seagull into a *memento mori*. In other words, the seagull continues to haunt the three artists, none of whom is capable of forming a whole picture out of isolated images. The rest of the characters hear of the bird's existence for the first and last time from Shamraev and appear to be too busy with their game of lotto to pay any attention. Unlike the characters of, for example, *The Cherry Orchard*, all of them would be very surprised to see it in the title of a play about their lives. The only omniscient mind that can endow the seagull with some overarching significance is that of the audience—provided that, unlike Trigorin, it keeps track of its metamorphoses.

In *The Coast of Utopia* Stoppard creates a zone or a current of the bizarre whose meaning in the dramatic whole is similar to its implications in Chekhov. Stoppard materializes the Chekhovian connection in a small object lifted from the three sisters' living room and planted in Herzen's apartment in

---

[22] Dunnigan, *Chekhov: The Major Plays*, 92.

[23] Ellen Chances, "Chekhov's Seagull: Ethereal Creature or Stuffed Bird?" in *Chekhov's Art of Writing: A Collection of Critical Essays*, ed. Paul Debreczeny and Thomas Eekman (Columbus, OH: Slavica Publishers, 1977), 27–34.

[24] Dunnigan, *Chekhov: The Major Plays*, 24.

Paris. In a long episode placed in the center of *Shipwreck* and thus of the entire trilogy, Herzen's deaf-mute son Kolya plays with a spinning top, which he then leaves on the floor. The next figure we find, "on his knees on the floor," is Belinsky, attracted by "some small flat wooden shapes, one of the toys" (*Shipwreck*, 36). Racking his brains over a children's puzzle, Belinsky attempts to make a square of what is designed to form a circle. In *The Three Sisters*, the top is a gift from Fedotik that delights Irina on her saint's day, and its demonstration prompts Masha's recital of Pushkin's lines about the tomcat going round and round the oak on his golden chain, although she herself fails to see the connection ("Why on earth do I keep saying this?"[25]). A token of lost childhood, and of time's irreversible yet circular motion, the top is a Chekhovian object par excellence that could be cherished by many Chekhov characters; in his magisterial staging of *The Cherry Orchard* in 1974, Giorgio Strehler has placed it in Gaev's and Ranevskaya's old nursery, and its spinning accompanied their return home.[26] In Stoppard, the flat circle against the full-bodied spinning top seems to spell the eternal return as the answer to life's puzzle—or, perhaps, it parodies the idea of an answer.

The long episode, broken into two by a leap into the next year's events, concludes with Kolya's returning and playing with his top. The silent child's connection with the spinning toy has a mysterious, mystical overtone. The deaf-mute boy isolated from human exchanges serves as a common denominator for all characters in their failures of judgment and understanding; yet in his serene poise he also seems to know something that others fail to grasp. His accidental, absurd death in a shipwreck is the last argument for Herzen's revolt against the Great Purpose: "Where is the unity, the meaning, of nature's highest creation? ... If we can't arrange our own happiness, it's a conceit beyond vulgarity to arrange the happiness of those who come after us" (*Shipwreck*, 100). However, Kolya's death is associated with a bizarre detail, belonging perhaps in an underlying design that Herzen fails to see—just like Belinsky fails to see the circle in the pieces of the puzzle. Kolya's body is never found, but the sea returns to his father his glove, which "for some reason," Herzen says, "was in his grandmother's maid's pocket," and the maid was rescued (*Salvage*, 56). Having found the glove in *My Past and Thoughts*,[27] Stoppard provides it with a stage history. The news of Kolya's death in 1851 comes in one of the last episodes of *Shipwreck*, and the glove is mentioned much later, halfway through *Salvage*, as a funeral that Herzen attends in 1857 stirs the image of his unburied child. However, in an intimate family scene that opens *Salvage*, the maid who looks after Herzen's daughters

---

[25] Ibid., 118.

[26] On Strehler's production see Senelick, *The Chekhov Theatre*, 267–72.

[27] Herzen mentions the glove in his account of the shipwreck in "A Family Drama," see *My Past and Thoughts: The Memoirs of Alexander Herzen*, trans. Constance Garnett (New York: Alfred A. Knopf, 1925), 4: 74.

makes a passing remark about Tata Herzen's having dropped a glove. Immediately following this the maid announces, "Oh, look, it's in my pocket!" (*Salvage*, 4), which, with its inscribed theatrical gesture ("Oh, look!"), brings the tiny object to the audience's attention and replays, uncannily, the incident that has already happened but is going to be revealed much later. Similarly, the remark of Herzen's absent-minded friend Worcell leaving his home, "I seem to be a glove short," has an uncanny overtone evident at the moment only to the startled Herzen: "A glove...?" (*Salvage*, 42). The next time Worcell's name comes up, two episodes later, at his funeral, and it is at this funeral that Herzen speaks of the glove to Natalie Ogaryov, who has recently returned from Russia and who is going to take the place of Herzen's deceased wife. A child's glove, like a child's puzzle, seems to contain a clue to the mystery of departures and returns, yet it may equally be empty of any meaning, signifying nothing.

The glove has a counterpart in the first play of the trilogy: Belinsky's penknife. (Although this may seem forced, I ought to mention that a little penknife is another charming gift Chekhov's Irina receives from Fedotik in *Three Sisters*.) Having fallen out of Belinsky's pocket in Moscow, the penknife is found by Lyubov Bakunin, who misattributes it to her beloved Stankevich. Upon discovering her mistake, the girl throws the false remembrance into a fishpond. The penknife returns to the astonished Belinsky, who happens to visit the Bakunins on their estate, in the belly of a carp fished out of the pond. Belinsky gives the incident a philosophical reading: "Lost objects from another life are restored to you in the belly of a carp," and eventually gives the penknife to his illiterate mistress. The miniature *Ding an sich* travesties the characters' current obsession with German philosophy, but its main function is to return, in a darker vein, in *Salvage*. The tragedy of the glove repeats the farce of the penknife with a complete coincidence of detail: the pocket, the loss, the water, the messenger, and the return. Both objects seem to bring from the hidden depths an intimation of life's secret. The odd pattern of coincidences, substitutions, and returns mirrors one of the main dramas of Herzen's life: his involvement in two love triangles with two women bearing the name of Natalie, first as a husband betrayed by a close friend, then as a lover of his best friend's wife. Contrary to Herzen's multi-dimensional image of a thousand gates, life seems to be driven by a circular force trapping human beings in its spin.

*The Coast of Utopia* ends with a thunderstorm breaking over Herzen's family circle as it looks in 1868. The thunder greeted by "cheerful responses of fright" concludes the cycle on an invigorating, optimistic note: the lightning finds an earthly counterpart in Mikhail Bakunin's cigarette denoting, for him, one of the seven degrees of human happiness; the joyful presence of Herzen's small daughter Liza inspires hope in the elemental forces of life (*Salvage*, 119). The thundering heavens may bring to mind the sound of a breaking string "that seems to come from the sky," but the tenor of the Herzen family gathering has little affinity with the restrained, melancholy (if not mournful) closures of Chekhov's plays. However, like the sound of a broken string, the thunder over the heads of the utopians is, above all else, self-referential: it alludes to its earlier occurrences, which can now be remembered only by the audience. In Chekhov, the characters that have been frightened by the odd sound are no longer there to hear it, and it has no effect on the deaf and dying Firs. In Stoppard, the recurring sound of distant thunder has been always associated with Kolya: one of the few sounds he was able to discern in the surrounding world, it has been his stage property, which, like his glove, stays on after his death. Thus in their last moments, both plays denote an absence and a return, but it is only the audience's memory that can make the connection: otherwise, Kolya may be forgotten like Firs. The bizarre patterns of existence are not visible to those who live them out, but even if granted an aerial view of their network, we hesitate to interpret them with confidence. Having followed "homeless wanderers" in their Shakespearean passions, Brechtian reasoning, and purely Stoppardian wit, one is moved to conclude, uncertainly, "If only we knew… If only we knew…"

# Chekhov and American Writing

# My Chekhov

## James McConkey, Cornell University

Eudora Welty became my friend through our mutual admiration of Anton Chekhov. Through the years, we had only one disagreement. It came during a visit my wife and I made to her home in Jackson, Mississippi. V. S. Pritchett's book on Chekhov had recently been published. Eudora valued her friendship with Pritchett, whose stories she had long admired. She told me that she had liked his book very much. If I had read it, didn't I think it a fine achievement, too? I said I had read it, but No, I hadn't liked it: the Chekhov that Pritchett responded to wasn't *my* Chekhov. My respect for both Chekhov and Eudora Welty has something to do with the integrity that marks their lives as well as their work; maybe I was trying to emulate them by being truthful here. But the quickness of my response, and the feelings the question had aroused, surprised me. I had found Pritchett's method of understanding Chekhov's life through his stories a congenial one, and maybe I felt it a personal affront that Pritchett, often using stories I particularly liked, had made of them something foreign to my own reading of them. To me, Chekhov's stories have a spiritual dimension that Pritchett never acknowledges. Surely a reader as perceptive as Eudora should have qualified her praise!

Such differences in opinion can never be satisfactorily resolved. Friends must accept the differences, knowing they retain much else in common. And yet much later I felt vindicated for disagreeing so strongly with Eudora when another friend Chekhov gave me—Simon Karlinsky, the well-known Slavic Studies scholar—told me that Pritchett's reputation in England, however well-deserved, was so pervasive that his misleading book on Chekhov had set back English studies on him for at least a decade. I am being so open about my feelings—which are as liable to error as anybody else's—because subjectivity of that sort about Chekhov is common among his admirers: each of us has her or his personal Chekhov. It proves how close he still is to us today.

Chekhov's insight into individual human beings encompasses, but passes no apparent judgment upon, all such differences. Welty's marvelous essay on Chekhov, "Reality in Chekhov's Stories," which was written as the concluding lecture of a Chekhov festival I organized at Cornell more than twenty-five years ago, is a commentary on this major aspect of his work. Here's one sentence from that essay: "Chekhov's perception of our differing views of reality, with its capacity to understand them all, may have done more than anything else to bring about his revolutionizing of the short story."[1] The observation, so typical of Welty's own creative abilities, delights me—it takes two of the most obvious characteristics of Chekhov's work, and demonstrates the linkage between them.

Today, the subjectivity of memory is an acknowledged fact, one easily proved. Memory may represent truth to each of us, but that truth is prone to fallacies both large and small. And yet our sense of reality, which we take for granted at each moment of our lives, comes entirely from memory. Our personal and collective memories hold the history of what has happened since Chekhov lived, and we're apt to be far more skeptical about the human future than he—an optimist in this regard. But his awareness that reality is anything but an absolute has much to do with his relevance to us today. Welty goes on to say, "What is real in life—and what a Chekhov story was made to reflect with the utmost honesty—may be at the same time what is transient, ephemeral, contradictory, even on the point of vanishing before our very eyes. So it isn't just *there*."[2] She illuminates this insight through specific examples of character behavior; for, like Chekhov, Welty knows the importance of details.

Doesn't the actual Chekhov—the human being who wrote the stories and plays—seem to elude us, as we read his words or attend a performance? That elusiveness is often attributed to his objectivity. He says that as a writer he can only pose questions; any answers belong to the jury—to his readers. Given that the elusive, shifting nature of reality is the basis of characterizations by a writer who would make us the jury, it is no surprise that each of us cherishes his or her own Chekhov.

I'll end with a brief mention of *my* Chekhov. I don't think he's been an influence on the style or subject of my writing; rather, he appeals to, and supports, something deep within my psyche. His influence comes from my sense of spiritual kinship with him—a kinship that simply couldn't exist if he were a purely objective writer. He's certainly not detached in the manner of the ideal scientist. If Chekhov were completely objective, we wouldn't respond to what Irving Howe has called his "dispassionate sympathy." (That's another way of describing his "compassionate irony," the subject of another fine essay at the Cornell festival by Ralph Lindheim.[3]) Nor would such an objective observer of our human dilemmas possess Chekhov's moral awareness of the injustices we inflict on others as well as the hurt we inflict on ourselves.

---

[1] Eudora Welty, "Reality in Chekhov's Stories," in *Chekhov and Our Age: Responses to Chekhov by American Writers and Scholars*, ed. James McConkey (Ithaca, NY: Center for International Studies, Council of the Creative and Performing Arts, Cornell University, 1984), 104.

[2] Welty, "Reality," 105.

[3] Ralph Lindheim, "Chekhov's Compassionate Irony in 'Neighbors,'" in *Chekhov and Our Age*, 213–36.

Actually, I find Chekhov's presence, or voice, to be everywhere in his work; and the greatest influence that presence had on me came while I was in Italy, trying to recover from the one period of my life in which I experienced spiritual paralysis—the result of my helplessness to resolve a bitter racial conflict at Cornell during the Vietnam War, for I was involved almost from that conflict's beginning in the attempts at reconciliation. My gratitude for Chekhov's assistance in preventing a possible breakdown is expressed as well as I can say it in *To a Distant Island*, a narrative which uses every resource available to me to explore the reasons for the greatest adventure of Chekhov's life, his arduous trip across Siberia to interview the convicts and their families at the remote penal colony on Sakhalin Island. Above all else, *To a Distant Island* represents my major attempt to capture his elusive voice.[4]

Why did Chekhov undertake such a trip? The motives he gave to others are contradictory. Alienated and nearing a breakdown himself, he seems to have wanted escape—escape both from himself and the society he now found so imprisoning. In my view—it is based on his letters and his book on Sakhalin as well as his stories—he was in search of "the most absolute freedom imaginable" that he once said was merely his wish. (Modified or not, "absolute" is a word seldom in his vocabulary.) Amid the suffering of those undergoing the hardships and harsh discipline of a lifetime in exile, he discovered that the convicts and other unwilling inhabitants wanted nothing more than the same freedom, which they identified with the Russia from which he had just fled. That kind of freedom is always to be found somewhere else. The knowledge of what he shared with the most hardened and illiterate person saved him from himself, and returned him to society as an even better writer: the evidence of that is apparent in "Gusev," the story he wrote aboard a ship on his homeward journey, and the work that follows it. From Chekhov I discovered what I must have known without thinking I knew: that the part of my mind I consider my soul is, like the mind itself, a quality—a spiritual desire that would vanish along with my very being if ever it were granted me. The extraordinarily evocative conclusion of "Gusev" makes this story a masterpiece; and it implies, I think, a similar knowledge.

For me, the desire for a freedom beyond anybody's attainment—not here, not yet—underlies Chekhov's voice, and is the source of the particular kind of compassion and moral awareness we find in his work. It also helps to explain his desire for objectivity. I am grateful that he never achieved either of them.

---

[4] James McConkey, *To a Distant Island* (Philadelphia: Paul Dry Books, 2000; repr., New York: E. P. Dutton, 1984).

# Chekhov and Aspiring Writers

## Claire Messud, Writer

Some years ago, when I was teaching creative writing to junior and senior undergraduate English literature majors at the University of Maryland, I assigned them "Ward 6" to read. This was early in the semester, and we were only just "getting acquainted," as one might say, and while I was aware that this story might prove a challenge for them, I was nevertheless naïve. On the day we were to discuss the story, I thought it relevant, first of all, to put Chekhov, however broadly, in context.

"What can you tell me about Chekhov?" I asked.

There was a long silence. A single, wavering hand was raised. "My husband says he's Russian," offered a young woman with a hesitant voice.

"Yes, indeed. And what has he written?" I asked.

There was a still longer silence.

"Has anyone come across his plays?" Surely this would raise a response: after all, in the English speaking world, Chekhov's plays are more performed than those of any other playwright besides Shakespeare.

Silence.

"Okay, let's begin at the beginning. Is he alive or dead?"

In answer to which, my friends, there was still nothing but silence. The joke has subsequently been made that my students were flummoxed by the seriousness of my intent: the answer to that question indeed depends on how you mean it. Literarily, of course, if not literally, Chekhov is more alive than most. He who said wistfully to Bunin that he would be read for only seven years would have been amused, doubtless, by the anecdote. By my naïve certainty that he, of all authors, would be known to aspiring short-story writers. By the bovine indifference of the students, whose primary interest was in their own deathless prose. By my prim shock at their ignorance. By the underlying, undeniable fact that he, of all authors, *should* be known to aspiring short story writers; and that, indeed, even if only indirectly, he always already is. To know the work of Welty, or Cheever, or Carver, or Penelope Fitzgerald, or Alice Munro is to know the influence of Chekhov. To take almost any creative writing workshop is to be raised upon Chekhov's literary philosophy. To have any understanding of the form of the contemporary short story is to have internalized Chekhov's principles.

Eventually, I managed to prise from one student only—and she one of my strongest—an opinion about "Ward 6": "It was really long, and kind of

*Chekhov the Immigrant: Translating a Cultural Icon.* Michael C. Finke and Julie de Sherbinin, eds. Bloomington, IN: Slavica Publishers, 2007, 169–75.

confusing, and a little bit slow?" Which might have satisfied Chekhov, of course, as a succinct assessment of life itself. And writing life as it is—in its fantasies, pettinesses, grandeur, tedium, and confusion; as clearly and dispassionately as possible—this was his enterprise.

To trace the influence of Chekhov on contemporary fiction is like searching for the original cutting from which a vast plant has grown. Precisely because he produced so many stories and such a variety of them, a wide and disparate range of traits can be deemed Chekhovian. (Even while he, who abhorred labels and categorizations, would shake his head in dismay at the irony of this.) He can almost be all things to all people. Limning the threshold of modernism while still making use of traditional techniques and, in his early pieces, of elements of folk tale, he can be found, if you look, in everything from the dirtiest realism to its most magical outposts (what is the ending of "Gusev" if not a flight of magical realism, in its best sense?) He can be hailed as an optimist or a pessimist; as a master of the shortest story, or of the longest. A natural storyteller. A natural playwright. A natural. His precepts, tidily summarized, provide the basis of much of the "teaching" of creative writing that occurs in this country today: show, don't tell; make every word count; don't take sides; write about simple things. A tireless advocate of simplicity, he was wise in his advice; and if only the students listened, those of us who teach creative writing frequently tell ourselves, we wouldn't have to read so many disastrous and deadly stories.

But the students have listened, as the short stories emanating from writing programs over the past twenty-five years amply illustrate. They have listened carefully, and whether in direct homage to Chekhov or through the filter of one of his many literary descendants, they have attempted to reproduce the same quotidian, unexplosive, deceptively casually structured fictions which are, we have all learned, the stuff of life. (As he said to Gorky: "Why write about a man getting into a submarine and going to the North Pole to reconcile himself with the world, while his beloved at that moment throws herself with a hysterical shriek from the belfry? All this is untrue and does not happen in reality. One must write about simple things: how Peter Semyonovich married Maria Ivanovna. That is all.")

The result of so much careful listening, of such religious study, of such heartfelt reverence for Chekhov and his work, is a mountain of the mundane, a vast sea of undifferentiated stories: pages upon pages of fiction that is simple, precise, clear, honest, and terribly, painfully, unmemorably dull. Stories set in supermarkets, around the dinner table, at class reunions, at family reunions, stories set at the beach, stories set in diners, in the woods, in boats, in fields, in wars, in the office, stories upon stories with nothing wrong with them, and nothing distinguishably right.

In consequence, over the past decade, there has been a rebellion: the novel, at least, has seen a vigorous turning away from so-called Chekhovian principles. The burst of focused energy around the short story form in the

'70s, '80s, and early '90s has dissipated (and by this I mean the explosion of writers who wonderfully peopled Bill Buford's *Granta* in its early days: Ray Carver, Richard Ford, Tobias Wolff, Joy Williams, and so on), and young writers gravitate increasingly towards the novel, an arena in which the equivalent of a man getting into a submarine and going to the North Pole has become commonplace. The exuberance of what James here has dubbed "hysterical realism" has great appeal—think of Zadie Smith, of Jonathan Franzen, of Aleksander Hemon, of Dave Eggers and Richard Powers and Jeffrey Eugenides—and it seems, in its jaunty madness, to capture the frenetic, unreflective spirit of our digital age. (There is an attendant discussion to be had, not here, not now, about the relationship of the marketplace to this type of fiction. More money is spent on "big" books than ever before; and I somehow can't imagine a publisher leaping to spend a fortune on a big, quiet, Chekhovian book. Interestingly, also, I'd note that at the time of the last Chekhov conference organized by Mr. McConkey, in the late '70s, the Master was also out of vogue: Pynchon superceded Hemingway, in that time. But the pendulum swings; and what is humanly true abides, regardless. In this sense, the vagaries of fashion may be of interest, but are irrelevant. Certainly Chekhov himself would have remained calmly detached therefrom.)

Gorky recalled that "in Anton Chekhov's presence everyone involuntarily felt in himself a desire to be simpler, more truthful, more oneself; I often saw how people cast off the motley finery of bookish phrases, smart words, and all the other cheap tricks with which a Russian, wishing to figure as a European, adorns himself, like a savage with shells and fish's teeth. Anton Chekhov disliked fish's teeth and cock's feathers; anything 'brilliant' or foreign, assumed by a man to make himself look bigger, disturbed him...." In this sense, we are living in a literary moment of fish's teeth and cock's feathers; and this at least in part in reaction precisely to the humble quiet and restraint of the short fiction of the '80s and early '90s, a fiction written in the name, and in the shadow, of Chekhov. (Think, of course, of Carver's late story "Errand," about Chekhov's death, fiction toying with biography, not merely in substance but in style, a piece the very story-ness of which is open to discussion: few fictional allegiances are so powerfully and openly reaffirmed.)

But that was a literary generation ago; and for the time being, between the mountain of the mundane and the flash of fish's teeth, readers have, by and large, chosen the flash. Dismayingly, and perhaps inevitably, this has coincided with, and perhaps directly stemmed from, a turning away from the supreme importance of character in fiction. That, for this reader, is Chekhov's most abiding legacy. As Eudora Welty wrote, in her splendid essay on "Reality in Chekhov's Stories," "In the whole population of Chekhov's characters, every single one, the least, the smallest, the youngest, the most obscure, has its clear identity. No life is too brief or too inconsequential for him to be inattentive to its own reality." And, as Gorky recalled, "No one understood as clearly and finely as Anton Chekhov the tragedy of life's trivialities, no one before him showed men with such merciless truth the terrible and shameful picture of their life in the dim chaos of bourgeois everyday existence."

Gorky doesn't mention Chekhov's humility, which is salient here. He wrote, in 1888, to Suvorin:

> It's time for writers, especially writers of real artistic worth, to realize, just as Socrates realized in his time and Voltaire in his, that in fact nothing can be understood in this world. The crowd thinks it knows and understands everything; and the stupider it is, the broader the compass of its perceived horizons. But if writers whom the public trusts could only bring themselves to admit that they understand nothing of what they see, that would be a great advance in the realm of thought, a great step forward.

Nor does he mention Chekhov's humor. But Welty does: "Chekhov showed us the implacable facts of existence, the illusions, the deceptions, the mystery, the identity, that reality variously stood for among many characters. How did he, himself, see it? What but the comic vision could accommodate so much, bring it all in? What other frame is generous enough? I think of that vision as an outreach of this artist's compassion—the careful attention to the human scale, a keeping to human proportions. It is the artist's deference, a kind of modesty, a form of ultimate respect, a reverence, for all living things."

For this reader, the joy of reading Chekhov lies in the clarity of that vision, in his knowledge—unadulterated by any ulterior agenda—of what each of his characters will notice, or think, or do. He does not presume to posit the significance of these gestures; but simply in observing them most precisely, he reveals his wisdom. Characters in fiction may be more knowable than in reality; but they must, in order to be true, react in ways that are simultaneously surprising and inevitable. One small example would be when young Yegorushka, in "The Steppe," rejoins his uncle Kuzmichov and Father Christopher after crossing the steppe in the company of the carters and their wagon train: "On first seeing his own people, the boy felt an irresistible urge to complain." This detail sums up the great complex of emotions that he feels: relief at being rejoined to them; resentment at his abandonment; pride at having survived the test; a childish need to be cared for and attended to; a need to maintain his dignity in spite of this; a desire to be heard, somehow to convey all that he has experienced which they will never know; and, of course, exhaustion plain and simple. It is the detail which alerts us to how well Chekhov knows *this* boy, and boyhood, and this boy in the face of *these* men, who are his guardians but not his parents. With his mother, would he not, perhaps, simply cry? And with his father, perhaps, lash out? To desire to complain is a response specific not only to the boy but to his circumstances, to the situation's dynamics of power and pride. A single Chekhovian detail about Yegorushka does more to characterize him than do pages of description from a lesser writer.

Chekhov is similarly effective in his comedy. His is not a broad comedy of situation, nor is it farce. His is the subtle comedy of the everyday, the small tragicomic ironies that are often internal, invisible. (Let it be said that if his disciples could learn and emulate his wit—but that, alas, is most singular—then those endless workshop stories would never be dull.) Again, significance lies in his use of details. In the town known only for the lay-reader who ate all the caviar at the funeral in "In the Ravine"; in the pickled mushroom waved by the priest in the same story; in the pony that tries to bite Gusev as he walks, for the last time, along the ship's deck; in the smell of fish that supplants Gurov's revelation of love in "The Lady with the Little Dog." Or indeed, from the notebooks, in the sentence, "The dog ran through the street and was ashamed of its crooked legs." In the way, as Gorky saw it, "His enemy was banality; he fought it all his life long; he ridiculed it, drawing it with a pointed and unimpassioned pen...." He fought it by seeing it, and taking note of it. He, one of Russia's great artists, whose corpse was returned home from Germany in a railway truck marked "for the conveyance of oysters."

This genius for the telling detail, for the wryly surprising, is perhaps Chekhov's greatest gift. For telling the world as it is, glorious, splendid, passionate, appalling, shabby, small, brutal, lonely, but always—even in death—fully alive. Welty carefully and rightly explores that which is so important in Chekhov's work, hand in hand with character: the question of reality, and what it is, for any given individual. This, surely, remains more broadly one of life's central issues; thereon hangs the question of what life *is*, or might be. The role of imagination, fantasy, subjective impression, the juxtapositions of the external world and the interior eye... endlessly fascinating, strangely simple, and the stuff of highest art.

As a writer now nearing middle age, I am drawn, in this regard, to Chekhov's great story, "The Black Monk," which—for all it features a whirling hallucination—seems to me one of the most accurate representations I have read of the individual's desire for greatness, for meaning, the illusion of its possibility, and the inevitable frustration of that illusion. Andrey Vassilyich Kovrin, a scholar on the edge of a nervous breakdown, goes to stay with his former guardian Pesotsky, the renowned horticulturalist, and his daughter Tanya on their luxuriant estate, where they "drank tea from old porcelain cups, with cream and thick pastries, and these small things again reminded Kovrin of his childhood and youth. The glorious present was fusing with the impressions of the past awakening in him; it was all rather overwhelming, but he felt good." While there, he first encounters the black monk, a vision from mysterious legend. He *knows* that he has conjured the monk; but he does not care: "'So you don't exist?' asked Kovrin. 'Think what you like,' said the monk, smiling wanly. 'I exist in your imagination, and your imagination is a part of nature, so that must mean I also exist in nature.'" The monk goes on to tell him: "'You are one of the few people who can genuinely be called one of God's chosen people. You serve eternal truth. Your thoughts and intentions, your astounding scholarship and your whole life have a heavenly, celestial bearing, since they are dedicated to all that is rational and beautiful, that is, everything which is eternal...'"

The monk continues in this vein, telling Kovrin all that he needs to hear in order to be inspired, in order—as he sees it—to take the risks of greatness. Kovrin knows the monk to be an illusion; and needs him nonetheless. He is willing to sacrifice his so-called sanity for his work; and not merely for his work, because it is in this state—inspired, you will recall, by the surroundings of his youth, the Proustian atmosphere in which he presumably first imagined that of which he might be capable—that he falls in love, for the first time, with Tanya. (Indeed how, one might ask, does the illusion of the monk differ from his illusion of Tanya, to whom Kovrin proclaims with great enthusiasm: "'I want a love which will envelop me completely, and only you can give me a love like that, Tanya. I am happy! I am so happy!'") All in all, he is willing to sacrifice his sanity for fulfillment of his soul, in work and in love; even if that fulfillment is illusory.

When Tanya and her father recognize his madness and insist on having him "treated," he is enraged at his loss: "'Why, oh why did you cure me? ... Maybe I was going insane, maybe I had delusions of grandeur, but I was good company, I was cheerful, even happy; I was interesting and original. Now I've become more down to earth and sensible, but I'm just like everybody else: I am a mediocrity, life is depressing... You've been so cruel to me! So what if I had hallucination—who cared? I am asking you: who cared?'" And further: "'The Buddha, Mohammed and Shakespeare were fortunate not to have their relatives and doctors cure them of their ecstasy and inspiration! If Mohammed had taken potassium bromide for his nerves, worked only two hours a day, and drunk milk, then he would have left as much to posterity as his dog.'"

Later still, when he is fully "cured" and resigned, long after he and Tanya have separated, "[Kovrin] thought about the high price life exacts for the insignificant or very ordinary benefits it can give a person. In order to be appointed to a chair by the age of forty, for example, to be an ordinary professor and articulate ordinary ideas, other people's ideas moreover, in a language which was stilted, boring and lifeless—in other words, to reach the position of an average scholar, Kovrin had to study for fifteen years, work day and night, suffer a serious psychiatric illness, experience an unsuccessful marriage, and do a lot of stupid and unfair things which it would be better not to remember. Kovrin now clearly recognized that he was a mediocrity, and he willingly reconciled himself to this, since it was his opinion that people ought to be happy with the way they were."

That Kovrin's first vision of the monk takes place on his guardian's estate, the site of his happy sensory memories of childhood, is no coincidence. In youth, he imagined, as we all do, that greatness was close, the way my little girl, when she was two, asked me to reach up and bring her the moon. (And when I said it was too high to reach, she said, "Then get a stool. And get it for me.") Only with age did its vast distance become apparent; only then did insidious doubt assail him. Against which he deployed the black monk, who might have saved him—but who proved instead his downfall, who ensured that ultimately he knew, he lived, his limitations.

Is this not the trajectory of all of us who aspire, in any realm? Surely it is the trajectory of all who wish to create. As Flaubert famously put it, "Human speech is like a cracked kettle on which we tap crude rhythms for bears to dance to, while we long to make music that will melt the stars." Life's lessons, whether suffered in extremis, as by Kovrin, or in more banal and mundane ways, are the lessons of less-ness, of how little can be done in a day, or a life; of how crucial the dream is to the attempt; and of how all this is born in childhood, in the physical world, in a wholeness before our Fall, when everything seems possible. Kovrin, at his death, is granted a last vision of the black monk; and most generously, the restored sight of the possibility of wholeness which was his joy: "He was calling out to Tanya, calling out to the large gardens with their luxurious flowers, sprinkled with dew, he was calling out to the park, to the fir trees with the furry roots, to the rye field, to his wonderful scholarship, to his youth, to his daring, to his joy, and he was calling out to his life which was so beautiful."

That, too, is the gift Chekhov grants us: it is vital to Chekhovian reality. Whether scholars or privy councilors or peasants, we may be brutes and failures, mean, small, lesser beings; but each of us—Kovrin, or Gusev, or Ragin in "Ward 6" who sees the silently running deer—has his own vision of grace. And in some form, sooner or later, the black monk appears to us all—I know he has appeared to me. He may be false, and he may be hope, but he is real, in his way, and essential, as Chekhov well knew.

# Learning from Chekhov*

### Francine Prose, Writer

*Francine Prose spoke during the panel on "Chekhov and American Writing" at the NEH Chekhov Symposium. Unfortunately, all but her opening words were lost due to mismanaged recording; we have therefore replaced her presentation with "Learning from Chekhov" (with permission from HarperCollins Publishers). Here are those opening words from her presentation:*

> *I feel like what I'm going to say is sort of a combination or conflation of what James has said, and Claire. For me, also, I discovered how much I needed Chekhov really* de profundis *at a moment of spiritual paralysis, but for me that moment was when I was teaching. [laughter] I think that one of the reasons or maybe the principle reason I was invited here was because I wrote an essay. I was thinking about it a few days ago: I was shocked and appalled to realize that it was almost twenty years ago. The essay is called "Learning from Chekhov," and it appeared first in the* Western Humanities Review, *then it was anthologized, and I think was passed around in this sort of photocopied samizdat form by desperate creative writing teachers all over the country.*
>
> *It started in the following way. This was the academic year probably of 1985–86; it was, I can say, without a doubt so far the worst year of my life. My father was dying, and I was teaching at Sarah Lawrence College, which was the worst job of my life. I was commuting, which was even worse: we were living in upstate New York and once a week my husband would drive me to the bus station, I would get on the bus, I would take the bus for two hours, and I would take a cab; I would go there and I would teach students—at that point you could major in creative writing there, so I had students who hadn't read anything but each other's work, and they didn't want to read anything else. And then I went home the next day. I'd do the same thing in reverse.*
>
> *What saved me that year: Ecco Press had just published the thirteen-volume edition of Chekhov. I bought the entire thing, and I just read it from beginning to end. I'd read it on the bus. It was really the thing that kept me on the bus instead throwing myself under the wheels of the bus as I was leaving to go down there.*

This past year I taught at a college two and a half hours from my home. I commuted down once a week, stayed overnight, came back. Through most of

---

* "Learning from Chekhov," © 1987 by Francine Prose, as taken from *Reading Like a Writer* by Francine Prose, © 2006 by Francine Prose. Reprinted by permission of HarperCollins Publishers. "Learning from Chekhov" originally appeared in *Western Humanities Review* 41: 1 (Spring 1987): 1–14.

*Chekhov the Immigrant: Translating a Cultural Icon.* Michael C. Finke and Julie de Sherbinin, eds. Bloomington, IN: Slavica Publishers, 2007, 177–88.

the winter I took the bus. The worst part was waiting to go home in the New Rochelle Greyhound station. The bus was unreliable, as was the twenty-minute taxi ride I took to get there, so I wound up being in the station, on the average, forty minutes a week.

One thing you notice if you spend any time there is that although the bus station is a glassed-in corner storefront, none of the windows open, so the only time air moves is when someone opens the door. There is a ticket counter, a wall of dirty magazines, a phone, a rack of dusty candy. It's never very crowded, which is hardly a comfort when half the people who *are* there look like they'd happily blow your brains out on the chance of finding a couple of Valiums in your purse.

Usually I bought a soda and a greasy sugar cookie to cheer myself up and read *People* magazine because I was scared to lose touch with reality for any longer than it took to read a *People* magazine article. Behind the counter worked a man about sixty and a woman about fifty, and in all the time I was there I never heard them exchange one personal word. Behind them was a TV, on constantly, and it will give you an idea of what kind of winter I had when I say that the first ten times I saw the *Challenger* blow up were on the bus station TV. I was having a difficult time in my life, and every minute that kept me from getting home to my husband and kids was painful. Many of you who have commuted will probably know what I mean.

Finally the bus came; the two drivers who alternated—the nasty younger one who seemed to slip into some kind of trance between Newburgh and New Paltz and went slower and slower up the thruway, and the older one who looked like a Victorian masher and had a fondness for some aerosol spray which smelled like a cross between cherry Lifesavers and Raid. The bus made Westchester stops for half an hour before it even got to the highway.

As soon as I was settled and had finished the soda and cookie and magazine from the bus station, I began reading the short stories of Anton Chekhov. It was my ritual and my reward. I began where I'd left off the week before, through volume after volume of the Garnett translations. And I never had to read more than a page or two before I began to think that maybe things weren't so bad. The stories were not only—it seemed to me—profound and beautiful, but also involving, so that I would finish one and find myself, miraculously, a half hour closer to home. And yet there was more than the distraction, the time so painlessly and pleasantly spent. A great sense of comfort came over me, as if in those thirty minutes I myself had been taken up in a spaceship and shown the whole world, a world full of sorrows, both different and very much like my own and also a world full of promise, an intelligence large enough to embrace bus drivers and bus station junkies, a vision so piercing it would have kept seeing those astronauts long after that fiery plume disappeared from the screen. I began to think that maybe nothing was wasted, that someday I could do something with what was happening to me, to use even the New Rochelle bus station in some way, in my work.

Reading Chekhov, I felt not happy, exactly, but as close to happiness as I knew I was likely to come. And it occurred to me that this was the pleasure and mystery of reading, as well as the answer to those who say that books will disappear. For now, books are still the best way of taking great art and its consolations along with us on the bus.

In the spring, at the final meeting of the course I was commuting to teach, my students asked me this: if I had one last thing to tell them about writing, what would it be? They were half joking, partly because by then they knew me well enough to know that whenever I said anything about writing, I could usually be counted on to come up—often when we'd gone on to some other subject completely—with qualifications and even counterexamples proving that the opposite could just as well be true. And yet they were also half serious. We had come far in that class. From time to time, it had felt as if, at nine each Wednesday morning, we were shipwrecked together on an island. Now they wanted a souvenir, a fragment of seashell to take home.

Still it seemed nearly impossible to come up with that one last bit of advice. Often, I have wanted to somehow get in touch with former students and say: remember such and such a thing I told you? Well, I take it back, I was wrong! Given the difficulty of making any single true statement, I decided that I might just as well say the first thing that came to mind—which, as it happened, was this: the most important things, I told them, were observation and consciousness. Keep your eyes open, see clearly, think about what you see, ask yourself what it means.

After that came the qualifications and counterexamples: I wasn't suggesting that art necessarily be descriptive, literal, autobiographical or confessional. Nor should the imagination be overlooked as an investigational tool. Italo Calvino's story, "The Distance of the Moon," about a mythical time when the moon could be reached by climbing a ladder from the earth, has always seemed to me to be a work of profound observation and accuracy. If clearsightedness—meant literally—were the criterion for genius, what should we do about Milton? But still, in most cases the fact remains: The wider and deeper your observational range, the better, the more interestingly and truthfully you will write.

My students looked at me and yawned. It was nine in the morning, and they'd heard it before. And perhaps I would not have repeated it, or repeated it with such conviction, had I not spent the year reading and rereading all that Chekhov, all those stories filled and illuminated with the deepest and broadest—at once compassionate and dispassionate—observation of life that I know.

I have already told you what reading the Chekhov stories did for me, something of what they rescued me from and what they brought me to. But what I have to add now is that after a while I started noticing a funny thing. Let's say, for example, that I had just come from telling a student that one reason the class may have had trouble telling his two main characters apart is that they were named Mikey and Macky. I wasn't saying that the two best friends in his story couldn't have similar names. But, given the absence of other distinguishing characteristics, it might be better—in the interests of clarity—to call one Frank, or Bill. The student seemed pleased with this simple solution to a difficult problem, I was happy to have helped. And then, as my bus pulled out of New Rochelle, I began Chekhov's "The Two Volodyas."

In that story, a young woman named Sofya deceives herself into thinking she is in love with her elderly husband Volodya, then deceives herself into thinking she is in love with a childhood friend, also named Volodya; in the end, we see her being comforted by an adoptive sister who has become a nun, and who tells her "that all this is of no consequence, that would all pass and God would forgive her." What I want to make clear that the two men's having the same name is not the point of the story; here, as in all of Chekhov's work, there is never exactly "a point." Rather, we feel that we are seeing into this woman's heart, into what she perceives as her "unbearable misery." That she should be in love—or not in love—with two men named Volodya is simply a fact of her life.

The next week, I suggested to another student that what made her story confusing was the multiple shifts in point of view. It's only a five-page story, I said. Not *Rashomon*. And that afternoon I read "Gusev," one of the most beautiful of Chekhov's stories about a sailor who dies at sea. The story begins with the sailor's point-of-view, shifts into long stretches of dialogue between him and another dying man. When Gusev dies—another "rule" I was glad I hadn't told my students was that, for "obvious" reasons, you can't write a story in which the narrator point-of-view character dies—the point of view shifts to that of the sailors burying him at sea and then on to that of the pilot fish who see his body fall, to the shark who comes to investigate, until finally—as a student of mine once wrote—we feel we are seeing through the eyes of God. What I have found—what I've just proved—is that it's nearly impossible to *describe* the end of this story with any accuracy at all. So I will quote the last few marvelous paragraphs. What I want to point out—what needs no pointing out—is how much would have been lost had Chekhov followed the rules.

> He went rapidly towards the bottom. Did he reach it? It was said to be three miles to the bottom. After sinking sixty or seventy feet, he began moving more and more slowly, swaying rhythmically, as though he were hesitating, and, carried along by the current, moved more rapidly sideways than downwards.
>
> Then he was met by a shoal of fish called harbor pilots. Seeing the dark body the fish stopped as though petrified, and suddenly turned round and disappeared In less than a minute they flew back swift as an arrow to Gusev, and began zigzagging round him in the water.
>
> After that another dark body appeared. It was a shark. It swarmed under Gusev with dignity and no show of interest, as though it did

not notice him, and sank down upon its back, then it turned belly upwards, basking in the warm transparent water, and languidly opened its jaws with two rows of teeth. The harbor pilots are delighted, they stop to see what will come next. After playing a little with the body the shark nonchalantly puts its jaws under it, cautiously touches it with its teeth, and the sailcloth is rent its full length from head to foot; one of the weights falls out and frightens the harbor pilots, and, striking the shark on the ribs, goes rapidly to the bottom.

Overhead at this time the clouds are massed together on the side where the sun is setting; one cloud like a triumphal arch, another like a lion, a third like a pair of scissors.... From behind the clouds a broad green shaft of light pierces through and stretches to the middle of the sky; a little later another, violet colored, lies beside it; next to that, one of gold, then one rose-colored.... The sky turns a soft lilac. Looking at this gorgeous enchanted sky, at first the ocean scowls, but soon it too takes tender, joyous, passionate colors for which it is hard to find a name in human speech.

Around this same time, I seem to remember myself telling my class that we should, ideally, have some notion of whom or what a story is about—in other words, whose story is it? To offer the reader that simple knowledge, I said—I must have been in one of my ironic moods—wasn't really giving much. A little clarity of focus cost the writer almost nothing and paid off, for the reader, a hundredfold. And it was about this same time that I first read "In the Ravine," perhaps the most heartbreaking and most powerful Chekhov story I know, in which we don't realize that the peasant girl Lipa is our heroine until almost halfway through. Moreover, the story turns on the death of a baby—just the sort of incident I advise students to stay away from because it is so difficult to write well and without sentimentality. Here—I have no pedagogical excuse to quote this, but am only including it because I so admire it—is the extraordinarily lovely scene in which Lipa plays with her baby.

> Lipa spent her time playing with the baby which had been born to her before Lent. It was a tiny, thin, pitiful little baby, and it was strange that it should cry and gaze about and be considered a human being, and even be called Nikifor. He lay in his cradle, and Lipa would walk away towards the door and say, bowing to him: "Good day, Nikifor Anisimitch!"
>
> And she would rush at him and kiss him. Then she would walk away to the door, bow again, and say: "Good day, Nikifor Anisimitch!" And he kicked up his little red legs and his crying was mixed with laughter like the carpenter Elizarov's.

By now I had learned my lesson. I began telling my class to read Chekhov instead of listening to me. I invoked Chekhov's name so often that a disgruntled student accused me of trying to make her write like Chekhov. She went on to tell me that she was sick of Chekhov, that plenty of writers were better than Chekhov, and when I asked her who, she said: Thomas Pynchon. I said I thought both writers were very good, suppressing a wild desire to run out in the hall and poll the entire faculty on who was better—Chekhov or Pynchon—only stopping myself because—or so I'd like to think—the experience of reading Chekhov was proving not merely enlightening, but also humbling.

Still there were some things I thought I knew. A short time later I suggested to yet another student that he might want to think twice about having his character—in the very last paragraph of his story—pick up a gun and blow his head off for no reason. I wasn't saying that this couldn't happen, it was just that it seemed so unexpected, so melodramatic. Perhaps if he prepared the reader, ever so slightly, hinted that his character was, if not considering, then at least capable of this. A few hours later I got on the bus and read the ending of "Volodya":

> Volodya put the muzzle of the revolver to his mouth, felt something like a trigger or a spring, and pressed it with his finger. Then he felt something else projecting, and once more pressed it. Taking the muzzle out of his mouth, he wiped it with the lapel of his coat, looked at the lock. He had never in his life taken a weapon in his hand.
> 
> "I believe one ought to raise this," he reflected. "Yes, it seems so."
> 
> Volodya put the muzzle in his mouth again, pressed it with his teeth, and pressed something with his fingers. There was the sound of a shot. Something hit Volodya in the back of his head with terrible violence and he fell on the table with his face downwards among the bottles and glasses. Then he saw his father as in Mentone, in a top hat with a wide black band on it, wearing mourning for some lady, suddenly seize him by both hands, and they fell headlong into a very deep dark pit. Then everything was blurred and vanished.

Until that moment we'd had no indication that Volodya was troubled by anything more than the prospect of school exams and an ordinary teenage crush on a flirtatious older woman. Nor had we heard much about his father, except that Volodya blames his frivolous mother for having wasted his money.

What seemed at issue here was far more serious than a question of similar names and divergent points of view. For as anyone who has ever attended a writing class knows: the bottom line of the fiction workshop is motivation. We complain, we criticize, we say that we don't understand why this or that character says or does something. Like parody method actors, we ask: what is the motivation? Of course, all this is based on the comforting supposition that things, in fiction as in life, are done for a reason. But here was Chekhov telling us that—hadn't we ever noticed?—quite often people do things—terrible, irrevocable things—for no good reason at all. No sooner had I assimilated this critical bit of information than I happened to read "A Dull Story," which convinced me that I had not only been overestimating, but also oversimplifying the depths and complexities of motivation. How could I have demanded to know clearly how a certain character felt about another character when—as the narrator of "A Dull Story" reveals on every page—our feelings for each other are so often elusive, changing, contradictory, hidden in the most clever disguises even from ourselves?

Clearly Chekhov was teaching me how to teach, and yet I remained a slow learner. The mistakes—and the revelations—continued. I had always assumed and probably even said that being insane was not an especially happy state, that the phrase "happy idiot" was generally an inaccurate one and that, given the choice, most hallucinating schizophrenics would opt for sanity. And maybe this is mostly true, but as Chekhov is always reminding us, "most" is not "all." For Kovrin, the hero of "The Black Monk," the visits from an imaginary monk are the sweetest and most welcome moments in his otherwise unsatisfactory life. And what of the assumption that, in life and in fiction, a crazy character should "act" crazy, should early on clue us into his craziness? Not Kovrin, who, aside from these hallucinatory attacks and a youthful case of "upset nerves," is a university professor, a husband, a functioning member, as they say, of society, a man whose consciousness of his own "mediocrity" is relieved only by his conversations with the phantasmagorical monk, who assures him that he is a genius.

Reading another story, "The Husband," I remembered asking: What is the point of writing a story in which everything's rotten and all the characters are terrible and nothing much happens and nothing changes? In "The Husband," Shalikov, the tax collector, watches his wife enjoying a brief moment of pleasure as she dances at a party, has a jealous fit and blackmails her into leaving the dance and returning to the prison of their shared lives. The story ends:

> Anna Pavlovna would scarcely walk. She was still under the influence of the dancing, the music, the talk, the lights, and the noise; she asked herself as she walked along why God had thus afflicted her. She felt miserable, insulted, and choking with hate as she listened to her husband's heavy footsteps. She was silent, trying to think of the most offensive, biting and venomous word she could hurl at her husband, and at the same time she was fully aware that no word could penetrate his tax collector's hide. What did he care for words? Her bitterest enemy could not have contrived for her a more helpless position. And meanwhile the band was playing and the darkness was full of the most rousing, intoxicating dance tunes.

The "point"—and, again, there is no conventional "point"—is that in just a few pages, the curtain concealing these lives has been drawn back, revealing them in all their helplessness and rage and rancor. The point is that lives go on without change, so why should fiction insist that major reverses should always—conveniently—occur?

And finally, this revelation. In some kind of fit of irritation, I told my class that it was just a fact that the sufferings of the poor are more compelling, more worthy of our attention than the vague discontents of the rich. So it was with some chagrin that I read "A Woman's Kingdom," a delicate and astonishingly moving story about a rich, lonely woman—a factory owner, no less—who finds herself attracted to her foreman... until a casual remark by a member of her own class awakens her to the impossibility of her situation. By the time I had finished the story, I felt that I had been challenged, not only in my more flippant statements about fiction but in my most basic assumptions about life. In this case, truth had nothing to do with social justice, or with morality, with right and wrong. The truth was what Chekhov had seen and I—with all my fancy talk of observation—had somehow overlooked: cut a rich woman and she will bleed just like a poor one. Which isn't to say that Chekhov didn't know and know well: the world being what it is, the poor do get cut somewhat more often and more deeply.

And now, since we are speaking of life, a brief digression, about Chekhov's. By the time Chekhov died of tuberculosis at the age of forty-four, he had written—in addition to his plays—588 short stories. He was also a medical doctor. He supervised the construction of clinics and schools, he was active in the Moscow Art Theater, he married the famous actress, Olga Knipper, he visited the infamous prison on Sakhalin Island and wrote a book about that. Once when someone asked him about his method of composition, Chekhov picked up an ashtray. "This is my method of composition," he said. "Tomorrow I will write a story called 'The Ashtray.'" Along the way, he was generous with advice to young writers. And now, to paraphrase what I said to my class, listen to Chekhov instead of me. Here are two quotations from Chekhov's letters, both on the subject of literary style:

> In my opinion a true description of Nature should be very brief and have the character of relevance. Commonplaces such as "the setting sun bathing in the waves of the darkening sea, poured its purple gold, etc."—"the swallows flying over the surface of the water twittered merrily"—such commonplaces one ought to abandon. In descriptions of Nature one ought to seize upon the little particulars, grouping them in such a way that, in reading when you shut your eyes, you get the picture.
>
> For instance you will get the full effect of a moonlit night if you write that on the milldam, a little glowing star point flashed from the neck of a broken bottle, and the round black shadow of a dog or a wolf emerged and ran, etc....
>
> In the sphere of psychology, details are also the thing. God preserve us from commonplaces. Best of all is it to avoid depicting the hero's

state of mind; you ought to try to make it clear from the hero's actions. It is not necessary to portray many characters. The center of gravity should be in two people: he and she.

You understand it at once when I say "The man sat on the grass." You understand it because it is clear and makes no demands on the attention. On the other hand it is not easily understood if I write, "A tall, narrow-chested, middle-sized man, with a red beard, sat on the green grass, already trampled by pedestrians, sat silently, shyly, and timidly looked about him." That is not immediately grasped by the mind, whereas good writing should be grasped at once—in a second.

Another quotation, on the subject of closure:

My instinct tells me that at the end of a story or a novel I must artfully concentrate for the reader an impression of the entire work, and therefore must casually mention something about those whom I have already presented. Perhaps I am in error.

And here are a number of quotations on a theme which comes up again and again in his letters—the writer's need for objectivity, the importance of seeing clearly, without judgment, certainly without prejudgment, the need for the writer to be, in Chekhov's words, "an unbiased observer."

That the world "swarms with male and female scum" is perfectly true. Human nature is imperfect.... But to think that the task of literature is to gather the pure grain from the muck heap is to reject literature itself. Artistic literature is called so because it depicts life as it really is. Its aim is truth—unconditional and honest.... A writer is not a confectioner, not a dealer in cosmetics, not an entertainer; he is a man bound under compulsion, by the realization of his duty and by his conscience.... To a chemist, nothing on earth is unclean. A writer must be as objective as a chemist.

It seems to me that the writer should not try to solve such questions as those of God, pessimism, etc. His business is but to describe those who have been speaking or thinking about God and pessimism, how and under what circumstances. The artist should be not the judge of his characters and their conversations, but only an unbiased observer.

You are right in demanding that an artist should take an intelligent attitude to his work, but you confuse two things: solving a problem and stating a problem correctly. It is only the second that is obligatory for the artist.

You abuse me for objectivity, calling it indifference to good and evil, lack of ideas and ideals, and so on. You would have me, when I describe horse thieves, say: "Stealing horses is an evil." But that has been known for ages without my saying so. Let the jury judge them; it's my job simply to show what sort of people they are. I write: you are dealing with horse thieves, so let me tell you that they are not beggars but well fed people, that they are people of a special cult, and that horse stealing is not simply theft but a passion. Of course it would be pleasant to combine art with a sermon, but for me personally it is impossible owing to the conditions of technique. You see, to depict horse thieves in 700 lines I must all the time speak and think in their tone and feel in their spirit, otherwise ... the story will not be as compact as all short stories ought to be. When I write, I reckon entirely upon the reader to add for himself the subjective elements that are lacking in the story.

And now, one final quotation, which given my track record for making statements and having to retract them a week later, struck me with particular force:

It is time for writers to admit that nothing in this world makes sense. Only fools and charlatans think they know and understand everything. The stupider they are, the wider they conceive their horizons to be. And if an artist decides to declare that he understands nothing of what he sees—this in itself constitutes a considerable clarity in the realm of thought, and a great step forward.

Every great writer is a mystery, if only in that some aspect of his or her talent remains forever ineffable, inexplicable and astonishing. The sheer population of Dickens' imagination, the fantastic architecture Proust constructs out of minutely examined moments, etc., etc. We ask ourselves: How could anyone do that? And of course, different qualities of the work will mystify different people. For me, Chekhov's mystery is first of all one of knowledge: how does he know so much? He knows everything we pride ourselves on having learned, and of course much more. "The Name Day Party," a story about a pregnant woman, is full of observations about pregnancy which I had thought were secrets

The second mystery is how, without ever being direct, he communicates the fact that he is not describing The World or how people should see The World or how he, Anton Chekhov, sees The World, but only one or another character's world for a certain span of time. When the characters are less than attractive, we never feel the author hiding behind them, peeking out from around their edges to say: "This isn't me, this isn't me!" We never feel that Gurov, the "hero" of "The Lady with the Pet Dog" is Chekhov, though, for all we know, he could be. Rather we feel we are seeing his life—and his life transformed. Chekhov is always, as he says in his letters, working from the particular to the general.

The greatest mystery for me—and it's what, I think, makes Chekhov so different from any other writer I know—is this matter he keeps alluding to in his letters: the necessity of writing without judgment. Not saying, Stealing horses is an evil. To be not the judge of one's characters and their conversations but rather the unbiased observer. What should, I imagine, be clear, is that Chekhov didn't live without judgment. I don't know if anyone does, or if it is even possible except for psychotics and Zen monks who've trained themselves to suspend all reflection, moral and otherwise. My sense is that living without judgment is probably a terrible idea. Nor, again, is any of this prescriptive. Balzac judged everyone and found nearly all of them wanting; their smallness and the ferocity of his outrage is part of the greatness of his work. But what Chekhov believed and acted on more than any writer I can think of is that judgment and especially prejudgment was incommensurate with a certain kind of literary art. It is, I believe, what—together with his range of vision—makes him wholly unique among writers. And why, for reasons I still can't quite explain, his work comforted me in ways Balzac just simply could not.

Before I finish, I'd like to quote Vladimir Nabokov's summation of his lecture on Chekhov's story, "The Lady with the Pet Dog":

> All the traditional rules of storytelling have been broken in this wonderful story of twenty pages or so. There is no problem, no regular climax, no point at the end. And it is one of the greatest stories ever written.
>
> We will now repeat the different features that are typical for this and other Chekhov tales.
>
> First: The story is told in the most natural way possible, not beside the after-dinner fireplace as with Turgenev or Maupassant, but in the way one person relates to another the most important things in his life, slowly and yet without a break, in a slightly subdued voice.
>
> Second: Exact and rich characterization is attained by a careful selection and careful distribution of minute but striking features, with perfect contempt for the sustained description, repetition, and strong emphasis of ordinary authors. In this or that description one detail is chosen to illume the whole setting.
>
> Third: There is no special moral to be drawn and no special message to be received.
>
> Fourth: The story is based on a system of waves, on the shades of this or that mood.... In Chekhov, we get a world of waves instead of particles of matter....
>
> Sixth: The story does not really end, for as long as people are alive, there is no possible and definite conclusion to their troubles or hopes or dreams.

Seventh: The storyteller seems to keep going out of his way to allude to trifles, every one of which in another type of story would mean a signpost denoting a turn of the action ... but just because these trifles are meaningless, they are all-important in giving the real atmosphere of this particular story.

Let me repeat one sentence which seems to me particularly significant. "We feel that for Chekhov the lofty and the base are not different, that the slice of watermelon and the violet sea and the hands of the town governor are essential points of the beauty plus pity of the world." And what I might add to this is: the more Chekhov we read, the more strongly we feel this. I have often thought that Chekhov's stories should not be read singly but as separate parts of a whole. For like life, they present contradictory views, opposing visions. Reading them, we think: How broad life is! How many ways there are to live! In this world, where anything can happen, how much is possible! Our whole lives can change in a moment. Or: Nothing will ever change—especially the fact that the world and the human heart will always be wider and deeper than anything we can fathom.

And this is what I've come to think about what I learned and what I taught and what I should have taught. Wait! I should have said to that class: Come back! I've made a mistake. Forget about observation, consciousness, clearsightedness. Forget about life. Read Chekhov, read the stories straight through. Admit that you understand nothing of life, nothing of what you see. Then go out and look at the world.

# Chekhov's Simplicity

## James Wood, Writer

Here are four sentences: "And it still seemed that there was some most important thing which he did not have, of which he once vaguely dreamed, and in the present he was stirred by the same hope for the future that he had had in childhood." "He began to play, himself not knowing what it was, but it came out plaintive and moving, and tears flowed down his cheeks... 'Ah, ah!' he said, as the tears crawled down his cheeks and splashed on his green frockcoat." "What was certain was that his own mother had never known him to embrace her, so she had never done the same to him either." "Ivan Ilyich's life was most ordinary, therefore most terrible."

The first is from Chekhov's story "The Bishop," and the second from "Rothschild's Fiddle." The terrifying line about how "what was certain was that his own mother had never known him to embrace her, so she had never done the same to him either" is from Giovanni Verga's great story, "Rosso Malpelo," and the last sentence, of course, is from Tolstoy's novella *The Death of Ivan Ilyich*. We know the sound of simplicity when we hear those lines: the direct access to deep emotion, the clarity of phrasing, the willingness to use vernacular and conversational language and repetition rather than obviously literary constructions, the sense that literary artifice has been pushed out of the way by the coarse elbow of metaphysics. There is a fearlessness in this writing, which in turn is fearful; a simplicity which in turn is complex.

We know that simplicity has always been an ideal, because of the abundant testimony to it in ancient and modern literature; and we know that it is rarely achieved because of the abundant complexity with which it is idealized. Plato, in the *Republic*, warns against such gratuities as Attic pastries and Corinthian girlfriends. These superfluities are likely to distract the soldier and make him sick, he says, just as unnecessary embellishment in songs and lyric odes gives rise to licentiousness. Simplicity and temperance is all. Such notions are familiarly found in the ancient treatises on rhetoric, such as Quintilian's *Institutio Oratoria*.

But in modern literature, simplicity tends to be elegiac; it is that which has been mysteriously lost, and cannot be re-found. Simplicity is honored in the breach, as in Yeats's little poem, "The Fascination of What's Difficult," which complains about complexity:

> The fascination of what's difficult
> Has dried the sap out of my veins, and rent
> Spontaneous joy and natural content
> Out of my heart.

Many literary cultures seem to have their own favored examples of lost simplicity and naturalness. Moliere is sometimes invoked by the French, and Pushkin has long represented a founding simplicity for Russian writers; Gogol suggested that Pushkin was able to serve "art for art's sake" because, in some way, he had no complex anxiety about what art was: by contrast, "we can no longer serve art for art's sake," wrote Gogol, "without having first comprehended its highest purpose and without determining what it is given to us for. We cannot repeat Pushkin." The Czechs revere Jaroslav Hašek's easiness; Bohumil Hrabal marvelled that Hašek's novel, *The Good Soldier Švejk*, was "written as though he tossed it off with his left hand, after a hangover, it's pure joy in writing." And Cervantes has functioned this way for writers as different as Flaubert, Milan Kundera, and Dostoevsky.

All these writers are idealized as somehow simple, at one with nature, almost pre-modern; they are envied because they are seen as unencumbered by artifice. Schiller's essay, "On Naive and Sentimental Poetry" is both the greatest example of this modern nostalgia and the most sharply self-aware and dialectical commentary on it. Schiller sees modern poets as writers who have lost an antique simplicity, one of whose components was a direct concord with nature. Modern writers, says Schiller, in their relationship to the ancients, are like sick people lusting after health. Goethe, adds Schiller, is rare and remarkable, because although he is a modern poet—and therefore a "sick" one—he still retains an extraordinary premodern simplicity and directness.

The "sickest" modern writer (in Schiller's terms) is Flaubert, and it is hardly surprising to find him groaning that Rabelais, Cervantes, and Moliere had it easy because they were so simple. "They are great," he wrote Louise Colet in 1853, "because they have no techniques." Those three writers "achieve their effects, regardless of Art." Anyone who has read Cervantes knows of course that there is abundant "technique" in *Don Quixote*, and knows merely that Cervantes mobilizes all kinds of techniques that seem premodern only because they have not yet been identified as techniques. But for Flaubert these writers are mere beasts of instinct. Flaubert feels that he cannot be free as they were: "One achieves style," he writes, "only by atrocious labor, a fanatic and dedicated stubbornness."

Flaubert was not only a sick modern, but one who, as it were, infected everyone who came after him. He does indeed represent a watershed. After Flaubert, style in fiction will always be a problem, always a trapped decision, because it is an overwhelmingly aesthetic one. Even simplicity, after Flaubert, is no longer innocent, but is a simplicity that has become weary of congestion.

(Think of Hemingway's intensely self-conscious and artful simplicity.) He knew this; nothing is more nostalgic for simplicity than his story "A Simple Heart," in which he tried to prove that he could use his aestheticism to achieve a fable-like purity. And the moderns know it too: both Robbe-Grillet and Natalie Sarraute, those exponents of the *nouveau roman*, used to say that without doubt Flaubert was their "precursor."

What is remarkable about both Verga and Chekhov, who wrote at about the same time—that's to say, in the 1880s and 1890s—is that they seem to have evaded this law of modern sickness. They lived after Flaubert, but write as if they had never read him. (And both had certainly read him.) They are simple but without any modern nostalgia for simplicity. Indeed, Chekhov in some ways represents the "solution" to all of Flaubert's dilemmas. Where Flaubert complained that his characters in Madam Bovary were "deeply repulsive," Chekhov said that one should love one's characters—"but not aloud!" If realism was a stylistic agony for Flaubert, it was a moral necessity for Chekhov; if Flaubert retained and aestheticized an essentially religious and judgmental disdain for life, Chekhov paganized life; if Flaubert's people are all mistakes, Chekhov's are all always forgiven; where Flaubert's characters are doomed, Chekhov's are merely imprisoned.

Chekhov, as all readers feel, has an extraordinary natural and simple charm, which is inseparable from his gentle and comic temperament. But what is the literary nature of his simplicity? How does it work, and what attributes does it possess that make it so attractive to we sick moderns? We can see it in operation in two stories, "Rothschild's Fiddle," written in 1894, and "Gusev," written in 1890. Both are relentlessly bleak. In the later story, we are introduced to Jacob, a miserly coffin-maker. The tale begins: "It was a small town, more miserable than a village and almost all the inhabitants were old people, who died so rarely it was even annoying." Jacob cares about nothing but profit and loss. When he makes expensive coffins, for women and gentry, he gets out his iron rule, and measures with great attention to exact size. But he is never keen to make children's coffins, because they pay so poorly. He would knock them up contemptuously and carelessly without measuring them, writes Chekhov, complaining all the while that he couldn't be bothered by such trifles.

From time to time, the town's Jewish band, which usually played weddings, would ask him to play the fiddle, out of necessity, since neither the band nor Jacob enjoyed the experience. Jacob had to sit next to a man called Rothschild, named, writes Chekhov, with some sarcasm, "after the noted millionaire. Now this bloody little Jew contrived to play the merriest tunes in lachrymose style. For no obvious reason Jacob became more and more obsessed by hatred and contempt for Jews, and for Rothschild in particular. He started picking on him and swearing at him."

Quite suddenly, this disagreeable man's wife, Martha, is taken ill. The extraordinary brutality of the narration continues: "On the sixth of May in the previous year Martha had suddenly fallen ill. The old woman breathed heavily, drank a lot of water, was unsteady on her feet, but she would still do the stove herself of a morning, and even fetch the water." Jacob suffers his first stirring of remorse, as he realizes he may soon be without a wife: "As he looked at the old woman, it vaguely occurred to Jacob that for some reason he had never shown her any affection all his life." But ever practical, he measures her for her coffin, and enters his wife in his debit book: "Martha Ivanov: one coffin, 2 roubles, 49 kopecks." Jacob and Martha go to the hospital, but the doctor shrugs his shoulders and sends them home, telling Martha that she has done well to get this far and now it is her time to die. A few days later, she does die, succinctly appraised by Chekhov thus: "The priest came and gave the last rites, whereupon Martha mumbled something or other. By morning she was gone."

Returning from her funeral, Jacob has what amounts to a revelation. Again he reflects that in fifty-two years of marriage he had never shown any love for his wife, that in "all that time, he had no more noticed her than a cat or dog." But his remorse is interrupted by Rothschild, who has been sent by the band leader to ask Jacob to play at a wedding. They are in need of a fiddler. Jacob turns on Rothschild, and attacks him. "Scared to death," Rothschild runs away, pursued by a dog and some street urchins, shouting "Dirty Yid!" Jacob walks alongside the river, and sitting for a moment, he reflects upon real losses, not just the pecuniary ones.

As Jacob mourns his losses, the reader gathers that he and Martha suffered a real loss when they were young—that of a baby. And suddenly we think back to the story's opening page, and Chekhov's sentence about how Jacob made children's coffins contemptuously and carelessly. What had seemed, in our readerly innocence, an economic contempt—since children's coffins bring in less cash—is disclosed as the desperate repression of grief. We know, now, why Jacob cannot stand the way that Rothschild plays his flute, making all the cheerful tunes sound lachrymose. Jacob fears true feeling.

The next morning, he himself feels sick, and goes to the hospital, and with the same fatalism with which he attended his wife's death, now prepares for his own. "He reckoned that death would be pure gain to him. He wouldn't have to eat, drink, pay taxes, or offend people. And since a man lies in his grave not just once but hundred and thousands of years, the profit would be colossal. Man's life is debit, his death credit." Thinking of all this, "he started playing he knew not what, but it came out poignantly moving and tears coursed down his cheeks." Just then, Rothschild comes to his door, terrified, but again sent to ask Jacob to play. Jacob does not hit him this time, merely says that it's no good, he won't be able to play because he is ill. "He again struck up, his tears spurting on to the fiddle. Rothschild listened carefully, standing sideways on, arms crossed on his breast. His scared, baffled look slowly gave way to a sorrowful, suffering expression. He rolled his eyes as if in anguished delight. 'Ah, ah!' he said as the tears crawled down his cheeks and splashed on his green frock-coat." On his deathbed, that evening, Jacob asks the priest to ensure that his fiddle is given to Rothschild.

It is a very beautiful story, and it shows us, first of all, how great simplicity founds itself on the defiance of much that is considered conventionally literary. Our soft scruples instruct us that literature should avoid the didactic, the sentimental, the clichéd, and the repetitive. But here is Chekhov being frankly sentimental, and frankly didactic, as he often is in his writing: "Why are people generally such a nuisance to each other?... Without the hate and malice folks could get a lot of profit out of each other." And here is Chekhov, with his usual hospitality towards cliché and repetition: "scared to death," "his heart missed a beat and he felt sorry," and so on. (Tellingly, these were the "prosaicisms" in Chekhov that so irritated the aesthete Nabokov.) But this is a story very concerned with false measure and the proper overflowing of measure; Jacob learns, of course, to go beyond the rules—both the "iron rule" of his craft, and the iron rule of his emotional life. His tears, as Shakespeare has it in a different context, "o'erflow the measure," splashing onto his fiddle. In such a story, simplicity itself overflows our nice little literary measures, our protocols, our fine laws and conventions of artifice.

If this story's simplicity is in some sense anti-literary, then it is most anti-literary in its mode of narration. Listen, again, to the story's opening sentence: "It was a small town, more miserable than a village and almost all the inhabitants were old people, who died so rarely it was even annoying." "Who died so rarely it was even annoying"; clearly, this opening sentence, the one that conventionally sets the scene, is written as if thought by Jacob the coffin-maker. It is Jacob who thinks that the town's niggardly rate of death is annoying, because he wants to make ever more coffins. So immediately, at a moment when an authorial omniscience is more usual—"the town consisted of three streets and one large manor house" etc., etc.—Chekhov begins by telling the story from within Jacob's head, and in Jacob's own language. Of course, he does not stay exclusively inside Jacob's head. Instead, Chekhov combines ordinary third-person narration with narration from within Jacob's head.

The technical term for this kind of writing is free indirect style, which is really a way of paraphrasing something that would ordinarily be written directly, and of paraphrasing it in the language of one particular character. In its simplest form, it allows novelists to avoid having to represent all speech within quotation marks, and all scenes as actually happening at the moment they are described. An example might be: "He listened to the music in stupid tears." The same sentence rendered merely as "He listened to the music in tears," would be direct reported style, with no inflection. The addition of "stupid" inflects the narrative: it seems to be a word generated by the subject himself, not the author. It is as if the subject were saying to himself: "How stupid to be crying to this music."

Jane Austen and Henry James are superb and habitual users of free indirect style, which at its subtlest allows a novelist the freedom to move between third- and first-person narration without having to choose one or the other. In addition, it allows novelists to use irony, since the gap between what is written and what we actually know becomes bigger and bigger, and so the gap between a character's version of things and our knowledge of things increases.

Free indirect style becomes a profound technique—to use Flaubert's word—when, as in the case of Chekhov's story, it is hardly signaled at all, and barely perceptible, and yet infects the very language and bias of the narration. As in my example, we are prompted by the merest word or phrase to see a bias, a tilt, an allegiance, in a sentence that otherwise looks like normal third-person authorial omniscience. For instance, when Chekhov writes: "He was known as Rothschild after the noted millionaire. Now this bloody little Jew even contrived to play the merriest tunes in lachrymose style," we know perfectly well that the first sentence, about Rothschild being named after the noted millionaire, is written—as it were—by Chekhov, and that the second one is spoken—as it were—by Jacob, the anti-Semite, because only Jacob would use the phrase "bloody little Jew." But what of this: "On the sixth day of May in the previous year Martha had suddenly fallen ill. The old woman breathed heavily, drank a lot of water, was unsteady on her feet, but she could still do the stove herself of a morning, and even fetch the water." The brevity of the description, the lack of interest and compassion, the vested interest in Martha's continued domestic functioning, the very idea that to describe Martha's ailments all that will be needed is to say that "she breathed heavily and drank a lot of water"—all this suggests that this picture of poor Martha is really seen as if from Jacob's cruel eyes. And later, Chekhov writes: "The priest came and gave the last rites, whereupon Martha mumbled something or other. By morning she was gone."

"Martha mumbled something or other": this is how Jacob would describe the scene, were he speaking it, perhaps to himself. And if some of us might feel that it is not exactly how Jacob would put it, we could say instead that Chekhov here finds a third vantage, a third point of view from which to tell his story: he writes as if someone in the community were describing the event—without formality, fullness of detail, or for that matter, compassion. It is a style that perfectly matches both Jacob and the wretched little town he comes from, a place of cruelty, fatalism, and speedy injustice.

Chekhov's use of free indirect speech is exceptionally delicate, and the more one searches for it, the more one sees that it really constitutes the fabric of his storytelling, his special way of siding with his characters, of merging with them, of seeing the world as they see it, without judgement. It is far from simple, of course, but then *pace* Flaubert, simplicity is always a matter of complex techinique. But it is a technique that results in simplicity, because, in issuing from within the vision and language of a character, it tends away from literary narration and towards the idea of spoken narration.

More than that, however, this way of telling stories runs against the conventional literary idea that we read in order to know. If it is the fitting style for a community that is cruel, it is because it is the fitting style for a community whose cruelty has to do with its not being interested in comprehension. The doctor who turns Martha away simply feels that she has lived her threescore and ten. Her husband has always treated her like a cat or a dog, barely noticing her. Martha is not worth investigation. And doesn't Chekhov's story do the same really? "Whereupon Martha mumbled something or other." Martha is seen as fundamentally unknowable, because not worth the trouble of knowledge. Chekhov uses a technique of storytelling which mimics incuriousness; from deep inside the mind of one character, he lets us look at another character and see in her only the cloudiest outline. We might say that this style of Chekhov's, so common in his stories, is founded on the management of incomprehension. That is not to say, of course, that we don't learn anything from reading Chekhov, or that in this instance that we don't learn quite a lot about Jacob or about his town in the course of the story; merely that in order to do so we are made to travel through his lack of comprehension, inhabit his cloud of unknowing.

How this simplicity differs from out-and-out complexity can be seen by comparing Chekhov with Henry James. James is a great controller of point of view, like Chekhov, but it is generally essential for James that the character from whose eyes we see and interpret gathering events is also a source of finally deep understanding. James's characters, in this sense, are all readers—it is what links him again with Austen, for all that, apparently, he disliked Austen. Think of Isabel Archer, or of Austen's Fanny Price; they become readers of their situations, highly literate hermeneuts of the material we too are reading. And of course this is deeply satisfying: especially in James, the experience offers the satisfactions of complexity. Chekhov, is almost the opposite: we learn how to read the unreading, the hermenutical illiteracy, of his characters. If James's point of view is that of reading, Chekhov's is that of speaking.

The experience of reading Chekhov is often the experience of the frustration of conventional access, an experience which in turn becomes a very full, if unconventional experience. It is the very principle of his story "Gusev." This sad tale, if possible bleaker than "Rothschild's Fiddle," is about a soldier, an illiterate peasant, who is returning on a military ship to Russia from the Far East. He is in the ship's sick bay. Gusev is a simple man, who believes that when the winds howl it is because they have broken loose from their chains, like dogs. One of the other patients, an aspirant intellectual and political malcontent named Pavel Ivanovich, mocks him for such superstitious ignorance, and lectures him about how he will soon die, and how foolish Gusev has been to have allowed himself to be oppressed by his superiors.

Like "Rothschild's Fiddle," the story is a beautiful exercise in perspective, in which we largely see events from Gusev's point of view. And Gusev, as Pavel Ivanovich disagreeably points out, is a fool. Gusev, for instance, does not accept that he is going to die in a day or two, and fondly imagines that he will see his home village again, and his brother who drinks too much, and his little niece, and that they will go sledding in the snow. We live in Gusev's memory, as he remembers tiny details of his village, and thinks happily of burying his face in the cold white snow. The next day, the patients are playing cards, and one of the solidiers, in Chekhov's words, "calls hearts diamonds, he muddles the score and drops his cards, then he gives a silly, scared smile and looks round at everyone. 'One moment, lads,' he says and lies on the floor. Everyone is aghast. They call him, but he doesn't respond." The solider has just died, which might be the most casual, brushed-off death scene in literature.

Just Gusev and Pavel Ivanovich are left now, and again Pavel Ivanovich harangues Gusev for his stupidity and servility. Pavel Ivanovich refuses to accept that he will die. "Comparing myself with you," he says to Gusev, "I feel sorry for you. My lungs are all right, this is only a stomach cough... I have a critical attitude to my illness and medicines... but you—you benighted people, you have a rotten time, you really do." But in fact Pavel Ivanovich is the next to die. Gusev drifts in and out of tormented sleep, and the story's way of narration mimics Gusev's flickering consciousness. For this is how Pavel Ivanovich's death is told: "Evening comes on, then night, but he notices nothing, and still is dreaming of the frost. It sounds as if someone has come into the sick-bay, and voices are heard—but five minutes later everything is silent. 'God be with him,' says the soldier with his arm in a sling. 'May he rest in peace, he was a restless man.' 'What?' Gusev asks. 'Who?' 'He's dead, they've just carried him up.' "

And so Pavel Ivanovich has just died, barely noticed by Chekhov—a few noises, followed, "five minutes later," by silence. (It is an ironically quiet demise for the talkative intellectual.) Chekhov's story achieves the remarkable feat of allowing us to inhabit the mind of a man who is dying but who is not aware of dying, and who thus doesn't see people around him dying. Logically, if Chekhov's allegiance to Gusev's point of view is to be maintained, this will mean that Gusev himself must die without quite realizing it. And this is exactly what happens. Chekhov describes Gusev as again having tormented sleep: "He dreams that they have just taken the bread out of the oven in his barracks. He has climbed into the stove himself, and is having a steam bath, lashing himself with a birch switch. He sleeps for two days. At noon on the third, two soldiers come down and carry him out of the sick-bay. They sew him up in sail-cloth and put in two iron bars to weight him down. Sewn in canvas, he looks like a carrot or radish—broad at the head and narrow at the base." And that is the end of Gusev. He is chucked into the sea.

But note how Chekhov describes—or rather refuses to describe—the moment of death itself. "He sleeps for two days. At noon on the third, two soldiers come down and carry him out of the sick-bay." Those are two sentences, one following the other. But, in conventional storytelling there ought to be a break between them, since Gusev literally dies *between* these two sentences: "He sleeps for two days. At noon on the third, two soldiers come down and cary him out of the sick-bay." When the soldiers carry him out Gusev is already dead, yet the narration simply carries on without a break; in one sentence we are still with Gusev, alive (he "sleeps for two days"); in the next we are *still* with Gusev, but he is dead. Yet in some strange way he is not dead, because it is impossible to rid ourselves of the idea that we are still inhabiting his mind. We imagine at first that Gusev is still alive when the soldiers come for him, because just the sentence before we were with a living Gusev. But no, he is dead, they are sewing him up in a sack. So *when*, exactly, did Gusev die? Perhaps in those two days when he was sleeping? We will never know.

As in "Rothschild's Fiddle," the way of telling the story exactly matches the way the main character sees things: he doesn't see death, as it were, until it is staring him in the face, and by then—well, by then, he is dead. The entire story flows out of its simple, opening sentence: "It is getting dark, and will soon be night." Again, the writing literally merges with the characters—literally, not just figuratively. For once Gusev has been thrown into the sea and has disappeared, the story, astoundingly, continues to see the world as Gusev sees it, continues, in effect, to be narrated by Gusev, even though he is now dead! For how does Chekhov descibe the clouds that mass over the sea at the end of the story? "Clouds are massing on the sunset side—one like a triumphal arch, another like a lion, a third like a pair of scissors." Yet how is this way of seeing clouds any different from Gusev's way of thinking of the wind as chained up somewhere like a dog? The writer and his character are one; literary metaphor (the clouds that are like scissors) is exposed as merely a fancy form of somewhat imaginative peasant illiteracy, a form of folkloric picture-making. Again, simplicity of this order seems to enjoy stripping the literary of its pretensions, while simultaneously making use of all the complex resources of the literary. We might say that when Chekhov describes clouds as looking like lions and scissors, that, in the context of Gusev's primitive thought, metaphor is removed from its status as something written and returned to its primal impulse and function—as merely a simple, commonsensical way of visualizing or picturing everyday things, rather than a way of writing about how the picture looks, or what the picture resembles.

For Chekhov, then, simplicity is achieved by using complex literary techniques to break through literary complexity; by using literature against itself. Note how, in both stories, characters are described in terms of the simplest exclamations: the silly smile of the soldier who is dying in "Gusev"; the tearful grunts of appreciation given by the Jew in "Rothschild's Fiddle":

"Ah!" T. S. Eliot once wrote an essay about the difference between Dryden's version of *Antony and Cleopatra* and Shakespeare's. He was interested in the death of Charmian. Both poets had similar verse, except that Shakespeare added to the couplet the words, "Ah, soldier!" Eliot said that he could not quite identify why this was great, but said that he knew that this addition was the secret of literature. I think, after reading Chekhov, we know. "Ah, soldier." "Ah," "oh," just two vowels—it is the sigh of simplicity.

# Innovations in Chekhov Scholarship

# Chekhov's "Rothschild's Fiddle": "By the Rivers of Babylon" in Eastern Orthodox Liturgy

## Robert Louis Jackson, Yale University

In "'If I forget Thee, O Jerusalem': An Essay on Chekhov's 'Rothschild's Fiddle,'" published more than twenty-five years ago, I signaled the presence in Chekhov's story of three distinct references in the text or subtext to the Old Testament Psalm 137 (in the Russian Bible, Psalm 136), "By the Rivers of Babylon" ("Na rekakh Vavilonskikh"). I argued that these references to the psalm, with its central themes of exile and anguish for a lost homeland, offered the thematic clue to Chekhov's approach to Yakov's moral-psychological illness and crisis, and to the spiritual resolution of that illness. I affirmed that in Chekhov's design the music of Yakov and Rothschild, the music of Rothschild's "weeping flute" and of the violin that Yakov plays in his dying hours, is the song of man's exile on earth from his Jerusalem—a song conveying the message that man's return from spiritual exile can only be accomplished through suffering and through the recognition of suffering in others.[1] "Jerusalem," I suggested, was a metaphor for humanity's longing and need for spiritual harmony and reconciliation.

In this brief discussion I wish to draw attention to the Eastern Orthodox liturgical metaphorical perception of the Hebrew psalm "By the Rivers of Babylon" and of the "Parable of the Prodigal Son" (Luke 15:11–32), and then to pose the question of the place of this perception in Chekhov's representation of the moral-spiritual crisis of Yakov Ivanov (otherwise known as "Bronza") in "Rothschild's Fiddle."[2]

---

[1] See "'If I forget Thee, O Jerusalem': An Essay on Chekhov's 'Rothschild's Fiddle,'" *Slavica Hierosolymitana: Slavic Studies of the Hebrew University* 3 (1978): 55–67. The essay was reprinted with some additions in *Anton Chekhov Rediscovered: A Collection of New Studies with a Comprehensive Bibliography*, ed. Savely Senderovich and Munir Sendich (East Lansing, MI: Russian Language Journal, 1987), 35–49. It was translated into Russian by Maxim Shrayer under the title, "Esli ia zabudu tebia, Ierusalim!" O rasskaze Chekhova 'Skripka Rotshil'da,'" and published in *Tallinn: Literaturnyi zhurnal*, no. 13 (1999): 154–65.

[2] For an interesting unearthing and discussion of various "Chekhovian parallels [in 'Rothschild's Fiddle'] with events of Sacred history" (not including those discussed in this article), see Aleksandr Potapovskii's "K probleme rekonstruktsii bibleiskikh i liturgicheskikh alliuzii v 'Skripke Rotshil'da' Chekhova," in *Molodye issledovateli Chekhova. III. Materialy mezhdunarodnoi konferentsii. Iun' 1998* (Moscow: Chekhovskaia komissiia soveta po istorii mirovoi kul'tury rossiiskoi akademii nauk. Filologicheskii

*Chekhov the Immigrant: Translating a Cultural Icon.* Michael C. Finke and Julie de Sherbinin, eds. Bloomington, IN: Slavica Publishers, 2007, 201–06.

In the Eastern Orthodox liturgical services leading up to Lent the biblical "Parable of the Prodigal Son" serves as a model for the sinner's exile and return to God. The parable forms the theme of the Eastern Orthodox liturgy on the third Sunday before Lent—"Sunday of the Prodigal Son" (*Nedelia o Bludnom syne*). Psalm 137, the "psalm of exile," is sung on this occasion, and sung twice more on the last two Sundays before Lent.

Sergei Bulgakov stressed the metaphorical dimension of the psalm for the Christian: "['By the Rivers of Babylon'] arouses sinners to comprehend their unhappy state as captives of sin and the devil in the same way that the Jews in their Babylonian captivity understood their bitter condition and repented; it [the psalm] depicts the sorrow of the soul that longs for its heavenly homeland [izobrazhaet skorb' dushi, toskuiushchei o svoem nebesnom otechestve]."[3] As Father Alexander Schmemann succinctly put it, the 137th psalm "reveals Lent itself as pilgrimage and repentance—as *return*."[4] Man has strayed from God and his path, but just as the prodigal son in the evangelical sermon returns to a welcoming father, so the sinner can return to the Father and prostrate himself in humility and repentance.

Yakov's moral-psychological journey offers interesting parallels to the pilgrimage of the Christian sinner, though here there are significant divergences. We may briefly trace Yakov's spiritual journey with an attention to the evangelical signposts of remembrance, repentance, and return.

Yakov's wife, Marfa, perhaps the true Christian believer in "Rothschild's Fiddle," inaugurates the theme of remembrance on the eve of her death. Her

---

fakul'tet moskovskogo gosudarstvennogo universiteta im. M. V. Lomonosova, 1998), 84–93. With careful attention to the liturgical calendar of the Eastern Orthodox Church, as well as to Old and New Testaments, Potapovskii seeks to establish a governing Christian subtext and point of view in Chekhov's story. He notes that Chekhov originally situated the action of his story on the threshold of Easter (see Chekhov's observation in his notebook, *PssS* 17: 109). Chekhov subsequently moved the date of the story's action to May 6 and the following days. Potapovskii, stressing the Easter connection, observes that "the purification of [Yakov's] heart" and the "resurrection of his soul" that takes place at the end of his life "falls within the period of Great Lent, one that leads to the joys of the Resurrection" (86). Potapovskii's didactic perception of "Rothschild's Fiddle" at times interferes with his interpretation of the text. We can indubitably speak of a "purification of heart' in Yakov at the end of "Rothschild's Fiddle." However, the notion of a "resurrection of his soul"—if we are to understand this phrase in a strictly Christian religious sense—lies entirely outside the semantic field of "Rothschild's Fiddle," that is, outside of Chekhov's artistic-ideological design of his story. For another interesting discussion of folk and religious motifs in "Rothschild's Fiddle," see Nancy Pollak's "Monday, Monday, Bronze Can't Trust That Day," in *New Zealand Slavonic Journal* 37 (2003): 83–90.

[3] S. V. Bulgakov, *Nastol'naia kniga dlia sviashchenno-tserkovno-sluzhitelei* (Khar'kov, 1900), 492.

[4] Alexander Schmemann, *Great Lent: Journey to Pascha* (Crestwood, NY: St.Vladimir's Seminary Press, 2003), 23.

recollection takes place in the context of the first allusion to "By the Rivers of Babylon" in the story.

> "Do you *remember*," Yakov, she asked looking at him joyfully. "Do you *remember*, fifty years ago God gave us a little baby with blond little hair? We used to sit by the river and sing songs... by the willow tree (*verba*). Yakov strained his *memory*, but could in no way *recall* either the child or the willow. "You're dreaming this up," he said. (emphasis mine; *PssS* 8: 301)

Marfa's death will shake up Yakov's memory and conscience. Returning from the cemetery after Marfa's death, a "deep anguish" (*sil'naia toska*) seizes him; "all sorts of thoughts" creep into his head. He recalls again (*vspomnilos' opiat'*) his cruel treatment of his wife over the years (*PssS* 8: 301). Other recollections will shortly follow. He encounters Rothschild, but rebuffs him: "Lay off!"; he is in no mood for musical engagements. More than customary irritation with the Jew underlies his harshness at this point. Yakov is in a state of rising distress. In Chekhov's concrete image, "He wanted to cry" (*PssS* 8: 302). Yakov is not quite ready to cry, but his overwhelming desire signals the beginning of a tectonic shift in his whole moral-psychological being.

The motif of remembrance echoes again in the second allusion to "By the Rivers of Babylon." Yakov goes to the river and encounters the "old willow"—"green, silent, sad." The "tiny infant" and the "willow" of Martha's recollection now surface in his memory (*PssS* 8: 303). The reference to the "green" willow is noteworthy: On the eve of Palm Sunday (*Verbnoe voskresen'e*), the last before Easter, the Orthodox faithful, carrying green willows, celebrate Christ's entry into Jerusalem, singing "Praise to the Son of David, blessed be what is coming in the name of the Lord [Osanna Synu Davidovu, blagosloven griadyi vo imia Gospodne]." Of special significance for Chekhov's story is the fact that on Jesus' entrance into Jerusalem he is greeted by *both Christians and Jews*. Yakov's spiritual awakening is accompanied precisely by this note of ecumenical unity. He himself, however, will never enter his Jerusalem.

In a deepening mood of sorrow and loss Yakov, as he sits by the river, "begins to remember" what the river of life had offered him, but what he had let pass by. His whole sorrowing interior monologue (intersected at one moment by the narrator's over-voice) might be presented under the rubric of Isaiah 48:18: "O that Thou had paid attention to my commandments! Then your prosperity would have been like a river." The Lord continues: "Go out from Babylon, flee from Chaldea, declare this with a shout of joy, proclaim it, send it forth to the end of the earth: 'The Lord has redeemed his servant Yakov!'" (Isaiah 48:20). For Chekhov's Yakov there is awakening, cleansing, and spiritual redemption through suffering, but there are no shouts of joy, there is no "return" in the religious understanding of that word. His reflections at the river prelude a tragic realization that his losses, the life he might have lived, are irretrievable. "Ahead there is now nothing, and when one looks back, there is nothing, but fearful losses" (*PssS* 8: 303–04). Despair overtakes him. He has tormenting visions at night in which images, almost all with a strong Christian resonance, pass through his head: "a little infant, the willow, fish, slaughtered geese, and Marfa" (*PssS* 8: 304).

In the liturgy for "Sunday of the Prodigal Son," the prodigal son despairs as he looks back on his losses, but he turns imploringly to his God: "I have squandered dissolutely / all the spiritual gifts you gave me"; he begs to be saved from the "terrible wild beast" and to be reclothed as before.[5] In Yakov's restless dreams the "terrible wild beast" of the liturgy appears to be tormenting him. He is "besieged on all sides by snouts muttering about losses." But Yakov's repentance is not expressed in a cry for God's mercy or in a cry to be taken back; it is not accompanied by an announcement of his, Yakov's, return to the Father's fold, as in the case of the evangelical sinner.

Yakov is unable to verbalize his spiritual despair and anguish. Yet in evaluating his spiritual condition at the end of his life one must examine more broadly his sense of despair and repentance. In his discussion of the liturgical text for "The Sunday of the Prodigal Son" Hugh Wybrew stresses the importance of repentance in the Eastern Orthodox spiritual tradition and the prominent part it plays in the Christian life. "Repentance," he writes, "is recognition of sin, condemnation of faults, and blaming oneself.... It is both a change of heart, inner conversion, and a practical change in one's behavior, leading to the practice of virtues." But, drawing on a deep and pervasive view in Eastern Orthodox thought, Wybrew continues:

> These liturgical texts see in the Prodigal Son more than repentance: they speak of compunction—*penthos* in Greek. Repentance—*metanoia*—is personal and for specific sins. Compunction goes much further than repentance. It is a more general mourning for salvation lost, by oneself and by others. While repentance does not necessarily involve the emotions, compunction is a feeling, which expresses itself in tears. Tears play an important part in the Christian life in the Eastern tradition. They are a gift from God, and, like baptism, wash away sins. John Chrysostom says that a single tear extinguishes a brazier of faults and washes away the venom of sin.[6]

In the liturgy for "Sunday of the Prodigal Son," the evangelical sinner calls out: "Coming back to the merciful Father/I cry out with tears."[7] The almost wordless repentance that Yakov experiences and gives expression to, his anguish for the living life that he let pass by, is marked precisely by the *com-*

---

[5] See Hugh Wybrew, *Orthodox Lent, Holy Week and Easter: Liturgical Texts with Commentary* (Crestwood, NY: St. Vladimir's Seminary Press, 1997), 25.

[6] Ibid., 26.

[7] Ibid., 24.

*punction* that finds expression *in tears*. In the case of Yakov's repentance, these tears find deep esthetic and spiritual expression in music.

The dominant theme of the violin grows more intense as the story reaches its climax. As he sat by the river Yakov reflected that he might have "floated in a boat from farm to farm and played on the violin" (*PssS* 8: 303). Later he gets up five times at night to play the violin. He regrets that he cannot take the violin to his grave. "Thinking about life, ruined and full of losses, he began to play, without knowing what, but there came forth something pitiful and touching, and tears flowed down his cheeks. And the harder he thought, the sadder sang the violin" (*PssS* 8: 304). Yakov reflects on his life, but he articulates his anguished thoughts in the form of music. Yakov's violin "sings," that is, he "sings" his thoughts.

Rothschild appears on the scene while Yakov is playing. Yakov's mood has altered radically. He bids Rothschild to come closer. "'Come here, don't worry,' Yakov said gently, beckoning him over. 'Come here!' ['Podoiti, nichego,' skazal laskogo i pomanil ego k sebe. 'Podoiti']" (*PssS* 8: 305). Because of illness, Yakov explains, he cannot play in the orchestra. The motif of tears grows ever more intense. "And again he played and tears gushed from his eyes onto the violin." Chekhov emphasizes the baptismal, cleansing character of tears: they fall upon his violin and, as it were, sanctify it. Rothschild listens in ecstasy. And "tears slowly flowed down his cheeks, drops fell on his green jacket" (*PssS* 8: 305). The "green" here, as in the earlier reference to the "green" willow, underscores the motif of renewal.

The sense of the Russian word *umilen'e*—tenderness, a feeling often expressed in tears; a softening of one's being in the contrition of the heart; a humble and humbling sense of grief and distress—is felt in this scene. Yet Chekhov avoids sentimentality.

"And then all day Yakov lay and grieved" (*PssS* 8: 305).

Yakov's pathos and tragedy is that he simultaneously discovers and loses his earthly paradise. Here both Rothschild's and Yakov's journeys converge; they are joined by Yakov's music of suffering and loss. Yakov does not rise from his grave like Lazarus, but the coffin, or grave (the word *grob*, "coffin," in Russian has an older meaning of "grave"), figuratively speaking, opens up: the wooden coffin, whose emptiness on religious holidays Yakov bewailed, is replaced by another box, the violin, from which pours forth sublime music.[8]

---

[8] Yakov's obsessive preoccupation with coffins and death is perhaps symptomatic of a basically religious nature. "The tomb—is it an abyss without exit or is it the portal to another world [Le tombeau, est-il un abîme sans issue ou le portique d'un autre monde]?" asked François-Auguste-René de Chateaubriand, in one of his works. He replied in another work: "Religion was born at the tombs and the tombs cannot do without it [La religion a pris naissance aux tombeaux et les tombeaux ne peuvent se passer d'elle]." *Oeuvres complètes de M. le Vicompte de Chateaubriand* (Paris, 1826–28), 2: 287, 3: 197.

When the priest, confessing Yakov, asked him "whether he remembered any special sin, Yakov, straining his weakening memory, recalled again the unhappy face of Marfa and the despairing cry of the Jew when the dog bit him, and he said barely audibly: 'Give the violin to Rothschild' [Skripku otdaite Rotshil'du]'" (*PssS* 8: 305). Yakov's feeling of contrition manifests itself not so much in words as in images and sounds: the "unhappy face" of Marfa and the "despairing cry" of the Jew. These two images, an organic part of his experience and of the experience of Russian life, are iconic in their allusions to *another* despairing Jew, Jesus, and *another* grieving mother, Mary. Chekhov reminds us here that the power and grandeur of religious imagery are to be found in the simple and tragic ingredients of life.

There are parallels in Yakov's and the evangelical sinner's journeys. These parallel lines, however, do not meet in any Christian hosanna. The dominant fact and experience of the Prodigal Son is that he returns from exile to his church and to the bosom of God. Yakov, however, does not experience any religious passion at the end of his life. One cannot speak of an anguish on Yakov's part for a "heavenly homeland" (Bulgakov), or of a "general mourning for [Christian] salvation lost" (Wybrew). Yakov's moral-spiritual crisis is redemptive, but he is overwhelmed by a feeling of desolation. In his life a nominal Christian, Yakov dies a Christian. There is no indication, however, that he experiences any consolation in the Christian faith.

After Yakov's death Rothschild plays only on the deceased man's violin. The same "plaintive sounds" come forth as when he played his flute. When he tries to repeat what Yakov played at the doorstep, however, "something comes forth so melancholy and mournful that everybody weeps" (*PssS* 8: 305). This "new song" is so pleasing to the merchants that they insist Rothschild play it ten times over. Here, of course, is the third and final allusion in "Rothschild's Fiddle" to "By the Rivers of Babylon," in particular to the lines: "For there they that carried us away captive required of us a song; and they that wasted us required of us mirth, saying, Sing us one of the songs of Zion. How shall we sing of the Lord's song in a strange land?"

At the end of his life Yakov *remembers* and *repents* in his own deep, albeit wordless, way; he makes contact with his essential moral and spiritual self, and with Rothschild. Yet his *return* to his humane self is devoid of any manifestation of a deep relation to his Christian faith (except a purely formal one), or to the notion of the immortality of his soul, or to religion in general. In the end, Chekhov's dark, but affirmative story—affirmative in its humanistic faith in man's essential humanity and its belief in the power of art—leaves Yakov where it leaves Rothschild: in exile. What is equally certain, however, is that the psalm, "By the Rivers of Babylon," one central to both Jewish and Christian theological history and thought, lies at the heart of "Rothschild's Fiddle" and constitutes its overarching ethical idea.

# Chekhov's Anti-Melodramatic Imagination:
# Inoculation against the Diseases of the Contemporary Theater

## Svetlana Evdokimova, Brown University

In his letter to Leontiev (Shcheglov) of 7 November 1888, Chekhov complains about the state of contemporary theater: "Everything good is being exaggerated to the skies, while everything base is being masked.... Contemporary theater is an eruption, a bad disease of the cities. One has to chase this disease away, but to like it is unhealthy. You will start arguing with me and repeat an old phrase: theater is a school, it educates, etc. I will respond to this with what I see: contemporary theater is not above the crowd, but, on the contrary the life of the crowd is more intelligent and above theater" (*PssP* 3: 60). Several days later he continues to debunk contemporary theater with the same gusto: "Contemporary theater is the world of blockheads, Karpovs, stupidity, and windbags. The other day Karpov bragged that in his inane *The Crocodile's Tears* he satirized our 'yellow-beaked liberals' and that this was the reason his play was not well-received and was criticized. After that I began hating theater even more and developed love for those fanatics-martyrs who are trying to turn theater into something useful and harmless" (*PssP* 3: 65–66).

These harsh comments are not exceptions in Chekhov's criticism of contemporary theater and cannot be dismissed as mere rhetorical flourishes. His statements about theater, actors, playwrights, and the unenlightened audience range from openly critical to condescending, theater being playfully referred to as his "mistress" or as a pleasurable sport comparable to fishing. So why did Chekhov spend the last years of his life being so intimately involved with theater? Was he himself infected with this dangerous disease of the cities? And how did Dr. Chekhov try to cure it?

First, let us consider his diagnosis. Chekhov's criticism of Karpov's *The Crocodile Tears* (*Krokodilovy slezy*) and his sort of popular plays is a good point of reference: "The whole play, in addition to its crude naiveté, is a lie and calumny against life.... One of the heroines exclaims: 'And thus vice is punished and virtue is triumphant!' and with these words the play ends.... If I ever say or write anything similar, you have the right to hate me and have nothing to do with me" (*PssP* 3: 67). Equally critical are Chekhov's comments about the excessive scenery in popular entertainment and his opinions of the actresses who wring their hands or shed torrents of tears on stage. In other words, it is not theater *per se* that offends his artistic sensibility, but theater as practiced on the contemporary stage. Chekhov singles out those aspects of

*Chekhov the Immigrant: Translating a Cultural Icon.* Michael C. Finke and Julie de Sherbinin, eds. Bloomington, IN: Slavica Publishers, 2007, 207–17.

contemporary theater that are traditionally associated with melodrama or a well-made play (unrealistic plot, exaggerated emotions, dualistic morality underlying the structure of the play, a clear-cut division of characters into villains and their victims, and stylized manner of acting).[1]

It is worth noting that melodrama, as the genre most accessible to the bourgeois, was held in contempt by the intelligentsia. Chekhov too perceived melodrama as a distortion of realism and dangerous theatricalization of life that was distracting the audience from more mundane and real concerns. He viewed the melodramatic structure and melodramatic gesture as dangerous because of their potential to manipulate the audience for the sake of frequently dubious goals. Note that melodramatic behavior often figures in Chekhov's stories and plays as a tool of manipulation and abuse of human goodness.

The histrionic style of acting exercised in contemporary theater was also associated with melodrama as a genre, since melodrama relied heavily on non-verbal modes of expression and a stylized manner of acting that appealed to the bourgeois public's need for self-expression. The "bad illness of the cities" manifests itself as the prevalence of popular genres of urban theatrical entertainment, and especially of melodrama with its formulaic structure, spectacular effects, and conventional morality. Chekhov's dissatisfaction with contemporary theater, then, is primarily dissatisfaction with melodrama's "aesthetics of astonishment" (to use Peter Brooks' term).[2] I suggest, therefore, that it is as the result of his persistent struggle with melodramatic conventions that Chekhov created his new theater. Similar to the Western European innovators of the stage, such as Henrik Ibsen and Maurice Maeterlinck with his revolutionary theory of "le Tragique quotidien," Chekhov's path to theater is also a *via negativa*, that is, through the rejection of contemporary theater and its "theatricality." Similar to Maeterlinck, he wants to focus not on the exceptional moments of life, which generate awe, sorrow, or intense emotional response, but on the condition of life itself.

A doctor by profession, he knew that one often needs to introduce the virus of a disease into the body in order to prevent the illness. Chekhov uses melodramatic conventions as antigenic material injected into his plays in order to "immunize" the audience against the "dangerous disease." In his mature plays, he introduces some elements of melodrama and uses some of its classical topoi (the enclosed garden, the space of innocence, the theme of the interrupted banquet, the devastated family nest) only to subvert melo-

---

[1] For a classical discussion of melodrama's generic characteristics, see S. D. Balukhatyi, "K poetike melodramy," in *Poetika: Sbornik statei* (Leningrad: Academia, 1927), 63–86.

[2] See Peter Brooks, *The Melodramatic Imagination: Balzac, Henry James, Melodrama, and the Mode of Excess* (New Haven: Yale University Press), 1976.

drama.³ We easily recognize as belonging to melodrama such of his *fabulas* as, for example, the theme of dispossession in *The Three Sisters*, the abuse of virtue in *Uncle Vanya*, and the "tons of love" in *The Seagull*. But these melodramatic *fabulas* function precisely as an inoculation *against* the malaise of melodrama and reveal the prose of life as the main propelling movement of the plays. Even in *Ivanov*, which clearly relies on melodramatic coincidences and explosive scenes, Chekhov embarks on the destruction of melodrama and any melodramatic concept of the human being. Chekhov's dramaturgy, I suggest, is based on what the formalists identify as a minus-device—in this case the reversal of the aesthetics of melodrama. The final goal is the audience's complete insusceptibility to the "virus" of melodrama, and the final result is a new type of play—an "anti-melodrama."

The genre of melodrama became the most consistent target of Chekhov's criticism of contemporary theater. What Peter Brooks identifies as "melodramatic imagination" was antagonistic to Chekhov's fundamental beliefs and artistic sensitivity. Chekhov not only ridicules melodramatic characters and melodramatic behavior as a "calumny against life," and, therefore, a betrayal of realism in art, but also as a dangerous moral fallacy. The Manichean duality that Brooks views as the central metaphysical system underlying melodramatic narrative structure, and the conception of the world in terms of extremes, were, in general, quite alien to Chekhov's artistic imagination. Moreover, Chekhov was aware of the degree to which the aesthetics of excess were ingrained in Russian cultural history, and he openly objected to the "melodramatization" of thought and experience typical of both the Russian radical intelligentsia and lowbrow culture.

---

³ Ivan Kuznetsov lists some of the melodramatic clichés that Chekhov uses in his plays, such as the topos of the family nest, characters' analysis and self-analysis of their emotions, the principle of contrast, among other characteristics of melodrama as outlined in S. D. Balukhatyi, "Poetika melodramy," in his *Voprosy poetiki* (Leningrad: Izdatel'stvo Leningradskogo universiteta, 1990). Although Kuznetsov does not analyze in detail the function of specific melodramatic devices in Chekhov, he correctly observes that the melodramatic clichés are used in Chekhov's plays as a distancing device, a way to dissociate the author's point of view from the plays' characters. See Ivan Kuznetsov, "Melodramaticheskie klishe v dramaturgii Chekhova i Zudermana," in *Chekhov i Germaniia*, ed. V. B. Kataev and R.-D. Kluge (Moscow: Universitet, 1996), 70. On the remnants of melodrama in Chekhov's plays, see also Margarita Odesskaya, "Chekhov's *Tatiana Repina*: From Melodrama to Mystery Play," *Modern Drama* 42 (Winter 1999): 475–90. Odesskaya notes, "Chekhov exploited several clichés of melodrama, but ... having placed them in a different semiotic context or system, he fractured the stereotypes. As is well known, Chekhov actively engaged his literary predecessors in dialogue, employing their popular subjects, heroes, and devices as material for parody" (479). I am interested not so much in Chekhov's parody of melodrama and melodramatic clichés, however, but in his anti-melodramatic aesthetics.

It is no coincidence that Dostoevsky, the most "melodramatic" of the Russian classics, is frequently satirized by Chekhov for portraying what Chekhov perceives as melodramatic suffering. Chekhov had reservations about Dostoevsky's dramatizations of human encounters and his intense, excessive representations of life that place the essential conflicts in the realm of spiritual reality. His early story "A Mysterious Nature" ("Zagadochnaia natura," 1883) offers a vivid example of how Chekhov associates the excesses of Russian "mysterious nature" with the name of Dostoevsky. Talking to the young aspiring writer, the heroine of the story suggests he should describe her mysterious nature: "My life has been so full, so varied, so multi-colored.... But above all—I have been unhappy! I am a sufferer of the sort you find in Dostoevsky. Reveal my soul to the world, Voldemar, reveal that poor soul!" (*PssS* 2: 90). The writer's response shows his complete familiarity with the melodramatic convention and the discourse of excessive suffering that became part of the Russian cultural context: "'My lovely one!' murmurs the writer, kissing her hand close to the bracelet. 'It's not you I am kissing, but the suffering of humanity. Do you remember Raskolnikov? That is how he kissed'" (*PssS* 2: 91).

Russian melodramatic art tends to reveal (cf.: "reveal my soul to the world!") and is often confessional in nature. By contrast, Chekhov develops an anti-melodramatic mode of expression that conceals emotions, avoids all the excesses of self-expression, and focuses on that which is hidden. Significantly, when Chekhov offers advice to young aspiring writers, he always chastises them for melodramatic excesses in style and recommends restraint. Consider, for example, his recommendation that Gorky show more restraint: "First of all, in my opinion, you lack restraint. You are like a spectator in a theater who is so unrestrained in the way he expresses his enthusiasm that he prevents himself and others from listening.... This is not breadth, not a bold stroke of the brush, but simply a lack of restraint" (*PssP* 7: 352). Likewise, Chekhov objects to the excessive expressiveness in acting, insisting instead on grace and restraint: "The majority of people suffer, the minority experiences sharp pain, but where on the streets or at home do you see people rushing about, galloping, and snatching at one's head? One has to express sufferings the way they are expressed in life, that is, not with the help of one's legs and arms, but with the tone of voice and the expression of eyes, not with gesticulation, but with grace... You will say that such are the stage conventions. No stage conventions should be an excuse for a lie..." (to O. Knipper, 2 January 1900).[4]

Chekhov's famous statement of religious belief, which led Aleksandr Chudakov to identify him as "the man of the field,"[5] is a classic articulation of

---

[4] See also Chekhov's sketch "The Fashionable Effect" ("Modnyi effekt").

[5] See Aleksandr P. Chudakov, "Chelovek polia," in *Anton P. Čechov—Philosophische und religiöse Dimensionen im Leben und im Werk*, ed. V. B. Katev, R.-D. Kluge, and R.

his refusal to commit to ideological or philosophical extremes: "Between 'there is God' and 'there is no God' lies a whole enormous field which a true sage crosses with great difficulty. A Russian, however, knows only one of these extremes, the middle ground between them does not interest him; that is why as a rule he knows either nothing or very little" (*PssS* 17: 224). This polarizing perception of reality, which Chekhov associated with Russian national identity, is essentially melodramatic. For it is the melodramatic mode that excludes the middle condition: "The world according to melodrama is built on an irreducible Manichaeism, the conflict of good and evil as opposites not subject to compromise. Melodramatic dilemmas and choices are constructed on the either/or in its extreme form as the all-or-nothing. Polarization is both horizontal and vertical: characters represent extremes, and they undergo extremes, passing from heights to depths, or the reverse, almost instantaneously."[6] Chekhov's criticism of "the Russian man" is primarily a criticism of Russian Manichaeism, the Russian melodramatic sensibility that refuses to acknowledge the existence and importance of "the huge field," or "the middle ground."

It is the middle ground indeed that becomes the focal point of Chekhov's artistic representation. While Chekhov's Ivanov was eagerly recognized as an heir of the Russian "superfluous man," Chekhov insisted that the protagonist of the play represented essentially a new type. Indeed, what is new in Ivanov is not his inertia, his disillusionment, and his "superfluousness," but the fact that he is defeated because he sees everything in extremes and is unable to accept the middle ground. He oscillates between lofty aspirations and despair. The diagnosis that Chekhov gives to Ivanov's malaise in one of his letters to A. Suvorin (30 December 1888) points specifically to Russian predilection for excesses as a key to this malaise:

> Russian excitability has one specific quality: it is quickly replaced by exhaustion. A man, just off the school bench, rashly takes on a burden beyond his powers ... makes speeches, writes to the minister, struggles with evil, applauds the good, does not fall in love simply but inevitably with either bluestockings or psychopaths or Jewesses or even prostitutes whom he saves, etc. But hardly has he turned 30 or 35, he begins to feel weariness and boredom.... Disillusion, apathy, nervous instability and exhaustion are the inevitable consequences of

---

Nohejl (Munich: Verlag Otto Sagner, 1997), 301–08. Referring to Chekhov as "man of the field" (*chelovek polia*) who is "infinitely free" because he does not place himself on any of the two poles, Chudakov hinted, without fully developing this point, at the importance of the vision of the middle ground for Chekhov's poetics: "In its significance this phenomenon is comparable to the dialogic worldview of Dostoevsky; in its influence on art it may be even more important, as it marks the beginning of the twentieth century's literature and theater" (308).

[6] Brooks, *The Melodramatic Imagination*, 36.

excessive excitability, and this excitability is characteristic of our young people to an extreme degree. (*PssP* 3: 109–10)

The problem of Russian cultural identity, as Chekhov sees it, is its oscillation between extremes. It is no coincidence that he refers to Russian "excitability" as the key to Russia's cultural malaise. Indeed, excitability is an important feature of the literary characters that in Russian cultural consciousness were associated not only with popular melodrama, but also with Dostoevsky. Ivanov may rebel against the melodramatic plot imposed on him, but ultimately cannot escape it. His suicide is the final form of entrapment in melodrama's excess.

Shortly before his death, Chekhov complained about stage directors' misinterpretations of his plays: "I am describing life... It is a dull, average life... But it is not tedious whimpering... They turn me into either a crybaby or simply a boring writer. I have written several volumes of humorous stories... And criticism makes of me some kind of weeper. They invent something about me out of their heads, anything they like, something I never thought of or dreamed about... This is beginning to make me angry."[7] Chekhov's refusal to associate with extreme positions at a time when multiple new social, political, and economic institutions were rapidly emerging was easily misinterpreted as "lack of principle" by his contemporaries, who failed to recognize the novelty of his position, with its underlying aesthetics of the middle ground. His frequently quoted letter to Pleshcheev, which articulated his artistic credo, focuses precisely on his anti-polarizing stand:

> I am neither liberal nor conservative, nor monk nor indifferentist. I would like to be a free artist and nothing else.... Pharisaism, dull-wittedness and tyranny reign not only in merchants' houses and police stations; I see them in science and literature among the younger generation.... I look upon tags and labels as prejudices. My holy of holies is the human body, health, intelligence, talent, inspiration and the most absolute freedom imaginable, freedom from violence and lies, no matter what form the latter two take." (*PssP* 3: 11).

Claiming that he wanted to be neither conservative nor liberal but merely a free artist, Chekhov resisted extreme positions as a form of ideological tyranny and viewed the melodramatic mode, with its dualist narrative structure, moral certitude, and pervasive use of "labels" and "tags," as too binding. Ultimately, his anti-melodramatic imagination was in part rooted in his desire to dissociate himself from commercial culture, and in part stemmed from his attempt to negotiate the extremes of Russian cultural self-expression,

---

[7] Evtikhii Karpov, "Dve poslednie vstrechi s A. P. Chekhovym," in *Chekhov i teatr: Pis'ma, fel'etony, sovremenniki o Chekhove-dramaturge*, ed. E. D. Surkov (Moscow: Iskusstvo, 1961), 373.

which thrived on overstatement. In the process of these negotiations, he developed what could be called "the aesthetics of restraint" or "the aesthetics of the middle ground."

☙ ❦

Let us now consider how Chekhov's anti-melodramatic imagination influenced his theatrical experimentations, and the ideological implications of this new type of middle-ground theater.

Chekhov's mistrust of ideological extremes translated also into his deep mistrust of artistic principles governing the contemporary stage. His aversion to any type of polarization and to contemporary theater's turning everything into ideological warfare made him reconsider the nature of dramatic character and action and the very core of conventional theater—the clash of characters, or conflict: "Contemporary playwrights stuff their plays only with the angels, villains or buffoons—try to find these types in Russia! Well, you may find them but not in such extreme forms as these playwrights require.... I wanted to be original: I did not depict any single villain, or angel (although I could not refrain from buffoons), I did not condemn or justify anyone" (letter to Al. P. Chekhov, 24 Oct. 1887; *PssP* 2: 137–38). Likewise, commenting on one of the characters in Gorky's play, Chekhov gives Gorky the following advice: "But please, do not oppose him to Peter and Tatiana—let him be by himself, and them by themselves, they are all fine people independently from each other" (*PssP* 10: 96).

While the characters of melodrama openly pronounce their moral judgments of the world, Chekhov ridicules characters who thrive on explicit self-expression and melodramatic rhetoric (Voinitsky and Sonya of *Uncle Vanya*, Petya Trofimov of *Cherry Orchard* among many others). The typical example is Doctor Lvov from *Ivanov*, the so called "honest and straightforward man" who stands on stage and utters the unspeakable: "Nikolai Alekseevich, I have listened to you and now I have to speak frankly, in plain terms. [...] I cannot tell you, words fail me, but... but I profoundly dislike you" (*PssS* 12: 17). The doctor's melodramatic rhetoric is not only comical; it is also presented by Chekhov as a moral fallacy, for Lvov tries to impose his melodramatic vision of the world on everyone around him (he casts Sarah as a saint and Ivanov as a villain). His melodramatic rhetoric implicitly insists that the world is polarized; it excludes any middle ground. Significantly, Lvov cannot understand, he can only overstate. This kind of pure self-expression is always ridiculed by Chekhov. A man, Chekhov insists, cannot be understood in terms of set traits that lead him inevitably, deterministically, to some kind of action. That is why Ivanov, who is caught in the web of melodrama, rebels against the tyranny of melodramatic vision: "No, Doctor. We all have too many cogs, wheels, and valves to judge each other by first impression or by outward appearance. I do not understand you, you do not understand me, and we do not understand ourselves" (*PssS* 12: 54–56). The tragedy for Ivanov is that, being viewed as he is in melodramatic terms by everyone around him, he cannot escape the melodrama that is being imposed on him.[8]

Although Chekhov engages with contemporaneous social issues, he refuses to plot them in the melodramatic terms typical of the Russian intelligentsia and so-called "men of ideas." It is not extreme situations that are important, Chekhov insists, but everyday life, which is not dramatic, not emplotted as tragedy or melodrama. This everyday life lacks teleology and is essentially unorganized: "After all, in real life, people don't spend every moment in shooting one another, hanging themselves, or making declarations of love. They do not spend all their time saying clever things. They are more occupied with eating, drinking, flirting, and saying stupidities, and these are the things which ought to be shown on the stage… People eat their dinner, just eat their dinner, and all the time their happiness is taking form, or their lives are being destroyed."[9]

Chekhov's mature plays involve the middle ground, which is the hardest to depict on stage. In a letter to Suvorin he writes: "He who invents new endings for a play will start a new era. These nasty endings are so hard to manage! The hero either marries or shoots himself, there is no other way out" (*PssP* 5: 72). Chekhov decides this dilemma by rejecting the traditional finale. Life goes on, there is no ending in a traditional sense—such are the denouements of *Uncle Vanya*, *Three Sisters*, and *The Cherry Orchard*. Even in *Seagull* there is no sense that Treplev's suicide will bring significant change to the lives of the characters.

While melodrama resolves conflicts by reaffirming the existing order and can therefore be interpreted as having conservative implications, Chekhov's plays are open to the future.[10] They never end with the restoration of the lost order. If melodrama urges toward harmony in the construction of its final moments, Chekhov's denouements lack reconciliation. But unlike tragedy, in which the hero moves from ignorance to knowledge at the moment of his downfall, Chekhov's heroes do not have a final downfall and gain only limited knowledge. The existing order of things almost invariably proves inadequate (*Uncle Vanya*, *Three Sisters*, *Cherry Orchard*), and the audience is given the sense that there is no way back to the old ways. At the same time, Chekhov is skeptical about the possibility of radical change and of the tragic vision that is associated with such change: Sonya and Vanya will continue to

---

[8] Cf. Boris Zingerman's observation: "They push Ivanov into an old worn-out net of human relations—into the parameters of an old theatrical system" (Zingerman, *Teatr Chekhova i ego mirovoe znachenie* [Moscow: RIK Rusanova, 2001], 227).

[9] V. A. Feider, A. P. Chekhov, *Literaturnyi byt i tvorchesto po memuarnym materialam* (Leningrad: Academia, 1928), 160.

[10] Melodrama may be at the same time interpreted as democratic in its attempt to make its representation clear and accessible to everyone. See Brooks, *The Melodramatic Imagination*, 15.

labor although their lives are never going to remain the same; the three sisters may explore various options but most likely will not go to Moscow; the cherry orchard will be destroyed, but Ranevskaya will return to Paris. Chekhov's plays, therefore, are neither conservative nor radical in their ideological implications, but rather ironical. Chekhov complained of Stanislavsky, who made people cry at his plays: "I merely wanted to say to people honestly: 'Look at yourself, look at how bad and boring your lives are!...' The important thing is that people understand this, and when they understand it, they will, without fail, create for themselves another better life... What is there to cry about?"[11]

While relying heavily on unbelievable plots, coincidences and inflated emotions, melodrama strove to locate and convey some hidden ontology. Melodramatic representation therefore operated with signs that transferred significance into another context. Discussing the melodramatic mode in Balzac, Brooks argues that "the site of his drama, the ontology of his true subject, is not easily established.... We might say that the center of interest and the scene of the underlying drama reside within what we could call the 'moral occult,' the domain of operative spiritual values which is both indicated within and masked by the surface of reality."[12]

Chekhov's vision, by contrast, recoils from hidden ontology and from metaphoric perception of reality in general. Instead, Chekhov's use of signs and symbols is highly ironic. *Seagull* is an interesting example of the reversal of melodramatic symbolization. On the one hand, the play's key metaphors seem to suggest melodramatic formula. The dominant images of lake and seagull have formulaic associations with innocence, purity, and freedom. The spectator's contemplation of innocence (Nina) should become the main "motor" of the action for the production and stimulation of the spectators' emotions. But her seduction by Trigorin, which takes place off stage, does not lead to the spectator's agitation, and there is nothing that would reinforce and enable enjoyment of conventional morality. Chekhov therefore does not simply reverse the traditional symbolic meaning of the lake and the seagull, but uses signs and symbols to parody signs and symbols and their semiotic urgency. The seagull is only a seagull, the lake is but a lake. It is the characters of the play who read more into these images and assign higher spiritual meaning to the trivial details of life.[13] The metaphoric meaning exists only to the extent that the characters of the play, and possibly the audience, tend to interpret the world metaphorically. Thus, though Chekhov's images are open to metaphoric reading, they also resist it. Some of his key symbolic images

---

[11] Aleksandr Serebrov [A. N. Tikhonov], "Vremia i liudi: O Chekhove," in *Chekhov i teatr*, 371.

[12] Brooks, *The Melodramatic Imagination*, 5.

[13] Cf. an excellent essay by Carol Strongin, "Irony and Theatricality in Chekhov's 'The Seagull,'" *Comparative Drama* 15: 4 (Winter 1981–82): 366–80.

resist the semiotic tyranny associated with melodramatic and metaphoric vision of the world and attempt to liberate themselves from symbolic significance. "I am a seagull... No, that's not right" — these final words of Nina are the indication that she ultimately manages to escape the world of melodrama and liberates herself from "tags" and "labels." The seagull is a seagull, the actress is an actress. While Nina's rejection of symbols and metaphors proves liberating and helps her to persevere (she leaves behind her melodramatic personal life and melodramatic style of acting), Treplev remains caught in the complex web of signification: "I still keep on drifting in a chaos of dreams and images, not knowing why and for whose sake it has to be"(*PssS* 13: 59). Treplev's suicide further shows that, similar to Ivanov, he cannot escape the melodramatic plot. The play as a whole, however, represents Chekhov's struggle with the pervasiveness of symbolic vision. The seagull as a non-verbal sign is ultimately not the symbol of something else (purity, youth, innocence, lost opportunity), but merely a dead bird. Trigorin's refusal to interpret the image of the stuffed sea gull ("I don't remember!") points to the dead end of overinterpretation.[14] Likewise, the black dress of Masha, the symbol of mourning, as well as her highly melodramatic rhetoric—"I am in mourning for my life"— have anti-symbolic meaning. She seeks drama and relies on melodrama's clichéd symbolism. But her drama is that she is in search of drama. Chekhov uses symbols and images that may have symbolic meaning, but does it in such a way as to liberate them from the semiotic and metaphoric tyranny characteristic of melodrama. Symbolic images function only as a way to establish connections between various characters and the play's motifs, but they are not loaded with specific symbolic or metaphoric meaning.

Similar to his subversion of the "moral occult" and melodramatic system of symbols, Chekhov also reverses the conventional melodramatic use of music and sound. In melodrama, music is used to emphasize dramatic moments, to mark entrances and exits, to delineate the emotional states of the personages, and to put the audience into a particular emotional mood. Music is used toward the dramatization of life.

In Chekhov's plays, sound and music are not employed to dramatize events or emphasize the characters' emotional disposition; they are not used as secondary acoustic effects, but have a function independent of characterization. Thus, the sounds of the military march in the end of *Three Sisters* do not reflect the emotional condition of the heroines and do not even mark a particularly dramatic moment in the play, they rather contrast with the emotional state of the sisters. In *Seagull*, the sound of the Treplev's gunshot is presented to the audience as a bursting bottle of ether, which clearly deflates the

---

[14] "*Shamraev*: Once Konstantin Gavrilovich shot down a seagull, and you requested that I order to make a stuffed bird of it. *Trigorin*: I don't remember. (In contemplation.) I don't remember!" (*PssS* 13: 54–55).

sense of tragedy. Various sounds that Chekhov uses in his plays are anti-melodramatic in their function, since they do not intensify or create mood in accordance with the devices drawn from the musicological doctrine of the eighteenth century. These sounds introduce no emotional, but rather an ironical element. Such is Dorn's singing snatches of opera and sentimental songs in *Seagull*. Frequently, it is the characters of the play (as in *Seagull* or *Cherry Orchard*) who assign symbolic value to various sounds and try to interpret them. The audience, however, is expected to keep an ironic distance from the characters' search for symbolic meaning. To be sure, the sound of a breaking string easily yields to symbolic interpretation, but it may just as well be the incidental sound of a bucket that, in Lopakhin's words, "must have broken loose" (*PssS* 13: 224). Once again, Chekhov's middle ground position oscillates between the two poles of reading: the sound could have symbolic meaning but it is just as likely to have none. Chekhov plays with the audience's prowess at identifying symbols, he engages the audience in the game of deciphering symbols and establishing symbolic connections, only to show the futility of this project.

Chekhov's aesthetics of the middle ground are an ambitious project not only because they go against the grain of the popular and the accessible, but also because they embody a mode of perception that transcends traditional genre division. They are neither comic, nor tragic, nor melodramatic, and they parody Russian proclivity for self-dramatization and for the "accursed questions" of existence. By injecting the "vaccine" of melodrama in his plays in dosages that reverse the melodramatic impact, Chekhov "inoculates" the audience against the malaise of contemporary theater. In doing so, Chekhov creates a new "healthy" drama, a Chekhovian one.

# Doctor without Patients/Man without a Spleen: A Meditation on Chekhov's Practice

### Cathy Popkin, Columbia University

In memory of G. Patton Wright (1946–2005)

The title of my essay proceeds from the title of the panel that occasioned it: "Doctor/Patient, Author/Reader: Conflicting/Conflating Identities."[1] This catchy title in turn capitalizes on the fact that identity is ordinarily singular—not only grammatically but also semantically: identity denotes "sameness," "oneness," "individuality." Etymologically, it derives from a contraction of *idem et idem*, literally "the same and the same." Yet here we have a professional carrying more than one union card, more than one ID.

It is a plurality Chekhov himself framed as mildly illicit, famously referring to his double duty as an auspicious form of two-timing, medicine being his lawful wife, literature his mistress. "When I get tired of one," he liked to say, "I spend the night with the other."[2] And if consorting with more than one discipline begets multiple identities, the excess spawned by this dalliance is only compounded by the cascade of signatures Chekhov used to designate his early authorial self. The apparatus to the *Complete Works* lists 51 names (see Table 1 on p. 220), not even counting the playful aliases he assumed in his private letters. The public pseudonyms range from the essentially transparent "Antosha Chekhonte" to the tautological "Brother of my Brother"; from the oxymoronic "Young Old Man" to the palindromic "Ruver i Revur"; from "Chekhov" without the middle three letters ("Ch-v"), to "Chekhov" without the middle two letters ("Che-v"), to "Chekhov" missing the last four letters ("Ch"), to Chekhov with the last letter alone ("…v")—more incomplete Chekhovs and Chekhontes than I can count—and finally the eponymous "Doctor Without Patients" and his paradigmatic double, the "Man Without a Spleen"—which Chekhov uses dozens of times in full, sometimes with only "without" spelled out ("M. Without S.") or further abbreviated as "M. W.

---

[1] An earlier version of this paper was presented at the symposium session dedicated to the medical humanities.

[2] Letter to Suvorin, 11 September 1888; to Al. P. Chekhov, 17 January 1887; to I. I. Ostrovskii, 11 February 1893; and to his Czech translator in 1897. Cited in *Letters of Anton Chekhov*, ed. Avrahm Yarmolinsky (New York: Viking Press, 1973), 230.

**Table 1.** A. P. Chekhov: Pseudonyms (*PssS* 18: 337–38)

| | |
|---|---|
| А. П. | A. P. |
| А. П. Ч-в | A. P. Ch-v |
| Антоша | Antosha |
| Антоша Ч. | Antosha Ch. |
| Антоша Ч.*** | Antosha Ch.*** |
| Антоша Чехонте | Antosha Chekhonte |
| А-н Ч-те | A-n Ch-te |
| Ан. Ч. | An. Ch. |
| Ан. Ч-е | An. Ch-e |
| Анче | Anche |
| Ан. Че-в | An. Che-v |
| А. Ч. | A. Ch. |
| А. Ч-в | A. Ch-v |
| А. Че-в | A. Che-v |
| А. Чехонте | A. Chekhonte |
| Г. Балдастов | Mr. Baldastov (blockhead) |
| Макар Балдастов | Makar Baldastov |
| Брат моего брата | Brother of my Brother |
| Врач без пациентов | Doctor Without Patients |
| Вспыльчивый человек | Hot-tempered Person |
| Гайка № 5 ¾ (*dubia*) | Nut (as in bolt; as in 'he's got a screw loose') #5 (*uncertain*) |
| Гайка № 6 | Nut #6 |
| Гайка № 9 | Nut #9 |
| Гайка № 1010101010 (*dubia*) | Nut #1010101010 (*uncertain*) |
| Гайка № 0,006 (*dubia*) | Nut #0.006 (*uncertain*) |
| Грач | Rook |
| Дон-Антонио Чехонте | Don-Antonio Chekhonte |
| Дяденька | Uncle (*diminutive*) |
| Кисляев | Kisliaev (sour) |
| М. Ковров | M. Kovrov (carpets) |
| Крапива | Nettle |
| Лаэрт | Laertes |
| Нте (*dubia*) | Nte (*uncertain*) |
| Н-те (*dubia*) | N-te (*uncertain*) |
| -нте (*dubia*) | -nte (*uncertain*) |
| Прозаический поэт | Prosaic poet |
| Пурселепетантов | Purselepetantov (babble) |
| Рувер | Ruver |
| Рувер и ревур | Ruver and Revur |
| С. Б. Ч. (*dubia*) | S. B. Ch. (first letters of Spleen Without a Man) (*uncertain*) |
| Улисс | Ulysses |
| Ц. | Ts. |
| Ч. Б. С. | Ch. B. S. (first letters of "Man Without a Spleen") |
| Ч. без с. | M. Without S. |
| Человек без селезёнки | Man Without a Spleen |
| Чехонте | Chekhonte |
| Ч. Хонте | Ch. Khonte |
| Шампанский | Shampansky (champagne) |
| Юный старец (*dubia*) | Young old man (*uncertain*) |
| «…въ» | «…v″» |
| Z. | Z. |

S."—plus, for good measure, *his* logical complement, the "Spleen Without a Man" (or at least Spleen Without a Man without all its letters—"S. W. M."). "When I place the final period," concludes the narrator of Chekhov's waggish "My Ranks and Titles," "I am the 'Man Without a Spleen'" ("Moi chini i tituly," 1883; *PssS* 2: 231). Having placed his final period in this sketch *after* the phony signature rather than before it, Chekhov makes pseudonymity part of the very story.[3] Then, having established his prerogative to identify himself as variously and as prodigiously as he pleases (adducing fifteen possibilities in the space of two pages), Chekhov publishes this piece *without* attribution.

The title I have adopted is thus cobbled together from Chekhov's own assumed names, with an obvious eye to those that fall into his favorite subcategory, "X without Y"—or more specifically X without something normally entailed by and included in X itself. And while a doctor might conceivably go through a stint without patients, the guy missing a major vascular organ has genuine cause for concern.

For all the apparent *excess* of identities and names, in other words, both "Doctor Without Patients" and "Man Without a Spleen" (along with all those incomplete renderings of "Chekhov") emphasize what is *missing*, pointing to deficit and loss. *Pseudo-nymity* itself, as a way of maintaining *a-nonymity* (namelessness), gives you, in effect, not only the man without his spleen or the doctor without visible means of support, but also, significantly, a writer without a recognizable signature—instead of a *surfeit* of identity, a rather glaring lack. (In fact, if you consider how many of the attributions on the list of pseudonyms are uncertain—all those marked *dubia*—the indeterminacy seems all the more acute.)

But the object here is not to impugn Anton Chekhov's sense of *self*. What coalesces, rather, at this intersection of names and titles, personal and professional identities, and the condition of being "without" is Anton Chekhov's *practice*.

**Part 1: Identity**

If you run mentally through Chekhov's prose, you can cite dozens of ways in which identity looms thematically large—mistaken identity in "The Kiss," borrowed identities in "The Darling," status-driven ones in "Fatty and Skinny," not to mention the innumerable self-recognitions through which characters come into their own. In fact, it seems almost too pervasive a topic to be analytically useful. But I am thinking for a moment of identity specifi-

---

[3] Two scholars in particular have offered nuanced readings of the complex story told by Chekhov's pseudonyms. See Marena Senderovich, "Chekhov's Name Drama," in *Reading Chekhov's Text*, ed. Robert L. Jackson (Evanston, IL: Northwestern University Press, 1993), 31–48; and Michael C. Finke, *Seeing Chekhov: Life and Art* (Ithaca, NY: Cornell University Press, 2005).

cally in terms of individuation, and I am less interested in cases where such individuation emerges than in instances where it dissolves.

The *locus classicus* for this is Chekhov's penultimate story, "The Bishop" ("Arkhierei"), written between 1899 and 1902, during a period of the writer's ever increasing fame but ever declining health. Decline essentially describes the trajectory of the story as well, as the venerated and high-ranking Bishop Pyotr falls ill and in his weakening state finds it increasingly difficult to carry out the duties of his office. By the end he can no longer stand on his feet and ultimately is unable to communicate at all. Then he dies, is replaced, and is promptly forgotten.

In the course of his illness, the Bishop had agonized over the fact that his exalted position effectively separated him from the faithful; no one managed to approach him without bowing and scraping, his own mother least of all. The Bishop's dying vision is a liberation from all that, as he imagines himself a "simple, ordinary man, walking briskly and gaily through the field … free as a bird and able to go wherever he liked" (*PssS* 10: 200). Having progressively shed the burdens of authority—and then expelled them definitively in a final massive hemorrhage—he can be just another guy, a carefree "rank amateur" rather than a credentialed but tormented cleric. In the dying Bishop's final moments, his mother, too, ceases to be intimidated, and laments in as heartrending terms as any mother the imminent death of her child.

In an obvious sense, then, professional identity would appear to give way to personal identity. But this essentialist reading obscures the more salient fact that, having been divested of his "external" trappings (like rank and title), the Bishop does not now revert to some sort of "real," intrinsic self. Indeed, he is no more of an individual person in the end than he was at the outset: his "ordinary man" striding through the field has by definition NO distinguishing traits, no fixed identity. If anything, he is Musil's *Mann ohne Eigenschaften*, the man *without* characteristics. Moreover, for all Chekhov's unwavering insistence on individuality ("I believe in individual people!") and his apprehensions about his own individual self being swallowed up by "some shapeless, jelly-like mass,"[4] it is less clear in his work that the dissolution of discrete identity is necessarily pernicious, or that the self-less self on a formless field has lost his way. Here it may be the beginning of the story rather than its famous end that warrants a closer look.

Recall that the Bishop is conducting the service on the eve of Palm Sunday and experiences the attendees as an undifferentiated mass (if not gelatinous, then comparably amorphous), indistinguishable from any other group of worshippers and indivisible into distinct individuals with particular traits; men and women, old and young, all have identical faces with identical expressions, and no single person can be discerned. The one figure to emerge

---

[4] To I. I. Orlov, 22 February 1899; to M. O. Men'shikov, 16 April 1897.

briefly is equally likely to be Bishop Pyotr's mother or some other old woman resembling his mother. I want to speculate that this breakdown of individuation points to something beyond a symptom of the Bishop's illness, that the blur may introduce its own form of clarity. To be sure, the Bishop is unwell, *nezdorov*—his breathing is labored, his shoulders ache, and he is fatigued beyond measure—but even once his mother or her look-alike has melted back into the shapeless, jelly-like crowd and, again, he cannot distinguish any single individual from any other, "his soul was at peace and all was well" (10: 186). Indeed, the tears that well up in him "for some reason" communicate themselves to everyone else in the church, producing what might be read as one of very few moments of authentic communion in the story and a stirring example of access to somebody else's pain.

In a second instance of susceptibility to another's suffering, it is the dying Bishop who is infected by the tears of his young niece, Katya. But his failure to be fully present to Katya—to reach out at the *present* moment rather than promising assistance at a later date (*after* the "Resurrection," as if in a future life)—suggests that this communion is incomplete. Daria Kirjanov sees genuine communion in the much anticipated reunion between mother and son at the story's end.[5] But given that, by then, the Bishop is beyond comprehension, and the mother's access of emotion is neither reciprocated nor even registered by her dying son ("'Pavlusha, answer me!... My son, Pavlusha, please answer me!'"), that connection seems even more tenuous. Indeed, her eleventh-hour realization that he is her child, "near and dear" (and not just a potential source of financial assistance), is *her* epiphany rather than his. He has made his own peace ("How good it is!" he thought, "How good!") before she even enters the room. Her ministrations have no more effect on the Bishop than the useless consultation of the three doctors who arrive at the same time (*PssS* 10: 200).

In the opening scene, the momentary apparition of the mother does raise the enticing possibility of recovering one's very own, of embracing one's origin as indelible proof of unique identity; the Bishop's elation at the mother's fleeting appearance, which seems to transform everything from painful to peaceful, certainly points to the primacy of that sort of attachment. Yet the scene's unmistakable insistence on the profound sensation of continuousness—the indistinguishability of beings and the unity of experience—introduces the startling potential for relatedness, compassion, even oneness, among those who are simply present, whether mom is present or not. Her credentials, after all, are still *dubia*;[6] the communal weeping is a demonstrable

---

[5] Daria Kirjanov, *Chekhov and the Poetics of Memory* (New York: Peter Lang, 2000), 56–57.

[6] Indeed, even when her ID does turn out to be valid, her stilted behavior makes her unrecognizable, not identical with herself ("Ne ta, sovsem ne ta"; *PssS* 10: 194).

fact, and the "someone" who starts the empathic sobbing is no relation of the Bishop's. It is not the specificity of his own flesh and blood that propels him out onto that wide, wide field. As he leaves the church, the experience of fluidity and connection expands beyond his fellow man to include even the walls, crosses, birches, moon, sky, and village, "young" and "welcoming," whose "lives," too, are ineffably close to his (*PssS* 10: 187).

There are moments, in other words, that posit an alternative to particularity and individuality—in Zen terms, instances that point to the possibility of overcoming the dualism that artificially separates the individual self from other selves and from the world. In hinting at the possibility of suspending this separation, of overcoming the habitual perception of the self as a circumscribed subject surrounded by (and distinguished from) a world of objects, Chekhov's practice borders momentarily on a Buddhist one.[7] The Bishop's final vision of the "ordinary man" tentatively surrenders the compulsion to delineate, individuate, and thereby segregate the self, instantiating what Rinzai called the "true man without rank," the man who is "without form, without characteristics, without root, without source, and without dwelling place, yet is brisk and lively."[8] Rinzai's "true man" names not a permanent, intrinsic, particular self, the identifiable offspring of a specific mother, but a form of being "without rank," not predicated on a fixed identity or discernible position—as a metaphor for "Buddha nature," which is always manifesting itself as this or that but has no *fixed* form.

This radical departicularization points beyond the mere dissolution of *hierarchical* distinctions between bishop and congregant, or even any rigid division of labor between writer and doctor. It is an intimation, rather, in Chekhov's own terms, that we are "all part of one gigantic life form," whether it's Buddha nature or creation understood in more familiar terms, and that it may not ALWAYS be productive, as we have come to assume when we talk about Chekhov, to "individualize each case."[9]

---

[7] For a succinct exposition of Zen thinking on dualism and the separate self, see Barry Magid, *Ordinary Mind: Exploring the Common Ground of Zen and Psychotherapy* (Boston: Wisdom Publications, 2002), 45–46, 49.

[8] Rinzai is the Japanese name (a pseudonym, of sorts) for ninth-century Chinese Zen master Lin Chi, whose teachings reached Japan in the twelfth century. See Discourse XIV in *The Recorded Sayings of Ch'an Master Lin-Chi Hui-Chao of Chen Prefecture*, trans. Ruth Fuller Sasaki (Kyoto: Institute for Zen Studies, 1975), 15.

[9] The two passages are from "On Official Business" ("Po delam sluzhby," 1899; *PssS* 10: 99) and "About Love" ("O liubvi," 1898; *PssS* 10: 66), respectively. Neither of these antithetical propositions is framed as the author's own; both represent the conclusions of characters, and both invite scrutiny. There is no question, though, that Chekhov's own position is more commonly associated with the imperative to individuate; hence, the flirtation with de-individuation is noteworthy.

Nor need this fly in the face of Chekhov's well-documented suspicion of generalizations. The opposite of particularity here is not generalization but continuity. Much has been made of Chekhov's interest in *temporal* continuity, the connections between past and present, present and future, and "The Bishop" visits and revisits this problem as part of the basic structure of reminiscence. But the obsessive nature of the Bishop's preoccupation with the past, together with the fallibility of his memory, suggest that temporal continuity may not be the most auspicious form of connection. The unbroken *sequence* aspired to by Father Sisoy ("and then what?") and the smooth succession implied by "Syntax" (the name of a dog and the subject of Chekhov's earliest recorded note for the story) are unavailable—and not only in the grammarless signifiers favored by Syntax's owner ("betula kinderbalsamica secuta"; *PssS* 10: 189) or in the merchant Yerakin's conversational style "May God grant!" "Most certainly without fail! Depending on the circumstances, Your Most Consecrated Grace! I wish!"; *PssS* 10: 195). I want to posit instead a vision of a continuum—a rankless one—connecting and imbuing everything that exists at any *single* moment, a continuity that would make either the "conflict" or the "conflation" of identities beside the point.

Our Bishop ends up without rank at several levels: first, literally, in the sense that once he becomes incapacitated, he can no longer preside; then, imaginatively, as he constructs himself as an ordinary man making his way on that "formless field of benefaction,"[10] where positions and identities are unfixed and he can exist as a true man without rank, "without roots, without source, and without any dwelling place," "brisk and lively" in spite of being bedridden. Then, post-mortem, when his title is retroactively removed—or at least his bishophood is *dubia*: people are skeptical when his mother mentions that she once had such a high-ranking son (much as, in the opening scene, the status of the maternal mirage is uncertain).

Finally, the story itself has a "bishopectomy," as we conclude "The Bishop" without the Bishop—which is unnerving, since we have been inside

---

[10] The "formless field of benefaction," from the Zen "Verse of the Kesa," invokes both vastness and the liberation from fixed forms. Recall that Chekhov conjures up a similarly wide field (*gromadnoe pole*) to designate the vast expanse between "there is a God" and "there is no God." Only the truly wise man has the courage to roam, rootless and without dwelling place, the undifferentiated middle ground of that field (*PssS* 17: 33–34, 224). So essential is the topos of indeterminate motion on an enormous field that Aleksandr Chudakov refers to Chekhov as the "Man of the Field." See his "Chelovek polia," in *Anton P. Čechov—Philosophische und religiöse Dimensionen im Leben und im Werk*, ed. Vladimir B. Katev, Rolf-Dieter Kluge, and Regine Nohejl (Munich: Verlag Otto Sagner, 1997), 301–08.

his head all along.[11] His disappearance is so complete that we begin to suspect it might be true that his nephew the aspiring doctor "cuts up dead bodies" as we are told more than once (*PssS* 10: 191, 197). At the very least, the text's expeditious disposal of the Bishop's remains dramatizes one aspect of our perplexity about death: our complete lack of access to how the story continues without us. There is finally no answer to Father Sisoy's unremitting "and then what?"—"a potom chto?"[12]—which no doubt accounts for his favorite response: "I don'[t] like it!"—"Ne ndravitsia!" (*PssS* 10: 193, 190).

Sisoy is well cast as a parodic refraction of the true man without rank. Not only is he the only character unaffected by celebrity; like Rinzai's rankless man, Sisoy is rootless, lives nowhere and everywhere, and as someone who seems to have sprung forth a fully formed monk—a "headbirth"—is also without "source" (at least of the maternal sort that so beguiles the Bishop). Even Sisoy's ludicrous assertion that the Japanese are the same as the Montenegrins is a *reductio ad absurdum* of the proposition that beings are continuous with one another. Lest we assent too readily to this "oneness of all beings" posited, however tentatively, in the Bishop's experience, it is roundly travestied in the caviling, nay-saying Sisoy, surely not a man without spleen, who is always audible from the room next door.

And yet neither does the story allow us to shrug off the suggestion of interpenetrability, partly insofar as the voice of Father Sisoy *is* always audible from the neighboring room. The walls are porous, the cloister permeable. If the Bishop's isolation (*futliarnost'*) is figured concretely in the carriages, vestments, and titles that cut him off from both other people and the natural world,[13] that containment crumbles as the vessels and boundaries that maintain separation and keep us to ourselves give way.

The story presents a chronicle of seepage, spillage, and overflowing, along with nearly Dionysian breaches of bodily integrity. These range from ghoulish post-mortem dismemberment (chopping up cadavers) to the pre-mortem disgorgement of the Bishop's life blood; to the abundant shedding of tears, a purer bodily fluid; to the perpetual spilling of water (the ritual washing of feet—Christ's lesson in living ranklessly; streams coursing through ditches and overflowing their banks, and, above all, Katya's chronic bad luck

---

[11] Interestingly, the removal of the Bishop is telegraphed from the start in the same locution that definitively identifies the old woman in church as his own parent: "A tut, vashe preosviashchenstvo, vasha mamasha bez vas priekhali" ("Your Grace, your mother came while you were gone" [literally "without you"]; *PssS* 10: 187). Given the repetition, the rhythm, the assonance, the rhyme, and the Bishop's position as object of the preposition "without" ("bez"), the promise of attachment is inescapably marked and marred by truancy.

[12] For *potom* refers not only to what comes *next* but also what comes *afterward*.

[13] Kirjanov, Chekhov and the Poetics of Memory, 51.

with stemware). The last results in the frequent shattering of glasses so abhorred by Sisoy, who prefers his breakables intact. The unceasing clinking of glasses next door resounds as a constant reminder of the frailty of vessels of all kinds.

Sounds, in fact, intrude so indefatigably from the outside world that any separation between inside and outside must finally be seen as spurious. Cell windows are inherently open to coughs, clocks, bangs, shouts, and songs, especially in the segments recalling the Bishop's life abroad, *zagranitsei* (beyond another specious boundary). The frequent use of verbs customarily reserved for human subjects to describe the behavior of celestial bodies (which "glance" in those open windows) and forms of vegetation (which "wake up and smile") breaches the not-so-inviolable boundary between human beings and the natural world. And in a final stroke of genius, the artificial distinction between inner and outer worlds, between me and not me, collapses as the Bishop is consumed by the noise of a door opening and closing, which turns out to be the rumbling of his own internal organs, the reverberation of what he himself has ingested.

So what are the implications of all these permeable membranes? What are we to make of the fluidity that erodes firm contours and uncorks water-tight identity? Can we do without the "rank" of an essential, particular, and jealously guarded self, as Chekhov's "man" does without his spleen? Judging from "The Bishop," being without something normally thought of as essential—like indelible individual identity or a luminous future life or attachment to a "significant other" (or mother)—might not be such a bad thing, but rather a surprisingly good thing, a liberating thing, for "field work."

"The Bishop" is a story of the dissolving self—the mother who fades in and out of view, the Bishop who fades in and out of existence. The concrete representation of that disappearance comes in the form of the Bishop's palpable shrinking; he grows smaller, thinner, weaker, and less significant before everyone's very eyes. Interestingly, as the world recedes from the dying man, we get an image of reverse creation, as everything that has existed up until now returns to the formless void, and the Bishop confirms that "it is good" (*PssS* 10: 200). Indeed, if the biblical Creator did his work by tirelessly separating light from dark and day from night, by securely dividing the world into sea and land, waters and firmament, and drawing firm distinctions between animals and men, men and women, creatures and Creator, the reverse process is in force in "The Bishop," where substances commingle and boundaries come undrawn.

But the Bishop only imagines that the world is vanishing and won't continue, for the world persists; the disappearance is the Bishop's own. His is the experience of an individual who will shortly cease to be, whereas existence at large will not; the world continues, unimaginable though it is, without us. The dissolving of the ego, then, is more than a liberation from a self-centered existence; it is equally a meditation on impermanence.

But that individual evanescence also defuses death: surrendering his fleeting selfhood, the Bishop is freed to merge with that larger, ongoing existence, of which he is a part. Is this broader continuity being advanced, then, as a consolation for the fact of mortality? Or are we perhaps to read the story's apparent progression from Sisoy's "I don['t] like it!" to the Bishop's "How good it is!"[14] as a suggestion that "what comes next" is more enticing than earthly existence, and that the best is yet to come? But "The Bishop" envisions no future at all for its individual hero;[15] nor, notwithstanding the first Gospel that so moves the Bishop, does the story suggest that he or anyone else is "not of this world," which would be to dissociate him from existence here and now, reinstating the spurious boundaries between self and world and restoring the dualism that compassion had overcome. Moreover, both "this stinks!" and "how great!" are extremes, like the final frontiers of the field that stretches between God and godlessness, and *longing* for death—whether for its anticipated blessings or as a release from suffering—is no more liberating than dreading it.

Perhaps, rather, we can trace a path from the lure of attachment—to life, to permanence, to particular things and people (maybe that's my mother!)—to the detachment and freedom of the ordinary man on the boundless field. For the field is significant not only as Chekhov's trademark space between faith and atheism. "Walking the fields" is a proposition scattered throughout Chekhov's correspondence in 1901 and 1902, as he imagined himself more than once on precisely such terrain, wandering through the open air "without source, without dwelling place, without characteristic habits," and, significantly, "not wanting anything"—inhabiting life as it is.[16] *Lacking*, we note, does not imply *wanting*; being "without" engenders not desire but a sense of freedom from the designs of a sovereign subject. Like the moonlit landscape the Bishop passes through, whose "life" he feels is intimately connected with

---

[14] Parts 1 and 2 end with Sisoy's negative assessment; 3 and 4 (or at least as far as the Bishop lasts in part 4) culminate in the Bishop's approbation.

[15] Indeed, while the story of Bishop Peter hews closely to the formulaic patterns of saints' lives, it departs radically in scrupulously withholding the *potom*. "The Bishop" ends *without* the obligatory wonders that occur after the saint's death, and thus also without his posthumous recognition and canonization (Alevtina P. Kuzicheva, "Ob istokakh rasskaza 'Arkhierei,'" in *Anton P. Čechov—Philosophische und religiöse Dimensionen*, 439–40). Instead, our Bishop disappears completely, and the only survivor to recall him is met with skepticism.

[16] See his letter to Olga Knipper, 17 March 1902. The words that so closely echo Rinzai's description of the "true man without rank" ("ne imet' rodiny, osedlosti, privychek") are Knipper's, but she is prompting Chekhov to recall his own vision of "true life" (letter of 2 September 1901; *PssP* 10: 342). Recognizing the terms of her description, Chekhov affirms that this would give him the space "to breathe freely and desire nothing" (letter to O. Knipper, 6 September 1901).

his own, like the fields just outside of town, where the song of the larks merges with the singing of the choir, beckoning him to peace, and the "immense, boundless, blue sky stretches endlessly overhead" (*PssS* 10: 196), the field onto which the Bishop's ordinary man emerges assimilates him (he is a bird!) into the natural world (under the same boundless sky). And if in its longevity nature reveals to us our impermanence, it also "makes you reconciled," as Chekhov wrote to Suvorin, "that is, it gives you equanimity. And you need equanimity in this world. Only people with equanimity can see things clearly, be fair, and work."[17] In this practice of equanimity, in this non-resistance to natural flow and transience, in this non-attachment, this acceptance of impermanence,[18] the boundary between life and death is less in need of a sentinel, and assenting to death is not renouncing life but affirming being.

**Part 2: Names and Titles, or Life Without Champagne**

Bishop Pyotr, it turns out, like Chekhov, had been working under an assumed name. Ultimately, he is not only divested of his dizzying title, "Your Grace" (*vashe preosviashchenstvo*), but behind this Pyotr lurks Pavel—instead of Peter he is Paul, or more affectionately, Pavlusha, the form of address his mother reverts to in the end.

To return to Anton Pavlovich Chekhov's many aliases, toward the end of the list in figure 1 you'll find the word Chekhov used at the very end of his life, "Champagne" (spelled in this instance as a surname: "Shampanskii"). In a way, when Chekhov signs off with his famous "It's been so long since I've had champagne" ("Davno ia ne pil shampanskogo"), he is signing with one of his pseudonyms the story of his own death (much as "My Ranks and Titles" concludes by invoking the Man Without a Spleen),[19] or maybe even drafting his own obituary, given that he's commenting on life *without* champagne. As

---

[17] 4 May 1889. My translation owes much to Michael Heim, whose inspiration it is to render the thrice-repeated *ravnodushnost'* as "equanimity" rather than the customary "indifference." *Anton Chekhov's Life and Thought: Selected Letters and Commentary*, ed. Simon Karlinsky, trans. Michael Henry Heim (Evanston, IL: Northwestern University Press, 1999), 139. The Bishop, incidentally, hails from Lesopole (literally "forest-field"). Stepping out imaginatively onto that sunny field at his most infirm moment, the Bishop is figuratively out of the woods.

[18] The formulations are Magid's, *Ordinary Mind*, 57.

[19] For an interesting reading of Chekhov's death scene as Chekhovian text, see Katherine Tiernan O'Connor, "Chekhov's Death: His Textual Past Recaptured," in *Studies in Poetics: Commemorative Volume Krystyna Pomorska (1928–1986)*, ed. Elena Semeka-Pankratov (Columbus, OH: Slavica Publishers, 1995), 39–50. Janet Malcolm's treatment of the "factual," memoiristic, and downright fictionalized accounts of Chekhov's ending is also compelling. *Reading Chekhov: A Critical Journey* (New York: Random House, 2002), 62–74.

in "The Bishop," what goes missing is *him*, and not only insofar as pseudonyms endanger an author's figurative immortality.

Moreover, as it turns out, champagne is a pseudonym not only for Chekhov, but for death itself, and the death of a doctor in particular. Doctors treating doctors, it seems, never told their ailing colleagues directly that the end was near; it was common practice, rather, to order a bottle of champagne to be brought to the patient's bedside.[20] When Dr. Schwöhrer has champagne delivered to the dying Chekhov, the latter's matter-of-fact "Ich sterbe" ("I'm dying") suggests that he can read the code. When he follows this avowal with a reflection on drinking champagne, his several identities intersect and merge: the dying doctor, whose champagne has come, the dying writer who, in citing the champagne alias, is voicing his own pseudonym, and the "ordinary man" who takes his final sip—note that in the roster of Chekhov's pseudonyms, "Ch" stands for both "Chekhov" and "Chelovek" (man).

In speaking of champagne, Chekhov is also citing titles, specifically of two of his own stories. A glance at "Champagne: Thoughts From a New Year's Hangover" ("Shampanskoe: Mysli s novogodnego pokhmel'ia," 1886; *PssS* 4: 282) and "Champagne: The Story of a Rogue" ("Shampanskoe: Rasskaz prokhodimtsa," 1887; *PssS* 6: 12–17) reveals that the beverage has been associated with death all along. A "gilded coffin full of the bones of the dead," champagne is generally drunk "to toast someone with one foot already in the grave." "When you die your relatives drink it out of joy that you've left them an inheritance." Revelers drink it to celebrate the New Year, emboldened by their foolish certainty that they will still be around next year to drink some more. Moreover, such celebrations call not for just any old champagne, but for Veuve Cliquot (Cliquot's widow). In spite of the narrator's opening admonition, "Don't trust [believe] champagne," this sparkling inebriant seems less to lie than to tell an ineluctable truth.

It is, at the very least, in all instances *telling*. Dropping the bottle augurs ill (*PssS* 6: 13). Ordering one (under certain circumstances) betokens death. What does it mean (under those same circumstances) to drain the cup? As an alternative to the kind of clamorous tea-partying the Bishop's survivors carry on endlessly in the neighboring room, accepting *this* glass means to cease denying that the end is near (the posture usually attributed to Chekhov),[21] to

---

[20] M. A. Sheikina, "Davno ia ne pil shampanskogo," in *Tselebnoe tvorchestvo A. P. Chekhova: Razmyshliaiut mediki i filologi*, ed. M. E. Burno and B. A. Voskresensky (Moscow: Rossiiskoe obshchestvo medikov-literatorov, 1996), 42–45.

[21] See O'Connor's suggestive article on Chekhov's letters, which takes issue with the assumption that Chekhov was "in denial" about his illness, arguing that his correspondence reveals a more artful form of dodging when his letters are not simply taken at face value but rather accorded the same close scrutiny as his stories. "Anton Chekhov and D. H. Lawrence: The Art of Letters and the Discourse of Mortality," in

stop avoiding at all costs life's last drop ("Stay away from champagne!"; *PssS* 4: 282). Importantly, though, taking the cup (like Socrates, like Jesus) and raising it with a smile to one's own death suggests not craving, but assent, equanimity; Chekhov's gesture in taking leave of his life—and his wife—is peaceful (*pokoino*). And the remarkable popping of the cork in the silence after Chekhov succumbs recalls the rupture of containers and release of fluid in "The Bishop," where separate, self-contained being is transcended and reabsorbed into forest and field, flux and flow. In other champagne fests, the "then what?" is explicit (champagne now, hangover later). In Chekhov's death scene, as in the Bishop's final field trip, Father Sisoy's question remains open, and being without an answer (and without a future) is no longer cause for discomfort.

**Part 3: Being Without**

*Without* (*bez*), as it happens, is the ninety-sixth most frequently used word in Chekhov's stories, right behind *God* (*Bog*).[22] Let it be said, though, that the tally, based on the text of 150 stories, was compiled *without* any of the stories entitled "Without...,"[23] including "Without a Title" ("Bez zaglaviia," 1888), which originally had a title that he made a point of removing. The inclusion of "Without a Title" (and others) would certainly have bumped "without" up a few notches.

The story is set in an isolated monastery surrounded by a vast and impenetrable wilderness. Here, in perfect seclusion, live a father superior and his devoted monks. The old man has such extraordinary powers of speech and such extraordinary musical talent, that whenever he plays the organ, reads his verses, or speaks of the most ordinary things, it is impossible to listen without a smile or without tears. The monks sometimes tire of nature's gifts (trees, flowers, the song of birds, the rush of the sea), but they are in absolute thrall to the artistry of the old man. His power, we're told, is without limits.

---

*American Contributions to the Twelfth International Congress of Slavists*, ed. Robert A. Maguire and Alan Timberlake (Bloomington, IN: Slavica Publishers, 1998), 128–41.

[22] *Chastotnyi slovar' rasskazov A. P. Chekhova*, ed. G. Ia. Martynenko (St. Petersburg: Izdatel'stvo Sankt-Peterburgskogo universiteta, 1999), 15.

[23] "Story Without an Ending" ("Rasskaz bez kontsa," 1886); "A Woman Without Prejudice" ("Zhenshchina bez predrassudkov," 1883); "Without Hope" ("Beznadezhnyi," 1885); "Defenseless Creature" ("Bezzashchitnoe sushchestvo," 1887). "Illegitimacy" ("Bezzakonie," 1887); "Without a Place" ("Bez mesta," 1885); "Knights Without Fear and Beyond Reproach" ("Rytsari bez strakha i upreka," 1883); "The Uneasy Guest" ("Bespokoinyi gost'," 1886); "The Wordless Fish" ("Ryba bezglasnaia," 1886, *dubia*); and his early, unpublished drama, "Fatherlessness" ("Bezottsovshchina," 1878).

One day, to everyone's astonishment, an "ordinary man" (in this case an "ordinary sinner") appears, having traversed, in his ramblings, the vast expanse between God (the province of the monastery dwellers) and godlessness (the depraved city across that wasteland). He castigates the monks for sequestering themselves and saving their own souls, while their debauched urban "brethren" sink ever deeper into iniquity. The father superior takes the reproach to heart, and sets off to the city to do his spiritual duty.

The stricken monks are left without music, without his speeches and verses, in a kind of fifth-century "Day Without Art" that lasts three months. When the old man finally returns, he speaks about the depravity he's seen with his own eyes—drunkenness without restraint, beautiful women without shame and without clothes. So vivid is this master orator's depiction of the pleasures of the flesh, that the next morning, when he gets up, there is not a single monk left; they have all raced to the city. Deserted by his flock, the charismatic father has been reduced to the monastic equivalent of the doctor without a practice; certainly he is as impotent to save his charges as the Bishop's physicians were theirs. Moreover, given that the old man's powers and ministrations have been more artistic than religious—his creations trump God's—he is also, in the end, an author without an audience, a condition fatal to any artist striving for immortality.

What this instant diaspora of monks makes clear is that the stark disjunction contrived by the cloister is spurious. Neither the distance nor the formidable obstacles surrounding the monastery really separate the monks from the sinners, the soul from the body; obviously the monks are subject to the same longings as their iniquitous brethren. Even before their mass exodus, the monks' attachment to their peerless leader is fraught with desire: they NEED his music; they crave his verse; they cannot live without his voice; they drink in his words greedily.

Assimilation notwithstanding, then, while discarding some of the artificial distinctions that separate the self from the world and from other selves, while resigning their spiritual "rank" and collapsing the distance between monastery and metropolis, afterlife and real life, the errant monks are still incontrovertibly discrete subjects in quest of objects outside the self, and theirs is lack at its most lascivious. Driven toward what they feel they are missing (all that monks vow to live *without*), they step out onto the great, murky middle ground, not "as free as a bird" and ready to roam, "without root ... and without dwelling place," but desperate to traverse it A.S.A.P.

Curiously, what concentrates their unbridled lust (more than the tawdry strip tease) is the city's wine, which, the narrative voice speculates, "must have been irresistibly sweet and aromatic, because everyone who drank it smiled blissfully and wanted only to drink more. The wine itself answered the drinkers' smile with a smile of its own and sparkled ecstatically when it was drunk, as if it knew what devilish charms lay concealed in its sweetness"

(*PssS* 6: 458). The demon drink stimulates an insatiable craving, a greedy thirst entirely absent from the tranquil sipping of champagne and the equanimity in the face of death it bespeaks.

This intimation of mortality may not be misplaced. If, as we are told, the city is perdition itself, and its inhabitants are dying into hell (*PssS* 6: 456), then insofar as the monks, too, are dying to get there, they are choosing death—and ardently. Significantly, their eagerness to perish is as problematic as the opposite extreme, the aversion to drink ("Stay away from champagne!") and the denial of impermanence that is its corollary.

Reticent as Chekhov may have been about how soon his own impermanence was to assert itself, his story about the dwindling Bishop began to take shape as early as 1899. He had become interested in the biography of Bishop Mikhail Gribanovsky, a bishop-turned-monk (like Chekhov's Pyotr, who mentally demoted himself from bishop, to priest, to deacon, to "simple monk" before making the final imaginative leap to "ordinary man"), who had just died of tuberculosis. It was at this time, Chekhov told Olga Knipper later, that he began "getting ready to die" himself.[24]

What, in practice, might such preparations entail? I suspect these labors were chiefly epistemological: to attempt to rise to the nearly insuperable challenge of taking in one's own mortality, to fully apprehend the breathtaking fact that one fine day you'll breathe out and never breathe back in. A few short pages before Bishop Pyotr embraces both his own impermanence and the world's continuation, stepping calmly and joyfully onto the field in the guise of ordinary man, he is still "unprepared to die," for "even though he had faith, something was not clear, not fully understood." He becomes agitated by this conviction that "something was lacking," and "there was some most important thing that he did not have" (*PssS* 10: 195), a lack that generates hope and desire not unlike the urgency that propels the libidinous monks toward their object.

What, then, ultimately enables the Bishop to pass through the "gateless barrier"—the Zen term for the artificial obstacles thrown up by what we feel we lack?[25] What gives him the equanimity (another Zen term, but one that's

---

[24] Letter to O. L. Knipper, 9 January 1899. See also Kirjanov's discussion of Gribanovsky, 37–38, 46–48, 54. For other possible prototypes of the Bishop, see *PssS* 10: 453, 458–60.

[25] *The Gateless Barrier*, compiled by Zen master Wu-men in thirteenth-century China, is a collection of koans "all about the problem of separation, about the artificial barriers we experience between ourselves and life as it is" (Magid, 6, 31–32). "We discover that life and death are the same as no-life and no-death; the other is no other than myself; each being is infinitely precious as a unique expression of the nature which is essential to us all." Robert Aitken, introduction to *The Gateless Barrier: The Wu-men Kuan (Mumonkan)*, trans. Robert Aitken (New York: North Point Press, 1991), xiv.

indigenous to Chekhov) to abandon his "hopes for the future" (*PssS* 10: 195), his "unbearable longing to go abroad" (*PssS* 10: 199), his desperate need for an interlocutor, and his wistful yearning for his mother's love, and be absorbed instead into the life of the field, much as Chekhov himself was shortly to digest his champagne? It is not that he has somehow found what was missing any more than he has successfully reunited with mom; rather, he has absorbed the fact that this is it. It takes practice simply to *experience* being "without" rather than straining to fill the void. While inextricably in a world of other beings, we are inescapably unaccompanied in death (as the Bishop's abortive conversation with Sisoy confirms), and fixating on particular entities is but a futile attempt to ward off the inevitable.[26] The Bishop sails through the gateless barrier onto the borderless field because he embraces life as it is, privations and all, which includes assenting to the facticity of death.

Thus, the Bishop takes the walk of his life, through a portal open to all walks of life—doctors, patients, writers, readers, bishops, monks, saints, sinners, and even Zen masters,[27] the "enormous field" accommodating all subfields, professions, identities, and practices without distinction. And despite the levity and agility signaled by Chekhov's association of his own professional dualism in terms of the female company he keeps, wives and mistresses are still attachments, and spending the night with one or the other is still part of an economy of desire. Setting out onto the formless field, however, the Bishop/ordinary man/Chekhov is neither cleaving to a wife (with her clattering teacups) nor pursuing a mistress (craving wine), but making friends with death (and toasting that friendship—that equanimity—with champagne).[28]

---

[26] Stephen Batchelor, *Alone With Others: An Existential Approach to Buddhism* (New York: Grove Press, 1983), 63. Interestingly, Batchelor dedicates this book to *his* mother.

[27] It is probably worth noting here how many of Chekhov's stories take their title from a professional identity, and that his oeuvre runs the gamut from the "Death of a Clerk" (1883) to the death of a cleric. Interestingly, the former dies as a result of forced access to a high-ranking official; the latter gains peaceful access to death by shedding his own high rank.

[28] Freud speaks of "making friends with the necessity of dying" in his discussion of *King Lear*. The superannuated king must renounce his no-longer-age-appropriate desire for the love of women (the flattery of Goneril and Regan) and choose instead the silent daughter—the third of the three fates, the inexorable Goddess of Death. The motif of selection imaginatively converts the inevitable into a matter of choice. "The Theme of the Three Caskets," in *The Freud Reader*, ed. Peter Gay (New York: W. W. Norton and Company, 1995), 520–22.

## Coda: Inadmissible Evidence

Chekhov was no student of Zen, though he had sufficient exposure to Tolstoy and Bunin for Buddhist thought to be on his radar screen.[29] He was also adequately steeped in the literary-philosophical polemics of his age to have absorbed the contemporary debates about "nirvana" and the relationship between desire and suffering. As for his access to actual texts, so many of the key European sources and even the Pali originals were being translated into Russian and widely read in the 1890s and early 1900s that Chekhov could scarcely have escaped the deluge. We do know that he sent a copy of Auguste Barth's *Religii Indii* (*The Religions of India*) to Taganrog for the library's collection. What is less clear is whether he himself was familiar with the volume or was simply fulfilling the library's request.[30]

---

[29] Tolstoy had a longstanding interest in Buddhism and, having read both primary and secondary sources in German, French, and English, eventually adapted and translated a number of Buddhist texts into Russian ("Life and Teaching of Siddartha Gautama Called The Buddha that is The Most Perfect One"; "Siddartha Called Buddha, that is The Holy One, His Life and Teaching"; "Sunday Reading: The Buddha"; "Karma"; "Kunala's Eyes"; "It is You"). For a sustained treatment of Tolstoy's views and a bibliography of sources (both the ones he used and the ones he produced), see Dragan Milivojevic, "Tolstoy's Views on Buddhism," in his *Leo Tolstoy and the Oriental Religious Heritage* (New York: Columbia University Press, 1998), 1–17.

Ivan Bunin's protracted engagement with Buddhism, which deepened during his travels in Ceylon, took shape principally in the years after Chekhov's death. His reading may have come earlier, though, as the Buddhist discourses that interested him were available in Russian as early as the 1880s and '90s. Moreover, Bunin's underlying sensibility—his great joy in being alive (undampened by the inescapable fact of impermanence); his belief that man is part of and continuous with the whole of creation; and his conviction that to live as an individual ego is to fall prey to delusion—is already palpable in his early works ("In the Field" ["V pole"], written in 1895 when Chekhov and Bunin first became acquainted, and "The Fog" ["Tuman"], written in 1901 at Chekhov's dacha in Yalta). Chekhov worked out the terms of his "field vision" (wandering without roots, without birthright, without "rank") in conversation with Bunin, and when he writes to Knipper about wandering "without wanting anything," he signs off with the exclamation "Bunin is full of joie de vivre" (6 September 1901 and *PssP* 10: 342). Bunin, in turn, had a special affinity for "The Bishop" ("Chekhov," in *I. A. Bunin: Sobranie sochinenii* [Moscow: Moskovskii rabochii, 2000], 8: 235–37). See also Thomas Gaiton Marullo, *If You See the Buddha: Studies in the Fiction of Ivan Bunin* (Evanston, IL: Northwestern University Press, 1998), 3–16; and James B. Woodward, *Ivan Bunin: A Study of His Fiction* (Chapel Hill: University of North Carolina Press, 1980), 19, 33–34, 71–72, 109–14.

[30] Letter to P. F. Iordanov, 11 August 1899. Barth's *Les religions de l'Inde* (Paris: Sandoz et Fischbacher, 1879) appeared in Russian translation in 1897. For a comprehensive and well annotated list of the relevant sources published in Russian during Chekhov's lifetime, see N. A. Rubakin, *Sredi knig* (Moscow: Nauka, 1913), 2: 238–39, 265–66, 1: 115.

I mention Chekhov and Zen in the same breath, though, in order to open up by analogy something that is difficult to access otherwise, in this case an aspect of Chekhov we usually miss because of what we already "know" about him; the references to Zen are thus meant not to advocate its practice but to give voice to another sensibility keenly attuned to the problems raised by "The Bishop," as well as by Chekhov's own approaching death. Recognizing impermanence is, in any case, more a matter of "clear seeing" than of doctrine, which is why Chekhov's own practice is, if anything, a "Buddhism Without Beliefs," not a set of precepts but a way of being in the world.[31] For that matter, Kirjanov accounts for all the dismantling of dualism without recourse to alien traditions, recognizing in the Bishop's reabsorption into the "universal unity" of life Russian Orthodoxy's ideals of compassion and of *sobornost'*, and in the field fantasy not Rinzai's rankless man, but the holy procession (*Krestnyi khod*) of Bishop Pyotr's youth.[32] Certainly in the exegesis of the self-effacing Bishop Mikhail (Gribanovsky), whose pamphlet on the Gospels Chekhov read with interest while beginning "The Bishop" in 1899, man's connection with all forms of life in "this world" at this very moment, right here and now, accords nicely with the teachings of Zen.[33]

Even without such obvious points of intersection, though, the introduction of "inadmissible" evidence (like Zen) can make for unexpectedly clear

---

[31] See Batchelor's seminal book of that title, *Buddhism Without Beliefs*, which argues that Buddhism is precisely a practice rather than a set of beliefs, concerned with what you do rather than what you believe (New York: Riverhead Books, 1997).

[32] Kirjanov, *Chekhov and the Poetics of Memory*, 37–60. Her emphasis on journeying "toward God" and arriving at that terminus, however, seems less in keeping with Chekhov's image of wandering the middle ground of the wide field (between "God" and "No God") without a clear destination.

[33] Ibid., and Episkop Mikhail (Gribanovskii), *Nad Evangeliem* (St. Petersburg: Satis', 1994, originally 1896). See, for instance, Gribanovsky's rereading of John 15:9: "We Christians are not of this world. But that does not mean that our world is somewhere thousands of versts away, somewhere beyond the infinite universe. Not at all. It is inside our very selves, in the nature that surrounds us, in each and every place, in every soul.... Its light and breath are immediately close to us; they suffuse me from the innermost depths of my spirit this very minute, right here, in this place where I am writing, within my very own soul, which I feel right now because of that very same nature and environment that surrounds me at the present moment" (12–13). He also urges his fellow man not to simply move through nature "distractedly" (without mindfulness) or make use of it "egotistically" (as a subject avails itself of objects), but to "try to apply one's deep and entire attention to every living thing that surrounds us, to everything that exists around us, each blade of grass and object, to enter with tranquil heart that luminous and wonderful reality that infuses everything and is reflected in everything" (14). For Gribanovsky, it seems, everything—including the Gospels—is infused with "Buddha nature."

seeing. Tom Peters, the business strategy guru, arrives at the same conclusion from the other side: "The most successful scientists, inventors and entrepreneurs draw upon wildly disparate sources (art, movies, sailing, flower arranging) to infuse new life into nagging problems, or to create new combinations of familiar things." What does this mean concretely for Peters? "When I get on a plane," he avers, "I look to see who's reading Chekhov."[34]

---

[34] "Chekhov and Business Strategy," *TP Times*, 2 November 1988, http://www.tompeters.com/col_entries.php?note=005222&year=1988. Peters himself has been most inspired by: a management mentor who was also a beekeeper; a business professor steeped in fourteenth-century politics, arcane mathematical theorems, and Sauterne; a consulting boss with degrees in physics and law and an interest in Eastern mysticism and folk singing; a chief financial officer trained as a merchant seaman and passionate about the London theater. Identities—like beings—neither conflicting nor conflating, but coalescing.

# Incapacity

### Spencer Golub, Brown University

> "Our lives are all incapacity."
> —Curtis White, *Memories of My Father Watching TV*

The sound of the breaking string in the sky overhead bothered him a good deal less than it did the others. "I am Yepikhodov," he said to no one in particular (reflecting the world's apparent disregard). "I am Yepikhodov, breaker of worlds and their false objects, maker of words with their false subjects." These words are not tortured, as they are when he speaks aloud, each word a hedge against dismissal from the scene, the stage. He does not stammer in his dreams.

Yepikhodov trusted his artistic intuition of the word, even if the world refused to recognize the articulation of his fractured artistry. He did, it was true, sometimes dream of being a celebrated public speaker in St. Petersburg or Moscow. However, he had not so much as visited those cities, did not even know what a city was, for that matter, having lived his entire life inside the confines of his small, provincial village. Where he lived, getting up to speak in a public place might get you arrested or at least labeled a "crank," an "eccentric," or worst of all, a "misfit." Occasionally, some haggard-looking stranger might wander through and speak aloud out of a habit he developed in some other no doubt larger and faraway place. Most often, though, the motive for such speech was hunger rather than genuine self-expression. This being said, Yepikhodov limited his speaking to a small circle of social acquaintances, who, for the most part, did not acknowledge his right to belong or even, as it seemed to him, his reason for being.

Even without encouragement, though, Yepikhodov allowed himself to believe that the world conformed to his vision of it. "I act with *complete* certainty," he reasoned. "But this certainty is [completely] my own."[1] He believed that the three overlapping clouds he saw enveloping the tallest wooden building in the village signaled smoke and thereafter fire, or more generally, calamity sent from above. "Only convictions that arise from terror

---

[1] Ludwig Wittgenstein, *On Certainty*, ed. G. E. M. Anscombe and G. H. von Wright, trans. Denis Paul and G. E. M. Anscombe (New York: HarperRow, 1972), 25e.

*Chekhov the Immigrant: Translating a Cultural Icon.* Michael C. Finke and Julie de Sherbinin, eds. Bloomington, IN: Slavica Publishers, 2007, 239–50.

are authentic," he thought.[2] Out of great fear comes a "behavior of doubt" that comes from an even greater certainty.[3] This truth was acknowledged by Ludwig Wittgenstein in the world that came after the world that Yepikhodov knew and that he knew would end when he did.

Yepikhodov's vision measured a vertical anxiety, which was perhaps unconsciously designed to offset his fear of inevitably being made horizontal, of lying and moldering in the grave. His fear was more concrete than that of the others, something he lived with and through without trying to rationalize or censor. Their fear was merely visited upon them. They denied or at least rationalized its presence in their lives by ascribing to it "realistic" motivations that lay outside of themselves. "Reality?" a clever man writing about "fakes" would one day say, "Reality is the toothbrush waiting at home for you in its glass, a bus ticket, a paycheck, and the grave."[4]

"All that the eye can rationalize is white," Yepikhodov heard himself saying about their cherry orchard, which metaphorically instanced their delusional thought, metaphor perhaps being itself a form of delusion.[5] Thus, they offered, the sound they heard in the sky overhead was "an echo from a mine shaft. But it must be far away."[6] "How utterly ludicrous!" Yepikhodov thought. The idea of an event-causing image appeared to him to be dubious at best, although not so much impossible as improbable. "Every life is, on the whole, improbable," he reasoned.[7] If this echo, this image clarified anything, he thought, it is that they (that is, other people) invent everything, including real events in real time, "as a last resort for structuring the runaway feedback of mind looking upon itself."[8] Well, it takes one self-syllogizing mind to read another('s), as Tristram Shandy might have said, with each such mind "tiring

---

[2] Vladislav Ivanov, "Michael Chekhov and Russian Existentialism," in *Wandering Stars: Russian Émigré Theatre 1905–1940*, trans. Sergei Ostrovsky and Laurence Senelick, ed. Laurence Senelick (Iowa City: University of Iowa Press, 1992), 142.

[3] Wittgenstein, *On Certainty*, 33e–34e.

[4] Orson Welles said this in the film he wrote and directed, *F for Fake* (1973).

[5] Curtis White asks, "Is a metaphor a delusion?" in *Memories of My Father Watching TV* (Normal, IL: Dalkey Archive Press, 1988), 69. The statement "All that the eye can rationalize is white" was made by Mike Laws, a student in my course *Mise en scene*, taught at Brown University, Fall 2002.

[6] Anton Chekhov, *The Cherry Orchard*, in *The Plays of Anton Chekhov*, trans. Paul Schmidt (New York: HarperCollins, 1997), 358 (Act II).

[7] Jacques Roubaud, *The Great Fire of London: A Story with Interpolations and Bifurcations*, trans. Dominic Di Bernardi (Elmwood Park, IL: Dalkey Archive Press, 1991), 247.

[8] Richard Powers, "Literary Devices," http://www.salon.com/books/feature/2002/ 11/28/literary/index.html.

out the patience of any flesh alive."⁹ The forever-mortified Yepikhodov was himself a demanding and a fatiguing presence.

Wittgenstein famously proposed that all philosophical problems assume the shape of the question, "I don't know my way around."¹⁰ Spoken like a man living in a world that has already ended, Yepikhodov might have thought had he still been around to think it. Yepikhodov's was a directional anxiety. Theirs was, to coin a phrase, misdirectional. They employed an amateur magician as their children's governess, and her misdirectional act was as blatantly fake as the custodial function she was hired by the family to perform. In truth, her act of misdirection served as an objective correlative to the family's own lack of focus which was supported by their tacit belief that they could trick time into doing their bidding. In this, the amateur magicians effectively fooled themselves. Neither real time nor even real event had ever been theirs to invent.

Of the lot, only Gaev articulated a directional anxiety, but his mental perambulations in the form of a catastrophic mental billiards game ending abruptly with the white ball being pocketed like a gentleman's handkerchief was regarded as the sort of posturing the family generally ascribed to outsiders like Simeonov-Pishchik and even Yepikhodov himself. The introspection born of age and experience of the old family retainer Firs, who only Gaev heeded or even truly heard, was misread as being mere retrospection. But then Firs was himself as guilty of doing this, as were they. When Firs saw clouds folded together like smoke, his mind traveled back through clouded memory to some actual event rather than leaping forward to some prefigured one. And that was on a good day. More often, Firs saw clouds folding in on themselves as being memory itself in its present form as an abstraction of the real and a dimming of the mind towards death. How can you believe someone who himself does not believe that memory can do anything but derealize the world given enough time?

Yepikhodov may also have used his three-fold cloud trick of the eye to situate himself in time, to wrest it away from the Firs-es and Gaevs of this world and again make it and himself seem real. Yepikhodov viewed his baroque mental play, which he called "The Three Folds," as a means to an end, a limit that he could acknowledge by expanding, breaking and overlapping. Unlike Gaev, who through his books in their bookcase memorializes memory (a family trait), Yepikhodov breaks free of memory and memorial constraint, fictionalizing both history and philosophy while seeming to play the fool.

"The infiniteness of the threat has broken every limit," intoned Yepikhodov, repeating the sound the sky made when the string broke, to borrow

---

⁹ Laurence Sterne, *The Life and Opinions of Tristram Shandy, Gentleman*, ed. Ian Campbell Ross (Oxford and New York: Oxford University Press, 1983), 37.

¹⁰ Ludwig Wittgenstein, quoted in Tom Sellars, "Question Marks" (review of two Peter Handke plays), *Theater* 2–3 (Spring 1997): 163.

their metaphor for what they thought they heard.[11] Does this sound like a fool speaking, or a pessimist, or, in their pedestrian coinage, a complainer? It is true that he said to them, "Every day something awful happens to me," however being quick to add, "But I don't complain."[12] Why is it that they register his complaint(s) without for a moment even trying to understand the enormity of the reality that is pressing in upon him about which he does not complain, *except as a mode of performance*? "Can it be that I am invisible, or have I simply gone unnoticed," ventriloquized Yepikhodov, who in so doing stole a page from Charlotta's book of magic tricks and pronounced an echo from the future.[13]

Yepikhodov's third-person performance is like that of the drowning man who looks into the emptiness and holds up a sign that he has handwritten in advance that reads: "HELP! I AM DROWNING!" In the later acts of his 1976 production of *The Cherry Orchard* at Moscow's Taganka Theatre, director Anatoly Efros took away Yepikhodov's voice and gave him a sign. On this sign, Yepikhodov wrote his lines that were then read aloud by the other characters. "Surely," he thought, "this will make them see me more clearly and even accede to my requests." However, Yepikhodov's signing only served to further inscribe his muteness. Yepikhodov's inability to be heard elided uncomfortably in his mind with Firs's inability to hear, aging the younger man appreciably and disastrously when he regarded himself in his mind's figurative mirror.

The signs of his impotence are everywhere and most often of his own creation. It is true that Yepikhodov carries in his pocket a pistol, but he carved it out of wood and painted it with boot black for effect. Needless to say, it is also unloaded. It makes no sound. It makes only a sign. His guitar sounds like gunfire, though, which must be why the others put their hands to their ears and either freeze or move away when they hear the playing and the braying of this failed Scaramouche.

"No," thought Yepikhodov, "that which defeats them will not defeat me. I carry as I quiver 'Zeno's Arrow,' not so much aimed at as naming and embodying a catastrophe that never comes." "There is no reaching the disaster. Out of reach is he whom it threatens, whether from afar or close-up, it is impossible to say: the infiniteness of the threat has in some way broken every limit."[14] "Blanchot wrote this last part about the disaster, but I could have said it," said Yepikhodov, although it is nowhere written that he said it but here. "The most that sentient being can say," said Wittgenstein, again invol-

---

[11] Maurice Blanchot, *The Writing of the Disaster*, trans. Ann Smock (Lincoln: University of Nebraska Press, 1995), 1.

[12] Chekhov, *The Cherry Orchard*, 334 (Act I).

[13] This quote is taken from the film *Russian Ark* (2002), written by Anatoly Nikiforov and Alexander Sokurov; directed by Alexander Sokurov.

[14] Blanchot, *The Writing of the Disaster*, 1.

untarily echoing the mute Yepikhodov, "is 'I thought I knew,'" and it is not said often enough, perhaps because it is more than sentience can remember to say.[15]

The sound of the breaking string in the sky overhead bothered Yepikhodov a good deal less than it did the others. That is, it bothered him only to the extent that as a metaphor (delusional in itself), it was philosophically misconceived. Perhaps, it would be more accurate to say that the metaphor was dysfunctionally conceived as yet another form of misdirection in the family plot that is the cherry orchard and *The Cherry Orchard*.

Yepikhodov was accustomed to tripping over objects and lines that were both real and imagined (although not necessarily imaginary), to walking backwards into rooms that he had entered before, to falling and even tumbling. So to him, the breaking string, whether it was only in the act of breaking or well and truly snapped (depending upon how the ear made its translation), was the sound that fear makes, fear of loss and of falling. For Yepikhodov, this sound signaled tripping without falling, what was for him a state of philosophical and behavioral suspension in which his ear, like his foot, was well rehearsed. Yepikhodov believed that he possessed a secret agency, and like any good secret agent, he used his body to break his fall. For him, it was a simple matter of translating the metaphysical into physical terms. "Others carry umbrellas to ward off the rain. I trip so that the sky will not fall." Yepikhodov could have said this, if he owned an umbrella and was not so much a character drawn to rain.

In some part of his being, Yepikhodov was glad that the sky produced music as awkward as his own. In the even more secret recesses of his being, he felt not merely vindicated but acknowledged, as if he were somehow personally responsible for having composed this music and setting it in play. "Has all of this been staged for me?"[16]—Another distant echo sounded inside his head, where it knocked against the low ceiling of the glowering sky. In the most secret recesses of his being, Yepikhodov thought that maybe this sound was meant to acknowledge the ordinarily unacknowledged, a category of person or thing to which he belonged.

Yepikhodov tapped a tabletop and contemplated its flatness but also the surface of the secret world that flatness concealed and sought to renounce. He held his hand before his eyes and, seeing the space between his thumb and forefinger, saw the index of something that was nothing, that was secret too. The teeth in his comb, much more regularly spaced than those biting the writing implement in his hand, could not disguise with their evenness the secret places to which these spaces might lead and how far, by analogical extension, this writing might go.

---

[15] Wittgenstein, *On Certainty*, 3e. Wittgenstein also wrote: "My mental state, 'the knowing,' gives me no guarantee of what will happen" (*On Certainty*, 46e).

[16] Quote taken and paraphrased from the film *Russian Ark*.

Inside this secret world, Yepikhodov is a notable, possessed of a secret agency that is entirely his own. To access this secret world first you have to navigate a collection of mental clutter that is materialized like furniture and accessories in a room that has been physically overtaken. This clutter renders the mental space of the room featureless and the life that produced it not so much inhabited as remaindered or put on hold, as in storage. It takes a random mind to assemble such a collection of parts, a mind that in public dissembles a wholeness at which it can only guess. This mind has too many stories to tell, but, having stored them up for so long, has difficulty in sequencing the parts into even a single, cohesive narrative form. The internal density and overlap of these parts make them operationally dysfunctional in any logical sense, although associatively performative in what appears to be an abstract language of non sequitur and nonsense. These stories quickly exhaust the patience of their audience, as does the storyteller who does not merely articulate but embodies them. However, this affront to logic and recognition is at the same time an invitation to unsee the world as it is socially perceived in favor of how it is made and remade by the individual who has the will to account for it and to make it accountable to his own intuitive terms.

The unwillingness of others to take him seriously, when they noticed him at all, used to torment Yepikhodov because he ascribed it to unwillingness on their part to recognize him for who he was. Now he saw their aloofness as being symptomatic of a more profound disengagement from life, as *their* incapacity. On this level, Yepikhodov could empathize with them. It was like looking at himself in a crooked mirror, and written on the surface of this mirror, like an epigraph to his story, were the words: "Our lives are all incapacity."[17]

This realization came to him as something of a relief. For a long time (or so repetition made it seem), Yepikhodov had enacted a disruptive, disabled agency that was too easily dismissed and that threatened to make his self-image go up in smoke. He began to feel that maybe he had no center, only a behavioral perimeter on which were located a series of behavioral performances adapted from fictions. He was Gogol's Bobchinsky/Dobchinsky in *The Inspector General*, the one tumbling over the other in a spastic counterfeit of their desire to draw attention by conveying a message, even the *wrong* message. Or maybe he was Griboedov's Repetilov in *Woe from Wit* cannily stumbling across the same threshold repeatedly as a way of symbolically drawing a prefigured future unnoticeably closer to the reason why he had been so named.

Repetilov, the mock-Decembrist before the fact, might represent "the emergence of the New *as* repetition," or what Kierkegaard called "inverted memory"—"The repeated event ... re-created in a radical sense," in a re-

---

[17] White, *Memories of My Father Watching TV*, 103.

worked coinage by Deleuze.[18] Yepikhodov, whose passage is linked to the setting of the sun and to the sound of the breaking string that follows (and so too to the sudden appearance of the Homeless Man/the Stranger/the Passerby), epitomizes a self-correcting passage in time that to the human eye and ear is never gotten right. Yepikhodov (like Repetilov) is a vampire disguised as an *untermensch* tripping over unseen lifelines that flow to secret rather than to future worlds, through the rehearsals of secret societies for a future that is always past, to an event that gives the appearance of always being just about to happen and so forever out of reach.

The Ranevskaya Family Players suffer individually and collectively from a partial blindness and so are unable to see or even to imagine a future that is not only imminent (as they see it) but also immanent (as they do not). The immanence of non-arrival is eclipsed in them by the arrival of imminence. This is the real fear of a family that feels compelled to return to the preserved nursery of a home they feel no compulsion to save. They fiddle while Rome burns not out of madness or neglect but out of fear that Rome will burn. And so, it does, inevitably. Fear will do this. It is written in the sky. The disaster only arrives once the future becomes unimaginable.

It is immanence that weighs heavily upon Yepikhodov, like the spider that presses down upon his stomach or his chest in a figurative sense at the precise moment when it is time to crawl out of death in dreams. Imminence is not his problem. Imminence, he reasons, will take care of itself. There is no stopping the thought of it happening. Imminence cannot abide a placeholder, talisman, or memorial. Imminence is not the memory of what was or of what will be. The future is always being tried on, as is the past, and both of them are worn, although neither of them is ever worn out, because neither one is ever entirely here or there. This much our shoes with escape holes in their soles (*The Seagull*'s Trigorin), our galoshes that are misplaced and left behind at parting (Trofimov), our bookcases that falsely materialize memory (Gaev), and our orchards that are remembered only to be forgotten (Ranevskaya) tell us. Nothing has ever really happened, not yet, except, that is, in the sense of the great and humble "Not Yet" itself.

En route to the estate, Yepikhodov tripped over two stones in the road and two wooden sidewalks that were missing some slats. He became anxious at the appearance of symmetry without pattern and so walked out of his way to the end of a dirt road where he knew he would find a wooden stoop upon which to sit. That action having been accomplished, he contemplated getting up and immediately forced himself to trip for a third time to see whether by breaking symmetry he could uncover design.

In the process of forming this thought, he had again started walking, and during this process absentmindedly circled a wooden wagon counter-clock-

---

[18] Slavoj Žižek, *Organs without Bodies: On Deleuze and Consequences* (New York: Routledge, 2004), 12, 13, 15.

wise, as he was not wont or ever wanted to do. In his present (sentient) condition, he could ill afford to run into the Wittgensteinian statement "I don't know my way around" coming at him from the other direction, like a mythic future.[19] Suddenly awakened by this ill-conceived action, Yepikhodov felt compelled to retrace his path around the wagon in a clockwise direction and then to recommence walking from that point on, now that it had been sanctified by this baptism by re-circulation.

Suddenly, he found himself in the door or more precisely the doorframe pursuant to the doorway that separated the where-he-was-going from the where-he-had-been. Firs, as was his custom, was not there to greet him, having gone off somewhere to rehearse his own eulogy in dreams. As a result of this, the door, against whose frame Yephikhodov's frame was pressed, was still unopened.

Standing stock-still in the haptic space inside the doorframe, the mind frame, Yepikhodov was now figuratively in the eleventh minute of the eleventh hour of the eleventh day of the eleventh month, lost in the fractured unevenness of a Gogolian re-circulation. In the windowless sky inside his mind, he saw a phalanx of black birds that became white as they crossed an invisible horizon line.[20] But did he really see what he thought he saw or was he belatedly remembering something he forgot he had seen? Whatever the reasonable explanation, if indeed one could be found, the reality of unreality was now, as always, on the wing.

Yepikhodov migrated, as though homeless, from frame to frame and through the spaces that divided the frames that led to rooms and to the people inside them. These were the spaces containing the lines that divide into pauses and silences, lines of dialogue that turned white space into black and black into white again, like migrating birds crisscrossing an invisible line in the sky. In the spaces and lines were the sleepers who spoke and dreamers who heard the flutter of wings as being the absence of sky.

Yepikhodov again saw the migrating birds, but this time in his mind's eye, as if he were a character in a play or even the creator of that character in a play. He looked to the sky and spoke, to his ear, as would a bad actor who had studied aesthetics only well enough so as to be able to impersonate an aesthetician in a play—which is to say, not well enough at all. "I fear seeing the white and unseeing the black traversing the sky," he intoned. "I fear that I may be losing my visual footing, losing sight of the ground that configures the figure and of the line subtly separating the still-to-be and the yet-to-be-seen, the future that is imminent and the future that is immanent." Still, phobia explains so little about whatever is deemed by the sufferer to be too much.

---

[19] Wittgenstein quoted in Sellars, "Question Marks," 163.

[20] The reference here is to M. C. Escher's woodcut *Dag en Nacht* (Day and Night, 1938).

Something broke on what may or may not have been the door's other side releasing "reflection into the real world" of thought in the form of a masked thirdness, a fear of dispossession and homelessness.[21] A homeless man, a stranger passed by on his way to or from somewhere or someone else. He was, perhaps, a homeless thought, entertained but not fully hosted by Yepikhodov, whose mind obsesses, then wanders off. This embodied thought is also, perhaps, "the simultaneity of a becoming whose characteristic is to elude the present.... the paradox of infinite identity (the infinite identity of both directions or senses at the same time—of future and past, of the day before and the day after, of more and less, of too much and not enough, of active and passive, and of cause and effect)."[22] The homeless man is an excess of thought, a fear of the remainder, a run(ning) on but also a running out and a running over time.

"Know when to stop," thought Yepikhodov, but Yepikhodov's thought never did know when to stop. Yepikhodov tried, as always, to say something clever to cover his unspoken thought: "I cannot abide the climate here," he said aloud to everyone and to no one in particular or to that someone, that anyone who might allow himself to become this thought's addressee.[23] Yepikhodov sounded more like a failed spokesperson for the art of conversation than an actual practitioner who was knowledgeable in the art. "—I never have abided it, ever," he continued, again without receiving either stimulus or response and further expressing the incapacity of his thought as a means of social expression.

Suddenly, Yepikhodov felt awash in "the absolute passiveness of total abjection."[24] "Crushed," he intoned, as if by a spider, and in this "as if" he recognized the performance that was his life that made everyone regard him *as if* he were a character in a play—but *what* play?

In the absence of witness (aside from his own relentless self-surveillance), Yepikhodov turned the knob of the door inside the frame of door and mind in both directions, three times each way, three times inside the one simultaneous

---

[21] Andrei Bely, *Petersburg*, trans. Robert A. Maguire and John E. Malmstad (Bloomington: Indiana University Press, 1978), 109 ("reflection"); White, *Memories of My Father Watching TV*, 146 ("masked thirdness").

[22] At the conclusion of the first chapter of *Petersburg* (36), Bely has this to say about the mental agency of another "stranger": "Once his brain has playfully engendered the mysterious stranger, that stranger exists, really exists. He will not vanish from the Petersburg prospects as long as the senator with such thoughts exists, because thought exists too." The quote concerning "the simultaneity of becoming" and "infinite identity" is taken from Gilles Deleuze, *The Logic of Sense*, trans. Mark Lester with Charles Stivale, ed. Constantin V. Boundas (New York: Columbia University Press, 1990), 1, 2.

[23] Chekhov, *The Cherry Orchard*, 334 (Act I).

[24] Blanchot, *The Writing of the Disaster*, 15.

time in which his homelessness is discovered. He was already dissatisfied with himself from the moment this action commenced to the moment it ended (which despite his planning always seemed to him to be arbitrary). Obsessive compulsion, like familiarity, breeds (self-) contempt. Disappointment, self-admonishment, and an admission of defeat await him at every turn and in every frame.

Yepikhodov sometimes imagined that he had two bodies, the one that entered and the other that delayed, much as he had two faces, the one that looked in the mirror and the other that looked back. In both instances, there was an irreparable disjunction which made the face that saw itself in the mirror and the entering body that saw itself arrested at the entrance that much more anxious and disjoined. In this way, Yepikhodov felt, physically felt, that there was more to him than met the eye, more than the eye could be trusted to tell. Why then did he so often feel with equal authority that there was *none* of him that met the eye, that he was truly invisible to everyone but himself, an unrevealed secret trapped in a world of its own eccentric design?

Yepikhodov remembered a sign that he saw, saw but did not believe, in passing, in his role as the Stranger, the Homeless Man, the Passerby. The sign read as follows:

> You are invited to
> ARE YOU FEELING ANXIOUS?
>
> An informational session featuring
>
> Doctor [Here the doctor's name is unreadable!]
>
> This Thursday [No date is given!]
>
> 12 noon-1:00 p.m.
>
> Attendance limited to 20 participants.

"Attendance limited to 20 participants"?! Why was attendance limited and why to 20 participants? Certainly 20 is a high (and an *even*) number, but is it *high enough*? Which Thursday is *this* Thursday? Or alternatively, how can one know whether "this Thursday" is the "this Thursday" of this week when there is no date on the announcement? Even if it is the "This Thursday" of this and not some other week and if 20 is a high enough number (high enough *and* even) to include even him, who or what is to say that he will even be available and want to attend the meeting. In any case, is a meeting advertised for both "12" and "noon" even worth attending? Why can't the writer of this announcement, the maker of this sign, the doctor offering a cure for this anxious condition get his story or his stories straight? Perhaps, he also has too many stories to tell and signage that frustrates rather than facilitates getting the word and the world out.

One way of understanding the multi-story sign is to regard "12 noon" as being representative of the conjuring sign, the immaterial sign inside the material sign or advertisement. This immaterial sign marks "the 'in-side' of the limit," where "internal past and external future face one another."[25] Again there is the image of Repetilov tripping across the limit of Chatsky's proairetic space of revolution in *Woe from Wit*. The physical sign that frames the conjuring sign is one of those "strange objects," like the eight-handed watch in Lewis Carroll's *Sylvie and Bruno*, that Deleuze says makes "two series of events with internal differences" appear to be simultaneous in the form of "the temporal occurrence of the event, but not the Event itself."[26] What the physical sign may represent is not the event that is advertised but rather the event that reading about the advertised event produces. The event-anxiety that is immanent in the act of reading the sign reinscribes the sign's question, written in capital letters so as to arrest the eye and shock the reader into an anxious stillness: "ARE YOU FEELING ANXIOUS?" It is, in this text and context, a rhetorical question. "A redundant one," Repetilov chimes in in a piping voice that is intended to annoy as it also repeats.

Instead of asking the question "What does the sign represent?", one can adapt art critic W. J. T. Mitchell's question, "What do pictures really want?" to read "What does the sign really want?" Mitchell writes: "What pictures want in the last instance ... is simply to be asked what they want, with the understanding that the answer may well be nothing at all." Might not the same thing be said about the sign, especially as it relates to Yepikhodov, the marginal man, the uninvited guest?[27] The sign is what Slavoj Žižek calls the Deleuzian "reality of the virtual." This is the sign of the purest form of Yepikhodov's being, the sign of this being's pure immanence, Yepikhodov's most "absolute, immediate consciousness," his anxiety of wanting.[28] Wishing or wanting will not make it so, and so the anxiety of wanting inscribes a non event or alternatively the event of not-making-it-so. It is in this way that Yepikhodov constitutes a vital link to the other characters in the play, although they cannot see it, as they are lost in their own multi-story sign of wanting, wherein the cherry orchard is lost.

Does the non-space separating the sign's numeral "12" and the word "noon" perhaps expose the fiction of the cure, or does it acknowledge the true

---

[25] "The entire content of internal space is topologically in contact with the content of external space at the limits of the living.... To belong to interiority does not mean only to 'be inside,' but to be on the 'in-side' of the limit: At the level of the polarized membrane, internal past and external future face one another." Gilbert Simondon, *L'Individu et sa genese physico-biologique* (Paris: P.U.F., 1964), 260–64, quoted in Deleuze, *The Logic of Sense*, 104.

[26] Deleuze, *The Logic of Sense*, 42.

[27] W. J. T. Mitchell, "What Do Pictures *Really* Want?" *October* 77 (Summer 1996): 82.

[28] Žižek, *Organs without Bodies*, 3, 5.

nature of the obsessive-compulsive symptom? The Doctor's name has been rendered unreadable, no doubt by an angry patient who realized that the Doctor was more interested in extracting information from him than in imparting information to him. "The same thing is true of authors in relation to their characters," thought Yepikhodov.

"YOU ARE INVITED TO FEEL ANXIOUS," is how Yepikhodov now misread the misremembered sign, a sign that he himself might have made. However, he did not misread the disorderly sign of anxiety itself, which had become clear to him at last in an articulatable form that mirrored but also actualized his general mode of performance. Not event, but event-anxiety had brought forth image after all. The sound inside his head was like a string about to break or snap. The time ran out inside his mental ticking. His boots squeaked a warning, unheeded, and Yepikhodov crashed into a mirror through which his reflection again emerged into the real world, where, as of this writing, he still considered himself to be a fake.[29]

---

[29] The language on the sign that I have been discussing is a slight paraphrase of an e-mail announcement that I received.

# Performance Practice

# Finding the Boy Band in Chekhov's *The Seagull*: LightBox's *Gull*

## Ellen Beckerman, Artistic Director, LightBox (New York City)

For a director who enjoys the act of interpretation, there's a great freedom in directing a classic play like *The Seagull*. Any obligation I might feel to give an audience *The Definitive* production of the play is eased by two factors: the first is of course the fact that there is no such thing as a definitive production; the second is the realization that my production will take place in a *Seagull*-rich environment. Anton Chekhov's *The Seagull* has already lodged itself in our collective conscious, so I can count on the majority of my audience knowing the play. This familiarity is invigorating because it gives me the freedom to interpret as boldly as I choose.

It also gives me a fun and important tool to play with: the audience's expectations. With *The Seagull*, I know the kinds of productions people will have seen and what they will expect when they walk into the theater. My production can work with or against their expectations to wake up their experience of the play: if they expect a samovar, tea drinking and lots of rugs on the floor, I can take all that away and give them a big empty space. If they expect period costumes and period behavior, I can take that away and give them a contemporary sensibility in all aspects of the production. If they expect emotional catharsis, I can turn all the actors to face forward and develop a restrained physicality that keeps the emotion simmering. And if that doesn't thoroughly refresh the play for them, then yes, I can add a surprise boy band dance number between Acts III and IV. Oh yes I can. And I will.

In fact, I probably have to. Because the disadvantage of directing such a well-known play is that familiarity can lead to numbness. It is likely that my audience will arrive at the theater with a static admiration for a deadened text. How did the text become dead? It has been crushed by that peculiar brand of preciousness that some Chekhov admirers impose on the texts. They adore the plays as if they are quaint, fragile scenes in a snow-globe. This opinion that Chekhov must be dealt with carefully and adoringly can be a burden to those of us who stage the plays. And the sense that Chekhov is inaccessible or requires special understanding leads to belabored performances, as if Chekhov's characters represent some strange breed of person in some world other than ours.

But this pomp is not Chekhov and this is not *The Seagull*. *The Seagull* is a searing critique of sentimentality. The play is like the smack of a Zen master's stick, slapping us awake and demanding our presence in this moment, and

*Chekhov the Immigrant: Translating a Cultural Icon.* Michael C. Finke and Julie de Sherbinin, eds. Bloomington, IN: Slavica Publishers, 2007, 253–58.

this one, and this one. Its characters are sharp-edged and contemporary. They cringe in the awkwardness of their own existence, but they are not dampened by mood, they are not heavy: they are light and crackling with energy. They are like us.

And *The Seagull* is not fragile. Although its sensibility is delicate, the play itself is as resilient as Shakespeare. Whatever crazy experiments I do in rehearsals, the text remains strong, and shows me what it needs, as it did in 2000 when I started working on it with my theater company, LightBox.

LightBox presents ensemble-driven, physically heightened productions of classics and new plays. LightBox productions are kinetic events, meant to reach an audience on a gut level as well as intellectually. The company works collaboratively, with actors, designers, and the director creating each piece together. We train year-round to be able to produce virtuosic performances. We intend that when the LightBox ensemble steps on the stage, the actors are so attuned to each other and the audience that if someone shifts his weight, everyone else reacts intuitively. This sets up a goose-bump-raising charge in the room, akin to the feeling one gets at a great sports event or rock concert.

This type of electrifying theatrical experience can only happen when the actors are fully occupying their bodies. It depends on their ability to be present in every cell, breathing deeply and tuned in to one another at a very high level. It may sound easy but the truth is that we live mostly in our heads and it takes quite a bit of work to open up the body and live fully in it. So LightBox trains year-round to maintain that level of physical presence and the trust and history required of great ensemble work.

Here's another good reason to work physically: it creates a vibrant platform for the text. If we want the text to be heard in its richest form, then we have to create an environment that supports it. This environment starts with the body that speaks the words. Speaking on stage is a profound act that should not be taken for granted. The way an actor delivers text must be deliberately designed according to the type of language that is spoken. Shakespeare, Chekhov, Neil Simon, David Mamet—each writer's language requires different things from the body that speaks it. This is not just about the voice, but about the whole body and how its density or lightness helps to frame the language it speaks.

How actors breathe, move, and speak on stage creates the three-dimensional world in which the play takes place. They shape the space around them and give rise to the physical atmosphere in the room. Very few theater artists take advantage of this, and that is why so many productions fail to create a palpable atmosphere on stage that has its own integrity and vigor. But the potential is always there, and with training and experimentation, a physicality can be designed that puts just the right edge into the air to envelop the audience in an extraordinary theatrical event. (How often does that happen to you in the theater? It should *always* happen.)

So, as I began work on *The Seagull*, my first inquiry was into the exact physical body and atmosphere that would best deliver this language, in all its richness, to the audience.

When I work on a play with LightBox, the process has several phases. First, it's just me and the play in a room together. I read it, and it delivers to me a visceral sense of itself. In order to create the three-dimensional physical world I've described, I have to first know it in my own imagination. This intimate personal connection to the play is the foundation of all that will follow.

With *The Seagull*, I perceived a world that vibrated with longing and loneliness, but also with great hope and an almost heartbreaking optimism. These characters were aching for connection to one another. They felt small and vulnerable in a big, overwhelming world. They shimmered with hope, tiny in a big space—this is how I imagined them on stage.

It was imperative to me to keep that loneliness and desire for connection front and center. I did not want to bury it under layers of behavior. It had to be there, pulsing in the space. Because this state of being was the link between Chekhov's characters and our audience, and the reason to do the play in the first place. I knew our audience could relate—we all feel that disconnect and overwhelm in our lives now, and we know too well the feeling of loneliness in a crowd. Through *The Seagull*, we would reflect this existence back to our audience.

So the question became how to keep that loneliness present in the space without requiring the actors to emote it constantly. In fact I never wanted them to act lonely—I just wanted that vibration in the space, to provide a kind of landscape against which they could play. This image of small bright bodies in a big dark space had stuck in my mind, so I decided we would not have a "realistic" scenic design, but would keep the space void. There would be no props to clutter the environment (no teacups, no notebooks, no dead seagull, no bandage—these things would be evoked). We would dress the actors in shades of white, so they appeared a little bit like ghosts. I knew that the space in between the actors would be of special significance in this production. That was where the lack would resonate, and we would have to charge that space with a particular quality of longing and desire.

To go further, I brought the actors into rehearsal and we started to explore. Their feedback and ideas were critical to advancing of these initial thoughts.

To create the real atmosphere of lack, I restricted the actors' physical vocabulary. They were to face forward, and they were not allowed to look at each other or touch each other except under special circumstances. This deprivation created a real, actual sense of lack of connection in the actors, and charged the space between them on stage with their desire to reach out to each other. And with such limited movement, each small gesture took on monumental significance. If an actor leaned even slightly toward another, it yielded lushest intimacy.

It was challenging to arrive at exactly the right quality of physical stillness for *Gull*. We found that if the actors were *too* still, they were not able to engage in the scenes—and the body tension rendered them unable to speak. But if they were too loose, the staging veered towards naturalism and did not provide the tautness we were looking for. With the actors' constant feedback, we went back and forth between very restrained and very loose movement until we found the exact right balance.

## Meta-theatrical Setting

For each play I do, I like to create a meta-theatrical setting in which the performance of the play itself takes place. This means that when the actors step on stage they are not yet characters in the play, and the play has not quite begun. There is a world on stage that is greater than the world of the play, and it gives context to the play's delivery. In our production of *Hamlet*, the meta-theatrical setting is Purgatory, where the characters perform the actions of the play again and again, searching for an alternate ending—one that won't produce so many dead bodies. This means that inside the play *Hamlet*, each twist and turn of plot and every offhand remark is important because it has the potential to change the play's outcome.

With *The Seagull*, I was interested in the fact that none of the characters was able to live fully in the present moment. They either pined for a sentimentalized past or obsessed over a rose-colored future—but none was able to live fully and comfortably in the present. I wanted to create a meta-theatrical setting that accentuated our awareness of time. So we created The Afterlife. We drew a box on the floor, and inside the box was the world of Chekhov's *The Seagull*, where characters were wracked by the ups and downs of daily life. Outside the box was The Afterlife, where characters move with a lightness and ease, and are able to look back with a sense of humor and greater perspective. It was incredibly moving to see characters walk towards the box with a half-smile on their faces, gentleness in their walk, and then jolt over the line into the box and suddenly become charged with hopes and needs.

One day actor Margot Ebling came into rehearsal with a volume of the Chekhov-Knipper letters.[1] Amazed, we learned that Olga Knipper had continued to write to Chekhov even after his death. These letters worked perfectly in our Afterlife, where characters could recite little odes to the ones they love and miss. So the play, which was quickly transforming itself from *The Seagull* to *Gull*,[2] began with Masha in the Afterlife, speaking to an unidentified dead companion (it could be Konstantin, whom she loved, or Trigorin,

---

[1] *Dear Writer, Dear Actress: The Love Letters of Olga Knipper and Anton Chekhov*, ed. and trans. Jean Benedetti (London: Methuen Drama, 1996).

[2] We titled our adaptation of the play *Gull* to signal its difference from the original. We have since learned that *Gull* is a more accurate translation of Chekhov's original Russian title, *Chaika*, than its common rendering in English, *Seagull*.

who showed some sympathy, or even Medvedenko, who tolerated her cruelty). Later in the play other characters step into the Afterlife to recite excerpts of Knipper's letters to a loved one long gone.

## A Problem Becomes A Solution

About ten days into the rehearsal process, we were hit with the unexpected departure of the actor playing Dorn. Caught without an easy replacement, I made the choice of proceeding without the character Dorn. This felt momentarily crippling, because the conversations that Dorn has with Sorin about Sorin's illness and impending death were absolutely central to exactly that question of how to live fully in the present moment and how to deal with our own mortality.

One of the huge benefits of working collaboratively is that great ideas come from all over. This time I don't remember who came up with it, but someone or a group of us found the solution to the Dorn problem, which turned a one-time problem into one of the strongest aspects of our adaptation. We decided to transform the Sorin-Dorn conversations into a series of dreams, or nightmares, that Sorin has as he enters the final stage of his life (some of us had lost parents or close relatives, and had witnessed such intense sleep/dream cycles first hand). The whole company learned Dorn's lines, and we shaped these dream sequences as conversations between Sorin and the entire community, as they help him come to accept the fact of his own death. The dreams were haunting and very different in tone from the rest of the play. The community spoke as one voice, but crisply, not in a strange lethargy that usually takes over choral speaking. In the dream world, people seemed taller, more vertical.

So, as we had been working on *The Seagull*, slowly our interpretation of the play was morphing into a real adaptation of the play. The elements so far: dreams, the Afterlife, and a restrained, forward-facing physicality.

## Bye Bye Bye

Between Acts III and IV in *The Seagull*, two years pass. And in those two years the mood shifts from wired desperation to grim disappointment. The play reaches its emotional peak in Act III. We faced the interesting question of how to change the atmosphere on stage and how to show the passage of time. (We use none of the usual tricks: intermission, costume change, scenery change.)

In the past, LightBox has made good use of the well-placed surprise dance number. We did an astonishing rendition of Michael Jackson's *Thriller* in *Hamlet* (the players scene). And at a pivotal plot point in *Orestes*, the characters rocked the house to The Jackson 5's "I Want You Back." These moments are exhilarating for the audience and for the actors. They lift the energy in the room and are far more refreshing than an intermission. When the actors finally stop dancing, there are hoots, hollers, screams, and applause. Everyone (nearly everyone) loves a great surprise dance number.

In trying to bridge Acts III and IV, a dance number was an obvious solution to us. I'm not a big boy-band fan, but I found the lyrics to 'Nsync's "Bye Bye Bye," and they seemed to express exactly the kind of frustration that each of the characters was feeling at the end of Act III. Trigorin has had enough of Arkadina's manipulation and is about to bust into a sexy tryst with Nina. Nina has put up with enough of Konstantin's dramatics, and will recklessly leave town for Trigorin. Masha and Konstantin have reached a head, sending Masha flying into her tortured marriage to Medvedenko. Arkadina is desperate to escape the claustrophobic farm and her withering brother. Everyone has reached a breaking point.

So... We bought an instructional video that actually taught the steps to "Bye Bye Bye," and the actors learned the dance.

It was beautiful. The sheer energy of it was exhilarating. After dancing their hearts out the actors dropped right into the sad fourth act with the proper level of exhaustion.

Of course, the real test of the surprise dance number came the first time we showed it to an audience. And we had gotten it right. Most audience members recognized the song within the first few notes, and the younger ones even recognized the dance moves from the video. They started clapping and even singing a little bit. The energy in the room soared.

Of course not everyone loved the dance. A few people always bristle, and I can certainly understand their point of view. But we've just gotta dance.

Not every play needs a surprise boy-band dance number, but maybe every Chekhov play does. Not because Chekhov needs supplementation but because we have to find ourselves again in his plays. Anything to get us away from that sense of preciousness. Think of the possibilities for *Three Sisters*, *The Cherry Orchard*, *Uncle Vanya*. When do the characters need to dance, absolutely NEED to? And what music is it? Doesn't that plug you right into the heart of the play? It does for me.

# "Must There Be a Cherry Orchard in *The Cherry Orchard*?": Understanding and Staging Chekhov

## Carol Rocamora, Tisch School for the Arts, New York University

In 1993, I went to Russia as a guest of the Moscow Art Theatre. At the time, I was artistic director of the theater in Philadelphia at the Annenberg Center, and we had just begun a four-year Chekhov Cycle of productions of my new translations of the major plays.[1] Anatoly Smeliansky, my host and the Art Theatre's literary director at the time, had been to Philadelphia earlier that year to see a performance of *The Seagull*, which I'd translated and directed, and wanted to talk to me about bringing our production to an international Chekhov festival in Moscow. The festival never materialized, but on that trip to Moscow I was given another gift, one of inestimable value.

Anatoly knew that, while in Moscow, I wanted to talk to Russian directors about their experiences in directing Chekhov. Oleg Efreimov was ill at the time, so at the last minute Anatoly arranged for me to visit the artistic director of the Army Theatre and a veteran director of Chekhov's plays. He had only an hour to spare, and I found myself in his drafty, Soviet-style office, explaining that I was "in search of Chekhov," had translated his major plays, and would be grateful for any insights into understanding them and staging them. He paused, and smiled. Then he jumped up from behind his desk. "Come with me," he said.

A moment later, we were making our way through the choked streets of Moscow. Soon we were standing at the door of the Tretyakov Gallery. I followed him up the staircase to the second floor, into a large room filled with portraits. He led me over to one in the center of the room, stood before it, and said in Russian: "There. Pure Chekhov. That's *it*."

The painting hanging in the center of a long wall was smallish and unassuming. And yet it had an unmistakable charisma. I looked at the title: "Girl with a Peach" by Valentin Serov. Its subject, a young girl, sits alone at a dining table, her hands holding a ripe peach. Behind her, a window, with a hint of springtime beyond. She gazes at us, calmly, intently (Figure 1 on the following page; note that Figures 2–8, illustrating the 1995 staging of *The Cherry Orchard* at the Annenberg Center in Philadelphia, discussed in this

---

[1] This essay is dedicated to the memory of Doug Wing, Fred Shaffmaster, and Marcia Mahon, who played Gaev, Firs and Lyubov Andreevna—respectively—in my staging of *The Cherry Orchard* at the Annenberg Center.

*Chekhov the Immigrant: Translating a Cultural Icon.* Michael C. Finke and Julie de Sherbinin, eds. Bloomington, IN: Slavica Publishers, 2007, 259–68.

article, are arranged on pages 261–67). I took in every detail. The bloom of that soft young face, reprised in the round fruit. The vibrance of the rosy chemise, the bright white cloth and walls, the dark, dark eyes. What warmth, what harmony! A portrait of purity, static and yet dynamic. A pose of serenity, innocent and yet elusive. A stolen moment, captured and yet not captured. "Is she smiling?" my host asked. And above all, the light coming in from the window, illuminating it all…

**Figure 1.** Valentin Serov, *Girl with a Peach*

I took that moment home with me (along with a book of Serov paintings), and over the next three years, as we continued to work through the Chekhov

Cycle, as the company of actors and I gathered to read my new translations, as the designers sat around the drafting table—the Serov book lay open, and the "Girl with a Peach" smiled (or not) out at us. (My actors called her "the Russian Mona Lisa"). Pure Chekhov. What was her secret? What was the magic? Something about the light... There was another element, too. While standing in the gallery, my colleague had offered another insight—or what I came to call his second principle in understanding Chekhov. "Chekhov felt nature keenly," he said. So I also bought a book of Levitan's paintings—Levitan, Chekhov's friend, after whom the character of Konstantin Gavrilovich in *The Seagull* was inspired; Levitan, the artist, whose luminous landscapes evoke the natural settings of Chekhov's plays. And of course, my director friend was right: Chekhov was a supreme observer both of nature and of *human* nature, and their symbiosis. Every one of the major Chekhov plays begins in the spring, with the birches in bloom, and ends in the autumn, the trees barren and bare. And each of the four acts in each of the four major plays is extremely specific vis à vis hour of the day, temperature, month, season, and weather. The time, the elements, the light...

My Moscow colleague gave me yet a third principle to work with. "I'll tell you another secret about Chekhov's plays," he said, riding back to the Mos-

**Figure 2.** *The Cherry Orchard*, Annenberg Center, Philadelphia, 1995, see pp. 266–67

cow Art Theatre from the Tretyakov. "Every act has a *zerno*." A core, a kernel, an essence. My designers and I considered this principle as we started to conceptualize the design for our upcoming production of *The Cherry Orchard* in January 1996. What is the *zerno* of each act? Let us find it, and build the design around it. Take Act I. Clearly, it is to be found in the moment when Lyubov Andreevna, who has returned to the beloved home of her childhood after years of exile in Paris, flings open the windows of the nursery. It's 2:30 on a fresh, spring morning, and she looks out onto her beloved orchard.

> VARYA: (Quietly opens the window). The sun is up now, it isn't cold anymore. Look, Mamochka: what glorious trees! My God, the air! And the starlings are singing!
>
> LYUBOV ANDREEVNA: O my childhood, my innocence! Once I slept in this very nursery, I'd look out on the orchard, right from here, and happiness would awaken with me, every morning, every morning, and look, it's all the same, nothing has changed. (*Laughs with joy.*) White, all white! O, my orchard! After the dark dreary autumn, the cold winter, you're young again, blooming with joy, the heavenly angels have not forsaken you... If only this terrible weight could be lifted from my soul, if only I could forget my past!

**Figure 3.** *The Cherry Orchard*, Annenberg Center, Philadelphia, 1995, see pp. 266–67

GAEV: Yes, and the orchard will be sold to pay off our debts, strange, isn't it?

LYUBOV ANDREEVNA: Look, there's my mother, walking through the orchard... all in white! (*Laughs with joy.*) There she is.

GAEV: Where?

VARYA: God bless you, Mamochka.

LYUBOV ANDREEVNA: There's no one there, I only dreamed it... Look, to the right, on the way to the summer-house, a white sapling, bowing low, I thought it was a woman...[2]

How do we design it, so that the moment happens? How do we stage it? She can't very well deliver the line facing upstage, can she?! No, we'll lose her. Facing stage right, or left? Hardly. No, she must face downstage, looking out on the orchard. So then where is the window? Where are we going to place it? And what does the orchard look like? After all, we *must* have a cherry orchard in *The Cherry Orchard*! It's obvious!

Or is it?

**Figure 4.** *The Cherry Orchard*, Annenberg Center, Philadelphia, 1995, see pp. 266–67

---

[2] Anton Pavlovich Chekhov, *The Cherry Orchard*, in *Chekhov: Four Plays*, trans. Carol Rocamora (Lyme, NH: Smith and Kraus, 1996), 226–27.

David Gordon, our set designer, reviewed landmark productions of *The Cherry Orchard*, beginning with Simov's design for the premiere at the Moscow Art Theatre on January 17, 1904. Stanislavsky had a cherry orchard. Giorgio Strehler's lyrical production at the Piccolo Teatro in Milan, 1955 (again in 1974; designer Luciano Damiani) had a cherry orchard. The Teatro Valle in Rome, 1966 (designer Ferdinando Scarfiotti) had a cherry orchard. The Taganka Theatre in Moscow, 1975 (designer Valery Levental) had a cherry orchard. So did the memorable 1977 production at the Vivian Beaumont Theatre (Lincoln Center), directed by Andre Serban and designed by Santo Loquasto (starring Irene Worth, Raul Julia, Meryl Streep), with its magical, frosted trees gleaming upstage in full view.

Then came the legendary production of *The Cherry Orchard* at the Theatre des Bouffes du Nord in Paris in 1981, which ultimately made its way to the Brooklyn Academy of Music in 1988, directed by Peter Brook and designed by Chloe Obolensky. "O my orchard..." Wait... where is it? Brook and Obolensky's visionary *mise en scene* consisted of the exposed brick walls of the theatre upstage, stage right and left, and a bare floor on which a number of oriental carpets were lain, one overlapping the other. The loges stage right and left became entrances and exits. Nothing else. An empty space. But the cherry orchard was there, in the faces of Natasha Parry and Erland Josephson, playing brother and sister in that magical moment in Act I when the invisible

**Figure 5.** *The Cherry Orchard*, Annenberg Center, Philadelphia, 1995, see pp. 266–67

window opens downstage and they look out onto all that spring splendor. It was there in their eyes, in their transcendent expressions.

Other directors and designers considered this question in the 1980s, too. Perhaps you don't need the orchard on stage, after all. Note the minimalist production (Jurgen Flimm/Hermann and Clarchen Baus) at the Teater der Stadt in Koln, 1983, with its towering floor-to-ceiling walls and severe wooden planes. Or Jacques Berwoot's highly conceptual, reductionist design for *The Cherry Orchard* in Belgium, 1987, consisting of Gaev's billiard table. Or the LaJolla Playhouse spare production in 1990, directed by Tom Moore and designed by Heidi Landesmann, shadowy and ephemeral.

Since the nineties, it has been open season on orchards. Some productions with, some without. The Redgraves (Vanessa and Corin, sister and brother), played Lyubov and Gaev frolicking on the nursery floor in the Cottesloe of the Royal National Theatre (2000, Trevor Nunn directing)—no orchard there. Nor was there one in Adrian Noble's production in the mid-nineties at the Royal Shakespeare Company on the West End, which focused on the house itself, featuring staircases and a second floor in full view. In contrast, I vividly recall Peter Stein's earlier, Wagnerian-scale production at the Schaubuhne in Berlin, which I saw when it was transported to the Moscow Art Theatre in the mid-nineties. In Act I, the curtains of the nursery were drawn apart, and

**Figure 6.** *The Cherry Orchard*, Annenberg Center, Philadelphia, 1995, see pp. 266–67

blackened branches of grotesque, gnarled trees appeared ominously through the open windows.

Meanwhile, for us in Philadelphia in 1995, the question remained: orchard or no orchard?

In the end, we returned to what we called the "Serov principle." We did it with light. We, too, had an empty space—the Harold Prince Theatre of the Annenberg Center, a deep, high, black box with three-quarters-in-the-round audience seating. Anything was possible. David Gordon and Jerold Forsyth, our resident set and lighting designers, and I agreed—we wanted something suggestive, evocative, not literal. So, the designers began with a platform on the theatre floor, which they painted white ("white, all white," as Lyubov says, so the designers wanted that color to be present). On it, they placed a single carpet. For the backdrop, they found a synthetic material called Contra-H, consisting of broad bands of a bubblewrap-like substance, which they wove together to make a textured, opaque sheet. Then they hung it in a frame that David built, covering the entire upstage wall. Jerry hung the lighting instruments behind it. A bit downstage of the backdrop, stage right, David built a single arched window, and dressed it with a diaphanous curtain, which could cover it at the pre-set, and then be drawn aside by Varya on cue (Figure 2 on p. 261). And hanging from the grid overhead, a suggestion of branches,

**Figure 7.** *The Cherry Orchard*, Annenberg Center, Philadelphia, 1995, see pp. 266–67

sprayed silver, suspended over the downstage edge of the platform and the heads of the audience in the first row. The stage is set for Act I (Figure 3, p. 262), ready for the moment. As Varya draws the curtains, the lighting cue turns the backdrop a pink/blue (Figure 4, p. 263), and as Lyubov's moment passes, the backdrop fades into a semi-realistic blue sky (Figures 5–8, pp. 264–67). Now, for the cast. Gathering the company together on the first day of rehearsal, the designers made their presentation of the set model. "But where is the cherry orchard?" asked Bill Wise, a veteran New York actor playing Lopakhin. (A pause.) "The cherry orchard is in your hearts," I explained to my cast.

Be very careful what you say to actors; I learned that lesson quickly. The next morning, the company arrived at rehearsal, and when we reached that moment in Act I in the text, Lopakhin opened his jacket to reveal, on his shirt, cut out of construction paper, a large red heart. The rest of the cast followed suit. And so it went throughout rehearsals, in a spirit faithful to Chekhov's instructions ("It's a comedy!"), ones which Stanislavsky never followed to Chekhov's satisfaction.

One learns many lessons, discovers many secrets, directing Chekhov. My favorite, having now directed all four plays, is as follows: there is a moment in each of the plays when there is an empty stage. A fleeting moment. And yet, what a *frisson* one feels when it happens! It occurs in the oddest of places.

**Figure 8.** *The Cherry Orchard*, Annenberg Center, Philadelphia, 1995, see pp. 266–67

Random ones. For example, in *The Seagull*, it's at the end of Act III, when Arkadina and her retinue exit, and the company follows for the offstage farewell. (A moment later, Nina and Trigorin enter for their stolen encounter.) In *The Three Sisters*, it's in Act IV, before Andrei comes on with the baby carriage for the second time. In *The Cherry Orchard*, it's in the very last moments of Act IV, after Lopakhin has locked up the house and before Firs's final entrance. One wonders if Chekhov had done this intentionally. Intentional or no, each of these subtle, evocative moments is an epiphany. For it is in these moments that the mysteries of his luminous plays reveal themselves, if only fleetingly...

Back to the question of "must there be a cherry orchard in *The Cherry Orchard*?" Ultimately, my cast and I think we may have found an answer—inspired, again, by my colleague in Moscow. It was his fourth principle of understanding Chekhov, and the last gift he gave me in that brief meeting in 1993. "Chekhov saw Russia through the eyes of a dying man," he said as we parted. In the time between the spring of 1902, when Chekhov conceived of the idea for the play (which he insisted was a comedy), and January 1904, when it opened at the Moscow Art Theatre, he fell into a steep decline. His consumption was progressing rapidly. On opening night, when he was called onto the stage at the end of Act III, he could hardly stand. When he died six months later, in July, at the age of 44, he looked 74. "My darling, how hard it was for me to write that play," he wrote his wife Olga, who would play Lyubov Andreevna (*PssP* 11: 271). "And life has passed by, somehow, as if I never lived it at all," says Firs.[3]

If you understand this, bear this in mind, and smile, you have your cherry orchard, and you can do the play.

---

[3] Ibid., 269.

# Seminar in the Medical Humanities

# A Conversation with Dr. Robert Coles: Anton Chekhov and William Carlos Williams

## Dr. Robert Coles (RC) and Michael Finke (MF)

MF

Dr. Coles, at the Symposium you were going to speak about William Carlos Williams, and particularly, about what William Carlos Williams thought of Chekhov. I was wondering if we might begin with that: would you perhaps share with us some of your recollections of Williams and thoughts about what Chekhov meant to Williams?

RC

Well, I met William Carlos Williams when I was a college student at Harvard College, because I wrote my thesis on him for Perry Miller, who was a professor of English there. When I finished my essay, Miller suggested that I send it to Williams, but I said, "I can't do THAT!" I'll never forget what Miller said to me then: "What, don't you have the money for the postage? You're a student at Harvard and you can't find his address?" And he laughed, and the long and the short of it is, I sent the essay off to Williams and I got back a note from W. C. Williams, M.D., 9 Ridge Road, Rutherford, New Jersey—no zip codes then. And he wrote on one of his prescription blanks, "Dear Mr. Coles, thank you for your paper," adding, after a dash: "not bad for a Harvard student." And then he asked me to come by and visit. It took a lot of effort, psychologically, for me to get the courage up, but I eventually wrote a letter and afterwards went down to see him.

And soon Williams was taking me along on his house calls; now that was an experience! Meeting American people in their homes with this busy doctor, who was carrying that black bag with his stethoscope and his neurological hammer and whatever else; I was meeting Americans at the side of a physician. It was because of this that I thought I should try to go into medicine, and because of this that I ended up in medical school at Columbia, across the the Hudson River from where Williams was. I remember, at this time he was older but still practicing medicine, and I would go to see him and distract myself from studying anatomy and histology and physiology and the whole business: I was getting to see a great hero of mine.

And it was around this time that he would urge Chekhov on me, because he knew I was a medical student. And *then* came "Anyuta." He said, "Read 'Anyuta.'"

*Chekhov the Immigrant: Translating a Cultural Icon.* Michael C. Finke and Julie de Sherbinin, eds. Bloomington, IN: Slavica Publishers, 2007, 271–84.

MF

That was the first story he urged you to read?

RC

The first story he urged me to read. He said it wouldn't hurt all the medical students over there at Columbia to read "Anyuta." Then he would always wax eloquent, going a bit over the top, and say, "In fact, it may be more important for you to read 'Anyuta' than some of those medical school textbooks that they're throwing in your face." [*Dr. Coles laughs*] I was struggling with those textbooks, they were in *my* face and I was trying to learn from them, and here he is telling me to read "Anyuta." Well, I said, "I'll try and find it." He said "I'm gonna give you the story." He went up to his study and he came down and he had Chekhov's story "Anyuta"—a volume from the public library, by the way. He said, "Take this with you back to that medical school of yours." That's how he referred to it: "that medical school of yours."

I read "Anyuta." I'll never forget my first year of medical school. *Gray's Anatomy*, and the histology and the physiology—difficult material. But "Anyuta," too, is a tough story to read. It's about a medical student who is learning medicine and developing a fine big medical head, but who has no heart or feeling for another human being. Furthermore, it's about an artist who lacks that too. Art and science are both in a way skewered in that story.

When I was a college student, I had read Søren Kierkegaard, the great Danish philosopher—once again, at the urging of Perry Miller. Incidentally, another great American physician and author, Walker Percy, whom I would later meet, was a great reader of Kierkegaard. In any event, Kierkegaard was continuously talking about the moral and the aesthetic and the dangers inherent in both. In a way, these are the postures of our humanity, psychological and intellectual, and I began to realize that this posturing is what Chekhov was skewering in that story. In a short story—indeed, in a short, short story, relatively speaking—he adopts a perspective like Kierkegaard's glimpse of the Danish intellectual bourgeoisie, which leaves it in ashes. And Chekhov leaves us to wonder about what kind of people we're going to become if we don't watch ourselves very carefully: smart doctors, talented painters—all indifferent to a fellow human being; manipulatively self-serving; cold and callous in our own terrible way. Talk about the occupational hazards of medicine, but also those of life!

And, you know, years and years ago Allen Wheelis, a very distinguished California psychoanalyst, wrote about the vocational hazards of psychoanalysis (in an essay published, I believe, in the *International Journal of Psychoanalysis*). But I think that before Wheelis came Chekhov, writing about the occupational hazards of medicine, of being a professor, of being an accomplished artist, of being a human being. Failing, even as we aspire to greatness of mind and thought—the heart dying, and when the heart dies, we become wordy caricatures of ourselves. This is what Chekhov knew. Young, feverish during a good part of that short-lived life, knowing that he was going to die young and persisting and fighting in order to speak and write and be heard. Chekhov was fighting against the death that he knew awaits all of us—the ultimate silence—and he was haunted by that silence as well as invigorated by the challenge of taking it on and affirming himself. A remarkable story and a remarkable person.

I mentioned to you the fire of youthful dying. We see it in Orwell, who also died in his forties; we see it in James Agee, who died in his forties; we see it in Simone Weil, the great French writer, philosopher, thinker, theologian of sorts, observer of her fellow humanity, who died young of tuberculosis. Williams once said to me when we were going on house calls, he said, "You know I've lived to be too old," and I wondered what he meant by that. He said, "I've lived to be so old that I'm further and further away from all the fire of my youth, and when you lose that," he said, "then you're really old. Then you have died."

MF

I'm wondering, do you think that Williams actually to a certain extent identified with Chekhov? Did Williams view Chekhov as a model for himself?

RC

Oh, very much so. Williams saw Chekhov as a doctor who also really knew how to write. Williams was an aspiring playwright as well as a writer of stories, not to mention his poetry, but he was above all a *doctor* who wrote, and he saw Chekhov as a *doctor* who wrote ... and wrote and wrote! Once Williams even said to me—when he himself was quite old—he said, "You know, he died so young ... and look what he did, look what he gave us; and some of us, we last and we last..." And he was being a bit reflective and self-critical, because, after all, Williams lived to be eighty or eighty-one, from 1883 to 1963. That's eighty years, which is twice what Chekhov had—twice. And look at what Chekhov gave us in that impassioned, strenuously lived, vulnerable life, ailing and yet, in his own way, on top of things. That trip across Russia—ancient Russia, if I may call it that, compared to the era we live in now: to go all the way across that continent! We're not talking about getting on an airplane or even on the Trans-Siberian Railroad, which wasn't yet built. You talk about an effort!

MF

Well, that's a point of connection, I think, between Chekhov and you and your professional career. As you know, Chekhov had two great aspirations he never realized: he wanted for a time to write a novel, which, he thought, would have put him in the central tradition of nineteenth-century Russian literature; and he also wanted to get an advanced degree in medicine and actually made a couple of starts on a dissertation in medicine. But the closest he came to achieving either of those goals was his documentary monograph on Sakhalin Island, which is the longest work that he ever wrote. I've wondered what you think of that, of him and of that trip, of his reasons for going, of the value of *Sakhalin Island* as a very odd, odd piece of literature.

RC

I think that that trip to Sakhalin was an effort to get away from what he felt to be the hold of stale death, or to forge out on his own and explore the world and show himself the master of his own fate and the observer of the fate of others—and who knows—maybe to break away from the privileged, aristocratic world that was beginning to treasure him and dote on him. This can be its own kind of death.

I remember my wife saying to me—when we started our work and I was getting offers to teach here or teach there—I remember she said to me, "We've got to get away from this... If you end up being engulfed by these institutions you'll lose all the interest you had in people and finding out about how they live. You'll be teaching, which is is a fine and respectable thing," she said, "but the fire in you that enables you to go out and meet people and write about them and try to understand them, you'll lose *that*." Maybe she was a little overwrought about it, but she was worried about the dangers for us of buying into our "academic"—which equals "conventional"—success. And I think Chekhov perhaps wanted to get away from something, on the one hand, and find something else on the other, and maybe even start a new life. And I remember, when we went from New England to New Mexico—we went just to be there with some ordinary people in the small towns of northern New Mexico—and I remember my wife saying to me, "We've got to stay away from Santa Fe. That's the first 'must.' We're going way out there to get away from here, and if we stay in Santa Fe, you'll become lost in a world that's very similar to Cambridge." And so she took me—by her insistent spirit—to little towns—El Valle, Truchas, you know the sort—to get away... And then we lived in Albuquerque, so as to be with ordinary Spanish-speaking people and precisely not in that elegant world of Sante Fe—which, with all due respect, is obviously a beautiful city, but I think you know what I am talking about. And I think that for Chekhov to leave Moscow and St. Petersburg and that world, so as to be among prisoners and try to understand them—I would say maybe this was a leap and a liberation. Maybe it's Kierkegaard's leap of faith, but I think that for him it was chiefly finding himself and what he could do to understand others, and to comprehend them, by finding himself away from what came all too readily, what was close to him and easy for him: a liberation.

Remember, there's a parallel between Chekhov going to Sakhalin and Tolstoy renouncing his privileged life and wanting to work alongside the laboring peasants; a parallel with Tolstoy, who asked in one of his essays: "Are the peasant children to learn from us or are *we* to learn from the peasant children?" In a way, Chekhov was going to learn from the penal colony, he was going to find a whole new moral, even intellectual world. This is Tolstoyan, and it's Dostoevskian, too, the Dostoevsky of *Notes from the House of the Dead*... This is in the Russian tradition of abandoning privilege, power, celebrity, and through the loss of this world gaining another: a fresh breath of air—I keep coming back to that—and a sense of renewal. It's a matter of turning toward the suffering and the poor not in a patronizing way, but with the understanding that we have to learn from others and be part of their lives lest we become all too privileged, and smug, and narrow, and full of ourselves, and read and applauded for what we write.

MF

As you know, Chekhov's first idea for a Ph.D. in medicine involved writing a theoretical Darwin-and-Spenser-influenced study of gender inequality. But in the end what he did as his bit of scientific research and contribution to medicine—to pay back his debt to medicine, as he explained his journey to Sakhalin—was traveling, meeting people, and telling stories. I'm wondering what you might have to say about the value of this kind of action; about the kind of knowledge and understanding that's available through stories documenting real lives, and how that passes or doesn't pass as legitimate scientific or medical research. If I'm not mistaken, what Chekhov accomplished as a scientific researcher was in many respects close to a central theme of your career, was it not?

RC

Well, you lose yourself and you gain this new world of other people. Remember, he was a doctor who wanted to attend people and understand them; that was his training. And maybe he wanted to find a part of the world where sickness was right on the table, a world of pain and suffering and hurt and tragedy. And by the way, it may have been a way to renew his medical career; otherwise, what could he have done? Treat those wealthy people who would come to him because he was a famous writer, or because they just thought he was a good doctor, well known in their social world? Once again, there's that metaphor of losing something to gain something.

I think Chekhov was curious about people: he wanted to see and understand their world and explore it, and this for him was a huge realm of possibility. And I want to emphasize again that while this is in the Russian tradition, it also characterizes someone like Dickens, too, who was exploring the world and trying to impart, through his fictional creations, how poor people live and suffer, but also a certain kind of transcendence that takes place because of this, and the price they pay for it; this comes across in some of Chekhov's writings, too. I see Chekhov as a spiritually inclined doctor who was trained to work with other people, who wanted to understand them, also, as a writer. And he was a writer who also had the good sense to worry about getting lost in the world he had been placed in by his increasing prominence as a playwright, as a "successful" person who knew how to give us something in the theater. I think he ran from that in some way. I think this was someone saying, "Valuable as it is to be a playwright, there's another part of me that's a doctor and an observer and maybe a traveling person" ... the way Williams used to travel...

Williams would take me from city to city in New Jersey, and he'd teach me how to look and understand the town: the drugstore, the five-and-ten-cent store, where the library was, where the school was. He taught me to look at the people, at what they were wearing, and to get out of the car and listen to them. I remember asking him, "Well, how do you do that?" He said, "For crying out loud! You go into a drugstore and ask for a soda. And someone's going to give you a soda, and there'll be somone sitting beside you... Talk with them! You don't have to get an affadavit! You don't have to get them to sign something. They're around... Go into the five-and-ten and try and buy something, get in and talk with the saleslady. She has a story to tell you ... about five cents, ten cents, her struggle for life... Never mind *your* difficulties in this five-and-dime store where she's working in as a saleslady." And the kind of language I heard from Williams—a language of exhortation, which was of course self-exhortation—was, I think, a conversation that Chekhov had within himself.

Who am I to presume what went on in Chekhov's mind? But one would surmise that when someone leaves St. Petersburg and Moscow and fights his way across a whole world of impasses and dangers and suffering to be in a penal colony... I think this is, I repeat, liberation, affirmation, exploration, and this is what makes for our writers. They want to be free to connect with others. They want to liberate themselves from themselves, so that through their language they connect with the reader, they and the reader becoming one, so to speak. And they of course want to find themselves through their words, never mind helping others to find themselves through their words.

MF

Well, bringing it back to William Carlos Williams, were there other Chekhov stories that Williams discussed?

RC

"Ward 6." He told me to read "Ward 6." He said—I remember very clearly—he said, "It's a confusing story, because at the end it's gonna make you wonder who was the doctor, who was the patient, and what's the difference between the two." And he said, "*You* should be thinking about this now that you're going to be a doctor." When is the doctor the patient, when are patients helping the doctor or even healing the doctor, and when might the doctor working with patients belong among them in ways that he or she doesn't even understand—maybe even be one of them? This and the whole business of the arbitrariness of medical authority and power as against the connection between medical authority and patienthood is, I think, what Chekhov is exploring in "Ward 6," which is where, one assumes, among other places, he lived ... where maybe all of us doctors ought to understand we live, as we think about ourselves and think about others...

Boy, do I still remember patients whom I treated in Boston psychiatric hospitals, and who taught me so much more than I realized at the time. But as I would discuss the work with my psychiatric and psychoanalytic supervisors, I began to realize that in a way I was a student learning about the mind not only from people whose minds were troubled, but from people who—in talking to me about themselves and about life, in sharing some of their thoughts—were helping me to understand some of my own thoughts. And this, by the way, is what Freud—a contemporary of Chekhov's—is getting at when he talks about "transference" and "countertransference": it's a two-way street. There is the doctor responding to the patients out of things in his life or her life, but there is the patient in a way responding to the doctor and helping the doctor along and enabling the doctor to understand things in ways that otherwise might not have been possible. The doctor as a learner or student as well as teacher; the doctor as authority and healer who is also healed by patients while going about his or her life-work—that, I think, is what Chekhov may be getting at in "Ward 6" and elsewhere.

MF

Well, this notion of the physician who himself needs to be healed makes me want to ask you a question about Chekhov's illness—tuberculosis—which you mentioned earlier. There's always been a point of argument among Chekhov scholars regarding the degree to which Chekhov knew and understood what his condition was but simply bore it very stoically, or whether he might have actually been in a kind of denial about his condition and blind to it. I'm wondering what your hunch is about about Chekhov's own illness—what it meant for him to be ill, and what it meant for him to either, let's say, stoically ignore and not acknowledge that illness in spite of being fully conscious of it, or, on the other hand, what was going on in him if he was actually able to disavow this devastating illness in himself?

RC

Look, he was a doctor and he had an illness that is not silent and secret. I know as a physician what tuberculosis is. I treated some tuberculous patients many years ago in medical school, and you *know* when you have tuberculosis. You cough up blood. You feel chest pain. There is an illness there—we're not talking about something spreading like cancer cells for a long time that aren't even known. This is a tangible, physical, concrete, palpable phenomenon of the body that Chekhov knew; he knew it as a physician, and he also knew it because at that time tuberculosis was a major prevalent illness. Of course he knew it. He knew that he was dying. He knew he was dying as a human being knows... I had patients, I remember, when I was an intern—they knew they were dying at times, even though I didn't tell them that they were dying, but they knew. They were in the Presbyterian Hospital, Columbia Presbyterian Medical Center; they knew they were dying, but we were talking about whether we should tell them! I remember my medical supervisor, Robert Loeb, once said to us once—I'll never forget it—he said, "You are trying to figure out whether you should tell these folks. Maybe you should ask them to tell you what they know, and you'll learn a lot." And Yale Kneeland, whom I also mentioned in that piece I wrote about Chekhov,[1] he was always telling us that our patients are our teachers. Time and again we underestimate what they know about their fate, and maybe what they know about *us*—indeed, they may know that we *don't* know many things! We were just medical students, trying to learn, but there are some doctors who—talk about denial—can't admit to themselves, let alone to their patients, how vulnerable all life is, everyone's, because that would take away their grandiosity. They are the all-powerful individuals!

A little humility—that is what Chekhov, I think, keeps asking for from us, from all of us; a little humility. And the absence of that humility shows the arrogant, smug side of us, and there—since we're talking about tuberculosis—there's a sickness worse than tuberculosis; there is metastatic cancer. You know, smugness and arrogance—including among, unfortunately, doctors, lawyers, politicians, teachers, all of us—it's *this* that Chekhov is getting at: human vulnerability, human neediness, and the challenge to us to learn from ourselves and maybe with the help of others to become a bit better... The others, handing us along, giving us a bit of a boost, are often patients helping doctors and teaching them and maybe healing them.

I remember a patient I had who was dying when I was an intern—Oh, my lord, do I! This was in Chicago, at the University of Chicago Hospital; he was dying of lung disease, fibrosis of the lungs, that he got through poisoning in one of the factories south of Chicago. I would come to see him with my stethoscope, and my neurological hammer, and my cocksureness as, now, an M.D., an intern; and I'll never forget—his name was Bill Park, I still remember his name, though we're talking now about forty-plus years ago, almost forty-five years. He looked at me, and he said, "Doctor, you look tired." And I said, "Well, I'm fine." But he said, "You look tired, you look as if you need a good night's sleep." Actually, I hadn't had that much sleep for a long time, I'd been up nights on calls, and he told me that he was worried about me. And he had some food that had been brought to him,

---

[1] Robert Coles, "The Wry Dr. Chekhov," *Times of Surrender: Selected Essays* (Iowa City: University of Iowa Press, 1988), 49–56.

some candy bars and stuff, and he insisted that I take some of it. He said, "It'll give you a little bit of energy." Who was the doctor and who was the patient? I still remember this, I can picture it; I remember Robert Ebert, who was the attending, and who would later go on to be the dean of Harvard Medical School, I remember him putting his hand on my shoulder—I was telling him about this—and I'll never forget how he looked at me and said, "You see how our patients take our pulse and help us sometimes to figure things out about *ourselves*, never mind about them."

This, I think, is what Chekhov was getting at in some of those stories—the patient as a healer, the vulnerable person as someone who reminds us of our own vulnerability, and maybe the doctor who has so much to learn from those whom he or she would be treating. It's what Martin Buber called "I-Thou." This runs through Chekhov, not because he was a philosopher or a theologian, but because he was a sensitive human being and reached out to people. That trip from conventional and privileged Russia to Sakhalin Island—I can only think of it as, again, in the tradition of the Hebrew prophets, of Isaiah and Jeremiah, and of Jesus of Nazareth: reaching out to the poor and knowing that the poor in a sense will heal us and give to us and help the impoverished part of us. In that sense, it was a trip of *need*. We know about the the physical hazards of this journey, and maybe even about its danger to his health, but I think he knew there was a greater danger to his health than primitive travel across Russia: the danger of a kind of smug insularity. To leave insularity in Moscow or St. Petersburg for an island off of Siberia was for him, I think, redemption, and discovery, and self-discovery, and a Judeo-Christian connection of suffering with fellow sufferers—as in healing from fellow human beings who themselves need healing. Going to Sakhalin, therefore, for this ailing doctor, was perhaps a trip toward some kind of self-discovery, but also toward what I would call a kind of invigorated new life, albeit short and tenuous.

This is Orwell, aging and dying young, trying to find out how the poor live, going among the down-and-out in London and Paris and writing about it. Chekhov too was exploring; he was trying to understand people, because I think he felt, "My lord, as frail as I am, this can give me some kind of strength that otherwise would be denied me, and no medicine in the world is going to give me that." This is Chekhov pursuing medicine in an Isaiah-Jeremiah-Jesus fashion, where being with the poor will heal us and give us ourselves.

I remember when I worked in Dorothy Day's soup kitchen on the Lower East Side, when I was a medical student, and I used to wonder: how does she do this work—with all these down-and-out people, many of them alcoholics and very troubled. I'll never forget, she took me aside and she said, "You know, you're a medical student. There's healing that goes on here all the time." And I thought, "Oh, the healing is her giving soup to the needy people of the Lower East Side"; but she saw that in my face, in my look, and she shook her head and said, "*We* are healed here. We are given an opportunity to link arms with people in some way that makes us stronger." At the time I didn't quite understand it, but it was a kind of a connection and an identification with others that was something to witness and try to understand. I'll never forget when I first went there to meet her, I waited and waited, the impatient, privileged medical student. She was talking to someone; I looked across the room, and I could tell that this was an alcoholic—a down-and-out Bowery bum, to be tough about it. She saw me fidgeting, and there I was in my suit—I was a medical student, full of himself. She picked herself up and walked across the room. She looked at me—I'll never forget that look on her face—she said, "Are you waiting to meet one of us?" "One of us," she said! For her, she and that person she was talking to—they were one. And in her own quiet way she was telling me a Chekhovian story: "Big shot, you have a lot to learn... And maybe you can think a little bit about yourself, never mind all the troubled people around you whom you're gonna 'help.'" A Chekhovian moment, in a way.

MF

Are there other Chekhov stories or plays that you would routinely teach in your courses or that you remember Williams talking about with you?

RC

"Anyuta" and "Ward 6" all the time. "The Student"—there's another one. The theology student, who has so much to learn; and he's learning the Bible, and he's learning his theology, and I think Chekhov is saying in that story: "Listen, look around you and try to understand how that narrative that you're studying has flesh and blood right here, never mind in the biblical story." There's always that turn-around in a Chekhovian presentation, at least to people like me who need it so badly and desperately. You want to understand something? You might think about this—not only in Scripture but in life. That's the distinction I think he's drawing.

I'm thinking about some of the others, such as "A Boring Story." Well, of course you know what used to interest Williams—I should mention this—Williams, who was obviously very word-conscious, told me several times, "Before you read Chekhov, go to your dictionary and look up the word 'boring.'" And I looked at him and asked, "Boring?" and he said, "Boring." I'll never forget it. And then I got a Williams moment from him: he said, "Boring bores through you. Boring makes you a bore," and I didn't know what he was talking about. Years later, thinking about Kierkegaard, I realized that this was what Kierkegaard was talking about in a much more complicated way: how we become lost in details, growing inert, all too consumed by detail and routines, and we become boring ourselves, we bore others, and we're bored. We've lost a sense of liveliness and vitality, we're caught in a humdrum life. This is what the existentialists are getting at. What Chekhov was getting at when he talked about "boring" is what the existentialists—Sartre and Camus—were talking about when they spoke of how, at a certain point, we lose our capacity for spontaneous awareness, and become humdrum, almost like slaves of detail and adjustment. Every once in a while there may be a moment that jolts us out of this, and then we're no longer in that boring mode, and suddenly—well, Kierkegaard talked about it, calling it a "rotation." And what he meant is: in *that* moment, when we remember, *then* we're free of the assembly-line, boring life. We're sprung loose and we find ourselves, and we never forget that. We never forget the place, the occasion when it happened, and I think Chekhov knew this. He didn't have to read Kierkegaard, or be anticipating Camus and Sartre, to understand that you can be in a boring, humdrum, driven state without working on a factory assembly line. And I think that's what Williams was telling me—not quite the way I'm doing it—but he kept emphasizing the fact that all too often we become bored, and then we lose our own lives, and we lose a connection with other lives. He said, "When I find myself living 'A Boring Story' on my rounds, I know the time has come to go home and sit with Flossie and have a glass of sherry or read some poem that'll give me back my life; because in going on my rounds, the rounds have taken me over." He's become a bore, he's boring, and he's bored by others, which equals indifference, callousness—what Chekhov knew to fear and rendered for us lest we ourselves fall prey to this. He knew that we can become slaves to life's peccadillo moments—the small things and sins that seize us—and then we're lost.

MF

I'm wondering if you would feel comfortable answering a question that might be kind of unfair to ask, but which I'd still like to put it to you: What in your mind is the most important thing about Chekhov? What would you tell someone coming to Chekhov for the first time—maybe one of your medical students in a course on medical humanities—is the most important thing to get from Chekhov?

RC

Well, here was someone who lived, and saw, and heard, and then rendered for others—out of his mind and heart and soul—what he had seen and heard, so that he gave us not only descriptive writing or evocation, as in the social sciences or as in documentary work, but soulful and heartfelt writing. He gave us writing that asked us to stop, that gave us pause, even as, I think, he was given pause by life's ironies and complexities, the inconsistencies, the near tragedies that are just around the corner for any of us, the accidents and incidents that suddenly, out of nowhere, either end a life or give it a new shape—like the arrival of tubercle bacillus in one's lungs. He knew all this, and he rendered it in plays, in stories, and in his personal reflections on his own life. In a sense he said, "I've been here addressing you and me, the future; I've witnessed these matters, and I want to share them with you, and I hope I'm doing so in such a way that this will give all this life that I've been a part of the new life that a reader or a theatergoer gets from watching a play being put on, from reading the story: these experiences offer the possibility of suddenly becoming, in a sense, a new person." And by the way, it's not only writers who can offer this possibility, but also doctors, who help us become somewhat different, as do teachers—indeed, we all do this for one another as fellow human beings. And I think that Chekhov was an extraordinarily talented fellow human being, determined to share the within-side of his life, the interior aspect of it, in such a way that it became part of our within-side, our interior; and the medium, of course, was his talent—his ability, no question about that—as a gifted storyteller and playwright.

But, you know, let's not separate the gifted person from the fellow human being, and let's not separate Chekhov, actually, from some of those sad and forlorn people he gave to us. Their pathos and their neediness and their failures—these were his, too; after all, he created them, and those people were a nod to his fellow human beings, and maybe, to himself. And I hope that those of us who are critics and scholars, in coming to Chekhov, feel the fire and the breath—yes, the feverish, tuberculous breath—of this extraordinary life, which lives on through his words. And I hope—and I think he would hope—that such a fire lives on in us when we experience our own Chekhovian moments: when we are stopped in our tracks, when we think of the Anyutas in our lives, when we walk through a ward 6, or a legal office, or the office of a newspaper, or an office at an academic institution or university. You know, those are Chekhovian moments, too. It's about how we are with people.

I remember when 9/11 took place—just recently, I'll never forget the time—it was a Chekhovian moment. I was at Harvard University getting ready for my lecture, and a janitor came up to me and put his hand on my shoulder to tell me what had just happened in New York. This is a janitor whom I had never "seen" before. Oh, I'd seen him in the literal sense; but here suddenly it was a different moment. I said, "Oh, my God," and then I told him something: I told him that my son and daughter-in-law with their children were supposed to be on a plane going to California, and that their plane might be one of those planes—I didn't know otherwise at the time, because this had just happened—and then he said, "Oh, my God." He gave me a hug, I gave him a hug, and then I went to find out whether, in fact, my family had been on this plane. And I found out that they had missed the flight by a Chekhovian moment. There was a traffic jam, and they were late arriving for this flight, and therefore their lives were saved. Why were they late? They were late because my son—another Chekhovian moment—is a doctor, a pediatrician. One of his patients had fallen ill. He had to tell his wife that he wasn't sure they could make that flight. He attended the kid. They *desperately* tried to catch that flight, and they missed it. There's

Chekhov in our lives now! When I heard that, I thought of Chekhov. I thought of Bill Williams. I thought of fate, and chance, and circumstance, and luck—good and bad. And then I had to get up before a class of 800 students and talk about what had just happened to this country and to the world, and about those airplanes crashing into those buildings. And I thought: "This is our life. This is how we live." And this is something I think Chekhov would've known, and probably worked into a play or a story, and I think that out of those tragedies that he knew: not the tragedies of airplanes crashing into twin towers, but you know, thousands die all the time (he knew that) not on planes, but in homes and in hospitals. They die in their tracks on streets. And he reached out to all of that life and tried to give it the substance of respect, of affirmation, of recognition. He was a storyteller, reminding us of who we are, whence we came, and where we're headed—all of which he knew. He was like Gauguin, when he asked us to think about all that in his triptych: Where do we come from? What are we? Where are we going? That famous triptych that's in the Boston Museum of Fine Arts—my mother used to take us to look at it when we were children. Those are the questions that Chekhov asked us as an artist (since we're talking about Chekhov and the artist in "Anyuta"); Gauguin asked those questions. In fact, my mother, who was an artist herself, once said to us: "When an artist has to put words at the bottom of a painting, the artist, in a way, is in trouble." But Gauguin wasn't in trouble. He knew to give us words as well as pictures, and I think Chekhov knew to give us words and to give us the pictures that words can convey, and thereby to help us to understand what life is about, its meaning and purpose.

MF

It sounds like you really feel that you see the person of Chekhov in these stories. You know, many people find that he's quite hidden in his narratives.

RC

No, I think those stories are doctor stories, just as I think Williams' stories were doctor stories. One of Williams' stories in *The Doctor Stories* is about a person who is dying. Williams is working with the person, and it's a very tough story because what he's really telling you is that the person is dying, while he—Williams—is dying to keep the person alive, and he knows he's going to lose: the patient is dying and Williams knows it's impossible to save that patient, and all this is shared and the two are connected. This is what Williams knew to do. Look at the story, "The Use of Force": this is about a doctor trying to help. He's a good doctor, but he's getting angrier and angrier at the patient, and at the impossibility of his accomplishing what he wants to accomplish. It's really a confessional story. What he's telling his readers is, "You see, I can lose control. There's a temper in me. I can be frustrated. I can be angry. You don't necessarily see that, but I'm going to confess to you what can happen in a doctor's life." And I think Chekhov was also confessional in that sense—in that Augustinian sense. In some of those stories he was telling us that, as a fellow human being, he could falter at times. He could lose his patience. He could want to be done with someone or a situation. He could consider life boring and people boring, and he could struggle against that—engage in a hard and mean struggle against it—hoping somehow to affirm and redeem his life as a healer and (I think this is very important) as a believer in humanity, in people and their worthwhileness. After all, he paid them such attention and gave them to us with such carefulness and thoughtfulness.

We know that Tolstoy much admired him; and I think that over time Tolstoy saw in him a fellow walker through life: a suffering, gifted, redemptively charged and alive person, maybe at times terribly troubled about himself and others (in the Judeo-Christian sense of walking through life, and glimpsing it, and paying attention to it, and offering it to others—seeing life and then offering the gift of what is seen to others). The gift of life witnessed, then life rendered by the writer—so that the reader will become more alive through that gift. The writer as the middle person, as in *Middlemarch*! I'm referring to the novel but, you know, I'm playing on the word "middle-march." The writer as the middle marcher, the observer, and the writer in this case is the one who lived it all out: suffering, hurt, vulnerable, traveling across the world, a fellow prisoner of fate. Chekhov was himself jailed—as though on Sakhalin island—by his own kind of life, by illness, by what Paul Tillich the theologian called "finitude." To draw on Kierkegaard: such are life's limits, which we all both live with and rail against. In the case of Chekhov, operating with his pen, he gave that story, his story, to others: as fate described, and in a way transcended—as a writer can sometimes do, and as a healer or doctor can sometimes do.

# Heal Thyself, Hide Thyself: Why Did Dr. Chekhov Ignore His TB?

## Michael C. Finke, University of Illinois at Urbana-Champaign

According to the written record, Anton Chekhov's first bout of blood-spitting occurred in 1884—the very year of his graduation from the medical faculty of Moscow University. Chekhov soon adopted a policy of refusing to submit to examination by other physicians until a massive hemorrhage in 1897 left him no choice. Biographers, including his brother and sister, have always struggled with what has been aptly called Chekhov's "massive denial."[1] It is my contention that how Chekhov coped (or didn't) with his illness makes sense in the larger context of his acute sensitivity—manifest in many aspects of his biography, as well as in distinctive thematic and stylistic features of his art— to how he was seen, and how he saw himself. This broader topic is the subject of my recent book, *Seeing Chekhov: Life and Art*.[2]

No major nineteenth-century Russian literary figure tried harder than Anton Chekhov to keep his personal self apart from his literary products and inaccessible to his readers. In a tradition where most key figures tended to insert themselves into their works in one way or another, Chekhov stands out for insisting that his verbal art speak for itself.

"I have autobiographophobia," he wrote his medical-school colleague and friend Grigorii Rossolimo (11 October 1899), who was assembling the biographies of classmates for an anniversary celebration; and Chekhov was not joking. That same year Chekhov's publisher Adolf Marks objected to his instruction that no photograph or biography of the author appear in the first volume of his collected works.[3] In Chekhov's journals, according to the Russian scholar who has studied them most closely, the pronoun "'I' sounds almost like the third person ... he seems estranged from his very self."[4] Never

---

[1] Cathy Popkin, "Historia Morbi and the 'Holy of Holies'—Scientific and Religious Discourse and Čechov's Epistemology," in *Anton P. Čechov—Philosophische und Religiöse Dimensionen im Leben und im Werk: Vorträge des Zweiten Internationalen Čechov-Symposiums, Badenweiler, 20–24 Oktober 1994*, ed. Vladimir B. Kataev, Rolf-Dieter Kluge, and Regine Nohejl (Munich: Verlag Otto Sagner, 1997), 366.

[2] Michael C. Finke, *Seeing Chekhov: Life and Art* (Ithaca, NY: Cornell University Press, 2005).

[3] Ernest J. Simmons, *Chekhov: A Biography* (Boston: Little, Brown and Co., 1962), 488.

[4] Zinovii Papernyi, *Zapisnye knizhki Chekhova* (Moscow: Sovetskii pisatel', 1976), 9–10.

*Chekhov the Immigrant: Translating a Cultural Icon.* Michael C. Finke and Julie de Sherbinin, eds. Bloomington, IN: Slavica Publishers, 2007, 285–97.

mind the roughly fifty pseudonyms with which he signed his early fiction (but see Cathy Popkin's article on p. 220 for a list); even most of his *publitsistika*—editorials and obituaries in which he could be expected to express strong personal opinions—was published anonymously.[5] The most striking exception to Chekhov's impulse to keep his self out of his writing was, ironically enough, his great "scientific" work, *Sakhalin Island*; that is to say, Chekhov's person is most present in the work where we might least expect it.[6]

As a result, there is something quite special about how we see Chekhov: We frankly acknowledge considerable blindness in regard to his inner life; and yet, that blindness notwithstanding, we have made him the ego-ideal of Russian literature—he has the reputation of being the most emotionally balanced and objective of all its authors and the unparalleled model of an *intelligentnost'* still relevant to all educated Russians.[7] Thus the *samizdat* and emigrant author Sergei Dovlatov wrote, "You can delight in Tolstoy's mind, Pushkin's refinement, and Dostoevsky's deep psychological penetration, but the only one you can wish to be *like* is Chekhov."[8] So too our collaborator James McConkey, in his autobiographical work that simultaneously retells the story of Chekhov's journey to Sakhalin, admits: "Perhaps my love of T. [Chekhov] is narcissistic; perhaps he is but a mirror of my ideal self."[9]

We particularly admire how Chekhov saw the world, and more often than not, this special vision is attributed to Chekhov's medical training. For it is clearly the case that, as a physician, Chekhov's professional identity depended on a certain kind of seeing. Chekhov's keen powers of observation have been acclaimed by both memoirists who knew him well and scholars who approach him only through the written record. Aleksandr Kuprin's remarks are entirely characteristic: "In his extraordinary objectivity, standing above personal sorrows and pleasures, he saw and understood everything"; and, "His eyelids hung somewhat heavily above his eyes, as one so often ob-

---

[5] Among noteworthy exceptions are appeals he published for donations to support construction of a sanatorium or pension and other assistance for destitute consumptives flocking to Yalta, where Chekhov even offers his home address (see *PssS* 16: 374).

[6] See the contribution of Conevery Valenčius to this volume for a discussion of *Sakhalin Island* as belonging to the genre of medical geography—a genre of scientific research congenial to and by no means undermined by the kind of authorial presence we find in *Sakhalin Island* (299–314).

[7] The term *intelligentnost'* is impossible to translate into English. It indicates a high level of education and cultural refinement, good manners, a responsible and professional attitude in one's occupation, and attention to ethics.

[8] Emphasis mine. Cited from Gennadii Shaliugin, "Chekhov v krugu kolleg," in *Brega Tavridy*, no. 5–6 (1999): 276.

[9] James McConkey, *To a Distant Island* (Philadelphia: Paul Dry Books, 2000), 19.

serves in artists, hunters, sailors."[10] To apprehend Chekhov means seeing how Chekhov sees, and the author's remarkable vision is understood as deriving from his occupational or professional training and identity.

This is the rhetoric from which legends are made. Chekhov himself participated in creating the legend, but he also spoke about his seeing in ways that complicate the facile causal attributions of critics and biographers. While he often credited his medical training for endowing his vision with a range and comprehension other authors lacked, he also displays great sensitivity to the mystifying and ideological components to scientific seeing. His fictional treatments of physicians are apt to foreground the limits and troubling ethical ramifications of their seeing, and his work offers equally devastating critiques of how the gazes of judges, detectives, artists and others—characters whose professional identity is tied up with seeing—can, on the one hand, assume ruthlessly cold and inhuman characteristics under the rubric of objectivity, or on the other, become corrupted by calculated self-interest or sudden and involuntary accesses of affect.[11]

Chekhov also certainly understood that medical seeing could not be translated directly into literary showing or telling. The actor and future director Vsevolod Meyerhold reports Chekhov's annoyance at the naturalistic sound effects Stanislavsky's theater was inflicting on his *Seagull*, and his amusement at one actor's naive explanation of the croaking frogs and howling dogs: "'It's realistic,' said the actor. 'Realistic,' A. P. repeated with a laugh. And then after a brief pause, he remarked: 'The stage is art. In one of [I. N.] Kramskoy's genre paintings he has some magnificently drawn faces. What if we cut the painted nose from one of these faces and substituted a live one? The new nose would be "real," but the painting would be ruined.'"[12] Art has its conventions and demands a certain quota of mystification; in science and medicine, by implicit contrast, the objective eye is supposed to prevail.

---

[10] Kuprin, "Pamiati Chekhova," in *A. P. Chekhov v vospominaniiakh sovremennikov*, ed. N. I. Gitovich (Moscow: Khudozhestvennaia literatura, 1986), 532, 514.

[11] For explorations of the epistemological implications of this problem in Chekhov—the degree to which problems in seeing and being seen were problems of disciplinary knowledge for him—see the excellent work of Cathy Popkin, including: "Chekhov as Ethnographer: Epistemological Crisis on Sakhalin Island," *Slavic Review* 51: 1 (1988): 36–51; "Chekhov's Corpus: Bodies of Knowledge," in *Essays in Poetics* 18: 1 (April 1993): 44–72; "*Historiia Morbi* and the 'Holy of Holies'—Scientific and Religious Discourse and Čechov's Epistemology," in *Anton P. Čechov—Philosophische und religiöse Dimensionen im Leben und im Werk*, 365–77; and "The Objective Eye and the Common Good," with Louise McReynolds, in *Constructing Russian Culture in the Age of Revolution: 1881–1940* (Oxford: Oxford University Press, 1998), 57–76. See also Finke, *Seeing Chekhov*, esp. chaps. 2 and 3.

[12] Vsevolod Meyerhold, "Naturalistic Theater and Theater of Mood," trans. Joyce C. Vining, in *Chekhov: A Collection of Critical Essays*, ed. Robert Louis Jackson (Englewood Cliffs, NJ: Prentice-Hall, 1967), 66.

In regard to Chekhov's person, too, both seeing and being seen could be highly problematic. This applied in the most banal and literal sense: he once explained to Aleksei Suvorin, "In Moscow I went to the eye doctor. One of my eyes is farsighted, the other, nearsighted" (26 June 1896).[13] Chekhov's eyes caused him no little suffering, and complaints about them rank right up there with those provoked by hemorrhoids and intestinal cattarh. More interesting, however, and very much remarked in the memoirs of Chekhov's intimates and by scholars since, were the discomforts aroused by his own increasing visibility as an author and celebrity. In his last years Chekhov was particularly upset by published reports regarding his health.

In 1888 Chekhov responded rather vigorously to a letter from Aleksandr Pleshcheev—the venerable poet and editor of *The Northern Herald* (*Severnyi vestnik*)—who had criticized him for writing "The Name Day Party" ("Imeniny") as though he were afraid of being identified as a liberal. This was a story that had come off well, Chekhov boasted in a letter to Suvorin (15 November 1888), precisely because of his *medical* insight into pregnancy. To Pleshcheev he responded: "It seems to me that you might sooner accuse me of gluttony, of alcoholism, of flippancy, of coldness, of whatever you like, but not of wishing to appear or not appear.... I have never hidden" (9 October 1888).[14] And yet, Chekhov did have a powerful (and, some might argue, a rather un-Russian) inclination for privacy. In his notebooks he even experimented with a bio-evolutionary explanation making deference to it a defining feature of what it means to be human: "In animals there is a constant striving to uncover the secret (to find the [hiding] spot, and this is why people have respect for another's secret, as a battle against their animal instincts" (*PssS* 17: 51).

Although Chekhov was prone to making literary use of the private lives of his friends, his own he handled with great discretion, and he resisted attempts by his friends to read his writings as pertaining to his self. He grew extremely uncomfortable with the fame he earned as a mature author, and he showed no desire to exploit his personal history in creating a public persona. This striving for privacy while engaged in an activity that conventionally involved self-exposure reached a bizarre extreme in the notorious practical joke accompanying his marriage ceremony with Olga Knipper: Chekhov asked a friend to arrange a dinner party for him, then married in secrecy, with the fewest possible witnesses, and departed Moscow with his bride while con-

---

[13] This citation from Chekhov's letter to Suvorin serves as the epigraph to Savely Senderovich's path-breaking study of the St. George complex in Chekhov, *Chekhov—s glazu na glaz: Istoriia odnoi oderzhimosti A. P. Chekhov. Opyt fenomenologii tvorchestva* (St. Petersburg: Dmitrii Bulanin, 1994); there it serves as a metaphor for both how Chekhov sees, and how his verbal art ought to be read.

[14] See the exchange in *Perepiska A. P. Chekhova v trekh tomakh*, ed. V. Vatsuro et al. (Moscow: Nasledie, 1996), 1: 486–91.

fused guests waited. This was no simple act of shielding one's intimate life, but an exhibitionistic and theatrical staging of self-concealment.

Chekhov's resistance to prying eyes certainly plays out in his long avoidance of the status of medical patient. The very notion of seeking medical attention, he wrote Suvorin in 1891, disgusted him (18 November). Why this visceral reaction? I want to suggest that it's not just about privacy. Chekhov's medical knowledge placed him in a terrible double bind regarding his own consumptive body, which, in the scientific discourse of the day, was also, and importantly, "degenerate."

Even after the bacillus causing tuberculosis was discovered (by Robert Koch) in 1882, heredity continued to play a considerable role in scientific thinking about predisposition and susceptibility to the disease. Thus in 1891 the Petersburg organization "Russian Society for the Protection of Public Health" (Russkoe obshchestvo okhraneniia narodnogo zdraviia, or "Roonz") on the one hand officially recognized tuberculosis as an infectious disease, but nonetheless also considered prohibiting marriage for consumptives and their relatives down to the third generation. Given that there was no scientific evidence for the role of inheritance in tuberculosis, the commission set that proposal aside, and yet it still recommended that tuberculars avoid marriage, so as not to "pass on to their descendents a predisposition to consumption."[15] In spite of the latest science, then, in the medical community the body of the tubercular patient continued to be perceived as degenerate and dangerous to the hygiene of the species. We can only speculate about the extent to which this fact contributed to Chekhov's reluctance to have himself examined by another physician or to marry, but there is ample evidence that Chekhov did think of himself in such evolutionary biological terms.

Chekhov told Nikolai Leikin that the hemorrhoids from which he suffered were a result of the inherited tendency for his veins to widen (22 May 1887); he explained seasonal sleep disturbances among his family members as an "atavism," the phylogenetic memory of their serf heritage;[16] and in a letter to Suvorin he expressed befuddlement at his two elder brothers' chronic problems with alcoholism precisely because there had *not* been a history of alcoholism in the family (10 October 1888). Chekhov even applied the logic of evolutionary biology to poetics, telling his brother Aleksandr that the latter's nefarious literary tendency to subjectivity was correctable because "You weren't born a subjective writer... It's not an inherited trait, but an acquired one..." (20 February 1883). Chekhov's friend and literary colleague Vladimir Gilyarovsky, renowned for his strength, says that in the 1890s Chekhov joined the gymnastics club of which Gilyarovsky was chairman. This was only to please Gilyarovsky, however; Chekhov joked about how inappropriate any

---

[15] See R. B. Kaganovich, *Iz istorii bor'by s tuberkulezom v dorevoliutsionnoi Rossii* (Moscow: Akademiia meditsinskikh nauk, 1952), 9–14.

[16] M. P. Chekhov, *Vokrug Chekhova* (Moscow: Moskovskii rabochii, 1960), 250.

muscular ambitions might be for himself. And then Chekhov added, invoking the logic of evolution and degeneration: "There will come a time—perhaps in about a hundred years—when everybody will be strong, and there will be a lot like you...."[17] The widely reproduced photograph (taken by Isaak Levitan in 1892), of Gilyarovsky hauling Chekhov and his brother Mikhail in a barrow dramatizes this evolutionary difference between the Chekhovs and Gilyarovsky (Figure 1).

When in March 1897 Chekhov was stricken with a lung hemorrhage while dining at the Hermitage Hotel in Moscow, he soberly pointed out to Suvorin that his brother (Nikolai) and his cousin Elizavata Mikhailovna, nee Chekhova, both of whom had died of consumption, had suffered the same sort of hemorrhage from the same (right) lung.[18]

Figure 1. Vladimir Gilyarovsky hauling the Chekhov Brothers. Reproduced from Michael C. Finke, *Seeing Chekhov: Life and Art* (Ithaca, NY: Cornell University Press, 2005), 207.

---

[17] Vladimir A. Giliarovskii, *Moskva i moskvichi: Ocherki* (Minsk: Narodnaia asveta, 1981), 258–59.

[18] M. P. Chekhov, *Vokrug Chekhova*, 272.

**Figure 2.** Chekhov recuperating at Melikhovo after his 1897 hemorrhage (from Gosudarstvennyi literaturnyi muzei, Moscow)

Now, there certainly were pragmatic reasons for denying the reality of his illness to others and perhaps to himself. Chekhov was no doubt multiply motivated: by the wish to shield his family, in particular his mother; by the lack of truly promising therapies for TB; by the financial and familial impossibility of pursuing the most typical therapy, i.e., travel to healthful climes and rest; and by the conventional medical practice of withholding dire prognoses from patients. But something else was at stake as well. The self Chekhov aspired to be—in particular his professional identity as a physician—very much hinged on his being the one who sees, rather than the patient of the medical gaze; and that in turn depended on a successful struggle to overcome certain inherited biological traits. For the degenerate was first and foremost *visibly* so: the theory of degeneration held that the malady's signs should be apparent to the trained eye, and that they could be codified in their visual aspects with help from such innovative and objective tools as photography. The degenerate patient was above all meant to be seen.[19]

---

[19] See the discussions in Daniel Pick, *Faces of Degeneration: A European Disorder, c. 1848–c. 1918* (Cambridge: Cambridge University Press, 1989); and Sander L. Gilman, "Hugh

The risks of being seen pervade Chekhov's fiction; and they are particularly dramatic in the cases of physician characters, who are supposed to do the seeing. Thus in "A Boring Story" (1889), the professional eye turned inward—upon himself and his family—paralyzes the mortally ill professor of medicine. Where once he shone when all eyes and ears were upon him in the lecture hall, now he reads in the mirrors of these eyes, rather than his professional potency, his physical and emotional decomposition. In "Ward 6" (1892), the whole story's trajectory may be delineated by the translocation of the central character, Dr. Ragin, from the position of physician to that of patient. Ragin shirks his professional duty to see—he hates examining patients, and he turns a blind eye to the corrupt and cruel behavior of the hospital staff under his supervision. He is forced out of his position as hospital chief, taken on a journey abroad—during which he refuses to sight-see—and in the end himself becomes the object of others' examination, at which point he understands he is finished: "When they tell you that you have something like bad kidneys and an enlarged heart, and you start undergoing treatment, or when they tell you that you're crazy or a criminal, that is, in a word, when people suddenly pay attention to you, then you might as well know that you've fallen into a vicious circle from which you'll never emerge" (*PssS* 8: 118–19). No surprise that Chekhov avoided entering that vicious circle.

But it wasn't just about being medically ill. In addition to the tuberculosis plaguing his family, the Chekhovs were beset by alcoholism, bankruptcy, and an ancestral heritage of servitude. Chekhov was quite sensitive to the legacy of his class, as his explanation of seasonal sleep disturbances among his family members suggests: he was separated from serfdom by only one generation. In one of his brighter moments—he had just won the prestigious Pushkin literary prize, his brother Nikolai was still alive, and his own health was relatively good—he famously described the self he had become as the result of a lengthy and painful process of squeezing the tainted blood of his recent ancestry out of his own veins "drop by drop" until, one day, he awoke feeling "real human blood" coursing through his vessels.[20] I take this metaphor quite literally. For Chekhov, submitting to treatment, subjecting *himself* to the medical gaze, would have exposed the vulnerabilities of this hard-won selfhood.

---

W. Diamond and Psychiatric Photography," in *The Face of Madness: Hugh W. Diamond and the Origin of Psychiatric Photography*, ed. Gilman (New York: Brunner/Mazel, 1976).

[20] Letter to Suvorin, 7 January 1889. It should be noted that, although Chekhov most definitely writes about himself here—and such has been the correct understanding of all the biographers and critics who invariably refer to it—he nonetheless does so in the third person: after speaking of his own literary career to that point, and the lengthy process of acquiring "virility" and a "feeling of personal freedom," he encourages Suvorin to "write a story about … a young man, son of a serf, former shop-boy, choir-boy, gymnasium and university student.…"

When that self does collapse, it will be because of a biological inheritance that cannot be disavowed. Now *that's* material for disgust.

Among the unused anecdotes or ideas for stories in Chekhov's notebooks is the following sketch of just such an unwanted patrimony:

> Doctor N., born illegitimate, never having lived with his father and knowing him little, his friend from childhood Z. tells him in embarrassment: "The thing is, your father has gotten melancholic, sick, asks permission to cast at least one eye on you." The father has [the restaurant] "Switzerland." Fried fish, which he handles with his hands, and only afterwards with a fork. The vodka he serves is like fusel oil. N. went, had a look, ate—no feeling other than irritation that this fat peasant with graying hair trades in such garbage. But once, passing by at 12 o'clock at night, he glanced through the window: his father sits hunched over a book. He recognized himself, his mannerisms… (*PssS* 17: 88)

This doctor's selfhood has been based on rejecting the bloodline of his father; to see himself in that "fat peasant"—whose mannerisms can only have been transmitted biologically, since the son was raised apart from him—poses the most troubling questions about who he actually is.

Chekhov—who, incidentally, had ample opportunity to observe his own father, of peasant birth, trading in foul goods and hunched over holy books—was faced with a similar conundrum. And confronting how he ought to view himself led him to interrogate the very nature of medical knowledge and,

Figure 3. Chekhov's father (from A. P. Kuzicheva, *Chekhovy: Biografiia sem'i* [Moscow: Artist. Rezhisser. Teatr, 2004], 49)

in particular, the professional gaze with which the physician (as well as other professionals) regards his object.

Now, Chekhov the medical student had been entirely capable of displaying considerable hubris. There is evidence, quite out of character for the humble Chekhov of biographic legend,[21] that in the early years his self was vulnerable to an inflation in proportion to the growing powers, as he understood them, of his professional seeing; all the more so when regarding the inferior female gender, as in his plan to write a dissertation on the topic of evolutionary inequalities between males and females. But Dr. Chekhov swiftly matured into a ruthless deconstructor of all such megalomaniacal identities.[22] We can observe how Chekhov's dismantling of professional, gender, and class identities operates in a nutshell through one of his unused journal entries: "Conversation during a congress of physicians. First doctor: everything is cured by salt. Second doctor, a military one: everything is cured by not using salt. And both are demonstrating this—one on his wife, the other on his daughter" (*PssS* 17: 143).

Indeed, by the 1890s the thin ethical ice from which one objectifies and categorizes another human being as inferior on the evolutionary scale or "degenerate" would become the central theme of major post-Sakhalin works.[23] You can tell a lot just by looking at the three projects Chekhov considered for a doctoral dissertation in medicine. After the "History of Sexual Dominance" came "A History of Doctoring in Russia" ("Vrachebnoe delo v Rossii," *PssS* 16: 277–356). Around the time Chekhov graduated Moscow University he began collecting materials on the healing arts going back to the earliest written records, including folk remedies, shamanism, superstitions. In what we know of this project, the position of the "doctor" has already been radically reconceived through its historicization; one might say that Chekhov's project defines it as culturally constructed. His own position as researcher has changed, too, from the more narrowly medico-scientific model of the first dissertation proposal. The Sakhalin project involved a further, even more radical leap: not only does Chekhov's person appear in the finished narrative; he literally goes to the place he is talking about, he inserts himself into the scene he will describe, and he does so as the result of a hard journey that casts him as a suffering hero making a descent to hell—this work includes an

---

[21] Exemplary in this regard is Ilya Ehrenburg's "On Re-reading Chekhov," where Chekhov's "humility" is a central theme; see his *Chekhov, Stendhal, and Other Essays*, trans. Anna Bostock et al. (New York: Alfred A. Knopf, 1963), 3–79.

[22] On the project for a history of sexual dominance and its reverberations in the mature Chekhov, see Finke, *Seeing Chekhov*, esp. 99–107, 120–28, 134–35.

[23] See, for example, the treatment of "Duel" in Vladimir Kataev, *If Only We Could Know! An Interpretation of Chekhov*, trans. Harvey Pitcher (Chicago: Ivan R. Dee, 2002), 112–19.

unmistakable mythopoetic dimension.[24] Although Chekhov visits, thinks, and then writes about Sakhalin still very much influenced by the conceptual frameworks of evolution and degeneration, the position he creates for him*self* as scientific observer in this project could not be more different from the one he imagined in connection with his "History of Sexual Dominance."

Chekhov ascribed the transformation of how he, in his capacity as a physician, saw himself and others, to his experience as a suffering patient—even as he stubbornly refused to present himself as a patient to another physician. In the mid-1890s it briefly (and mistakenly) appeared that Chekhov's book on Sakhalin might earn him a doctorate and position at Moscow University, where he aspired to teach the introduction to internal medicine to first-year students. In discussing this prospect with his old friend Rossolimo, who was now on the faculty, Chekhov imagined imparting a new way of seeing the patient and, arguably, anticipated today's field of medical humanities. He said, "I, for instance, suffer from intestinal catarrh"—notice the evasive diagnosis—"and well understand what such a patient feels, what sort of mental tortures he experiences, but this is rarely comprehensible to a doctor. If I were a teacher, then I would try to draw my audience as deeply as possible into the realm of the subjective feelings of the patient, and I think that this could really be of use to the students."[25] There is a deep irony here: while virtually all of Chekhov's readers have tended to celebrate the author's "objective" eye and attributed it in some measure to his medical education, Chekhov's teaching plans involved a deliberate de-objectivizing of the medical gaze. And it should be pointed out that these discussions with Rossolimo took place at a time when Chekhov was still stubbornly refusing to present himself as a patient to another physician.

But the plan Chekhov elaborated to Rossolimo was also a kind of fantasy, a never-realized wish that the position of teacher might unify his disparate identities as doctor, patient, and verbal artist: in his lectures as a professor of medicine, it will be his literary skill—and in particular how he handles narrative point of view in telling a patient's story—that conditions how his "audience" sees that patient (or character); and it will be his experience as an ill man that will allow that seeing to be maximally empathetic. Chekhov's most powerful mature stories are often studies in the manipulation of narrative point of view and, correspondingly, the reader's projections of self into the text.[26] Among the roughly ninety stories on medical themes that a Soviet

---

[24] On the descent theme in Chekhov, see Finke, *Seeing Chekhov*, 155–71.

[25] See G. I. Rossolimo, "Vospominaniia o Chekhove," in *A. P. Chekhov v vospominaniiakh sovremennikov*, 436.

[26] The most striking examples, perhaps, of such manipulative handling of narrative point of view are to be found in "Gusev" (1890) and "Ward 6"; on the latter, see Finke, *Seeing Chekhov*, 111–20.

doctor-*chekhoved* identified,[27] I'd wager that the ones that stick most in readers' minds are those portraying illness from the internal perspective. And these are by no means limited to maladies Chekhov himself experienced, though readers of limited imagination have at times supposed otherwise: thus his treatment of the young professor's descent into psychosis and death from tuberculosis in "Black Monk" was so compelling that Chekhov's friends famously thought that he must be suffering from mental illness.

It is to the point that, when approached by Rossolimo, the Dean found the idea of awarding the *author* Chekhov a doctorate in medicine and a teaching position too ridiculous for response. If the empathetic approach promised benefit to patients, it could also entail dangers for the physician. Thus when Chekhov was younger, healthier and more sanguine about the detached and objective position he assumed as in his role of physician, he wrote critically of his new friend and colleague Elena Lintvareva for her—distinctively female, since he calls her "the lady doctor"—propensity to identify too fully with her patients: "she is anxious to the point of psychosis over them"; "where death is obvious and inevitable, my doctor friend reacts quite unprofessionally" (to Suvorin, 30 May 1888).[28] Even if Chekhov's thinking about the medical gaze evolved past this position, it remained with him, viscerally, until the end, and this perhaps helps explain why he might have strongly resisted acknowledging his medical condition so long as possible.

When Chekhov finally became the patient and moved to Yalta for his health, he donated the lion's share of his library to his hometown's public library. He held on to his medical books, however,[29] and in the last years of his life, when he no longer practiced, these volumes presumably served the same function as the medical instruments that always lay on his desk: symbolic affirmations of an identity that remained important to Chekhov. So too at the other end of his career, on his first vacation from the university (July 1880), he had carried to the south a human skull in his bag.[30] At the apex of his literary success, Chekhov was still apt to make remarks like, "Listen, I'm not a playwright, I'm a doctor."[31] As Mikhail Gromov put it, "Chekhov

---

[27] I take the number from M. B. Mirskii, *Doktor Chekhov* (Moscow: Nauka, 2003), 95; he in turn refers to V. V. Khizhnikov, *Anton Chekhov kak vrach* (Moscow, 1947).

[28] Cited from *Anton Chekhov's Life and Thought: Selected Letters and Commentary*, trans. Michael Henry Heim and Simon Karlinsky, selection, commentary, and introduction Simon Karlinsky (Berkeley: University of California Press, 1973), 102.

[29] I. M. Geizer cites a letter of Mariia Chekhova about this point, and about Chekhov's professional identity as a physician, in *Chekhov i meditsina* (Moscow: MEDGIZ, 1954), 45.

[30] Evgenii D. Ashurkov, *Slovo o Doktore Chekhove* (Moscow: MEDGIZ, 1960), 7.

[31] For instance, to Stanislavsky, regarding Hauptmann: "He's a real dramatist. I'm not a dramatist. Listen, I'm a doctor" (cited from Simmons, *Chekhov*, 304).

would have never have said: 'I'm a good writer.' But he said many times: 'I'm a good doctor.'"[32] A playwright is a celebrity who is seen; a doctor sees.

In his memoirs, Dmitry Likhachev—the great scholar of Old Russian culture—recalls a conversation he had (while in a prison camp on the Solovetsky islands) about the idiosyncratic dress of all significant turn-of-the-century writers; only Chekhov abstained from adopting a unique and statement-making appearance. His interlocutor "considered this and said: 'Yes, but Chekhov dressed like a typical doctor.'" He was right, Likhachev writes: "No doubt Chekhov had had a 'doctorly self-awareness' in his dress."[33]

If I am right, and Chekhov's thirteen-year disavowal of his ill bodily self issued from a broader set of concerns about how he was seen, and how he saw himself, then careful attention to clothing, and rigid adherence to a semiotics of dress whose signification was clear and unchanging—dressing "like a typical doctor"—might well be construed as a strategy for rendering the body otherwise unreadable, for obscuring telltale signs of the degenerate patient masquerading as a physician.

---

[32] Mikhail Gromov, *Chekhov* (Moscow: Molodaia gvardiia, 1993), 156. See also Evgenii B. Meve, *Meditsina v tvorchestve i zhizni A. P. Chekhova* (Kiev: Gosudarstvennoe meditsinskoe izdatel'stvo SSSR, 1961), 132.

[33] Likhachev was speaking with the artist Pavel Smotritsky; see Dmitry S. Likhachev, *Reflections on the Russian Soul: A Memoir*, trans. Bernard Adams (Budapest: Central European University Press, 2000), 147.

# Chekhov's *Sakhalin Island* as a Medical Geography

## Conevery Bolton Valenčius
### Department of the History of Science, Harvard University

Read from the vantage point of history of medicine, Chekhov's *Journey to Sakhalin Island* makes sense. It makes sense not simply as an unfolding part of Anton Chekhov's career or his creative self-development, but on its own. It makes sense under a rubric of medico-scientific thought that was a lively part of Chekhov's intellectual world. Reading *Sakhalin Island* in those terms reveals coherence and argument in a text not widely known for either.

Chekhov structures his book on the Russian penal system at Sakhalin through the discipline of medical geography.[1] Medical geography as an aspect of nineteenth-century medical science was based on careful observation, measurement, and local knowledge, grounded in the conviction that human well-being existed only in a matrix of environmental factors. *Sakhalin* (the book) argues that Sakhalin (the place) represents a tragic failure to heed these forms of knowledge. The island colony has instead been formed in defiance of climatic and environmental wisdom, through a mournful process of bureaucratic inefficiency and accretion. We can thus profitably understand *Sakhalin Island* not simply as literary work or personal document, but as an argument for the importance of the form of medical and scientific knowledge termed medical geography, and a passionately trenchant set of observations on the human suffering created by defying those principles.

## Sakhalin Island

Broadly speaking, *Sakhalin Island* (which Chekhov published in 1893) has been understood either as a singularity of his work, or as simply and unproblematically consistent with his writings in literature. In most scholarly com-

---

[1] This is old news to Russian medical geographers. Over forty years ago, a Soviet historian of Russian medical geography asserted that *Sakhalin Island* "is not only a fine artistic work, but essentially a scientific geographic and medical-geographic study." A. P. Markovin, "Historical Sketch of the Development of Soviet Medical Geography," *Soviet Geography: Review and Translation* 3: 8 (October 1962): 12. Such recognition, however, has taken place in an intellectual village separate from literary study. I am deeply appreciative of Frank A. Barrett's willingness to share his wide-ranging expertise in the history of medical geography and his and Deborah Coen's extremely helpful comments on a draft of this essay.

*Chekhov the Immigrant: Translating a Cultural Icon.* Michael C. Finke and Julie de Sherbinin, eds. Bloomington, IN: Slavica Publishers, 2007, 299–314.

munities, it tends to get scooted out of the front parlor, where everything is well-arranged and polished to a sheen, into the back hall, alongside knobby bags of potatoes and half-broken umbrellas. It is not that academics want to throw it out the back door into the rubbish heap altogether—more that we don't want visitors looking too closely. They might notice the repetition, the lugubrious pace, the heaviness of language where all else of Chekhov's is so deft and quietly sure.[2]

Chekhov's book is indeed a challenge. It is long—especially in the context of Chekhov's other writing, which tends to be exquisitely crafted and often brief. Passages of insight and clarity are nestled amid discursive sections and long descriptions. Overall, Chekhov's *Journey to Sakhalin Island* has the feel of a book in search of form: not exactly a travel narrative nor yet a scientific report, not quite an exposé, and not precisely a diatribe, yet taking something of the style of each.

But historians of medicine have great use for knobby stubbornness. Much of what is so frustrating—even embarrassing—in a literary sense about this book looks familiar to those of us whose main reading is medical journals and health advice manuals and whose main concerns include the interchange between science and medicine. Rather than trying to stuff the book toward the back of a closet of literature, we can try to understand it as part of Chekhov's conversation with other scientifically informed observers—that is, with many educated people of his time—and as part of a debate about the extent to which scientific principles would govern Russian modernity.[3]

Chekhov begins his book with an account of his own overland journey from the center of metropolitan Russia into the far-flung edges of nation, continent, and civilization. In a carriage, he traces the long journey of exile made by those condemned under the often arbitrary Russian system of justice. Some had committed murder; others had simply stolen a few kopecks. Many others traveled as dependents—parents, wives, small children trudging for months through mud and snow or (the lucky ones) taking the shorter route of leaky ships to the various dispersal centers. Those who did not escape to a lifetime of anxious flight (if not outright brigandage) were finally

---

[2] As one biographer of Chekhov has noted, the book was much more widely read at the time than it has been by critics since (Ernest J. Simmons, *Chekhov: A Biography* [Boston and Toronto: Little, Brown, and Company, 1962], 305). All citations are to the excellently edited and annotated edition by Brian Reeve: Anton Chekhov, *A Journey to Sakhalin Island*, trans. Brian Reeve (Cambridge: Ian Faulkner Publishing, 1993), hereafter cited in parentheses as *SI* with corresponding page number.

[3] Keeping in mind Chekhov's continuing engagement with scientific conversations in his cultural world—as, for instance, the satiric critique he wrote in 1891 exposing a lab for animal experimentation as a deceptive boondoggle by a Moscow professor (Simmons, *Chekhov*, 249).

sent to penal centers, including the one with which Chekhov is concerned: the island agricultural colony of Sakhalin.

Off the eastern coast of Eurasia, periodically claimed by Japan, the island had flourishing fish runs but difficult ports and a climate challenging even by the hardy standards of Russian agriculture. Here, Chekhov found a discontented, often drunken, badly administered group of bureaucrats, guards, and ill-defined staffers running a sprawling penal system. Some of the condemned were in prison—these, Chekhov found, at least got regular meals. Many others—those still serving their formal sentences (and their families), as well as those whose sentences were over but who were still under stricture of permanent exile from Russia—were "settled" in crowded, poorly-planned communities and enjoined to create flourishing agriculture. Chekhov found filth, disease, and discouragement; he reported hunger and illiteracy among old and young; he recorded with wounded tenderness the spiritual numbness, moral degradation, and pervasive brutality that characterized Sakhalin's people.

Much of the book is based on interviews Chekhov conducted with an astounding number of the islanders, as well as his talks with government officials. Against those who argued for the efficiency and desirability of a system of penal colonization, he marshaled evidence that it did not punish fairly, it did not effect reform, and it did not serve to advance the farming frontier or, by extension, the national interest. *Sakhalin Island* is uneven. The book can be arid; it can also be devastating. It is hard to read, not simply because Chekhov's style is so difficult to pin down, but also because he documents situations that are painful to the heart. Compared to his other writings, it is a difficult book to place. Yet the many, seemingly disparate elements of the book—the threads of travel and of reform, the combination of moral fire and pitiless reportage, the emphasis on numerical tabulation even when grossly inadequate—can be understood as part of a coherent whole when it is read as a medical work as well as a literary one.

## Medical Geography

One key to understanding Chekhov's medical conversations is his use of a form of scientific inquiry known as medical geography.[4] Current medical

---

[4] Related categories—many of which overlapped at various periods—include medical topography, medical cartography, and geomedicine. I use "medical geography" as the broadest umbrella covering the scientific investigation of relationships between health and environment. See Gregg Mitman and Ronald L. Numbers, "From Miasma to Asthma: The Changing Fortunes of Medical Geography in America," *History and Philosophy of the Life Sciences* 25 (2003): 391–412, esp. 392–93. For recent scholarship on the history of medical geography, see Frank A. Barrett, *Disease and Geography: The History of an Idea* (Toronto: Atkinson College, York University, 2000); Nicolaas A. Rupke, ed., *Medical Geography in Historical Perspective* (London: Wellcome Trust Centre for the History of Medicine, 2000), esp. Conevery Bolton Valenčius, "Histories of

practitioners may well be familiar with the modern forms of this discipline. In the Soviet Union, medical geography (often called "landscape epidemiology") was not simply a major area of research, but an important institutional form.[5] For much of the twentieth century, Soviet researchers used the frameworks of medical geography to understand environmentally linked medical phenomena as diverse as tularemia, frostbite, and rates of different kinds of cancers.[6] In the Anglo-American world, medical geography has in the last few decades become a contemporary form of analysis in the discipline of geography (examining, for instance, how likely people are to die of heart attack depending on how far they live from a hospital, or the geographic and seasonal variations in the spread of malaria).[7] My interest here is in medical geography as a form of knowledge in the nineteenth century, flourishing from its late-seventeenth-century antecedents up through the 1890s—and, especially in Russia, even further.

Medical geography took the form of reports, often including maps and tables, usually (though not always) in medical literature. Medical geography identified regions of disease or healthfulness, but it also went further, searching for the wealth of factors that would create those correlations. Medical geographies described a particular environment, although definitions could vary considerably—from one small neighborhood to an entire geographic

---

Medical Geography," 3–28; and Bimal Kanti Paul, "Approaches to Medical Geography: An Historical Perspective," *Social Science and Medicine* 20: 4 (1985): 399–409. I focus here on medical geography as a formalized intellectual project, but I have argued elsewhere that it drew from widespread cultural beliefs; see Conevery Bolton Valenčius, *The Health of the Country: How American Settlers Understood Themselves and Their Land* (New York: Basic Books, 2002). The foregoing citations have a clear Western European and North American bias. I acknowledge my own limitations—especially that of language—and feel a certain temerity in venturing conclusions about medical geography so far to the north and east of well-traveled scholarship in the subject. I do so hoping that this brief essay might help stimulate further and much-needed research into Russian-language medical geography.

[5] Markovin, "Historical Sketch"; O. V. Shkurlatov, "The First Soviet Conference on Problems in Medical Geography," *Soviet Geography: Review and Translation* 4: 9 (1963): 55–57; and Frank A. Barrett, personal communication, 2 March 2005. The history of medical geography in Russia and central and eastern Eurasia is both fascinating and largely undeveloped. One crucial exception is the work of A. P. Markovin ("Historical Sketch" and *Development of Medical Geography in Russia* [St. Petersburg: Nauka, 1993]).

[6] I take these particular examples from *Soviet Geography: Review and Translation* 3: 8 (October 1962): V. P. Byakov, "Materials on the Medical Geography of Mountain Landscapes," 20–41; G. T. Ivanov, "Some Data on the Medical Geography of the European North of the RSFSR," 42–58; A. V. Chaklin, "The Geographical Distribution of Cancer in the Soviet Union," 59–68.

[7] Medical geography is a main theme, for example, of the British journal *Social Science and Medicine*.

region. Yet the basic approach was consistent, even if the scales of analysis zoom in and out disconcertingly. Medical geographies could be written of well-settled regions, but they also represented one way in which eighteenth- and nineteenth-century scientific thinkers tried to come to terms with and assimilate new regions.[8]

Medical geography represents a combination of technique and intellectual approach. Its central practices were careful observation and description, exact measurement, and locally-based knowledge. Medical geographers, who were usually physicians but could also come from the more holistic approaches and disciplines of the eighteenth and nineteenth centuries, drew on the post-Enlightenment movement for quantified knowledge.[9] Tables and charts appear frequently in their reports. Medical geography drew explanatory force from the power of comparing specific, measured quantities with one another, whether they were of dew point, rainfall, number of cases of cholera, or number of people or livestock living in a certain district. Such measurement demanded local knowledge—that is, on-the-ground observations rather than grand theories. A characteristic of medical geography is therefore that people in obscure regions become important sources whom texts grant significant authority.

I characterize the work in such broad terms because most of all medical geography represented an intellectual approach: we can only understand human well-being when we understand the total environment in which people live and move and have their being.[10] This form of inquiry emerged from the widely-shared environmentalism of pre-twentieth-century medicine. Human beings do not simply inhabit a place, they are influenced by a matrix of factors like heat, humidity, landforms, clouds, volcanoes, seasons, elevation, and a host of other aspects of their surroundings. Accounting for those many factors is the only way to comprehend what makes people sick or keeps them well in that particular place.

Perhaps the most instructive parallel with Chekhov is the massive, two-volume, mid-century American medical geography compendium by physician Daniel Drake, *A systematic treatise, historical, etiological and practical, on the principal diseases of the interior valley of North America, as they appear in the*

---

[8] I develop many of these and the following points further in Valenčius, *The Health of the Country* (esp. chap. 4).

[9] Thomas Sydenham's investigations into London epidemics are generally viewed as important for this quantification of relationships between health and place. See Valenčius, "Histories of Medical Geography," 8.

[10] Frank Barrett has emphasized that even as medicine and other sciences began to specialize and narrow their focus of inquiry in the nineteenth century, geography retained generalization, holism, and integration across fields of endeavor as central aims. Barrett, *Disease and Geography*, 239.

*Caucasian, African, Indian, and Esquimaux varieties of its population.*[11] This book was published in two volumes, the first in 1850 and the second, posthumously, in 1854. To compose this immense medical geographic report, Drake wrote to a wide network of scientifically minded correspondents for information, he read extensively in the published literature (standard medical publications and also a variety of other reports on the Mississippi Valley), and then he rode off on a horse over several summers to gather information on-site. Drake collected local informants' information on epidemics and patterns of sickness, he searched out elaborate and exhaustive records of local weather, he gathered information on the course of diseases in different regions, and he asked regional practitioners what diseases they had treated. He researched the indigenous and the recently arrived populations and observed people himself—not just their health, but also many other aspects about them: their appearance, their recreations, the size of their families, their eating habits (how much coffee did they drink? how fast did they gulp their food?).[12]

Drake's *Systematic Treatise* represents a broad, connective kind of science. Investigating health and disease, Drake wanted to know about river flows, underlying mineral structure, trade patterns, ethnic differences, topography.... All these factors of his vast, sprawling treatise were intended to coalesce different elements of a place into a report on what kind of health challenges newcomers could expect to find if they went West.

Unlike Drake, Chekhov was writing at a time when many of the major discoveries of what we now call the "bacteriological revolution" were being made. He traveled to Sakhalin Island during what one historian of medicine has termed the "twenty-one golden years" between 1879 and 1900, when the micro-organisms responsible for many of humanity's major diseases were

---

[11] Even the ambition of the title tells us much about the scope and ideas of medical geography! Daniel Drake, *A systematic treatise, historical, etiological and practical, on the principal diseases of the interior valley of North America, as they appear in the Caucasian, African, Indian, and Esquimaux varieties of its population* (Cincinnati: W. B. Smith and Co.; New York: Mason and Law, 1850), and Second Series, ed. S. Hanbury Smith and Francis G. Smith (Philadelphia: Lippincott, Grambo and Co., 1854). On Drake as a medical geographer, see Frank A. Barrett, "Daniel Drake's Medical Geography," *Social Science and Medicine* 42: 6 (1996): 791–800; Barrett, *Disease and Geography*, 241–54; and Michael L. Dorn, "(In)temperate Zones: Daniel Drake's Medico-moral Geographies of Urban Life in the Trans-Appalachian American West," *Journal of the History of Medicine* 55 (2000): 256–91.

[12] Thus Drake has chapters on "Clothing, Lodging, Bathing, Habitations, and Shade Trees" and "Occupations, Pursuits, Exercise, and Recreation" (Drake, *A Systematic Treatise*, 1850, 676–84 and 684–91; on food and drink, see especially 653–57). On the broad social impact of medical geography, see Bonj Szcygiel and Robert Hewitt, "Nineteenth-Century Medical Landscapes: John H. Rauch, Frederick Law Olmsted, and the Search for Salubrity," *Bulletin of the History of Medicine* 74 (2000): 708–34.

being discovered at a rate of one every year.[13] Such investigations would seem to toll a funeral knell for work like Drake's. Medical geography might seem, after all, a pre-germ-theory notion of health, reliant on diffuse and overlapping environmental influences rather than specific, identifiable microbes to explain, predict, and analyze well-being. Yet in several different cultural contexts, the medical geographic approach proved robust in the face of changing medical epistemology.[14] It did not simply molder away with the onset of germs. Instead, medical geography remained a powerful form of analysis in medicine. A major European medical geography compilation roughly contemporary with Chekhov's—and also contemporary with discoveries in bacteriology—is August Hirsch's *Handbook of Geographical and Historical Pathology*, which was originally published in Germany beginning in 1881.[15] A historian of Russian medical geography has termed the latter half of the nineteenth century a "'Golden Age' of medical geography in Russia," one in which a wide range of practitioners contributed to active research on a broad range of regions.[16]

Such research led to a very different history for medical geography in the twentieth century in Russia and the Soviet Republics than in western Europe and North America. Russian researchers never repudiated explicitly medical-geographic tenets as many western European and American workers did. Medical geography was an important and recognized Soviet science, a way to gather crucial information about the far-flung and diverse geographic regions of the Soviet Union.[17] In the West, by contrast, medical geography as an explicit discipline fell out of favor as an old-fashioned, rather musty approach. Yet even well into the twentieth century, its emphasis on environments and their healthfulness continued in somewhat transmuted form in Anglo-American medicine as a crucial element of the study of allergy.[18] Only after World War II did western European and American geographers begin to call

---

[13] Roy Porter, *The Greatest Benefit to Mankind: A Medical History of Humanity* (New York: W. W. Norton, 1998), 442. "Science and technical knowledge," Chekhov wrote his close friend and publisher A. S. Suvorin in 1892, "are now passing through a great period, but for our sort the times are flabby, stale, and dull..." (Simmons, *Chekhov*, 301).

[14] On the challenges to medical geography from bacteriology and new medical sciences, see Barrett, *Disease and Geography*, chaps. 12 and 13.

[15] August Hirsch, *Handbook of Geographical and Historical Pathology*, trans. Charles Creighton, 3 vols. (London: The New Sydenham Society, 1883–86). On Hirsch, see Frank A. Barrett, "August Hirsch: As Critic of, and Contributor to, Geographical Medicine and Medical Geography" in Rupke, *Medical Geography in Historical Perspective*, 98–117; and Barrett, *Disease and Geography*, 297–305.

[16] Markovin, *Development of Medical Geography in Russia*, "Summary," 165.

[17] Barrett, *Disease and Geography*, 467.

[18] Mitman and Numbers, "From Miasma to Asthma."

for a reinvigoration of the field. That process has continued in fits and starts, with a particular emphasis in recent decades.[19]

In the lively and rapidly changing medical world of the 1880s and '90s, Chekhov thus had at his disposal the intellectual frameworks and approaches of medical geography as a widespread and important scientific discourse. In the course of his frenzied research preparations, he read widely in European and especially German literature, where medical geography was particularly strong.[20] The list of publications he consulted before embarking includes an explicitly medical geographic work, "Preliminary comparative study of the hygienic conditions of peasant life, and the medico-topography of the Cherepovetsk District" (1880).[21] His reflections on Sakhalin also make clear the comparative framework of his thinking. He drew comparisons, for example, to other settler colonies like North America's Virginia (*SI*, 275n5). As part of his preparatory work, Chekhov compiled the sort of statistical information that was typical of production of medical geographies.[22] He gathered a variety of ethnographies, travelers' reports and descriptions of Sakhalin's people, fauna, fish, and plants (especially the potentially marketable sea-kale).[23] He also familiarized himself with a number of other medical reports on the

---

[19] Valenčius, "Histories of Medical Geography," 21–22.

[20] His list of works consulted before his journey includes, for example, Dr. A. Th. Middendorf, *Reise in den aussersten Norden und Osten Sibiriens wahrend der Jahre 1843–44* (St. Petersburg, 1847); see *SI*, appendix 1, part 1, "List compiled by Chekhov before his journey to Sakhalin," 396. Chekhov's engagement with this literature validates the use of Euro-American primary and secondary materials to set the context for his thinking. On the European and heavily Germanic flavor of nineteenth-century medical geography, see, for example, Michael A. Osborne, "The Geographical Imperative in Nineteenth-Century French Medicine," 31–50, and Nicolaas A. Rupke, "Adolf Mühry (1810–1888): Göttingen's Humboldtian Medical Geographer," 86–97, in Rupke, *Medical Geography in Historical Perspective*.

[21] P. Griaznov, "Opyt sravnitel'nogo izucheniia gigienicheskikh uslovii krest'ianskogo byta i mediko-topografiia Cherepovetskogo uezda," dissertation for higher degree of Doctor of Medicine (St. Petersburg, 1880), cited (with adjusted transliteration) from *SI*, appendix 1, part 2: "Supplementary List of Works Compiled by Chekhov and mentioned in *From Siberia* or *Sakhalin Island*," 401.

[22] His reading list included, for example, A. D. Brylkin, "Statistical Data concerning the Southern Section of Sakhalin Island," *Proceedings of the Siberian Expedition of the Imperial Russian Geographical Society* (St. Petersburg, 1868), cited from *SI*, appendix 1, part 1, 394; and Decennial Report (*Survey of the Decade's Activity of the Central Prison Department, 1879–89*) (St. Petersburg, 1890), in *SI*, appendix 1, part 2, 400.

[23] Such travelogues and reports are exactly the kinds of work later credited by Soviet historian A. P. Markovin as pushing forward the field of medical geography; see Markovin, "Historical Sketch," 8, 12.

island.[24] Medical geography formed part of the intellectual framework that Chekhov had available and that he builds on in his book.

## Medical Geography in *Sakhalin Island*

Chekhov's motivations for his trip were complex and difficult to pin down. It is not clear whether he intended his work as a strictly scientific piece—the kind of dissertation, for instance, that would give a practicing physician academic credentials. Yet there were many contemporary Russian examples of dissertations based in medical geography, and certainly he approached his project as a serious scientific endeavor.[25] Grounding his text, Chekhov emphasizes that when it was founded, Sakhalin Island was scientifically unknown (*SI*, 279). It represented the kind of tantalizing possibility for description, evaluation, and appropriation upon which much of nineteenth-century medical geography was centered. To apprehend Sakhalin Island, Chekhov employed scientific methodology—he made, he claims, a census of every person on the island, "around 10,000 labour convicts and enforced settlers" (his own narrative makes clear that, strictly speaking, he fell short of this astounding feat—but he did certainly accomplish an impressive number of interviews).[26] All of this effort on the island was buttressed by the extensive

---

[24] These include Junior Doctor Sintzovsky, "Hygienic situation of hard-labour convicts in exile. Report from Sakhalin Island," *Health* no. 16, 31 May 1875 (*SI*, appendix 1, part 1, 398); "The southern section of Sakhalin—extract from military-medical report of Dr. Dobrotvorsky for 1868," *News of the Siberian Branch of the Imperial Russian Geographical Society* 1: 2–3 (1870); and N. P. Vasilyev, "A Journey to Sakhalin Island," *Archives of Forensic Medicine*, no. 2 (1870) (both cited from *SI*, appendix 1, part 2, 400, 402).

[25] Chekhov's often-quoted letter to close friend and publishing patron Suvorin notes that he ventures to Sakhalin "totally convinced that my trip will yield a valuable contribution neither to literature nor to science," but he will nonetheless write something "thus to repay a little the science of medicine, towards which, as you know, I have been a swine" (9 March 1890; *SI*, 370). Later he wrote to Suvorin from aboard the steamer *Baikal* in the Tatar Strait that "I don't know what will come out finally, but I've done quite a lot. There's enough for three dissertations" (11 September 1890, *SI*, 387). Historian A. P. Markovin cites many medical geography dissertations in the mid- and late nineteenth century (see Markovin, "Historical Sketch," 8, 10). He asserts, without further source attribution, that Chekhov "planned to write a doctoral dissertation on the topic 'Medical-geographic description of the island of Sakhalin'"; on a crucial exchange about this possibility, see also Simmons, *Chekhov*, 211, 344–45. Tracing intentions is tricky business, but Chekhov's own passages do strongly suggest that he took seriously the medical and scientific aspects of his journey, and that we as readers would thus do well to hold in mind the context of medical science at his time.

[26] Chekhov to A. S. Suvorin, 11 September 1890 (*SI*, 387), where he speaks of his index card system and adds: "In other words, there is not a single convict or settled-exile on Sakhalin who hasn't had a chat with me. The census of the children has been especially successful, and I am placing quite a few hopes on it...."

research he did to locate publications about Sakhalin before he even left metropolitan Russia, and that he continued once on Sakhalin.

In addition to setting about this scientifically in a broad sense, Chekhov uses many of the techniques and assumptions of medical geography. Chapter 7 features a long discussion on weather. Chekhov is interested in how weather affects agriculture and how it affects human well-being. His conclusions are grim: the weather is cold, winter lasts a very long time, it is gray and damp. At Alexandrovsk District, "the amount of warmth sufficient for the full ripening of oats and wheat has not been observed in one single year" (*SI*, 135). Moreover, this has direct consequences for the human form as well as ripening grains. "Such weather," he observes, "inclines one towards depressed reflections and despondent drunkenness" (*SI*, 135). People become brutal and lose hope. In chapter 15, he asserts that damp, cold weather makes outside labor unhealthy: he describes "a veritable *febris sachalinensis* [Sakhalin fever], with a headache, and rheumatic pains throughout the whole body, which derive not from infection but from climatic influences" (*SI*, 242). The environment—and ignorant, poorly managed use of it—literally makes people sick.

Bad weather, furthermore, affects different convicts differently. He notes that the exiles who risked escape attempts were often those "for whom the difference between the climates of Sakhalin and their home region is most perceptible" (*SI*, 342). Here Chekhov draws on longstanding frameworks of environmental medicine. Bodies, under the rubrics of medical geography, have to meld with their environments. Sudden and substantial dislocation requires a process of acclimation—an uncomfortable period in which the body physiologically adjusts to the demands and constraints of new surroundings (often accompanied by so-called "seasoning" illnesses). Distance from home was thus felt as somatic, as well as spiritual or social. One's own self was a keen instrument for registering the distance and strangeness of a place.[27]

In his discussion of weather, Chekhov is not simply impressionistic. He strives to collect for himself, and also convey to us, his readers, a quantified sense of just how unforgiving the weather is. His are arguments according to the medical science of his time, not just travelers' gripes. In chapter 7 he includes a chart of monthly temperatures that would be right out of many reports labeled "medical geography" (and indeed, in that discussion he footnotes Griaznov's report on medical geography; *SI*, 134, 140n3). In a note in a different part of the book, Chekhov discusses how the miserable state of data collection on Sakhalin weather could be improved: where and how weather stations should be set up, how "literate exiles" could effectively staff them

---

[27] Valenčius, *The Health of the Country*, 22–34, 240–43; Mitman and Numbers, "From Miasma to Asthma"; and Gregg Mitman, "Hay Fever Holiday: Health, Leisure, and Place in Gilded-Age America," *Bulletin of the History of Medicine* 77 (2003): 600–35.

and do the measurements necessary (*SI*, 207n7). Throughout the book, and on many subjects, his constant refrain is the need for better records in the Sakhalin bureaucratic morass and the need for clearer local informants.[28]

For Chekhov, medical geography provides the framework for critique of the Sakhalin administration. The lack of modernity of Korsakovsk Post, for example, is shown by the lack of telegraph office or meteorological station—hence Chekhov's frustration at drawing conclusions about climate (*SI*, 203–04). Further, the lack of local information is directly tied to a lack of personal engagement. Despite credible meteorological data (rare enough on Sakhalin!), Chekhov dismisses a recent report by the Inspector of Agriculture as being "a small, purely academic piece of work, lacking descriptions of any personal observation made by the writer...." (*SI*, 289n1).

Chekhov, like many researchers in the tradition of medical geography, draws on a broad understanding of well-being. His chapter 19 engages in a long analysis of food—like his predecessor Daniel Drake, whose excoriation of strong drink and hasty eating ran through his medical geographic work. Throughout, Chekhov sees the pervasive effect of environmental influences. He notes of interest in the supposedly high birth rates on the island that "people say that the very climate of Sakhalin disposes women to pregnancy...." (*SI*, 270). Such consequences extended to the moral and spiritual planes of life—medical geography encompassed the whole self, not only the tangible body.[29] Chekhov repeatedly notes the soul-deadening effect of coarseness and degradation, as in the "constant proximity of shaven heads, shackles, executioners..." (*SI*, 313). People are shaped not only by where they are or what they do, but what they witness daily. Decent people cannot last long in such a place: "The environment dragged them down into its filth, like an octopus" (*SI*, 313).[30] Here in his scientific work, as in fiction like "The Murder" (1895) or his haunting story "In Exile" (1892), Chekhov writes of the ways not just outer body but inner self are brutalized by life in a prison colony.

Chekhov does discuss infectious diseases, the strictly medical conditions that we are familiar with today as a main subject of medicine and that we might expect him to have focused on. In chapter 23 he analyzes the island's morbidity and mortality—to the extent possible given such poor base statistics. He concludes that "the acute infectious diseases have up till now found a soil unfavourable to their development" (though "[a]mong the exiled men you will not encounter any who are well nourished, plump and rosy-

---

[28] Prison records, for instance, were hopeless; some have noted on them, "Obviously untrue" (*SI*, 319n12).

[29] As Michael Dorn has effectively argued for Daniel Drake; see Dorn, "(In)temperate Zones."

[30] Similarly, in chap. 20 he discusses Sakhalin's degrading effect on prison staff as well as on inmates.

cheeked: even those settled-exiles who do nothing are gaunt and pale"; *SI*, 350). Sakhalin, he concludes, does not harbor malaria. Rather, consumption (what we would now call tuberculosis) is the main killer. Climate and harsh work and bad conditions cause it. Yet Chekhov does not focus on disease itself, as we would usually understand it today: the total environment concerns him, rather than any one particular disorder.

Throughout *Sakhalin Island*, Chekhov draws on techniques of medial geography: its columns of numbers, its seemingly a-theoretical gobbling-up of data, its striving for measurement, precision, and accuracy.[31] Most of all, he bases his work on a scientific faith that seems to us thoroughly paradoxical, that subjective experience—the way in which environments register in and through human bodies and each person's own sensations, states of health, and daily activities—is a telling and crucial element of any understanding of place.

### Re-Reading *Sakhalin Island*

So how might this change the way we read *Sakhalin Island*?

First, literary scholars have been right to be uneasy with this text. I do not think we can simply lump it in with the rest of Chekhov's written work. It is informed by other nonfiction medical writings in important and far more explicit ways than is his fiction (which is certainly affected by his attitudes toward medicine and science as well, but more subtly and often with ambiguity).[32] *Sakhalin Island* embodies an argument that hinges on medico-scientific principles—and the failure of those principles to be carried out.

Second, I want to therefore assert the analytic coherence of much of the book. Those who have read the entire volume may agree that this is perhaps an uphill battle ... but let me engage it!

Wrestling with *Sakhalin Island* in a 1992 article, Cathy Popkin has argued that we have to acknowledge "the waywardness and the excess of the book" where other scholars have tried to see clear and realized intention.[33] She calls our attention—quite rightly—to the riot of facts and the sheer sprawl of the book: for an author whose fiction is so brief and well-crafted, so trimmed of unnecessary flourish or sentiment, the density and repetition and wandering prose of *Sakhalin Island* do, I agree, signal that something else is going on.

---

[31] As Frank Barrett has observed, a hallmark of medical geography in the early to mid-1800s was the call to obtain more data. By the latter part of the century, researchers had begun to bewail that there was *too much* data (*Disease and Geography*, 370–72).

[32] On how Chekhov's medical background influenced his perception and his fiction, see Michael Finke, *Seeing Chekhov: Life and Art* (Ithaca, NY: Cornell University Press, 2005).

[33] Cathy Popkin, "Chekhov as Ethnographer: Epistemological Crisis on Sakhalin Island," *Slavic Review* 51: 1 (Spring 1992): 49.

Popkin argues—in a beautiful and well-observed article—that Chekhov encounters and is ultimately overcome by a deep epistemological frustration on Sakhalin. He goes to Sakhalin to know and make known this stubbornly foreign territory, but ends up unable to do so. His bulky footnotes, his hugely spiraling text, his contradictory statements about statistics and records—all indicates not a coherent, realized plan that we can discuss in the same way we talk about his jewel-like short stories, but rather evidence of failure to be able to make sense of the place. In the end, she argues, Chekhov abdicates an attempt to organize his material. He *enacts* rather than *reports* the failure of "sense-making capacity" on Sakhalin.[34]

In contrast, I would assert that Chekhov's *Sakhalin Island* makes sense. It does not make the same kind of sense his stories do, but through it Chekhov crafts a biting argument in terms of medical geography.[35] His vast accumulation of data does not simply represent his dumping it all in because he is frustrated, or overwhelmed, or cannot come up with a better plan (this is a not quite fair simplification of Cathy Popkin's argument), but because the accumulation of data (including all those seemingly bizarre long digressive footnotes) is part and parcel of the intellectual project—or at least one of the intellectual projects—that he undertakes.

Chekhov's seeming pile-up of data is absolutely typical of medical geographies. Even his tabulations look familiar. Popkin argues that Chekhov "creates peculiar correlations such as temperature tables" and "arbitrary" categories like "sick months."[36] Yet in the context of medical geography, such concepts and vocabulary are neither peculiar nor arbitrary. They are typical and useful. The seasonal variation of disease and its geographic distribution were fundamental and essential elements of a responsible environmental accounting of a place. All this information does not float without context—it is familiar to a form of medico-scientific reporting that Anton Chekhov and educated, science-minded people like him had before them at the time.

Furthermore—and most importantly—Chekhov uses this information as part of an argument. The framework of medical geography allows him to reveal the craziness of the Sakhalin system. He sets up the expectation of observation of natural laws connecting human beings to their environments, and then makes clear how un-natural the whole world of Sakhalin is. He argues, in other words, that this is the framework that should make sense of this place—and look how little sense it makes.

---

[34] Ibid., 51.

[35] And likely other scientific disciplines as well, as Juras T. Ryfa begins to explore; see his *The Problem of Genre and the Quest for Justice in Chekhov's "The Island of Sakhalin,"* Studies in Slavic Languages and Literature, vol. 13 (Lewiston, ME: The Edwin Mellen Press, 1999), chap. 6.

[36] Popkin, "Chekhov as Ethnographer," 45.

In chapter 12, Chekhov notes that climatologically, it is absurd that southern Sakhalin remains unsettled, even though that region would be much more welcoming of agriculture. Settlement, in other words, has not obeyed the dictates of climate (*SI*, 197). Weather and soil, he acknowledges, can be a "chief cause" of well-being—as at a small settlement he visits in the south where people are actually doing well—but these positive factors can be foiled by mismanagement, inefficiency, and subsequent overcrowding (*SI*, 210). Occasionally even the challenging environment of Sakhalin can seem promising. "The Korsakovsk Prison," he notes, "occupies what is the highest, and most probably the healthiest, spot in the post." Building there would seem to recognize the logic of health and environment. Yet in fact, "[t]he barracks-huts here are old, it is stuffy in the cells, the latrines are much worse than in the northern prisons, the bake-house is dingy, the punishment cells for solitary confinement are dark, unventilated and cold…." (*SI*, 204). Rather than building on the strengths of environmental connections, those in charge at Sakhalin have squandered what the environment is actually giving them (which is precious little).

His book resonates with indignation: those in power *should* give attention to all the factors of environment that shape well-being, but they do not. Throughout, he notes the unhappy consequences of not investigating the environment. Ignorance of the natural history of the local salmon called *keta*, for instance, prevents people on Sakhalin from taking advantage of it through efficient fishing (*SI*, 287). Further, those who could and should use such information are not even looking for it. He laments that Sakhalin's potential for farming has been misunderstood. The haphazard agricultural policy propagated down from the disengaged levels of the Russian bureaucracy has been based on simplistic information like "geographical latitude," not on more detailed assessments or on the local knowledge of "the people who plough and sow" (*SI*, 280). Sakhalin, in Chekhov's mournful and grim assessment, demonstrates a failure of appropriate knowledge-gathering, an absence of detailed observation or informative networks like Drake's. The island's evident tragedy represents a failure to apply the concepts of medical geography.

Chekhov's insight extends to a larger failure of sense-making, as Popkin so well puts it, that pervades life on Sakhalin (Chekhov recounts in chapter 16 that because of rations for prisoners, a certain woman accused of murdering her cohabitant will end up better fed if she is in fact convicted; *SI*, 265n11). Yet for him it is a failure on the part of the bureaucrats who manage from afar and the functionaries who run the place—not a failure necessarily intrinsic to the locale. He emphasizes again and again how bureaucratic behavior on Sakhalin belies stated goals and denies the actual environment. Logic is completely subverted by contradictions between officials' recognition of the failure of Sakhalin agriculture and official orders demanding it. His evidence forces the reader to acknowledge the backward cruel logic of a prison colony.

Chekhov's accretion of detail is not incidental; it does not show the failure of his analysis. Instead, his amassing of evidence actually demonstrates a structure like that of many more explicit and articulated medical geographies. He notes many examples, takes detailed local information, and then slowly—slowly—builds up a picture of a region. Chapter 18 sums up many of his implicit arguments about the failure of settlement, agriculture, and prison system. Yet instead of discerning underlying environmental laws from this picture, as medical geographers aimed to, he must instead reveal a portrait of science ignored, of principles flouted. The misery of all he encounters demonstrates the cost of doing so.

## Conclusion

Cathy Popkin has trenchantly argued that Chekhov demonstrates on Sakhalin "the complete failure of the human sciences."[37] She contends that he participates in that failure, finds himself subject to it, demonstrates that failure for us as readers through the conceptual murkiness of his own writing. Yet I contend that Chekhov argues for specific ways in which known laws of the human sciences, and especially those that relate environment to human well-being, are being transgressed, to the great suffering of those living on Sakhalin. Paying attention to this seemingly antiquated and fusty approach to medical investigation can help us see the withering insight with which Chekhov builds his case. Those with oversight of Sakhalin are not only immoral or inhumane in the degradation and misery they force upon those within their purview; even more than that, they refuse to investigate, to acknowledge, or to obey the far-reaching connections between people and their environments that close investigation of the kind that he engages in could reveal.

In a broader sense, Chekhov argues that for penal servitude to actually serve its purposes—for it to actually embody the enlightened, modern approach to crime that it is meant to—the whole enterprise must operate more scientifically. He is making not a political, but an evidence-based call for the use of science, in the broadest sense, to govern the enactment of Russian law.

He points out how science, in the form of investigation of the laws of environmental health, does not govern penal settlement, but laced through his text is the hope that it *could*—that weather reporting stations could tell settlement managers the best sites for new settlements, or that correlation of agricultural results (actual results, not the completely fictitious ones he finds in the files) could give useful information about what to plant the next year, or that careful record-keeping and actual tracking of who is in the Sakhalin system could help support families who have come with their loved ones voluntarily into penal servitude. In *Sakhalin Island*, Chekhov does not reject the entire system of penal colonization. He yearns to see it actually function according to principles that make sense, and that are immanent in the world

---

[37] Ibid., 40.

around him. Not simply Anton Chekhov as writer or intellectual figure, but Chekhov as physician and Chekhov as man of science emerge from a reader's journey through *Sakhalin Island*.

# A Few Words on the Seminar on Anton Chekhov and the Medical Humanities

## Richard Kahn, M.D.

On 2 October 2003 I received an e-mail from Michael Finke asking for help organizing a seminar in the medical humanities that was to be part of a Chekhov Symposium taking place one year later at Colby College in Waterville, Maine. Why me? It turned out that a mutual friend, a medical historian and former colleague from his days at Washington University, had suggested my name. While practicing as an internist in Maine for over thirty-two years I have maintained a strong interest in medical history and other areas of the medical humanities. And it was certainly relevant to this project that I had been a member of the Maine Humanities Council from 1986 to 1992. I agreed to help and suggested we contact the Maine Humanities Council for support and additional ideas.

In the period leading up to the Chekhov symposium I reread a number of Chekhov's medicine-related short stories, and I read some works that were new to me, too. As a medical historian, I particularly enjoyed Chekhov's *Journey to Sakhalin* (1895). That work raises numerous issues still confronting us today, including that of physician involvement in corporal punishment—and this was fifty years before Nazi Germany and 100 years before the U.S. invasion of Iraq. Conevery Bolton Valenčius's presentation on Chekhov's *Sakhalin* resonated particularly well with my interests. A historical work that Michael recommended for participants, Nancy Frieden's *Russian Physicians in an Era of Reform*,[1] provided some much-needed background on medicine in Chekhov's Russia.

I felt honored to be asked to take part in the program and enjoyed meeting Chekhov scholars on the centennial of Chekhov's death. I love words, and under the rubric of history of medicine I have studied the medical ties of the dictionary-makers Noah Webster and Sir James Murray (*OED*). It was therefore of great interest to me that Chekhov's best translators were participating in the program. The idea of commanding the nuances of two languages well enough to do justice to the works of an author like Chekhov is incredible. I thought of an article on Peter Mark Roget (of thesaurus fame) by Simon

---

[1] Nancy Mandelker Frieden, *Russian Physicians in an Era of Reform and Revolution, 1856–1905* (Princeton, NJ: Princeton University Press, 1981).

*Chekhov the Immigrant: Translating a Cultural Icon.* Michael C. Finke and Julie de Sherbinin, eds. Bloomington, IN: Slavica Publishers, 2007, 315–17.

Winchester,[2] in which Winchester pointed out that there is rarely more than one word that exactly fits the precise meaning of a particular sentence. Chekhov's translators helped us compare several different published translations of a given passage, and they shared something of the thought process guiding the translator's labors. Witnessing the translation of great Russian to great English gave me a new appreciation of the work of a translator.

Over the years I had many times heard variations on Chekhov's witticism, "Medicine is my lawful wedded wife, and literature my mistress," but I had not known to whom it originally belonged. In Chekhov's formulation it continues: "When one gets on my nerves, I spend the night with the other. This may be somewhat disorganized, but then again it's not as boring, and anyway, neither one loses anything by my duplicity."[3] That comment could itself be the subject for a medical humanities seminar. Some of the basic facts about Chekhov as a man and physician that stick in my mind are:

> Grandson of a serf and son of a poor shopkeeper;
> University of Moscow, graduated 1884. Worked his way through
>     medical school by publishing 200+ short stories;
> Suffered from and died of TB; first coughed up blood in 1884;
> 1888: winner of the prestigious Pushkin Prize;
> Trip to Sakhalin in 1890;
> Engaged combating the famine and cholera outbreaks of 1892
>     (620,051 cases and 300,321 deaths).[4]

I must say, I was a bit concerned about what might result from a discussion forum that included, on the one hand, devoted Chekhov scholars who live and breathe Chekhov, and on the other, a group of physicians, nurses, therapists, and counselors, who might have read a few of Chekhov's short stories, but nothing else, and who would—inevitably—respond to the material quite differently than the scholars. But I believe the forum's transcription provides the record of a very valuable and innovative sort of dialogue.

I remember, years ago, hearing Vartan Gregorian urge multidisciplinary and interdisciplinary learning, where the "interconnectedness" of disciplines would be stressed. This distinguished educator—past president of the New York Public Library and Brown University, and current head of the Carnegie Corporation—has encouraged educational reform for decades, and he has always emphasized multidisciplinary approaches that ask how scholars from

---

[2] "Word Imperfect," *Atlantic Monthly*, May 2001, 53–75.

[3] Chekhov to A. S. Suvorin, 11 September 1888, cited here from *Anton Chekhov's Life and Thought: Selected Letters and Commentary*, trans. Michael Henry Heim and Simon Karlinsky, selection, commentary, and intro. Simon Karlinsky (Berkeley: University of California Press, 1973), 107.

[4] Frieden, *Russian Physicians*, 325.

different disciplines observe, think, and write about a given problem.[5] This Chekhov symposium has been remarkable precisely for the multidisciplinary interaction it fostered. And nowhere was the disciplinary gap wider, and the dialogue more interesting, than when scholars of Russian literature, language, and history conversed about Chekhov with nurses, physicians, and other health care professionals. Each group brought their own knowledge, experience, and prejudices to the discussion; but they could and did talk together and learn from each other. Vartan would be happy.

---

[5] About Gregorian and his views, see: http://www.carnegie.org/sub/about/vgregorian.html and http://www.carnegie.org/sub/pubs/colleges.html.

# Seminar on Anton Chekhov and the Medical Humanities: A Discussion of Selected Chekhov Stories

## Moderators: Michael Finke, University of Illinois at Urbana-Champaign and Richard Kahn, M.D., Rockport, ME

*Note: Participants are identified whenever possible, because the personal and professional perspective from which each individual was speaking was an important part of the conversation.*

MICHAEL FINKE

In the next segment of the medical humanities program we'll be discussing some Chekhov stories on medical themes. This morning our number has been augmented by local health-care professionals attending the seminar under the auspices of the Maine Humanities Council, and these participants have read a selection of Chekhov stories in preparation for our meeting: "Anyuta," "Ward 6," "A Medical Case" (or, depending on your translation, "A Doctor's Visit"), and "On Official Business."[1] I suggest that we start addressing the stories more or less in the order in which they're presented in the handout we distributed prior to the Symposium, keeping open the possibility of shifting focus. If it turns out that people are more interested in talking about the Dr. Coles interview we just screened, for instance, that is also possible; and in fact, Dr. Coles made many interesting remarks about the stories we've read for today. If you'd like to return to the material from the preceding panel, that's also fair game. One thing to bear in mind: We have an even more heterogeneous mix of topics and participants this morning than has been the case in the Symposium thus far. In addition to professional Slavists very immersed in certain questions of Chekhov scholarship, historians, writers, translators, and theater people, we also have folks who are reading Chekhov in an entirely different discursive context, connected with their special life-experience and professional practice in health care. It will be a challenge, but also an interesting potential of our discussion here this morning, to truly talk with one another and achieve a common language, if not a meeting of the minds. We want to take care not to let the rather academic kind of discussion we've been having of Chekhov for the last two days steam-roll over other perspectives.

---

[1] Participants were directed to the translations in Anton Chekhov, *Stories*, trans. Richard Pevear and Larissa Volokhonsky (New York: Bantam Books, 2000).

*Chekhov the Immigrant: Translating a Cultural Icon.* Michael C. Finke and Julie de Sherbinin, eds. Bloomington, IN: Slavica Publishers, 2007, 319–36.

With that, shall we begin with the stories that we read for today? Several of these stories have gotten quite a bit of attention in the conference already, which tells us something. Let's open up the floor for discussion on "Anyuta." Here are three questions from that handout to help us get started:

- What emerges from the juxtaposition of the medical student and the painter and how they use Anyuta in this story?
- When, in your training or practice, might it have been necessary to "use" another person as Anyuta is used here? How were your ethical sensibilities assuaged, and how do you imagine the situation looked from the other person's point of view?
- What, if anything, is "comic" about this story?

I don't want to force discussion along these tracks, however; our time is short.

RICHARD KAHN

I would just say that for an individual starting out in medicine—and I'm thinking of the medical students I see today—it's difficult and embarrassing to develop a relationship with and examine somebody when you really don't know what you are doing. It's so tough to learn how to examine patients while being sensitive to their selves. And I think that's a very difficult time in one's career. I practice up in rural Maine. Preceptors come to work with me, and it's the medical student and me—that's all. You don't have a third-year student, fourth-year student, resident, and intern with you. There's a great advantage for the second-year student who is coming up to work where it will just be the two of us: it means that he or she is not the third or fourth person to examine somebody. And for anybody the least bit sensitive and uncomfortable to begin with, the idea of being the third or fourth person examining a patient is just terrible!

As for "Anyuta" being comic: I don't see anything comic about it at all. It's as Dr. Coles said—this should be shown to all medical students starting off in the field. How would you like to be on the other side of this, on the other side of the stethoscope? I can speak from my own experience as a physician later in life. The American College of Physicians is now using more "standardized" patients for training. People are hired to present as having a certain disease, and you are supposed to take a history, examine them, and so on. And I had been in practice for probably fifteen years when I attended a program on OB-GYN, where we were to work on pelvic and breast examinations. I was thinking about it a lot before I went, and I wasn't sure if I liked the idea at all. I was afraid that the women I'd be practicing on would be underprivileged, and that subjecting themselves to such examinations would be the only thing they could do for a living. And I felt terrible—I was really dreading that part of it. But what I found was that the subjects were generally feminists, and that they had themselves worked in clinics. These were well educated women who had made a very deliberate decision to help teach students and practicing physicians—for doctors are students too—how to better carry out examinations. And the program really ended up being not so bad, though I had been very apprehensive. Now, in the past—if you went back a generation—we did indeed learn medicine on poor people, but I think that's changed a great deal—it's really not like that anymore. No individual *has* to be examined today.

MICHAEL FINKE

Other responses? Do you see any connection between this artist character and this doctor character, beyond what Dr. Coles pointed out to us?

JIM HAZEN, CHESTERVILLE, ME

It's just so distressing to read about these people preparing to work in professions calling for sensitivity. This painter who's training to be sensitive so that he can respond to the world around him, and the physician... You'd expect the exact opposite of their treatment of this woman. And she has also been abused and used that way by other people, too; this is the fifth person she's been with in this role. It's really distressing to read this.

MICHAEL FINKE

Yes, that's the irony of the story. You have an amorous situation in which these two are living together, and the medical student is supposed to be looking at his woman with a loving gaze, but instead views her with this cold, professional eye. You would expect a completely different approach to seeing her body, and that's part of the story's irony.

MALE PARTICIPANT

But that's a major portion of the dichotomy of being a physician. Because in order to be able to appropriately isolate yourself from what's going on, the clinical aspects of the patient, you can't be saying, "Wow, doesn't she have nice looking breasts!" Perhaps you do, but it goes into a corner somewhere... It's a difficult situation in which you find yourself interacting with a human being, but doing odd, unnatural things. Most women, for instance, don't walk in and take their clothes off in front of a stranger. Their behavior is altered, and your response has to be altered—it's a basic artificiality. I think that in his story Chekhov is trying to recognize that you cannot totally isolate that and drive yourself entirely into an entirely personal or impersonal corner. Other aspects of one's response are there, and they have to be recognized. For example, when I run into an attractive woman in the clinical setting, I do still recognize that the attraction is there; it's part of the interaction, but it remains, if you will, a forbidden area. You can't go there. But you know it's there; which is different from ignoring it.

FEMALE PARTICIPANT

Right, because there can be compassion in that, and you can still see that individual as a human being. But I think, nevertheless, that so much of the medical world is trained to operate with so-called objectivity—a pseudo-objectivity, really—when in reality the second you encounter that person, such objectivity becomes totally impossible. But certainly that was being emphasized in Chekhov's medical background, because it was emphasized in mine—what I'm calling pseudo-objectivity, the idea that you could observe *anything* with no involvement.

MICHAEL FINKE

This is an area in which our collaborator Cathy Popkin has done some very interesting work, in particular in an article called "The Objective Eye and the Common Good."[2]

MALE PARTICIPANT

What she said is important. I think that what she called "pseudo-objectivity" is, somehow, a distortion of the necessary aspect of our training that helps us develop something called "isolation of affect." As a physician I can go into the emergency room and treat a kid who has been brutalized by his or her father and not go out and twist the father's neck. I treat that child, and I'm able to isolate that portion of my response. It's hard to do, and it's difficult to teach people to do that. Because we're humans, we essentially feel towards the other person. And to call this "pseudo-objectivity," I think, is going a little too far...

FEMALE PARTICIPANT

I'm a registered nurse and I work in an ambulatory care center, where every day we meet people for the first time, and work with them for maybe six hours—and then they're home again. But it takes very little time to be able to say, "Hello, how are you feeling today," or "Who's this with you?"—to be a human being and a friendly person with them, and yet *still* be objective... Oftentimes, if you show your humanity within the first few opening minutes they will open up to you a lot more, and you will get a lot more information from them than by just going in and being clinical. I think Chekhov was before his time in thinking that. And it's taken us so many years to even begin to realize how important that is.

MICHAEL FINKE

These are absolutely ubiquitous themes in Chekhov, and not just in connection with physicians. Early in his career he wrote a kind of mystery novel—

---

[2] Cathy Popkin and Louise McReynolds, "The Objective Eye and the Common Good," in *Constructing Russian Culture in the Age of Revolution: 1881–1940*, ed. Catriona Kelly and David Shepherd (Oxford: Oxford University Press, 1998), 57–76.

*The Shooting Party*—where the detective who is investigating a young woman's murder turns out to have been a lover of the victim, and not only that, in the end we learn that he was also her murderer. But the whole story is narrated from his point of view, so there's this play between his supposedly "objective" position as a professional investigator examining the case and his libidinal investment in it. And the points you raise are interesting in consideration of the biography of Chekhov, too. I have to tell you, when I first started thinking about this topic in Chekhov, I immediately jumped to very theoretical, psychoanalytic understandings about seeing and being seen—voyeurism, exhibitionism, shyness, and so on. And then it occurred to me that this was a huge leap, that we have to think also about how his training as a physician might have affected him in this regard.

Other points about "Anyuta?"

RICHARD PEVEAR, TRANSLATOR

I just want to point something out. We are talking about this as a medical story, but Anyuta isn't sick. And the story is called "Anyuta." How do we see this woman as a result of this story? Does Chekhov feel pity for her, or is he in contempt of her?

RICHARD KAHN

Or is he just telling it as it is? He wrote in 1888, "An artist should not be the judge of his characters and what they say, but only an objective observer." You read into it what you want: "Here's what I saw. Here's what the chart says."

RICHARD PEVEAR

This is the wonderful irony of Chekhov. He keeps saying that an artist should only be an objective observer; but is there anyone *less* objective than Chekhov? Chekhov is so filled with compassion, so filled with anger, so filled with rage! I see nothing objective about him. What he does is make us confront our own willingness to accept our detachment, and to look at how they treat this woman, Anyuta—as if she were a thing, they share her out and then they pass her on. This is a horror, whether it is a question of artists or doctors...

MICHAEL FINKE

Next to Cathy Popkin, who, by the way, has written a splendid article on "Anyuta."[3]

CATHY POPKIN

Just a small point. In terms of the story's symbolism, he has turned this woman into more than a thing, he's made her into a cadaver...

---

[3] Cathy Popkin, "Chekhov's Corpus: Bodies of Knowledge," in *Essays in Poetics* 18 (September 1993): 44–72.

RICHARD PEVEAR

Right, she has ribs drawn on her.

CATHY POPKIN

And the artist too... When she returns from the artist she's shivering blue. The reason he has to get Anyuta is that his last model's legs have turned blue. This ostensibly happens because her stockings weren't colorfast, but symbolically it's a sign of rigor mortis—she's become a cadaver. So the doctor and artist haven't just been insensitive, they have killed.

RICHARD PEVEAR

But this woman, she has also *allowed* herself to be killed.

CATHY POPKIN

Yes, that's right. But that was the only "how" she had to live.

CONEVERY VALENČIUS, PH.D., DIBNER INSTITUTE

Cathy Popkin's point gets to this in part, but I still want to ask why the medical student in that story also paints the woman. He marks on her with chalk. I think you're right that he's doing the marking as you would for an autopsy, but it is very interesting that, while the painter is painting her representationally, on a canvas, the doctor is marking her body. And I'm wondering why he does that, and what to make of this contrast. I'm interested in your sense of why Chekhov made sure to have the doctor-figure touch her, and not just touch her, but leave marks on her.

PAUL GRAYCE, M.D.

To further objectify and depersonalize her... It makes her a drawing board as opposed to a person. He could have used a blackboard. Again, if you allow me, since there's an opening here: Chekhov's view of women is very, very—how can I put it—interesting? I found some very provocative quotes on that topic in a biography I just read, but how he feels about women is also quite interestingly revealed, in my opinion, in this story. In the biography you learn of his own personal difficulties with women—going from one to the other—and that he made such remarks as: "There is no way I can tie myself to a woman, though there are a lot of opportunities. You screw her once, and next time you don't get in"; "Women are most unlikable in their lack of justice, because justice is organically alien to them. As head of the family, the man is clever, reasonable, fair and God-fearing, while the woman is... God help us!" This gives you a sense of where he sits with women...

MICHAEL FINKE

I can also recite a letter of Chekhov rebuking his eldest brother for not appreciating the complexity and intellectual advancement and character of his sister. Chekhov also had female colleagues, colleague-physicians whom he admired (though it's true that he drew certain distinctions between male and female doctors). And as a medical student Chekhov drew up a prospectus for a doctoral dissertation on sexual inequality, which he viewed as a distortion of nature and something that might be corrected. So it's a very complicated picture.

CATHY POPKIN

Just to respond a little bit to Conevery's question: I think we might consider the content of each man's painting. The doctor is drawing on her body and attempting to draw the body; the painting that the artist is attempting to achieve is of Psyche, a mythological subject, but which also means "soul." And he's desperately bad at capturing Anyuta's soul or anything like that. So we have two projects, one oriented toward the body, the material, and the other toward the soul, the immaterial—neither of which is gotten at by these two forms of inquiry.

MICHAEL FINKE

I'd like to return to Richard Pevear's questions about how we see the character Anyuta, and the authorial perspective on her. One way of working toward an answer would be to look very closely—as James Wood's paper yesterday instructed us to do—at the handling of narrative point of view in the story. As you can see very dramatically in "Ward 6," Chekhov is often very subtle in his manipulation of narrative point of view, shuttling his reader into and out of various perspectives, and this formal mechanism is key to how we see characters. So a study of point of view in the story might be one way of approaching an answer to Richard's question. Even if we can't go into close textual analysis here, it's worth thinking about how we might proceed if we had the time to thoroughly analyze one story.

Shall we move on to "Ward 6"? Have we said the last word about "Anyuta?"

PROF. MARTIN BIDNEY, SUNY BINGHAMTON

I would like to say one more word. I really think it's important to get a feel for the many-sidedness of Chekhov as a human being. He's not necessarily our great "Jesus" and teacher, although he had that aspect to him, and there are some parts of him that are very inspiring. But I remember having a real shock when I read this story. And there's "The Darling," which is about a woman and her several husbands. She identifies with every aspect of their professional lives. When she marries a provincial theater impresario, all she talks about is everything that has to do with his business; when she marries a lumber man, her life is all lumber. But at the same time she's eating this mate up. The fatter she gets, the thinner he gets, until he dies. And this happens multiple times. What this means is that the woman is figured as a total lack, in a positively Freudian way. She is filled up with male content in a quite vampiric and cannibalistic way. I'd like to suggest that Chekhov is not free from 1890s pathology.

MALE PARTICIPANT

A great admirer of Strindberg. [*laughter*]

MALE PARTICIPANT

You can also read that story—"The Darling"—as so clearly exaggerated in every phase that it has to be read as a parody. And Tolstoy, when he wrote an article about it, said: This is such a parody that we know that Chekhov doesn't really believe it. But I believe it; I, Tolstoy, believe it!

MICHAEL FINKE

We should try to keep to works that everybody has read for today. Shall we move on? To start us off on "Ward 6," perhaps we might consider the first question from the handout:

- If Chekhov were making rounds with you, where might he find a ward number six—or its analogue in the American system?

This question comes out of Dr. Robert Coles's article "The Wry Dr. Chekhov,"[4] in which he recalls a dying patient he was caring for as a third-year medical student back in the 1950s. This woman says to him: "I hope I'm not in Ward No. 6." First she tells him that she's going to die in the course of the night, which makes him think that she is completely off—in fact, he considers ordering a psychiatric evaluation—and then she says, "I hope I'm not in Ward No. 6." And he had no idea what she was referring to at that time, because he knew only Chekhov's plays. This patient was an English teacher, by the way, and she had been talking about literature throughout her hospitalization. Now she was dying of leukemia—a very young and attractive woman, to whom he had become very attached. And he set out trying to understand what she was trying to tell him. And that's what made me think of asking this question.

PROF. JANE COSTLOW, BATES COLLEGE

I teach Russian at Bates and live in Lewiston, which is an old mill town. Some years ago I had a good friend who was in family practice in Lewiston and also served South Paris and Farmington and other outlying towns off toward the mountains. And I remember him saying that the thing that was most difficult for him in this practice was seeing kids, where the problem he was being asked to deal with as a physician was not a medical problem. It was really either a mental health issue, or an abuse issue, or a kind of collapse of the family or its livelihood—problems along these lines. For me, this connects with "Ward 6," because I think that he was describing a kind

---

[4] Robert Coles, "The Wry Dr. Chekhov," *Times of Surrender: Selected Essays* (Iowa City: University of Iowa Press, 1988), 49–56.

of despair at what he could do, at the limits on his own abilities or powers as a physician. And I just wanted to put that on the table for comment from the local physicians. Do you find this relevant to "Ward 6?" And how do you as physicians deal with the sense of your own powerlessness and despair? Comparing Chekhov's medicine and medicine of today a layperson might think, "Oh man, look how much more they can do!" But does a sense of powerlessness and despair still come into play, and if so, how do you deal with it?

RICHARD KAHN

I want to talk about expectations. In Chekhov's time, I think, the general expectations weren't so high. You know, a hundred years ago people died, kids died, all around you people were dying. Not that they were happy about it, but it was more of a part of life. Now, one hundred years later, there are enormous expectations. We don't have answers to every problem, but the expectations are there. There's what we can do, on the one hand, and there's where expectations have gotten, on the other. And I think that for society in general there's this idea that we really shouldn't get sick, and we really shouldn't die—there ought to be some way to avoid that. Obviously it's not so, but I think that the expectations have gotten higher. No matter what the problem is...

And on top of that you have to look at the difficulties in doing what we *can* do. Medications today have gotten ridiculously expensive, and unless you're independently wealthy or have some insurance program that pays a great deal, you end up trying to finagle ways to get the medicine; and this is in the wealthiest country in the world. A doctor goes to a third-world country and spends a week or two helping out there, and you know, you can do something for a couple minutes and then you leave, and they don't get it any more. There's great frustration, on the local community level, on the national level, and at the world level—that's what we're dealing with. It has to do with fairness and how we treat others in society. I don't want to make any political statements right now, but we seem to have less interest in some of these issues now than in other times... And that's all I am going to say.

PAUL GRAYCE

The story struck me, principally, as an exposition of Chekhov's own struggle with his self. Chekhov has some very interesting difficulties in terms of his character structure, and for me, the two main characters were both Chekhov. Chekhov is looking at himself, first one way and then the other; and in fact he gets transformed. I see the patient Gromov as a representation of how Chekhov thinks society will look upon him if he really expresses some of his doubts and questions about it. Ragin's trip with the neighbor to Warsaw, and his turning his back to the scene, is another way of representing Chekhov's essential wish to refuse the nonsense he sees in society. You see the same struggle in his voyage to Sakhalin: he's trying to get his physician and servant self "out there" as opposed to going off having parties, submitting to the "la-dee-dah" of developed society. And I understand this as related to Chekhov's own difficulties in connecting with others, particularly with women: he can never form long-term relationships and be consistent, have a consistent sense of his self. That's what the story represents for me: here I am, both sides.

MARTIN BIDNEY

I just wanted to say one word, and then comment briefly on my word. The word is "double," or "Doppelgänger." We have in Chekhov the contemporary of Robert Louis Stevenson. These are two interesting characters; they're two aspects of one psyche. Your double is your Mr. Hyde, that part of your self that you wish to hide, otherwise known as the repressed unconscious. But both are parts of your self, and therefore they resemble each other to an uncanny degree despite their apparent contrasts. And that's why there's great difficulty in distinguishing between the two aspects of yourself—the part you want to affirm, and the part you want to hide—particularly when you're in an insane asylum, and Mr. Hyde appears to be driving you down into a great quagmire.

PROF. ANDREW DURKIN, INDIANA UNIVERSITY

I'd like to respond to that by asking Dr. Grayce further: which of the two characters is the more serious pathological case? It's always struck me that Ragin is really the one who is avoiding reality.

PAUL GRAYCE

Well, I think that depends on your own philosophical viewpoint. Can I read a rather interesting passage from Chekhov himself? "The best modern writers, whom I love, serve evil, since they destroy. Some of them, like Tolstoy, said: 'Don't have sex with women because they have mucous discharges. Woman is revolting because her breath smells.' These writers help the devil multiply the slugs and wood-lice we call intellectuals. Jaded, apathetic, idle philosophizing, a cold intelligentsia which is unpatriotic, miserable, colorless, which gets drunk on one glass and visits fifty-kopeck brothels." You have to answer your own question then: Which one does he think is worse? I think that was part of his struggle. I don't know that he ever solved the struggle, and as far as pathology itself, it's very difficult to tell from the story, because there are aspects of how the so-called "insane" man looks at society that are obviously more correct and more reasonable, while there are aspects of the "doctor," the "expert," that are quite twisted. That's why I said that to me there seems to be a blending of both. It's Chekhov's own struggle. There you go, take your choice. It's going to depend upon you.

MICHAEL FINKE

I just want to say, very quickly, something that must be flashing through the minds of the Chekhov scholars here. As I mentioned before in regard to his journals, one has to be very careful when reading Chekhov's letters. They are slippery terrain. One problem is that there are so many of them that you can almost find whatever you're looking for in them; another is that you have to consider who he's writing to, and in what context. That said, it's also extremely important to realize that Chekhov was indeed capable of certain modes of thought, and ideas, and expressions that are very often excluded from our sentimentalized or idealized view of the man and his personality.

DOROTHY THAYER, M.D., LIVERMORE FALLS, ME

I'm from one of those outlying towns that the professor from Bates alluded to earlier, and I'd like to address her question about what you do with the despair that you can't help feeling from time to time. In this story, I felt that until the doctor started talking to the patient in the psychiatric ward, he dealt with despair by ignoring his job, ignoring his patients, drinking, talking to the postmaster, and complaining about everybody around him. And then suddenly I see this glimmer of hope: he's talking with one of his patients. And I think that when we're faced with one of those hopeless situations in the office—and there are many of them that we can do nothing about, such as poverty, and the lack of medical care, and the lack of social supports, you can go on and on—the way I cope with that is to say: Well, I can make this fifteen minutes of your life more pleasant, I can think of you as a worthwhile person, and I can respect you and listen to your story, and then you have to say good bye; and that's it. And so I think a part of me does ignore the bigger problem, but you know, I'm not out there trying to solve all our world's problems…

ELLEN GRUNBLATT, M.D., FARMINGTON, ME

Dorothy, I'd just like to ask you, what do you make of the fact that when the physician in the story talks to the patient, the rest of the community, including the more orthodox part of the medical community, puts him into the institution. What do you make of that? What does anybody make of that? That's what really struck me about the story.

MICHAEL FINKE

It's a great irony, isn't it, because something therapeutic is actually happening. The doctor is actually able to bring Gromov out of some of his delusions, while speaking with Gromov has a therapeutic benefit for the doctor. Healing is happening there, but that gets defined as illness.

FEMALE PARTICIPANT

Well, many doctors and engineers and literary people that were before their time were shunned and ignored. I just think that they wanted to put him where he wouldn't get involved with anyone else.

PROF. KATHERINE O'CONNOR, BOSTON UNIVERSITY

I'd like to follow up on Jane Costlow's question on what a doctor does when faced with despair. That's obviously an issue in "A Medical Case," too, and it also relates very dramatically to Chekhov's "A Boring Story," where at the end the character Katya (who is certainly depressed about her life, though she's not physically ill), begs the professor: "I'm at the end of my road here; tell me what to do." And of course he doesn't, he can't answer. And I've always defended that—perhaps for my own reasons—I've always said, "What do you do?" We've all had friends who've been clinically depressed at times; what do you do when someone grabs you by the lapels and asks: "What can I do?" What do you say?

BRUCE FINKE, M.D., NORTHAMPTON, MA

My response has to do with Dorothy Thayer's comment, and also the question about our own despair. Dorothy describes one mechanism for dealing with that, an individual's reflective and therapeutic way, both for herself and for the person she's seeing. There are also a variety of institutional mechanisms for dealing with despair, most of which are pathological and have to do with distancing and objectifying, and busying: going on rounds together and seeing the patient that way, or being so *busy* that one doesn't have time to engage in the despair. And to the degree that the physician in "Ward 6" doesn't take advantage of those institutional mechanisms, he actually threatens the institution, and so there's a response by the institution. When he takes Dorothy's approach, there's a degree to which he's threatening the others.

PROF. RALPH LINDHEIM, UNIVERSITY OF TORONTO

I think that the story is much darker than we're making it. There are multiple levels of despair in the story, and despair increases in the story, until the greatest act of desperation: when the doctor finally realizes what it is that he has done, and he himself is locked in ward number six, when he himself is battered by the warder. What is his response to that? It's a response of complete desperation. What can he do? This is a conversion that has come too late, as occurs quite often in Chekhov. And the only thing he can do, or think of doing, is attacking his warder and, in effect, killing himself. There's no constructive way out of this bleak situation.

CYNTHIA SEEFAHRT, RN, PENOBSCOT BAY MEDICAL CENTER

I'd like to make one comment. The very first question you asked was: "Are there any ward sixes here, that we can see?" Well, I say that we need to be very, very careful in our society that we're not creating ward sixes for the elderly. For the institutionalized elderly, the despair can be beyond despair. In "Ward 6" it is the sufferer of mental illness who is isolated and locked up; but with us, an individual experiencing the normal aging process may not have the support of family or community. And I think we need to heed when we read "Ward 6," and truly, honestly look around in our own society, and make sure we're not creating ward sixes.

MICHAEL FINKE

If there's no follow up to that last point, I'll ask another question. Savely Senderovich earlier alluded to Lenin's evaluation of the story. Lenin talked about reading "Ward 6" late at night, and just being overwhelmed with horror and uncanny feelings. Do you have any ideas about where the *power* of this story comes from? According the annotators of Chekhov's collected works in Russian, there were cases of women fainting dead away on reading the story. Where does this kind of power come from?

PROF. JAMES MCCONKEY, CORNELL UNIVERSITY, NOVELIST

It makes us question how sane we are. How sane am I? What is the degree of mental health we each have? Do you ever wonder if you haven't exceeded the norms of your society? Very often! I'm speaking for myself... How do we determine sanity? I ask questions like that.

PAUL GRAYCE

Here's the answer to the question who's the sane one: whoever has the key. When you're in a psychiatric institution you can tell who the patient is, because that's the person who doesn't have the key.

PROF. CAROL FLATH, DUKE UNIVERSITY

To develop that thought further: I think that great writers often like to write about insane people because this theme offers a lot of potential for making comments about our society. But I have a question for the doctors. There *are* very sick, very insane people. There's *biology* involved. And so isn't it a little facile to suggest that the doctor/patient opposition so easily collapses, and that sane and insane are so close? That possibility makes me feel very desperate. After all, in "Ward 6" we're faced with a primarily literary image of madness, aren't we? Whereas there *are* people who are truly insane.

PAUL GRAYCE

Psychotic people still have a personality.

CAROL FLATH

Yes, but they need to be in the hospital, they need to see doctors, they need medication.

PAUL GRAYCE

We each have our own level of pathology; the question is, at what level does it become destructive to your life.

CAROL FLATH

Of course, and I guess we can all recognize that in our lives.

SAVELY SENDEROVICH, CORNELL UNIVERSITY

But notice, these are the only two interesting people in the story, the doctor and the patient. The other characters are not interesting at all.

RICHARD PEVEAR

That leads to a point worth making about medical cases and literature, which is that medical cases are not intrinsically interesting. Psychotic people are not good literary subjects—let's put it that way—because they are too specific. So when Chekhov is dealing with Gromov and Ragin, he's dealing with our own human qualities, not with some strange aberrations. The question is, as you said, who is sane and who is not? This story is often seen as Chekhov's rebellion against his former self, in particular, against himself as the author of "A Boring Story," where the doctor says, "By God, I don't know what to do, I don't know what to say!" In this story the doctor reacts, he revolts. The intensity may be why people faint—he revolts so intensely, and so late, and so hopelessly. And I want to ask: Is this a Tolstoyan Chekhov, that is, is this Chekhov saying we should all go out and become social activists and correct the faults of society, improve the hospitals, get rid of the bad medical work? Or as a colleague here has said, is there much deeper despair in it?

JIM HAZEN

I also thought that there were only two interesting people in the story, but I was struck by the fact that it was the other characters who had control. They were able to isolate and confine the two to the ward, and your question of why the story is so powerful, why it would drive people to tears, to faint even, is that it's easy to imagine ourselves being in a situation like this. It's easy to imagine that we might lose it, however momentarily, and then be in a situation where we had no recourse, just like these two had no recourse, having been caught, as it were, by a conspiracy of nasty people.

MICHAEL FINKE

By the way, that was Dr. Cole's explanation, many years later, for why the dying young woman said she hoped she wasn't in ward number six. She hoped that she wasn't losing it.

MARINA MADORSKAYA, GRADUATE STUDENT IN SLAVICS, UNIVERSITY OF MICHIGAN

I think that what was just said here is precisely the story of Gromov. He gets sick because he is so afraid of getting into a situation where he might be arrested.

MICHAEL FINKE

Yes, and if we've been talking about how the professionals Chekhov depicts look at other people, then Gromov's way of looking at other people is to really identify with them. He even identifies with criminals who are being led away by the police. And that supreme capacity for empathy seems to be what does him in.

I'd like also to offer one answer, having to do with form, to the question of the story's power. The story opens with a narrator who addresses the reader directly, saying, "If you're not afraid, let's go take a look at these madmen." It sets up a me-and-you-against-them situation. And the story begins with a great deal of distance on the hospital and characters. In the Russian original, the verbs are all imperfective, which in the Russian verbal system means in this case that they're iterative: this is the way it always is. And then we get slotted into the point of view of Dr. Ragin. The story shifts to free indirect discourse attached to Ragin's point of view, and that starts us seeing the world from his eyes—including what he sees and what it feels like as he's dying, which is really going to the limit of what an author working in the realistic mode can represent. It's a formal trick that has a lot to do with the story's effect on us: Chekhov starts us at a safe distance from the characters, and then he slots us into the perspective of the character Ragin. If you go back and look at the text, I think you'll be able to spot how this happens.

Shall we go on to "A Medical Case" or "On Official Business"? I fear we won't manage to talk about both stories in the little time left to us.

CYNTHIA MARSH, UNIVERSITY OF NOTTINGHAM

Can I ask a broad question, for the practitioners here? Is there anything in these stories, from the medical point of view—apart from what has changed historically and as the result of scientific progress—you would wish to dissociate yourselves from? I mean, we've taken a continually one-hundred percent positive attitude toward Chekhov, and I wonder if some of the discussion could have gone another way?

MICHAEL FINKE

Everybody wants to identify with Chekhov. [*laughter*]

FEMALE PARTICIPANT

I have a question: What do you think the girl in "A Medical Case" suffered from?

DOROTHY THAYER

From a medical point of view, she has anxiety causing a racing heart, which for someone with problems with anxiety or an anxiety disorder is a very frequent complaint. And then there's the watchman banging the boards at night, which is really quite the set-up for bringing out the anxiety and insomnia for anyone having problems sleeping. To me it seems that the root of the problem, though, is in her loneliness...

MICHAEL FINKE

She got the fifteen minutes that you were talking about...

KATHERINE O'CONNOR, BOSTON UNIVERSITY

Could any of the doctors—or anybody—comment on neurasthenia? Wasn't that malady a catch-all diagnosis for anybody who was vaguely depressed or suffered from other similar symptoms? And is it accepted today as a medically real condition?

DOROTHY THAYER

I've only run across the term in novels. Like "brain fever."

MICHAEL FINKE

We have some historians who might address this.

PROF. MARLI WEINER, UNIVERSITY OF MAINE AND MAINE HUMANITIES COUNCIL

I can answer that, as a practicing historian. There's a real danger in diagnosing backwards; indeed, there's great danger in going both backwards and forwards. You can't take a disease from today and assume that what was seen in the past was the same thing. Nor can you assume that the symptoms that were seen in the past would be diagnosed the same way today, particularly with diagnoses like neurasthenia—and there is a whole range of others, like hysteria, interesting for its gender component. You can't even assume that the same set of symptoms even exists today, because the symptoms themselves would look different and be perceived differently. And so diseases themselves have a history, they emerge and disappear in particular historical contexts. Here we're talking about psychiatric maladies, which are particularly difficult, but the same applies to medical diseases like the one I know best, malaria. Today you either have it or you don't, and doctors have no great difficulty in diagnosing it, but in the past there was a whole array of fevers, some of which corresponded to what we now call malaria, some of which didn't. So even with biologically clear-cut diseases—never mind with psychological ones—you can't do that.

RICHARD KAHN

While you were talking, I just looked up "neurasthenia" in Webster's, and it sounds very much like what we would now call depression. They define it as "easy fatigability, often a lack of motivation, feelings of inadequacy and psychosomatic symptoms," and 1856 is when the term started being used. But it's a question of how you frame disease, and to be sure, the same categories don't apply across time and cultures.

MICHAEL FINKE

There's a wonderful article, called "Russian Nervousness," which looks precisely at the idea of neurasthenia in Russia, its historically and culturally specific context.[5] And the author, Laura Goering, borrowed her title from that of another work of interest, a book on neurasthenia in the American context called *American Nervousness*.[6] These would be two excellent sources for addressing Katherine O'Connor's question about neurasthenia.

CATHY POPKIN

There's also a good article about neurasthenia and melancholy in Chekhov's "Boring Story" by Jefferson Gatrall, who has had medical training.[7]

RICHARD PEVEAR

Why, if we're talking about suffering from an ailment, is Chekhov always drawn to people who are suffering from the same ailment? This inability to do anything, the inability to act... The doctor in "A Medical Case" is clearly a much more trivial person. He comes, he's thinking his own thoughts about how nice the day is, he enjoys his drive there in his carriage, he examines her and feels that there's nothing he can do. He looks at the hideous place she lives in, this flashing fire, the devil's eyes. He goes off home feeling good again and leaves this poor woman. Why is Chekhov drawn to her if she's a special medical case? Does that mean, as Svidrigailov says in *Crime and Punishment*, that if certain things appear to be special cases, that's not because that's the only way that they can appear. He's talking about ghosts. But is there some grand, larger aspect of human suffering that isn't a matter of neurasthenia, and that Chekhov will not let go

---

[5] Laura Goering, "'Russian Nervousness': Neurasthenia and National Identity in Nineteenth-Century Russia," *Medical History* 47 (2003): 23–46.

[6] Tom Lutz, *American Nervousness, 1903: An Anecdotal History* (Ithaca, NY: Cornell University Press, 1991).

[7] Jefferson Gatrall, "The Paradox of Melancholy Insight: Reading the Medical Subtext in Chekhov's 'A Boring Story,'" *Slavic Review* 62: 2 (Summer 2003): 258–77.

of? He will not commit this girl to an asylum, he will not commit her to the care of a doctor. He pulls her out for us to look at her and say: This is *you*, this is *me*.

MICHAEL FINKE

And this is very much what Jim McConkey was getting at, much earlier, when he addressed the question of what underwrote our response to the stories; is that right?

JAMES MCCONKEY

Said much better!

# About Chekhov
# (An Excerpt)

## I. N. Altshuller

Once I visited Chekhov while he was reading an article about himself and as I walked in he greeted me with: "Look, my dear sir, who would guess that I am already in my *third* creative period?" Then he knocked off his pince-nez—a habit of his—comically shrugged his shoulders and, with a twinkle in his eyes, added: "Yes, it used to be no periods at all, and now there are three!"

I do not really know how many periods there were in Chekhov's literary life but my acquaintance with him undoubtedly coincided with a new period of his personal life in Yalta—the period that was destined to be his final.

In the end of September of 1898, I fled the harsh autumn of Northern Russia and arrived in Yalta. It was my first time there. I had a referral letter to local health officer I. P. Rozanov, and it was at his place that I met his cousin S. Ya. Yelpatievsky. Yelpatievsky himself had moved to Yalta only recently; he was building a summer house there, as Chekhov put it, "with appetite." Yelpatievsky was very fond of Crimea's South Coast; he convincingly argued that I, too, needed to abandon the North and informed me that, look, even Chekhov came here and intended to stay. Once, as we were strolling through the city park, he noticed Chekhov sitting on a bench. We approached and Yelpatievsky introduced us. The next day a mutual friend, well-known *zemstvo* physician I. I. Orlov, came over and somehow it turned out that the three of us began spending our days together. Chekhov lived in two small rooms in Bushev's summer house on Nikolayevsky Street.

That year's autumn was splendid even by Crimean standards. Chekhov was in an excellent mood. Back then he still looked upbeat and really no older than his age of 38; he had a slender, albeit slightly stooping figure. But the deepening wrinkles near his eyes and mouth, his sometimes weary eyes and—most importantly to a medical observer—his heavy breathing (especially when he walked uphill) and, due to the breathing, his slow gait and characteristic coughing—all this was indicative of an illness. Chekhov was the only one who avoided speaking about it. There were two effective ways to annoy him: talk to him about his health or about his writing.

Once when the three of us chatted, Dr. Orlov, who loved Chekhov and was very concerned for him, suggested jokingly that we should all listen to each other's lungs "just for a check-up." Chekhov gently declined, saying "Let's take a walk instead."

*Chekhov the Immigrant: Translating a Cultural Icon.* Michael C. Finke and Julie de Sherbinin, eds. Bloomington, IN: Slavica Publishers, 2007, 337–44.

[...]

Despite our long talks and living together, we did not discuss health issues; or rather we discussed them only indirectly—he did not approve of *my* coughing, recommended that *I* take good care of myself and so on.

[...]

Chekhov considered himself a practical man (perhaps it was true to some degree) and since I was furnishing my apartment at the time, he actively participated in this. He was horrified at the sight of my business card pinned to the front door. "It's completely unacceptable, serious doctors must have serious plaques—not a copper one! You must order from Moscow a black one of cast iron." Indeed, through his brother, I think, he got me such a plaque from Moscow. He assured me that without him I could not even buy a window curtain. He insisted that I should become a member of the Mutual Credit Society and pay with checks. When I told him laughingly that I would do that when I am rich, that now I could not make any deposit, he said without a smile that this was our typical Russian lack of culture—in the West, no one carried cash any more.

[...]

As is well known, Chekhov was a physician; he loved medicine. While still a student and during the first years afterwards, he worked hard studying medicine and did not plan to give it up. In the middle of the 1880s, he wrote, "medicine is my lawful wife, and literature is my beloved mistress." During his summer breaks from school, he studied in the Chikinsk hospital in the Zvenigorod district; later, he briefly substituted for a district physician, and in Moscow he saw patients. Apparently, he planned to write specifically on medical issues; for, after his death, among his papers were found several handwritten pages on the history of medicine in Russia. Unfortunately I did not think at the time to make a copy of them. These notes have not been published to this day. According to my research, the manuscript is now in the Central Archive. Chekhov, in fact, saw his *Sakhalin* as a sort of medical dissertation. In Melikhovo, he treated sick peasants who came for help and gave them medicine, of course at no charge. But even back then that was the extent of his involvement in medicine. During the last 10-15 years he was not involved in scientific medicine. It is true that in Yalta he received the medical weekly *Russkii vrach* [Russian Physician] from the office of *Russkaia mysl'* [Russian Thought]; but in it, he would only read news and the brief so-called "notes from practice." He sometimes liked to impress by asking, "Have you read about the latest cure for hemorrhoid?" "No, I haven't." "Well, dear sir, gambling with your practice, aren't you? I, on the other hand, have read it and already cured Kondakov with it. A great cure." On the left side of his desk, there were always a stethoscope, a plexor, and a current Rikker medical calendar. He always took active care in treating his family and servants. He also liked to give medical advice to his friends and often asked them about their conditions. However, the extent of his advice was usually to say, take serious care of yourself and see a doctor. He did have a soft spot, though, for writing prescriptions. Knowing this, I tried not to write him prescriptions myself but instead dictated them as he stood by the telephone and ordered them from the pharmacy. He especially savored the mouthing of Latin terms. Then he would make the pharmacist repeat the prescription and added at the end: (for the author) Dr. Chekhov.

That Chekhov was a physician may explain some particularities of the history of his own illness. Strange as it may seem, physicians more often than others fall into two extremes: they either overreact to their sensation of sickness and its symptoms, and fear the most unfavorable outcome they know about that particular disease, or they underestimate their condition— again justifying it through their professional knowledge.

I have already mentioned that in the beginning of our acquaintance Chekhov did not talk about his illness. One early morning in the end of November 1898 I received a note from him asking me to come with my "stethoscop*chik* and laryngoscop*chik*" [joking, diminutive names for the instruments—*Trans.*] because he was having hemoptysis. Indeed, I found him spitting up a lot of blood. My laryngoscope was unnecessary because there could be no doubt that it was coming from the lungs. A few days later when I could examine him more thoroughly, I was shocked by what I found. That was our first medical conversation; Chekhov told me that blood-spitting first began during his trip to Sakhalin (1890). Later, however, it turned out that the first occurrence was in fact in 1884 and after that it had recurred quite often. Since his college years he coughed a lot, feeling bad in spring and autumn and having fever, but he had explained it away as influenza, never saw a doctor, never allowed anyone to examine him so that "they would not find something there." He explained the blood-spitting as a throat condition and the coughing as a mere cold, although by his own admission he had sometimes lost a lot of weight, looking like a ghost. Back in 1888, he wrote to Suvorin in a doctor-like manner that "tuberculosis or other serious lung illness is recognized by a combination of signs, and this is precisely what I don't have." However, even after blood-spitting, which was the only symptom that left a lasting impression on him because "in blood flowing from one's mouth there is something ominous like in the redness of the sky at sunset," and even after his brother Nikolai's death from galloping consumption in 1889, he firmly stated that he would "not allow anyone to examine him." Only in the spring of 1897 when blood came out gushing, the insistence of his friends made him agree to go to Professor Ostroumov's clinic. Since that time, apparently, the worsening process never stopped. During my first examination of him I found already extensive damage in both lungs, especially in the right one, with several vomicae, traces of pleurisy, a very weak and degenerated heart muscle and bad intestines interfering with good nutrition. My attempts at the time to convince him to seek serious care led to nothing. He maintained that he abhorred going to doctors and taking care of his health; that nothing should remind him of the illness and no one was allowed to notice it. That was why he contrived this manner of speaking in a very soft voice, slowly and monotonously, stopping when he felt irritation in his throat to avoid coughing. And when he did cough, he would spit the mucus into a small paper bag hidden inconspicuously behind the books and throw it into the fireplace. Only with a very careful approach, as if by accident or using an innocent pretext, was it possible to listen to his lungs and make him do anything. Only after 1901 did he become a patient proper and himself often suggested: "Let's listen to those lungs, shall we?" But even then, to make him stay in a hospital, to undergo treatment or to make it his priority was impossible. He disliked talking about his illness not only with other people, he would hide his poor condition even from his family. He never complained; to the question "how are you feeling?" he would answer, "Very good now, almost completely well, just some coughing," or "just a headache," or something like that. Unfortunately, the process was already in that stage wherein there could be no hope for recovery. One could only attempt to slow down its development or to ameliorate the patient's state temporarily.

Alas, even to achieve that little, his circumstances were utterly unfavorable—first and foremost because of the environment he lived in. Strange as it may seem, he was deprived of proper care and certain conditions necessary for treatment. Chekhov was very close to his family; he loved his mother especially tenderly and treated her with touching care, the last words to his sister in his will being, "Take care of Mom." Yevgenia Yakovlevna loved her Antosha with equal tenderness. But what could she do, this sweet and adorable old woman? Could she really insist on anything or make anything happen? So it would turn out that despite all the instructions, he was given unsuitable food, his compresses were applied by an unskilled servant, and no one could take care of the thousand little things that constitute the regimen of a sick man. When the nature of his condition became apparent, his sister Maria Pavlovna was ready to quit both her job and Moscow and move to Yalta, but after his marriage it was cancelled for quite understandable psychological reasons. Anton Pavlovich married Olga Leonardovna Knipper in May of 1901 without warning anyone, as is well-known. From that time on, his lifestyle changed drastically.

As a physician who treated Chekhov—and strictly from a medical standpoint—I must say that those changes, unfortunately, could facilitate neither a treatment nor a betterment of his health. A famous French specialist on tuberculosis once said, "The consumptive patient must forget about laurels," and Chekhov's life seems to prove this. His bad fortune was, paradoxically, the very good fortune that came to him at the end of his life— the Moscow Art Theater and his marriage—and would eventually prove unbearable. I remember how nervous he was before the opening of *The Seagull* at the theater; how he could not hide his worries; how his nervousness manifested itself in the minutely detailed stories he would recall about the failure of the play at the Aleksandrinsky Theater. I also remember how utterly excited he was long after the celebration and triumph in Moscow. And he, who had promised himself to forget about the theater and never write plays again, went on writing specifically for this company. The Moscow Art Theater became the Chekhov Theater and immensely facilitated Chekhov's popularity during his final years. And then the marriage.

In the past one might hear from Chekhov, when he was in a particularly cheerful mood, how he and friends had had a good time in their youth. But I never heard either from him or others of any serious love relationship. He fell for Olga Leonardovna long before his plays were produced, having first seen her at a rehearsal of *Tsar Fedor*. I was abroad when I learned about their marriage from *Russkie vedomosti* [Russian News], and for some reason I then recalled one group scene I had witnessed. Olga Leonardovna came to Chekhov's home in the spring of 1900 and once I saw her standing on the top of the stairway with Maria Pavlovna while Chekhov stood at its bottom. She was wearing a white dress, looking very happy and healthy, the star of the Art Theater, the center of attention in Moscow and elsewhere, with great hopes and potential for the future. And he—emaciated, pale, quickly aging, irreversibly ill. And when their lives merged together in marriage, fatal consequences were only too quick to come. She had to stay in Moscow; he could not leave his "warm Siberia" without risking his health. Knowing Chekhov, the outcome was easy to predict—frequent trips from Yalta to Moscow and back. After almost every return from Moscow, he paid for it with either pleurisy, or blood-spitting, or a lengthy fever. And he consciously lied to himself about all this, substituting cause for effect when he pointed out that, of course, in Moscow it was not bad at all but once back in Yalta—sick again. He spent the winter months of 1901–02 and 1902–03 in Yalta feeling ill almost all the time, going through periods of acute symptoms.

By the end of this period, his appearance changed, too. His complexion became grayish; his lips lost their color; he lost even more weight and his hair turned noticeably whiter. His heart became progressively weaker; the process in his lungs intensified. Because of this, his heavy breathing occurred more often; symptoms of the tuberculosis were also affecting his intestines.

I have a letter from Olga Leonardovna written on January 9, 1902; that is, half a year after their wedding. She asked me to write to her about Anton Pavlovich's health in more detail and, among other things, she wrote: "This winter is very hard on me. The only thing that helps is that I am very busy. Such separation is unthinkable. I thought that Anton Pavlovich's health was in a better state than it really is and that it would be possible for him to spend at least the winter months in Moscow. But now, of course, I wouldn't even suggest it... So sad and difficult."

There was no way out. When Olga Leonardovna spoke about quitting the stage and moving to Yalta, Anton Pavlovich of course protested and would not even talk about it. Under the circumstances, it turned out, he was correct. In the spring of 1903, with the blessings of the famous Moscow clinical professor Ostroumov, the decision was made for Chekhov to spend winter in Moscow. But in the fall of 1903, he had an on-going fever, one bout of pleurisy after another, and also an indigestion which was hard to treat. He could not hide his bad condition any longer. But the Art Theater, keen on its high goals and pressed by production plans, rushed him to submit *Cherry Orchard* as soon as possible. Quite often I would find Chekhov in his armchair or on the couch but without books or newspapers. Unlike before, he no longer avoided discussing his work. He himself now complained how hard it was to write and re-write the play—now he could do it only in short snatches.

In October, I attempted for the last time to keep him in Yalta. I told him almost the entire truth about his condition; I begged him not to kill himself, not to go to Moscow, I said it would be madness. He wrote about it to Moscow, but by December he left. The rest is history. I will repeat that what happened under those circumstances was inevitable. Still, when we read in one of his letters to his wife "You will decide; for you are a busy person—a worker, and I just hang on in this world like an idler," we the readers of Chekhov cannot agree. And when in another letter he points out that in a new third-floor apartment rented in Moscow the stairway is too high and there is no elevator and that it will be difficult for him to climb considering his breathing problems, and then ends with, "Well, it'll be fine after all, somehow I'll climb," as a physician I cannot help but think what fatal effect that stairway must have had on his already extremely weakened heart.

In Moscow, he actively participated in the rehearsals of *Cherry Orchard* and worried a lot about the show. All this was happening in the midst of the theatrical season, and as usual there were multitudes of visitors.

Deep in his heart, did Anton Pavlovich fully realize his situation? In the foreword to his letters, Olga Leonardovna writes: "It was as if fate decided to pamper him at last and gave him in the final year of his life all that he cherished: Moscow, the winter, the production of *Cherry Orchard*, and the people he loved." Chekhov himself commented more than once on how he loved Moscow and everything there, how he missed the northern winter, how close the Art Theater had become to his heart, and how much he longed for the people and the environment of Moscow.

However, even in Moscow he would have those dark moods that were so familiar to me in Yalta. T. L. Shchepkina-Kupernik, an old friend of Chekhov's family who knew them all very well, described in her memoirs one visit in 1902: "I was amazed by the change in him... He was stooping, wrapped in some plaid, and often spit mucus in a small jar... That night Olga Leonardovna was to participate in a concert. An elegant V. I. Nemirovich, dressed in tails with an impeccable plastron, arrived to take her there. Olga Leonardovna came out wearing an evening gown and redolent of delicate perfume. Tenderly she said a sweet good-bye to Anton Pavlovich with some cute 'don't miss me and be good,' and disappeared. Anton Pavlovich looked after her, then started coughing—long and hard. When the fit passed, without any connection to our prior merry conversation about old memories, friends, and such, he said, 'Oh, my—it's time to die.'"

January 17 was the opening night of *Cherry Orchard* and the honoring of Chekhov by all of Moscow, but pale as death and coughing, he could hardly stand on the stage. In the middle of February he returned to Yalta feeling much worse but still full of Moscow impressions. He talked excitedly about the honoring, showed the presents he had received and complained jokingly that someone had apparently started a rumor that he loved antiques while he, in fact, could not stand them. Indeed, among the presents were a replica of the old Russian village, an old jewelry box and, among other things, an eighteenth-century inkwell. To my remark that it was all very beautiful and that I especially liked the inkwell, he answered: "Really? But we don't use sand any more—there is blotting-paper now, and no quills either." Then he added with his charming smile: "Well then, if you really like it, I will see to it that as punishment they will hand you this inkwell after my death." However ill he was, I could not imagine that in less than half a year the inkwell would be mine indeed.

He stayed in Yalta till the end of April, sometimes feeling upbeat, making plans for the future, wishing to go back to work, saying that there is so much in his mind ready to be put on paper. He was planning in the summer, health permitting, to go to the war that deeply worried him. He planned to go as a physician since physicians see more. But more often he was silent, deep in his thoughts. He, who had never before complained about his health, now often said that he felt tired, that he wanted to have some really restful time to regain his strength. He did feel the need for rest but in the end of April he left for Moscow again. On his way there he caught a cold, the symptoms worsened—pleurisy with a very high temperature—and he became bedridden immediately upon arrival. He got out of the bed only in order to go to Badenweiler.

The last letter I received from him came on May 26: "Dear Isaak Naumovich! Since I arrived in Moscow I have been in bed day and night—haven't dressed even once. Your request about Khmelev[*] I, of course, couldn't fulfill. But even if I were well, I could hardly do anything. Khmelev is very busy these days; to make an appointment with him is hard. The diarrhea has stopped; now I am suffering from constipation. Three days ago I caught an infection. After dinner I have fever and can't sleep all night. Less coughing, though. On June 3 we are going abroad to the Black Forest; in August I will be back in Yalta. Oh, how I hate these enemas... They already give me coffee and

---

[*] N. N. Khmelev was acting Chairman of Moscow County Council. The request to see him concerned the participation of the Moscow *zemstvo* in creating a sanatorium for war veterans. *(Note by I. N. Altshuller.)*

I drink it with joy, but eggs and soft bread are still not allowed. Take care, my friend. These days I spend on the couch and, having nothing else to do, I curse Ostroumov and N. A lot of fun. Yours, A. Chekhov." And then a postscript: "Last night was the first time when I slept well."

Olga Leonardovna later told me with outrage that while in Berlin's Savoy Hotel they had the well-known Professor Evald come and see Chekhov. Having thoroughly examined the patient, he only shrugged his shoulders and walked out without a word. That was of course inconsiderate, but he probably shrugged his shoulders in astonishment: where and why were they taking this patient?

And yet, however well I knew that the end was close, I was shocked when in the early morning of July 3, on the Riga coast, I received the telegram of his death.

Translation from Russian © 2006 by Eugene Alper

# Contributors

ELLEN BECKERMAN is the artistic director of LightBox, an avant-garde theater company that presents physically heightened, ensemble-driven productions of classics and also creates new work. For LightBox, she has directed *Ajax: 100% Fun, Shutter*, Charles Mee's *Orestes, Gull, Fanatics, Hamlet*, and *Embarkation*. Other directing credits include The Public Theater/New York Shakespeare Festival, New York Theatre Workshop, Soho Rep, New Dramatists, and The Playwrights Center. Beckerman is a recipient of the NEA/TCG Career Development Program for Directors (2003–05), a Drama League Fellow, and a member of the Lincoln Center Directors Lab. She is a graduate of Princeton University.

SHARON MARIE CARNICKE (School of Theatre, University of Southern California) has made landmark contributions to the study of Russian theater. Her books on theater directors Nikolai Evreinov (*The Theatrical Instinct*, Peter Lang, 1989) and Konstantin Stanislavsky (*Stanislavsky in Focus*, Harwood, 1998; Routledge, 2000) discuss precedents to contemporary performance studies and the radical differences between U.S. and Russian actor training. She has written numerous articles and presented dozens of talks on Russian theater, nationally and internationally. Her translations of Chekhov's *The Seagull, Three Sisters*, and *The Cherry Orchard* have received performances nationwide.

DR. ROBERT COLES (Department of Psychiatry, Harvard University; co-founder of *DoubleTake* Magazine), Pulitzer Prize winner and one of the first MacArthur Foundation "Genius" Fellowship awardees, has had an illustrious career in interdisciplinary fields—largely of his own invention—that involve work in psychiatry, psychoanalysis, anthropology, sociology, history, literary and cultural criticism, and social activism. Among his many published books are biographies of Anna Freud and Erik Erikson; books of poetry; the five-volume series, *Children in Crisis*; several childrens' books; and many volumes of essays of astounding range in subject-matter. He is the most prominent living American example of a medical doctor who is also an active player in the field of humanities.

*Chekhov the Immigrant: Translating a Cultural Icon.* Michael C. Finke and Julie de Sherbinin, eds. Bloomington, IN: Slavica Publishers, 2007, 345–52.

PETER CONSTANTINE is a freelance translator in New York City; he spent 2002–03 as a writer-in-residence at Princeton University. Constantine brought literary sketches from Chekhov's early prose to an English-speaking audience with translations published first in *Harper's Magazine* (November 1997), then as *The Undiscovered Chekhov: Thirty-Eight New Stories* (Seven Stories Press, 1998). Constantine's volume was awarded the National Translation Prize for 1999 by the American Literary Translators Association. Selected vignettes were performed by Vanessa Redgrave in 1998. The volume has since come out in paperback (2000). Constantine has produced acclaimed translations of Isaac Babel, Nikolai Gogol, Ismail Kadare, Felix Morisseau Leroy, Thomas Mann, Alexandros Papadiamantis, and the Hannah Arendt-Heinrich Blucher correspondence.

JULIE DE SHERBININ (Department of German and Russian, Colby College) was the co-founder of the North American Chekhov Society and served as editor of the *NACS Bulletin*, a biannual scholarly newsletter, from 1992–2000. She has published many essays on Chekhov, as well as other nineteenth- and early twentieth-century Russian authors. In her monograph *Chekhov and Russian Religious Culture: The Poetics of the Marian Paradigm* (Northwestern University Press, 1997), she identifies Chekhov as a literary ethnographer with profound understanding of the cultural psychology behind Russian Orthodoxy, who makes subtle and systematic use of its constructs in his narratives.

ANDREW DURKIN (Department of Slavic Languages and Literatures, Indiana University), author of a book on Sergei Aksakov *(Sergei Aksakov and Russian Pastoral*, Rutgers University Press, 1983) and specialist in nature-writing and the pastoral in nineteenth-century Russian literature, has presented on Chekhov at numerous conferences and published many articles on Chekhov. His articles tend to be close readings of individual stories; besides the theme of nature, in several he also explores that of art in Chekhov. He is currently completing a monograph on Chekhov.

SVETLANA EVDOKIMOVA (Department of Slavic Languages and Literatures, Brown University) is a specialist in nineteenth- and twentieth-century Russian literature. Her main areas of scholarly interest include Pushkin, Russian and European Romanticism, Tolstoy, Chekhov, relations between fiction and history, and gender and sexuality in Russian and European literatures. She is the author of *Pushkin's Historical Imagination* (Yale University Press, 1999) and the editor of *Alexander Pushkin's "Little Tragedies": The Poetics of*

*Brevity* (University of Wisconsin Press, 2003, which was selected as an Outstanding Academic Title for 2004 by *Choice*. She has published a wide range of articles on Pushkin, Gogol, Tolstoy, and Chekhov. She is currently completing a monograph, "A Genius of Culture: The Chekhov Phenomenon," that examines Chekhov's relationship with the Russian intelligentsia and its impact on the formation of his literary self.

MICHAEL FINKE (Department of Slavic Languages and Literatures, University of Illinois at Urbana-Champaign) has opened innovative psychoanalytic and metapoetic perspectives on Chekhov. Most recently, his *Seeing Chekhov: Life and Art* (Cornell University Press, 2005) explores the intersection between Chekhov's person and his writings with a psychobiographic approach that offers a new understanding of Chekhov's multiple identities as author, physician, and patient. A specialist in nineteenth-century Russian literature, he is author of *Metapoesis: The Russian Tradition from Pushkin to Chekhov* (Duke University Press, 1995); he also co-edited and introduced *One Hundred Years of Masochism: Literary Texts, Social and Cultural Contexts* (Rodopi, 2000).

CAROL APOLLONIO FLATH (Department of Slavic and Eurasian Studies, Duke University) has an accomplished record as a Russian interpreter, a translator of Russian and Japanese, and a Chekhov scholar. She has translated into English two books and several articles from Russian, and two books from Japanese. Her article "*Anna Karenina*: Translation, Literalism, and the Life of Art" (*Tolstoy Studies Journal* 14 [2002]) analyzes translations of Tolstoy's novel, including the recent translation by Pevear and Volokhonsky. In "Demons of Translation: The Strange Path of Dostoevsky's Novels into the English Tradition" (*Dostoevsky Studies*, New Series, 9 [2005]) she explores some links between Dostoevsky, his famous translator Constance Garnett, and some Russian terrorists. Flath has authored many articles on Chekhov.

SPENCER GOLUB (Departments of Theatre, Speech and Dance, Comparative Literature, Slavic Languages, Brown University) is a prolific theater scholar with a history as a script consultant and as a member of an artistic directorate for New York theaters. He has directed Chekhov's four major plays. His scholarly work on Russian theater includes a score of essays and two books, *Evreinov: The Theatre of Paradox and Transformation* (University of Michigan Research Press, 1984) and *The Recurrence of Fate: Theatre and Memory in Twentieth-Century Russia* (University of Iowa Press, 1994). The interdisciplinary foundation of Golub's work—which combines art and film criticism, theater, literary theory and aesthetics—is manifest in *Infinity (Stage)* (University of Michigan Press, 1999) and in a work in progress, *The Innocence Show*, a post-surrealist blend of theory and fictionalized memoir about the anxieties of innocence and desire filtered through film, literature, and performance. He is currently co-authoring a novel.

MICHAEL HENRY HEIM (Department of Slavic Languages and Literatures, University of California Los Angeles) has had a distinguished career as a scholar and a translator. He has produced professional translations from many languages. His Chekhov work includes the translation of Henri Troyat's well-known biography *Chekhov* from the French, and renderings of all of Chekhov's major plays—translations that have been performed in theaters in the U.S., Canada, and England, and were published in 2003 by Random House in the Modern Library series as *Chekhov: The Essential Plays*. He is well known for his translation of Chekhov's letters in *Anton Chekhov's Life and Thought* (University of California Press), a volume edited by Simon Karlinsky. It has undergone many reprintings and is widely regarded as a key source on Chekhov for non-Russian speakers in anglophone countries.

ROBERT LOUIS JACKSON (Department of Slavic Languages and Literatures, Yale University, *Emeritus*), a preeminent American Slavist and scholar of Dostoevsky, Tolstoy, Turgenev, and other Russian writers, organized The Third International Chekhov Symposium at Yale University in April, 1990, from which issued the volume *Reading Chekhov's Texts* (Northwestern University Press, 1993). Here, and in an earlier edited volume—*Chekhov: A Collection of Critical Essays* (Prentice Hall, 1967)—Jackson assembles some of the most influential voices in Chekhov studies. Jackson, a pioneer of symbolic readings of Chekhov, champions humanistic-moral interpretations, which emerge through his in-depth analyses of individual stories and plays in some fifteen articles. He is currently assembling his own work on Chekhov into a book.

RICHARD J. KAHN, M.D. practices internal medicine in Rockport, Maine. He founded the Maine Society for the History of Medicine; he is a long-time member of the Maine Humanities Hospital Reading Groups, and he has served on the Executive Committee of the Maine Humanities Council. His historical writings on American medicine have appeared in the *Journal of the History of Medicine* (Oxford), *Bulletin of the History of Medicine* (Johns Hopkins), *American National Biography* (Oxford University Press, 1999), and the *New England Journal of Medicine*.

JAMES MCCONKEY (Goldwin Smith Professor of English Literature, Cornell University, *Emeritus*). His writing as a literary scholar, fiction writer, memoirist, essayist and teacher of creative writing openly acknowledges Chekhov's considerable influence, most recently in the essay "On Being Human" (*American Scholar*, Winter 2003). He organized the Chekhov Festival at Cornell University (1977–78) and edited the volume issuing from it, *Chekhov and Our Age: Responses to Chekhov by American Writers and Scholars* (Center for International Studies, Council of the Creative and Performing Arts, Cornell University, 1984); and he has published two other books whose titles proclaim a deep involvement with Chekhov: the novel *A Journey to Sahalin* (Coward, 1971) and an account of Chekhov's journey to Sakhalin, *To a Distant Island* (Dutton, 1984). In this last work McConkey very literally makes Chekhov his own, incorporating Chekhov's biography into a narrative about his own life.

CLAIRE MESSUD (Writer and Critic, Boston) has published three widely praised novels and a volume of novellas, as well as book reviews for such periodicals as *The New York Times Book Review* and *Bookforum*. She has also held teaching appointments at a variety of American colleges and universities, where she has taught fiction writing. Her first novel, *When the World Was Steady* (Granta, 1994), and her novella *The Hunters* (Harcourt, 2001) were both finalists for the PEN/Faulkner Award. *The Last Life* (Harcourt Brace, 1999) has been translated into at least seven languages. *The Emperor's Children* (Knopf) came out to great acclaim in 2006. She is the recipient of a Guggenheim Fellowship, the Addison Metcalf Award from the American Academy of Arts and Letters, and the Academy's Straus Living Award.

ANNA MUZA (Department of Slavic Languages and Literatures, University of California, Berkeley) formerly taught theater and drama at the Russian Academy of Performing Arts (GITIS). She has published and presented conference papers on Chekhov and Russian theater of his time, and contributed chapters on Chekhov to the volume *Cold Fusion: Aspects of the German Cultural Presence in Russia* (Berghahn Books, 2000), and to the forthcoming Chekhov volume in the academic series *Literaturnoe nasledstvo* (Moscow). She has translated original and critical texts on theater and visual culture from English into Russian and from Russian into English, most recently for the collection *The White Rectangle: Kazimir Malevich's Writings on Film* (Potemkin Press, 2002), which she also co-edited.

KATHERINE TIERNAN O'CONNOR (Department of Modern Languages, Boston University) has delivered many talks on Chekhov and has broken new ground in a number of essays. She was one of the first to read Chekhov's letters as an integral part of his art. She has also offered a reading of Chekhov's death as "his textual past recaptured" and has explored how Chekhov's correspondence illuminates his relationship with Alexei Suvorin, his literary patron and friend. Her interest in Chekhov's letters on sickness and mortality took a comparative form in her study of the "discourse of mortality" found in the letters of Chekhov and D. H. Lawrence. Before concentrating on Chekhov, she wrote articles on Leskov and Nabokov, a book on Pasternak's *My Sister Life,* and translations (with Diana Lewis Burgin) of Chukovsky, Dovlatov, and most recently of Bulgakov's *Master and Margarita.* She plans to write a book on the art of Chekhov's letters.

RICHARD PEVEAR AND LARISSA VOLOKHONSKY are today's leading translators of Russian fiction into English. A husband and wife team living in Paris, they have translated all of Dostoevsky's major novels and two volumes of his shorter fiction, Tolstoy's *War and Peace* (now in press), *Anna Karenina,* and *What Is Art?,* Gogol's *Dead Souls* as well as a volume of his short fiction, Bulgakov's *Master and Margarita,* and most recently, two volumes of Chekhov's fiction (*Stories,* Bantam Books, 2000) and a volume of Chekhov's five longest stories (*Complete Short Novels,* Knopf/Everyman's Library, 2004). Their translations have won two PEN awards, and they have both received honorary doctorates. Pevear has also published translations from French and Italian, and two volumes of his own poetry. He has received numerous grants and awards, including a Guggenheim Fellowship, and is Adjunct Professor of Comparative Literature at the American University of Paris.

CATHY POPKIN (Department of Slavic Languages and Literatures, Columbia University) has in recent years published a series of studies on Chekhov's epistemologies as author and physician, on his staging of the epistemological insufficiencies of the medical gaze, and of the complementary way of knowing that is represented by narrative art. A summation of this work will soon be appearing in *Bodies of Knowledge: Chekhov's Corpus* (under contract to Stanford University Press). She has also published on Chekhov's narrative poetics, to which is devoted a section of her *The Pragmatics of Insignificance* (Stanford University Press, 1993). Popkin is currently editing a new Norton Critical Edition of *Anton Chekhov's Short Stories.*

FRANCINE PROSE is the author of ten novels, including *Blue Angel*, which was nominated for a 2000 National Book Award. Her most recent book, *Reading Like a Writer* (HarperCollins, 2006) includes the essay "Learning from Chekhov." Other recent books are *A Changed Man, After, Sicilian Odyssey, The Lives of the Muses: Nine Women and the Artists They Inspired*, and *Gluttony*. She is also the author of *Hunters and Gatherers, Bigfoot Dreams, Primitive People*, two story collections, and a collection of novellas, *Guided Tours of Hell*. Her stories, reviews and essays have appeared in *The Atlantic Monthly, Harper's, Best American Short Stories, The New Yorker, The New York Times, The Yale Review, The New Republic*; she is a contributing editor of *Harper's* and *Bomb*, and writes regularly on art for *The Wall Street Journal*. Prose has been the recipient of a Guggenheim Fellowship, a Fulbright Fellowship, two NEA grants, and a PEN translation prize.

CAROL ROCAMORA (Department of Dramatic Writing, Tisch School of the Arts, New York University) is a translator, playwright, director, and teacher. Her three volumes of the complete translated dramatic works of Anton Chekhov have been published by Smith and Kraus (1996–99). Her play, "I take your hand in mine…" (Smith and Kraus, 2000), based on the correspondence between Chekhov and Olga Knipper, premiered in September 2001 at the Almeida Theatre in London, and was later mounted at Peter Brook's Theatre des Bouffes du Nord in Paris, a production which toured Europe (2003–05). Her new biography, *Acts of Courage*, treats Vaclav Havel's life in the theater (Smith and Kraus, 2004). Rocamora is the founder of the Philadelphia Festival Theatre for New Plays at Annenberg Center, where she has directed all of Chekhov's major plays. She has written about theater for *The New York Times* and *The Nation*, and currently contributes to *The London Guardian* and *American Theatre*.

LAURENCE SENELICK (Fletcher Professor of Drama and Oratory, and Faculty Research Council Distinguished Scholar, Tufts University), is an eminent American scholar of Chekhov theater. He authored the authoritative *The Chekhov Theatre: A Century of the Plays in Performance* (Cambridge University Press, 1997)—one of twenty books on theater that he has written or edited in the last twenty-five years. He won the George Jean Nathan Award for best work of dramatic criticism for 2000 for *The Changing Room: Sex, Drag and Theatre* (Routledge, 2000). Senelick, a preeminent authority on the international history of Chekhov theater and the translation of Chekhov's drama into English, recently translated and edited *The Norton Edition of Select Plays of Anton Chekhov* (W. W. Norton, 2004) and *The Complete Plays of Anton Chekhov* (W. W.

Norton, 2005). He has most recently published *A Historical Dictionary of Russian Theatre* (Scarecrow Press, 2007) and entries in *The Encyclopedia of Erotic Literature* (Routledge, 2006).

CONEVERY BOLTON VALENČIUS (Departmental Associate, Department of the History of Science, Harvard University) is an environmental historian and historian of medicine currently researching a book on the New Madrid earthquakes of 1811–12. Her recent book, *Health of the Country* (Basic Books, 2002), won the George Perkins Marsh Prize from the American Society for Environmental History. It argued for rhetorical homologies between understandings of health problems and solutions for homesteaders and the land they were pioneering in the westward expansion of the United States. She has also published studies of American and Western European medical geographies.

JAMES WOOD is a Professor of the Practice of Literary Criticism at Harvard University and a Senior Editor for *The New Republic*, where writes and commissions book reviews, and where he has published several commentaries on Chekhov, including "No More Mr. Nice Guy" and "The Unwinding Stair: Can Literature Be Simple?" His major essay on Chekhov, "What Chekhov Meant by Life," appears in his collection *The Broken Estate: Essays on Literature and Belief* (Jonathan Cape, 1999). Recently he has published a novel, *The Book against God* (Farrar, Straus and Giroux, 2003), and a book of essays, *The Irresponsible Self: On Laughter and the Novel* (Farrar, Straus and Giroux, 2004). He is the recipient of an Academy Award in Literature from the American Academy of Arts and Letters (2001).

**DATE DUE**

BRODART, CO.                  Cat. No. 23-221-003